"Now, whenever I awoke in the middle of the night and listened to the convoluted rustle of the wind—as complex as speech—I imagined that someone in another compound might be lying awake, trying to interpret the hushed movements of spirits. I'd long believed that spirits were creatures of the imagination; now I felt that spirits indeed existed— because they were creatures of the imagination. The spirits lived within the Beng and therefore outside them as well."
—from *Parallel Worlds*

"*Parallel Worlds* is a remarkable memoir that both reads like a novel and meditates profoundly on art and the human condition. Gottlieb, a brilliant young anthropologist, and Graham, one of the most original fiction writers at work today, have together taught me wonderful things about culture and myth and the artistic process and, ultimately, about what it means to be human. This is a compellingly readable and richly enlightening book, a book that will endure."
—**Robert Olen Butler**, author of *A Good Scent from a Strange Mountain*

"As their lives converge and ultimately meld with those of the Beng people in common humanity—childbirth, celebration, sickness and death—this book becomes strangely affirming of homo sapiens. In alternating passages, Ms. Gottlieb and Mr. Graham plot that convergence in precise, often arresting prose. . . . It might be worth enduring the desperate material conditions of life in Bengland just to achieve such a heightened spirituality."
—**Marvin Hunt, *Atlanta Journal-Constitution***

"A wonderful book—I was captivated by the audacity, pluck, and innate humanity of this dauntless team, by the grace and wisdom of their writing, and above all by their integrity in striving to understand lives so different from their own. Graham and Gottlieb tell their story so vividly that the reader cannot help but feel like a fellow guest of the Beng people."
—**Lynne Sharon Schwartz**, author of *Disturbances in the Field*

"Powerful. . . . [The authors] lead the reader on an adventurous journey. . . . Offers Western readers a broader view of the state of affairs in Ivory Coast and of the continent's vast complexities."
—**Mwangi Ireri, *Christian Science Monitor***

"A splendid book, full of the poetry that anthropology values most of all."
—**Roy Wagner**, author of *The Invention of Culture*

"The book becomes a blend of two very different authors: on the one hand, the story of a writer living amid fascinating subjects for his craft; on the other, the story of a fieldworking anthropologist, striving to find a context in which to describe a unique group of people who live as much among their ghosts and spirits as in the world we know."
—*Washington Post Book World*

"An intricate play of multiple, paralleling worlds that are given to us with delicacy and an intimacy of perception rare in accounts of Africa."
—**Vincent Crapanzano**, author of *Waiting*

"A book of unusual candor, *Parallel Worlds* offers a unique introduction to Africa."
—*Library Journal*

"While loaded with all the funny First-World-meets-Third-World stories we have come to expect from those chronicling vanishing tribes, this account of the authors' yearlong stay with [the] Beng tribe in Africa's Ivory Coast is unique because its jokes do not come at the 'primitive' culture's expense."
—**Alex Raksin,** *Los Angeles Times Book Review*

"An engaging memoir that testifies to a loving partnership while it draws the reader into a remote society.... That to a large extent the [authors] eventually won the trust and friendship of their hosts attests to patience and skills that seem remarkable."
—**James Idema,** *Chicago Tribune*

"This volume breaks new ground by its artful integration of two writers' voices, offering a remarkable and engaging expression of parallel worlds."
—**George Marcus,** coeditor of *Writing Culture*

"At once a beautifully written depiction of a single culture and a fine account of how anthropologists do their work."
—**Gregory McNamee,** *Outside Magazine*

"Alternating perspectives from each author, this sensitive, suspenseful, and delicately textured narrative is a 'candid memoir of [the authors'] pain and joy.'"
—*Publisher's Weekly*

PARALLEL
WORLDS

ABOUT THE AUTHORS

❧   ❧   ❧

ALMA GOTTLIEB is the author of *Under the Kapok Tree: Identity and Difference in Beng Thought* and coeditor (with Thomas Buckley) of *Blood Magic: The Anthropology of Menstruation.* She has recently completed a Beng-English dictionary. She has contributed articles to many scholarly journals, including *Africa, Man, American Ethnologist,* and *Anthropology Today,* as well as to edited collections, and her work has been frequently anthologized. Gottlieb has held fellowships from the National Endowment for the Humanities, the Social Science Research Council, the Woodrow Wilson Foundation, the American Association of University Women, and the Wenner-Gren Foundation for Anthropological Research. She is an associate professor of anthropology at the University of Illinois at Urbana-Champaign.

PHILIP GRAHAM is the author of *The Vanishings* (prose poems) and *The Art of the Knock: Stories.* His short stories have appeared in *The New Yorker,* the *Washington Post Magazine, North American Review, Chicago Review, Fiction, Carolina Quarterly,* and elsewhere, and have been reprinted frequently both here and abroad. His novel, *How to Read an Unwritten Language,* and new story collection, *Interior Design,* will soon be published. The recipient of a National Endowment for the Arts Fellowship and of grants from the National Endowment for the Humanities and the Illinois Arts Council, as well as winner of the 1992 William Peden Prize in Fiction, Graham teaches creative writing at the University of Illinois at Urbana-Champaign, where he is an associate professor of English.

PARALLEL WORLDS

AN ANTHROPOLOGIST
AND A WRITER
ENCOUNTER AFRICA

ALMA GOTTLIEB
AND
PHILIP GRAHAM

THE UNIVERSITY OF
CHICAGO PRESS

Published by arrangement with Crown Publishers, Inc.
PEANUTS reprinted by permission of UFS, Inc.

Fifty percent of the royalties from the sale of this book is being donated to the Beng people.

The University of Chicago Press, Chicago 60637
Copyright © 1993, 1994 by Alma Gottlieb and Philip Graham
All rights reserved. Originally published 1993
University of Chicago Press Edition 1994
Printed in the United States of America

01 00 99 98 97 96 95 94   6 5 4 3 2 1

ISBN: 0–226–30506–6 (pbk.)

Library of Congress Cataloging-in-Publication Data

Gottlieb, Alma.
    Parallel worlds : an anthropologist and a writer encounter Africa /
Alma Gottlieb and Philip Graham.
        p.   cm.
    Includes index.
    1. Beng (African people)—Social life and customs.   2. Philosophy,
Beng.   3. Beng (African people)—Religion.   4. Ethnology—Côte
d'Ivoire—Field work.   5. Côte d'Ivoire—Social life and customs.
I. Graham, Philip, 1951–   . II. Title.
DT545.45.B45G73   1994
306.4′0899634—dc20   94–16533
                                                                CIP

⊗ The paper used in this publication meets the minimum requirements of
the American National Standard for Information Sciences—Permanence
of Paper for Printed Library Materials, ANSI Z39.48–1984.

To our parents:
Florence and William Gottlieb
William and Edith Graham

CONTENTS

꽃   꽃   꽃

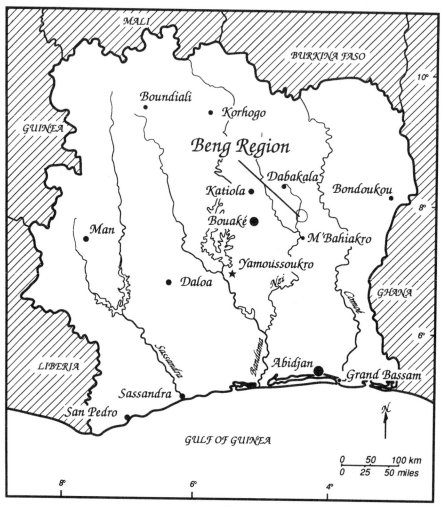

MALI

BURKINA FASO

10°

GUINEA

Boundiali

Korhogo

Beng Region

Dabakala

Bondoukou

8°

Katiola

Bouaké

M'Bahiakro

Man

Yamoussoukro

Nzi

GHANA

Daloa

Comoé

6°

LIBERIA

Sassandra

Bandama

Abidjan

Grand Bassam

Sassandra

San Pedro

N

GULF OF GUINEA

0   50   100 km
0   25   50 miles

8°

6°

4°

Côte d'Ivoire

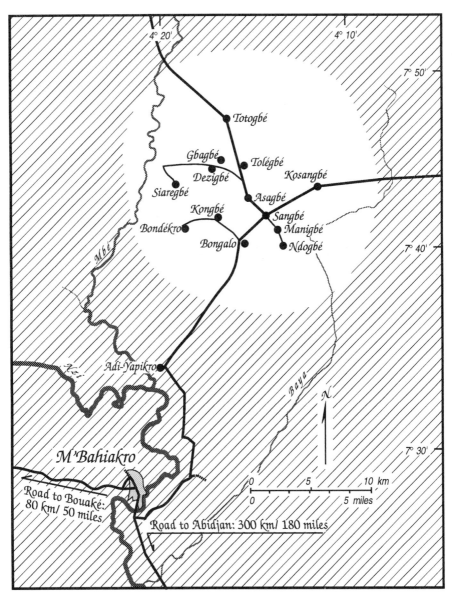

Beng Region

CAST OF CHARACTERS

❧ ❧ ❧

VILLAGE OF KOSANGBÉ

Wamya Kona: village *secrétaire;* our host
Sunu: senior wife of Wamya Kona
Busu Amla: junior wife of Wamya Kona
Moya: daughter of Wamya Kona and Sunu; our cook
Karimu: younger half brother of Wamya Kona

Wuru San: father of San Yao; formerly village chief
San Yao: village chief; Earth priest; rival of Wamya Kona
San Kofi: younger brother of San Yao
Nguessan: sister-in-law of San Yao
Yaokro: Nguessan's husband; younger half brother of San Yao
San Komenan: younger brother of Yaokro

Yacouba: village farmer, our close friend
Dongi: wife of Yacouba
Sramatan: wife of Yacouba

Gba Apo: mother of Ché Kofi and Honoré
Ché Kofi: oldest son of Gba Apo
Asaw: wife of Ché Kofi
Honoré: son of Gba Apo; younger brother of Ché Kofi; tailor in M'Bahiakro
Apu: nephew of Ché Kofi

François: our village landlord
Makola: wife of François
Kossum: younger brother of François
Afwé Ba: senior wife of Kossum
Andama: uncle of François

Kouakou Kala: village elder and Earth priest
Aya: wife of Kouakou Kala
Félice: their young son
Mo'kissi: their niece; reluctant wife of Domolo

Zang: village farmer
Afwé/Nakoyan: daughter of Zang; reluctant wife of Gaosu
Amlakro: daughter of Zang; reputed snake child

Kri Afwé: village elder
Ali Kouakou: her son; would-be husband of Kobla; passed over for village chiefship

Anzoumena: Jula immigrant farmer and healer

Apisé: village elder; reputed witch

Bani: Jimini immigrant farmer

Komena Kouassikro: village elder; would-be diviner

Kwamla Chakro: master drummer of village

Raogo: Mossi immigrant farmer

VILLAGE OF ASAGBÉ

Kouassi André: younger half brother of Bwadi Kouakou; uncle of Pascal
Marie: senior wife of André
Maat: junior wife of André

Bwadi Kouakou: village *secrétaire*
Jokwa: senior wife of Bwadi Kouakou; mother of Pascal
Kla: junior wife of Bwadi Kouakou
Kouakou Kouadio Pascal: son of Bwadi Kouakou and Jokwa; student at the National University of Côte d'Ivoire

Akissikro: mother of Akwé Amenan
Akwé Amenan: village farmer; Alma's principal research informant and friend
Kofi: Amenan's Ghanaian husband
Kokla (Aba) Kouassi: village Earth priest; uncle of Amenan
Evelyne: oldest daughter of Amenan
Amwé/Esi: daughter of Amenan

Ajua: diviner

Amwé: madwoman

Gaosu: husband of Afwé/Nakoyan

Lamine: diviner

OTHER VILLAGES

Akissi: diviner; from the village of Bondékro

Bondé Chomo: king of the Beng savanna region; Amenan's uncle; from the village of Gbagbé

Domolo: husband of Mo'kissi; from the village of Ndogbé

Kobla: would-be wife of Ali Kouakou; originally from Kosangbé, now living in city of Bouaké

Kona Kofi Jean: petty trader in Bongalo; Alma's research assistant; originally from village of Dezigbé

PREFACE TO THE 1994 EDITION

🍥 🍥 🍥

In 1979–80, as a novice anthropologist I lived with my husband Philip in a small West African village in the tropical rain forest of Côte d'Ivoire. There I struggled to learn the previously undocumented ways of the Beng people as Philip and I joined in the rounds of daily life, always hoping for acceptance. This wish was both well placed and misguided, for throughout our time in Bengland we felt alternately welcome and unwelcome, fulfilled and frustrated. Fieldwork, I discovered, was a never-ending series of negotiations. In recounting our experiences, we hope in this book to illuminate what may seem an exotic world and show it to be made of ordinary people. Yet familiarity does not necessarily bring understanding. My task as an anthropologist, and Philip's as a writer, has been to imagine the hidden reasons behind what people do—the *whys* that give life meaning.

The experiences of any traveler are unique, and so this book is not intended as a guide for future travelers or fieldworkers. Instead, it is meant as a candid memoir of the intense emotional involvement—both the pain and joy—that marked the stay of one couple living in what then seemed a foreign land. There are many decisions that Philip and I would have made very differently had we known at the time what we later came to understand. However, in this account we have chosen to resist telescoping that understanding, tempting though it was to let wistful hindsight revise our misjudgments. Instead, our narrative endeavors to recapture the immediacy of the moment by recreating for the reader the emotional landscapes that marked our immersion in a radically different culture. By presenting ourselves with sometimes brutal honesty in offering more than a few carefully chosen epiphanies, we hope to enrich a tradition of ethnographic writing that is curiously reticent about the difficulties that often continue *throughout* fieldwork.

The path to any significant level of mutual comprehension is as bumpy as the washboard dirt road we often traveled from M'Bahiakro to Bengland and back again. But given the motivation to learn from mistakes, a significant level of mutual understanding *is* imaginable, and through the many stories that follow, we try to illuminate the highs and lows of such imagining. In these attempts I have been grateful to my coauthor for his writerly skills in evoking interior as well as ethnographic worlds, and for his insistence that narrative itself can be revelatory.

Although the book covers much that occurred while we lived among the Beng, there are significant omissions: confidences we shared with our hosts and hostesses that we have not passed on. For this reason (as well as, in some cases, more practical considerations), we have used pseudonyms on occasion. We do, however, retain Beng names of their own villages, as well as the name "Beng" itself, which is what Beng people call themselves (they are known as the "Ngen" or "Gan" by others in Côte d'Ivoire). For all Beng terms and names, we have used spellings that will be readily pronounceable for an English-speaking reader.

—A.G.

"Why don't you write a novel?" I was once asked by a friend whom I'd regaled with yet another story about my life among the Beng.

I paused, only half-surprised by the question—I certainly felt as if I'd *lived* a novel. "Maybe I will," I replied, though without much conviction.

Yet for years I resisted the impulse to fictionalize my experiences, for I didn't want to represent the complex world of the Beng as a product of my imagination. Rather, I continued to write works of fiction that, though set in America, secretly charted how my imagination had been transformed by Africa. Meanwhile Alma continued to deepen her own understanding of Beng culture, producing articles and a full-length ethnography. And so, many years passed before we could begin to write this book. Our lives in Bengland had been so intense and overwhelming that neither of us wanted to offer glib judgments; I certainly didn't want to add to the dubious tradition of the literary travelogue, which too often channel surfs through the Third World, eschewing the commitment necessary to understand the realities behind exotic details. Instead, Alma and I were determined to do justice to our Beng friends and neighbors, as well as to chronicle honestly our intertwined experiences as we slowly shed our naive assumptions on a journey of cultural discovery.

When Alma and I finally felt we were ready, we pored through a daunting collection of evidence: carbon copies of several hundred letters that I had written and my three volumes of daybooks, Alma's thousands of pages of field notes and voluminous file of Beng vocabulary cards, as well as hundreds of our photos and slides. Virtually every day had been recorded meticulously—a record that sometimes, to our chagrin, contradicted our recollections. After choosing to tell our story as a chronological narrative of multiple mysteries, unfolding secrets and sometimes painful confessions, Alma and I first wrote our alternating sections separately and then served as each other's first editor. Happily, the normal strains of coauthorship were far outweighed by the pleasures of reliving and recreating a crucial time in our lives.

The result, finally, is a literary construction, a particular shaping of the unruly intricacies of our life in Bengland. In searching out the patterns behind complex events, Alma and I have tried to explore several sets of parallel worlds: the two perspectives of anthropologist and fiction writer that we brought with us to Africa; two cultural—and literary—traditions, Western and African; the two villages where we lived among the Beng people; the coexisting worlds of Beng daily life and the unseen but potent world of the forest spirits and ancestors. This multileveled cultural universe now inhabits us both, suggesting, of course, that these worlds are by no means mutually exclusive—even parallel lines can run infinitely close together.

When I returned to Côte d'Ivoire in 1990 for a brief visit as the American guest at that country's first writers' conference, I found a country racked by protests against the government's decade of mismanagement and corruption, the collapse of prices for farmers' cash crops, and the deterioration of an already inadequate health care system beset by increasingly drug-resistant strains of malaria and the continuing onslaught of the AIDS epidemic. The Beng have so far avoided the depredations of AIDS, but in nearly every other way their plight has worsened, as Alma and I discovered when we lived in Bengland with our son Nathaniel in the summer of 1993. If anything, our immersion in and commitment to what we consider our second home has further deepened. Our son is regarded as the reincarnation of the Beng ancestor he was named after, and my father, who'd recently passed away in America, was given a Beng funeral to allow his soul to enter the Beng afterlife. We in turn have dedicated half our earnings from *Parallel Worlds* to the Beng, and now, back in Illinois, we are hosts to a Beng university student— Kouadio Kouakou Bertin, the son of François, our landlord in the village of Kosangbé. And so we seem to have come full circle: Bertin hopes to write a book one day about his experiences in America, and we willingly offer ourselves as subjects for his own ethnographic imagination.

—P.G.

The only way to get out of Africa is to get Africa out of you.

—Ben Okri

... and they had never forgotten a thing. Not when they left, nor when they were over there, nor when they returned: they had never forgotten a thing. And now they had two memories, two countries.

—Eduardo Galeano

Here before me now is my picture, my map, of a place and therefore of myself, and much that can never be said adds to its reality for me, just as much of its reality is based on my own shadows, my inventions.

—M.F.K. Fisher

PART ONE

ARRIVING

1

PREMONITIONS

❦   ❦   ❦

(OCTOBER 1–NOVEMBER 5, 1979)

Alma: Head Burdens

THE BATTERED PEUGEOT TAXI SWERVED TO AVOID A POTHOLE, AND I CLUNG TO THE WINDOW crank, gazing out at the throngs of pedestrians on the crowded Abidjan city streets. Women walked with babies strapped to their backs, while they carried all manner of burdens piled high on their heads: an enamel tray of imported apples to sell in the market, an old-fashioned foot-pedal sewing machine, a vinyl pocketbook. Stationed at street corners, men dressed in brightly patterned print suits hawked gold-colored necklaces, snakeskin wallets, folding umbrellas. When would the view outside the open window reveal dirt paths winding through dense forest rather than paved roads leading from hotel to restaurant to bank? For I was on my way to meet a government minister—if he stamped my papers, my husband and I could leave this capital and inaugurate my research with the Beng people, a tiny ethnic group some two hundred miles to the north, deep in Côte d'Ivoire's rain forest.

The driver slammed on the brakes to avoid hitting two young girls crossing the street with their pinkies interlocked. The girls jumped aside, and the driver continued, muttering curses at them. Could those girls possibly be Beng migrants to the city? I had no way of knowing—I hadn't yet met any Beng people here in the capital; perhaps the driver might know some.

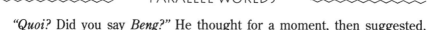

"Quoi? Did you say *Beng?"* He thought for a moment, then suggested, "Maybe they have another name. Where are they from?"

"Up around the town of M'Bahiakro," I answered.

"Non, I've never heard of them." He chuckled. "Imagine, a white lady from America teaching me about my own country!"

I laughed—I'd chosen the Beng precisely because they *were* a small and obscure group, appealing to the romantic in me. Because no Western scholar had ever studied Beng culture, I'd spent a year in my university library dredging up a few brief passages, which mentioned a people still devoted to their indigenous religion, farmers who also hunted and gathered in the forest. But here in the city, that life seemed so remote, impossible to imagine.

Finally the taxi reached the block of government offices, and I wandered among the tall buildings until I found the right tower and took the elevator up to the Ministry of Scientific Research. There, the receptionist greeted me with a crisp dismissal: "The minister will be in today, but I can't say when, so I can't make appointments. Have a seat, along with everyone else." She gestured to one of the few free chairs lining the wall, and I sat down to wait my turn.

By noon there was still no sign of the minister. Disheartened, we all left for the three-hour siesta. Once outside, I hailed a cab to take me back to the two-room apartment Philip and I had rented from the University of Côte d'Ivoire. As the taxi lurched and veered suddenly, I consoled myself: patience should be a valuable trait during fieldwork, for who knew what obstacles we'd encounter in the village? Indeed, the paths that led me to anthropology, and to Africa, were so circuitous, it seemed fitting that once arrived in Côte d'Ivoire, my journey would be full of unexpected twists and turns as well.

As a child in a largely secular family, the only ritual I knew was that of our yearly Passover celebrations in my grandmother's Bronx apartment. As a teenager, feeling the pull of ritual, I explored what the world's other religious traditions had to offer. In Manhattan I sometimes sat in an empty pew of St. John the Divine or St. Patrick's Cathedral, contemplating the emotional pull of those icons around me. In high school I read the classic texts in Buddhism and Hinduism, then I discovered the pacifist Hopi culture, with its continuous round of rituals—some solemn, some bawdy and ridiculous, all insisting on the integration of human life into the natural world.

But in college, offered a tempting array of courses in many of my latent interests, I put aside my readings in the non-Western world and instead devoured works in Western literature, psychology, music, and environmental science. Then my beloved grandmother died, and with her died my only link to the Old World shtetl culture of my ancestors. I left college to mourn. Adrift, I joined a crew of discontents and runaways on an old schooner moored off the southern tip of Texas. The captain, clearly an admirer of Ahab, made a honeymooning couple sleep in separate cabins, allotted the cook the grand sum of five dollars weekly to buy food for a crew of fifteen, bestowed each of us only two hours ashore every other week, and had fits if anyone missed a tiny spot in the daily sanding and polishing of the decks. After two months I left that floating pit of shared misery. But I craved to understand the hidden longings and commitments that bind people to one another in such small communities. I decided to return to college in the fall to study anthropology.⌡

Now, seven years later, I looked outside the taxi window: a young girl with a large tub on her head called out her wares: *"Yi glacé!"*—Ice water! Watching her step carefully to avoid spilling a drop of her precious load, I felt eager to balance my own multiple lives and begin my transition to a field-seasoned anthropologist.

"Hi, hon," Philip called out as soon as I opened the door to our apartment. Sitting on the tiny balcony, manuscripts stacked on the small table next to him, Philip stroked his mustache and gazed out at the expanse of the city. What did he think of it all? I nervously recalled my advisor's wife, who, having spent a year and a half in the Amazonian jungle, once remarked to me that fieldwork could make or break a marriage. There was much that excited Philip in our upcoming adventure—after all, before I'd met him, Philip had hitchhiked through Japan and canoed on the Yukon River. Still, he had left behind a satisfying literary life in America, and I hoped our relationship was strong enough to sustain him in a fifteen-month exile from his literary loves.

I dropped my canvas briefcase on the sofa—leather would rot, I'd been warned—and walked out to the balcony. "It looks like we might be stuck in this city a while—no sign of the minister and no way to make an appointment." I sighed. "How was your morning?"

"Oh, I scratched away at a story," Philip said quietly, "but then I went for a long walk." He paused. "This is a fantastic neighborhood! There's a wonderful little market just a couple blocks away—we can get brochettes there for dinner."

"Great," I said, eager both to see the market and be kind to our tight budget in this expensive city—the next installment of my grant wouldn't arrive for another three months.

"Oh, while I was out I saw a motorcade go by," Philip continued, "lots of cop cars and black Mercedes. People on the street got real excited—it seems Bokassa was in one of those cars. . . ."

"Bokassa?" I gasped. I'd read that the dictator had been given asylum in Côte d'Ivoire, but I never imagined our paths might cross, however remotely.

"Yeah, but the Ivoirians have demoted him—they shouted out, 'Bokassa

Zéro!' Anyway, the little parade stopped just down the road. We're living a couple of blocks from that bastard."

"Another reason to leave the city," I said.

The next day I returned to the minister's office toting a series of anthropology books: solace for my expected hours of waiting. Reading African ethnographies did indeed absorb me in alternate worlds—perhaps ones not too dissimilar from the one I would soon inhabit—but ironically, the act of reading made me oblivious of the Africans seated next to me who were waiting to present their own cases to the minister.

One long morning in the waiting room, I was intrigued to read that the Ebrié people of Côte d'Ivoire had a calendar that operated on a six-day week. I wondered how this fit with the modern world: did the Ebrié think in two systems simultaneously? My attention wavered when a man sitting across from me, who'd arrived a few minutes earlier, stuttered in agitation, *"Pardon, mesdames et messieurs,* I was so worried about my own problems that I didn't greet you."

Everyone in the room glanced up. The man rose and announced, "Good morning, ladies and gentlemen."

Some people frowned, some nodded with sympathy, but they all said quietly, "Good morning." At once I thought: These strangers greeting one another have transformed this anonymous urban waiting room into a temporary village, where everyone *must* know everyone else! Had I offended those in the room with my rude silence, or did they expect as much from a white person?

The next day I tried out my own formal greeting. Everyone looked up briefly, smiled, said, *"Bonjour,"* and went back to what I imagined were their own bureaucratic broodings. It was so easy to join in a simple custom that, I suspected, served as a marker of civilization. Living in a small village would no doubt require similar demonstrations of friendliness . . . but would months of it begin to feel stifling?

After several more days of waiting on an invisible line with no discernible order, the receptionist called out: "Madame Gottlieb, the minister will see you now."

I walked down the hall, trying nervously to remember the speech I'd memorized over the past week. The minister's door was partly ajar. I knocked, and a deep voice said, *"Entrez."* Elegantly dressed in a pin-striped suit, the minister was seated at a desk covered with neat stacks of papers that effectively proclaimed the burdens of an important person. I made my way to a cushioned chair and suddenly felt nervous: was my research project well conceived enough, my spoken French eloquent enough?

"What may I do for you?" the minister inquired in a polished but friendly tone. Forgetting all I'd planned to say, I resorted to dragging out the letters of introduction that various people had written for me: the president of the Social Science Research Council, certifying, with a red ribbon, that his agency had awarded me a fellowship; my advisors, attesting that I was bound for a respectable career in anthropology and would certainly obey the laws of a foreign country; the registrar at the University of Virginia, swearing that I already possessed a master of arts degree in anthropology from that institution and was currently a doctoral student in good standing.

"Yes, fine, but what may I do for you?" the minister repeated when he glanced at these offerings.

"Oh, yes," I said, suddenly remembering my lines, "I'm here to conduct research among the Beng people of the M'Bahiakro region. I wrote to you from America, and you were kind enough to reply, but you indicated you would need to see me before you could approve my research." Now I remembered, a bit belatedly, the most relevant paper of all: a copy of the letter the minister himself had sent me.

"This is fine, we encourage foreign students to conduct research in our country. We're delighted to have you here." He smiled. I beamed. "Unfortunately"—he sighed—"I can't sign your papers."

My eyes widened in dismay.

"I wish I could," the minister continued, "but we have a new regulation: research such as yours must first be authorized by the Ministry of the Interior. I advise you to make an appointment with that minister, then return to my office with a letter from him."

"Thank you very much, *Monsieur le Ministre*," I managed to say. But how long would it take to obtain an appointment with this second minister? And would *he* agree to my research?

I decided to take a break from waiting rooms and stock up on the supplies Philip and I imagined we'd need during a long stay in a remote village. The market was a daze of colors, tastes, smells: brightly patterned, wraparound, long skirts worn by traders and buyers alike—so these were the *pagnes* I'd read about; mounds of chili peppers, stacks of animal skins, rows of bicycle tires at our feet; pungent scents from the heaps of dried herbs and pieces of bark laid out on mats on the ground. Soon we discerned a hidden order to the merchandise: freshly butchered beef in one corner, advertised by the hordes of flies; mounds of cherry tomatoes, okra, pearl onions grouped in another spot; small wooden statues—ancient or cleverly made to look so—upstairs; and across from those, jewelry of colored glass beads, amber, ivory. Seated on the ground next to their wares, the sellers entreated us to buy from them,

not their rivals. "Madame, my price is lowest!" But the sound of this familiar cry only incited a competitor, who countered rapidly:

"No, monsieur, come to me, I can do better!"

We found batik fabrics to buy as presents for villagers we didn't yet know, wondering which of the floral and geometric prints they might prefer. And we discovered a collection of heavy, old-fashioned charcoal irons with a red wooden hen perched atop the compartment for charcoal: ironing, we'd been advised, should kill the eggs that tropical tumble flies laid in wet laundry hanging out to dry.

In a Lebanese-owned boutique, we bought a tall kerosene lamp that shed the light of a seventy-five-watt bulb from a delicate mesh mantle: ideal for Philip, who often wrote at night. The next stop was a local geographic society, where we were delighted to find detailed printed maps of the Beng region. Philip and I pored in wonder over the large sheets. "Look at those thin blue lines," I exclaimed, "they're streams that go right through the Beng area!" Seeing the landscape plotted out so minutely made our future home seem one layer closer to real.

At a pharmacy, we stocked up on tetracycline and Ganidan for assorted cases of dysentery; lotions and antihistamines for rashes and nasty insect bites; rolls of gauze and bottles of disinfectant solution for cuts; two dozen disposable syringes to avoid hepatitis from reused needles. Standing on the long cashier's line, we stared at this sobering medical arsenal, foolishly hoping that we'd never have to use any of these supplies.

The interior minister's office was located in a Quonset hut that must have been earmarked for the wrecking ball as soon as a new office building could be erected. The waiting room was hot: air-conditioning wasn't worth it for temporary quarters such as these. It was October, but these last weeks of the rainy season brought no cool breezes, only a thick humidity that made the people in this lounge look as if they'd melted into the moist heat of their chairs.

Like his colleague across town, this minister also took no appointments. In the lounge, I began to consider these delays from the ministers' perspectives. Why should high officials give priority to a lowly foreign graduate student who was seeking permission to study the social and religious life of a tiny minority group? The Beng may have been the main subject of my daily reveries, but clearly they were not a national priority.

I sometimes repeated these consolations like a mantra, because it took a week of waiting before I had my audience with the minister. He greeted me cordially but frowned slightly as he looked over my papers. Did he think I

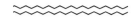

was studying the wrong subject? Maybe he was Christian and didn't approve of my interest in traditional religion. Finally, brows wrinkled, he asked, "But who are these Beng? I've never heard of them!"

If only I'd brought along my ethnic map of the country, to prove their existence.

"Why don't you live with the Baulé people?" he continued. "That's who all the anthropologists study."

But I had no interest in adding the Baulé to the repertoire of the standard anthropology joke:

Q: How many people live in the typical nuclear Mexican family?

A: Six: a father, a mother, three children, and an anthropologist.

As I tried to think of a suitable reply, the minister finally responded to my silence with a chuckle. "I suppose if you've come all this way to study an ethnic group I've never heard of, there must be something interesting there to find out. I'll write your letter of authorization . . . but I'm afraid the minister of scientific research must write me a letter first. Once he's done so, return to my office with his letter."

"But, monsieur," I said, almost in tears, "the minister sent me to you. He said *you* have to write *him* a letter first."

"Ah, he's mistaken," the minister declared, "we've recently received a new directive on that point."

"Monsieur le Ministre," I said with a sudden burst of courage, "would it be possible for you to phone him—to discuss the problem between the two of you? Because I know that if I return to him, he'll repeat what he said before."

A reasonable man, the minister agreed to my suggestion. He picked up the receiver of the French-style gray phone on his desk and dialed. I sat expectantly, hoping he would speak loudly enough for me to follow the conversation. *"Zut,"* he exclaimed, "the phone lines are down. I'm sorry, please come back tomorrow."

Philip: The Shifting Line

Throughout my childhood I was an avid reader of the Peanuts comic strip. Even now I enjoy turning to the back of the local newspaper for a brief immersion into a special nostalgia for Charlie Brown's unpopularity, Lucy's bossiness, Linus's security blanket, Schroeder's Beethoven worship. But of all those years of reading strip after strip, only one still stands out, virtually memorized. It's not an especially striking example of the Peanuts world, yet even when I first read it, years ago, I knew it said something fundamental about me. As Charlie Brown walks home from school with Patty, she asks, "How are you doing in school these days, Charlie Brown?"

"Oh, fairly well, I guess. I'm having most of my trouble with arithmetic."

Surprised, Patty says, "I should think you'd like arithmetic, it's a very precise subject."

"That's just the trouble," Charlie Brown replies, "I'm at my best in something where the answers are mostly a matter of opinion."

I agreed with him—math and science were always my poorest subjects, English and social studies my best. That comic strip clarified for me the secret reason for my preference—a single, unambiguous answer felt too confining—yet only later did I come to understand what it said about the way I viewed the world: that any one vision is always counterbalanced by another, and another again. Perhaps it was inevitable that I would become a writer, exploring the competing impulses of my fictional characters.

Perhaps it was also inevitable that I would marry an anthropologist. I can still remember the rush of excitement I felt in fifth grade when I discovered in the school library a novel about a young Incan messenger runner: I'd never before heard of the South American Indian civilizations, and I set about reading everything I could find on the subject, feeling my imagination tentatively trying on that different culture. Later, after indulging in a trashy infatuation with Edgar Rice Burroughs's pulp fiction ethnographies of Mars, Venus, and the core of the earth—oddly enough, Tarzan interested me only minimally—I discovered Tolstoy and Dostoyevski and immersed myself in a nineteenth-century Russian world. Then, in my early twenties I quit a lucrative job as a bartender in order to impersonate Santa Claus at a suburban branch of Saks Fifth Avenue: during the occasional lulls from the long lines of children and their adoration, I sat on my throne and pored through an anthology of non-Western poetry and creation tales, hoping to solidify my budding sense of mythic stature. Soon I was avidly investigating the literatures of the Third World, as if preparing for a journey.

The sights of Abidjan swept over me for days: the plaited hairstyles—as elaborate as baroque filigree—of well-to-do women who swept down crowded streets with haughty grace; children pushing pallet boards, their deformed limbs on display as they begged; Muslims on line in the bank who, as prayer time arrived, faced Mecca and prostrated themselves on the floor; market women selling stacks of bright pink fabric featuring the oval-framed portraits of Houphouët-Boigny—the president since independence in 1960—and his wife, Thérèse; men and women everywhere toting *baguettes,* as the people of this former French colony had developed a taste for those long loaves.

For years I'd been reading the work of African writers: Elechi Amadi's evocations of a traditional life untouched by colonial rule; Chinua Achebe's depictions of that life's destruction; Bernard Dadié's memoir of political resistance to colonialism; Wole Soyinka's bitter humor at the modern Africa. These works had created inside me a mishmash of a world I'd one day visit, and while Alma found herself increasingly baffled by bureaucratic niceties she'd never dreamed of, I roamed the streets near our apartment, trying out my frail French, listening to the profusion of African languages—perhaps one of them was Beng, the language I'd have to learn. Even the smell of the air I took in was new: musty, almost mildewed, and slightly sweet. In a way I was a child again, surrounded by overlapping secrets waiting to be deciphered, yet as I explored the streets of Abidjan I wondered how this vast, as yet unlived experience before me would affect my writing. I couldn't help thinking of the stack of manuscripts lying on a table back in our lodgings: my short-story collection, long in progress. Soon I'd have to return to my fictional families and the strange patterns they made of their lives.

Occasionally Alma and I had enough time together to continue the search for provisions, and one afternoon we visited the Treichville market. As we skirted the edge of the crowded stalls, we heard the distant, collective shout of an angry crowd. The sound drew nearer, repetitive, almost choral.

"What *is* that?" Alma asked.

"I don't know, but I think we'd better move," I replied, and we wended our way across the street to the wide entrance of a housewares shop. Soon we saw a surge of people surrounding a most unhappy man: tall and in rags, his arms held by two gendarmes. The crowd continued shouting in rhythmic unison, and finally we could make out the cry: *"Voleur! Voleur!"*

With much difficulty the gendarmes managed to shuttle the thief into a paddy wagon, but still the people roared, now shaking the car, rolling it in a wave back and forth. I felt something inside me urge toward the mob and something else resist it. For a moment I feared they might tear apart the car and everyone inside. But the horn blared frantically, and slowly the paddy wagon moved through the crowd. Everyone continued shouting *"Voleur!"* though now with a festive, laughing quality.

Alma and I had been warned about thieves in the markets, but our fear vanished after seeing the response that a thief, however desperate, knew he might have to face. Watching that paddy wagon pull away, I wondered what sort of moral universe we'd find in a village and how, as strangers, we'd fit in.

Through a notice at the university we found ourselves a used car—a Renault R6 that a faculty member wanted to sell. We assumed the roads upcountry would be formidable—dusty, cratered affairs in the dry season, mud-slogged swamps in the rainy season—so we wanted to make sure that whatever car we bought would hold up against untold future difficulties. The night before we were to examine the car, I paged through the automotive section of my Berlitz guide for hours, so I might ask pointed questions in my inadequate French. Remembering that spark plugs were *bougies,* that the ignition was *l'allumage,* was simple enough, but would I be able to calculate easily how many *kilomètres* we might expect per *litre* of *essence?*

None of this, however, would truly disguise the fact that I was absolutely ignorant mechanically. During our inspection I could only pace around the car, murmur enigmatically, and poke among incomprehensible wires and hoses in the engine. I regarded the stick shift dubiously—it stuck out horizontally from the dashboard. But the test drive was fine—shifting gears with the *arbre de transmission* and *embrayage* was no trouble—and the seller was a fellow scholar, an Ivoirian historian who nodded encouragement as Alma told him of her fieldwork plans. How could he possibly sell us a bad car when he knew how much we'd need to rely on it? So we haggled good-naturedly and finally settled on a price.

Within a week we had foresworn taxis—a loss, I thought, missing those daredevil cabbies and the bold slashes of their scarification marks. Driving in Abidjan was much different from being driven. I was now acutely aware of the virtual absence of street signs, stop signs, and traffic lights. In America we are told on almost every street where we are, where we are going, how fast we should continue on our way, and when we should stop, yet the drivers around me seemed to do well without these landmarks, improvising traffic rules as they roared down avenues and across intersections, cutting off other cars cavalierly. Our Renault performed well, though once, as I downshifted on an exit ramp, we heard a small explosion coming from the engine. I pulled over quickly and opened the hood, where I discovered that a spark plug, apparently loosely screwed in, had shot out of the engine block, denting the inside of the hood. Fortunately we had that day bought replacement parts at an automotive shop. I slipped in a new one and tightened it, nervously aware that I was on the edge of my mechanical competence, and we drove back to the apartment silently, afraid of another small explosion.

While buying the car and all our provisions, we made numerous trips to a bank on the Cocody plateau to cash our traveler's checks. One late afternoon as we arrived we noticed an unusually large crowd gathered in the parking area. But we were so anxious to exchange our money before the bank closed that we passed by and continued on until I saw, through the glass door, depositors with their arms raised while burly men pointed machine guns at them. I stopped and grasped Alma's arm. We were just outside the doors and could be seen at any moment.

"Alma, look," I whispered.

She caught her breath. Together we carefully, silently, walked backward, hoping to blend in with the crowd that was too far behind us. Wonderful, I thought, we've traveled to Africa only to be shot up in a bank robbery. Then Alma and I noticed a gendarme standing among a knot of people: he was *smiling*. Confused, I looked back at the bank: the robbery was still under way, though now I noticed an unusually bright light in the lobby and a man, standing near the three robbers, who balanced a large camera on his shoulders.

Eventually the cameraman left the bank, along with another man who, murmuring orders to a few assistants, appeared to be the director. They stood before us, preparing the camera angle for the scripted getaway. Then the bandits rushed from the bank, firing guns in the air, and they packed into a waiting car that lurched forward a few feet and stalled.

We all laughed at the botched escape. Alma and I were ready to settle in and watch the next take, but then we remembered how late it was and how much we needed to exchange money. We entered the bank and stood on line.

Soon the armed actors were back in the lobby—apparently the director wanted to cover himself and shoot a second take of each scene. Now *our* arms were raised before the menacing machine guns. The loot was grabbed once again, the escape finally accomplished smoothly.

After we returned to the teller's window and completed our transaction, I began to worry that during the editing of the film someone might notice the huge grin I hadn't managed to contain during the holdup. Would my obvious pleasure at being an extra in an African television drama break the illusion? And if I'd spoiled the scene so easily here, how would I manage to straddle what I suspected would be a far more subtly shifting line between art and reality in the intense, enclosed energies of a small village?

Alma: Trying to Say Hello

The ministers' spiderweb wove itself ever more elaborately. Even when the phone lines were restored, each minister asserted a different procedure must be followed, and I commuted back and forth between them, desperate to extricate myself from this bureaucratic tangle. Finally the two ministers agreed on who should be the first to write the other. When I obtained my letters I promptly made ten copies of each on a university Xerox machine and then scattered them: one in the large suitcase with my clothes; another in the aluminum camera case; another in Philip's typewriter case. I had worked for almost three weeks to obtain those documents—letters I imagined should greatly ease our entry into a Beng village—and I wasn't taking any chances. Only a short time remained for us in the capital. I asked virtually anyone I met—shop owners, market traders, restaurant waiters—if they knew any Beng people, but invariably I met with shrugs or blank stares. At last, a few days before our scheduled departure from the city, a linguist at the university told me she'd located a Beng student. I was elated—and anxious. Would we like each other? All our friend knew was that Kouakou Kouadio Pascal was majoring in English and that he seemed rather shy. We arranged for a rendezvous in our rented apartment.

Waiting in our living room, Philip and I formulated a long list of questions for Pascal. We hoped he'd be friendly and willing to talk about the village he'd left behind. When the expected knock came, Philip and I rose quickly from the couch to greet Pascal. The short young man at the door said, *"Bonsoir, are you Monsieur Graham and Madame Gottlieb?"*

"Yes, please come in—and call us Philip and Alma," Philip said.

"Bon," Pascal said tentatively, his eyes flashing around the room.

We all sat down in the living room, and I said, "I should tell you that I'm here as a college student, like you. I'm here to study the Beng—uh, your people. Forgive me"—I suddenly felt a wave of joy wash over me—"you're the first Beng person we've met! I'm *really* happy to meet you."

Pascal smiled encouragement.

"Well," I continued, slipping into a short version of the speech I'd repeated to the ministers, "I'm interested in Beng culture, especially traditional religion, and women's lives. Philip and I are hoping to live for about fifteen months in a Beng village."

Pascal nodded seriously and said, "I'm very pleased to meet you, too. And I'm happy that you'll be living among my people."

"I understand you're majoring in English," Philip said.

"Yes," Pascal said, switching to English, "I am studying your language." His speech became slow and deliberate, marked by a thick French accent. "I am very happy to speak with you. I do not know any Americans, and it is . . . rare for me to talk in English."

"Ah, I'm sorry we didn't meet earlier," I said, now in French—speaking English was clearly an effort for Pascal. "We could've taught you some good American slang, and you could've given us some lessons in Beng."

"Oui, that would have been very wonderful for me."

"But perhaps you could teach us a few words right now?" I suggested. I knew that the hardest thing about our first few months among the Beng would be communicating even the simplest needs, ideas, questions. Except for a few very brief reports, their language had never been studied.

"Yes, I'd be happy to," Pascal agreed readily.

"Great! Maybe we could start with the greetings," I proposed. When we showed up unexpectedly in our first Beng village, it would certainly be helpful to be able to say "Hello."

"Well," Pascal began, "there are a lot of different ways to greet people, depending on what time of day it is. So, let's start with the morning."

Pascal settled into the couch. As he switched roles from student to teacher, he seemed to gain confidence. "For you, Monsieur Philippe, when you see a man who's about your father's age, you can say, *'Aba ka drua.'* Then the man replies, *'Maa, ka kungli.'* Then you say, *'Maa.'* The man waits a second and says, *'Blini ka.'* You say, *'Nn-nn'* "—his voice dropped on the second syllable—"and he says, *'Ee-en.'* You reply, *'Dru kalé.'* Then he says, *'Maa, ma gwa no wé,'* and you say, *'No nyilé.'* "

Philip and I exchanged glances of alarm. How could we ever remember so many phrases?

"But what does it all mean?" I asked.

"Well, it's all to say, *'Bonjour, ça va?'* "

"But you just said that in French in three words!" Philip said, a note of despair beneath his laughter.

"Yes, you're right," Pascal agreed, "but in Beng it takes us a lot longer to say hello. Also, for you, Madame Alma, there are different phrases for your responses. And of course, the afternoon and evening have still other sets of greetings."

"Are those the only differences?" I asked, dreading to hear the answer.

"Oh, no. You must use other terms if a woman greets a man, or if two women greet each other, and so forth."

I fell silent, feeling sorry for myself. Why hadn't I taken the optional field linguistics course in graduate school? Finally I said, "You know, I learned French pretty easily in school, and I even know a little German, Spanish, and Russian. But Beng—*mon vieux,* it seems really complicated!"

"Oh, you'll learn it in no time," Pascal said confidently. "After all, we always learn other languages. English is my sixth."

"Okay," I said, renewing my determination, "can you teach us a short version of 'hello'?"

"Bon, I'll just teach you the afternoon greetings to an older person."

"Great," I said, hoping fervently that when we finally arrived in our first Beng village, it would be afternoon, and everyone we met would be a good deal older than us.

Pascal proceeded to recite the afternoon greetings for each of us. Inaugurating my first red, spiral-bound notebook, I tried my best to write down each phrase, syllable by syllable, guessing at an alphabet as I went along. When we finished the lesson I said, "I'm sure you must be tired after all this, but I wonder if you could tell us just a few things about the villages."

"I'm not tired at all," he said cheerfully. "What would you like to know?"

"We'll have to decide on a village to live in. How many are there? Could you tell us about each of them? We don't even know all their names."

"Sure," he answered. "There are about twenty, but, really, you should live in my village. That's Asagbé. It's pretty large—about twelve hundred people—and it has a good little general store. The bus usually passes by once a day for M'Bahiakro, the nearest town. And there are some Christians living there." He paused. "Also, my father is the *secrétaire.*"

"Excuse me?" I asked.

"In Côte d'Ivoire," Pascal explained, "all the villages have a representative to the PDCI."

"Ah," I said, suddenly realizing that the modest student before us, having reached the university from humble village origins, must have come from a locally influential family—the Parti Démocratique de Côte d'Ivoire was the country's single political party.

"Your village sounds lovely, but I think I'd prefer a smaller one that's more traditional." I looked up, hoping I hadn't offended Pascal, but he nodded noncommittally. I continued, "Also, I'd like to hire someone to help me in my research, someone who has an interest in Beng culture and who knows French, to translate for me and at the same time teach me your language. Can you think of someone who might be interested?"

Pascal was silent for just a few moments, then smiled. "There's a fellow named Kona Kofi Jean: he's a trader in a village market, but he could probably give that up to work for you—especially since he doesn't have any fields to farm. And he's not married, so he could probably move to whatever village you choose. Yes, I think he'd be perfect."

"He sounds great!" I said. Silently I compared his situation to those of other field assistants I'd read about. Often they were marginal to their own society: the Dogon hunter Ogotommêli became Marcel Griaule's trusted informant in Mali after being blinded in an accident; the renowned Ndembu healer Muchona the Hornet became Victor Turner's best informant in Zambia after he bought his freedom from his slave mother's master. Undoubtedly the precariousness of anthropologists' own roles during fieldwork attracted them to people who were themselves in one way or another marginal to their own societies. Perhaps Jean fit this pattern, too.

I looked out the window: the afternoon lizards were starting to scramble about outside, looking for evening shelter. Philip and I were ready to say good-bye, however reluctantly, when Pascal offered, "You know, you'll need a place to stay while you're choosing a village to live in."

We knew that all too well. Philip and I had often imagined driving into a strange village where we knew no one. It was hard to say who would find it more bizarre—the villagers or us.

"I'll write a letter to my uncle André," Pascal offered. "He speaks very good

French. He's the one who buys coffee from the village farmers to resell to the government. I'm sure you can stay with his family for as long as you need."

Philip: The Best of the Best

Alma and I spent the morning packing our belongings into the back of the Renault: suitcases stuffed with clothing, boxes of medicines, kerosene lanterns, a two-burner camping stove that eventually would be fueled by a large metal gas can. Where would we unpack all this, what home awaited us? Finally, armed with Alma's signed research papers and Pascal's letter of introduction, we began our long journey to the Beng.

Within minutes of leaving the city's suburbs we were confronted by an entirely different landscape: the huge trees of the rain forest filled the horizon with as much authority as had the skyscrapers of Abidjan. And nestled in the dense forest every few miles were small villages: clusters of mud houses, bare dirt courtyards cluttered with large wooden mortars and pestles, small stone hearths, and piles of firewood. The villages were invariably deserted, except for a few playing children, an old man or woman sitting in the dark entrance of a house, a young woman cooking. As we sped by, a few curious faces always peered at us. Soon we would be living in a village much like the ones we were passing, and the difficulties of such an endeavor seemed to magnify, even as we drove closer to its fulfillment.

But the paved road Alma and I had chosen for the beginning of our journey swiftly made us forget these long-term worries: merely miles from Abidjan, the road seemed to develop huge, gaping potholes before our eyes—craters that could easily swallow a tire. I had to weave in and out of the two lanes, sometimes swerving away suddenly from a speeding logging truck filled with gigantic sections of felled trees. By the time we reached the city of Bouaké that evening, 160 miles to the north, we were rattled and exhausted.

Alma had one last bureaucratic hurdle to clear—her already signed papers needed to be stamped by the *préfet* of Bouaké, under whose jurisdiction the Beng lived, but that potential problem we'd confront in the morning. For the moment our immediate concern was to find a hotel. We quickly located an Ivoirian-run establishment of small, well-kept rooms. After laboriously moving all our baggage into our room, we walked a few blocks to Tanti Sally, a restaurant the hotel manager had recommended. Famished, we ordered too much—chicken in peanut sauce, a Senegalese rice dish, plantains, oversize bottles of beer. The food was delicious but incredibly spicy, as if the meals had magically trapped inside them the fire with which they were cooked. Was this the kind of food we could expect in the village? I couldn't imagine eating like this every day, though with such a diet our mouths might be ideally primed for all those difficult greetings Pascal had tried to teach us.

From the friendly stares and smiles we received, we suspected that we were highly unusual additions to the clientele. We greeted the people sitting at neighboring tables and tried to strike up conversations in French. Alma was disappointed to hear that all government offices would be closed the next day for Tabaski, a Muslim holiday that celebrated God having prevented Abraham's attempted sacrifice of his son Ishmael. To applaud God's mercy, every Muslim family in the city would sacrifice a ram. When one of our restaurant neighbors said, "You should drive through the city tomorrow, thousands of sheep will be slaughtered in the streets," Alma drew out her notebook, now pleased with this latest bureaucratic delay. Then we learned that dancing would begin in the late afternoon, and we didn't want to miss this—though the Koran prohibited dancing, some African Muslims obviously had their own ideas about how to glorify God.

Still exhausted from our journey, we awoke late the next morning. Afraid we'd already missed too much, we quickly drove to Koko, Bouaké's Muslim section, and along the way we saw that the entire city was closed down. Under slate-gray clouds that threatened rain, long lines of Muslim men, straw prayer mats in hand and dressed in immaculate, flowing *bubus*—elegant, ankle-length gowns—were walking to the various mosques. Droves of skittish sheep were shepherded through the streets, their nervous bleats echoing through the air.

After half an hour of communal prayers, families returned home, and soon the slaughter began: on street after street, in virtually every household, two or three young men held down a struggling animal while an older man slit its throat. Then the carcass was cleaned and butchered. So much blood everywhere, so many lives taken for meals of celebration.

By late afternoon Bouaké's Muslim quarter was filled with the sound of furious, interlocking drumming patterns. I parked the car and we followed a large throng accompanying a dance procession through the streets. Many dancers wore headdresses of red felt, inlaid with bits of mirror, and a lock of sheep hair tied to the top that swung freely with the sharp shake of a head. The dancers were surrounded by appreciative, swaying onlookers, but when the crowd drew too close, a middle-aged man strode swiftly along the edge of the circle, snapping a leather whip, making the audience ripple away from him. At times a daring child darted forward, testing the range of the whip as people gasped and giggled at once.

For as long as I'd known Alma, she'd been a student of anthropology, but now she was an anthropologist, and this festival was a dry run for the hard work ahead. I watched admiringly as she asked questions of anyone who would stop to answer them: "Why is that man dancing with the women? Why are there mirrors on those headdresses? What's the name of this dance?"

The name was *didadi,* a word in the Jula language meaning "the best of the best." As the night drew on and the rhythms of the drums and the dancers' steps seemed all there was to the world, we had to agree.

To Alma's surprise, her papers were stamped by the Bouaké *préfet* with almost shocking swiftness, leaving us with one remaining task: the purchase of snake serum. Before we'd left for Côte d'Ivoire, Alma's professors had regaled us with the terrors of some of their choice snake stories—and gleefully so, for they had survived. Yet their underlying message of caution hadn't been lost on us, and we were determined to prepare for any sudden crisis that might occur in a remote village.

The only pharmacist who sold the necessary serum in Bouaké was the son of an influential politician; a large, relaxed man, he took an immediate interest in Alma's research. He also cautioned us to keep the vial cold at all times.

"But we'll be living in a small village," Alma reminded him, "where there's no electricity."

"You'll be near M'Bahiakro," he replied, "that's the seat of the *sous-préfecture;* there's electricity there."

"But we don't know anyone in M'Bahiakro," I said.

"There are two Protestant missionaries living there. One is a nurse, and I know they have a refrigerator. I'm sure they'd store the serum for you. The vial can keep for four hours in the heat. That should give you enough time to drive to M'Bahiakro and find them."

Alma and I glanced at each other nervously—what if we *couldn't* find them? Still, M'Bahiakro was only forty-five miles away, a short enough distance—we decided to take the risk. The serum was a form of insurance we didn't want to give up.

"Good," he said, smiling with satisfaction at our good sense. "I keep the vials stored at my home—they're quite expensive. Just before you leave for M'Bahiakro, you can come and pick one up. This will save you time."

We thanked him, and the next day we parked in front of a modest two-story building located on a crowded, dirty street. But when we entered the interior courtyard we saw a Rolls-Royce parked in the garage. Once in the pharmacist's home we found ourselves walking on marble floors and Oriental rugs, and we tried not to gawk at the huge ivory tusks mounted on wooden stands here and there among the leather couches or the plant stands made of gold. We couldn't believe the contrast between our surroundings and the life in the

dirt street outside: those children hawking bottles of peanuts, the gaunt old men pulling carts filled with sacks of rice. The pharmacist had a kind face, and we were grateful for his concern and advice, but I doubted that this politically well-placed son had built himself such a home from selling aspirin.

Fewer than ten miles outside of Bouaké, the paved road turned into a dirt washboard surface, with thick overhanging forest on either side. The hardened ripples rattled the car so alarmingly that I thought it might simply fall to pieces under us. I slowed to about fifteen miles an hour. But when Alma calculated how long it would take us to arrive in M'Bahiakro, I sped up, worrying about the serum. Once again the car shook as if possessed, and I felt that the nucleus of every cell in my body had a headache. If the car broke down from the strain, a vial of spoiled serum would become an extremely tiny problem. I braked again to slow down, and the dust plumes doggedly following us seeped into the car.

Our progress was further slowed by the roadside army checkpoints. Time after time we were flagged down by a soldier with a machine gun slung over his shoulder, and we stopped to present our passports, international driver's licenses, and Alma's signed and stamped research permissions. We tried not to appear impatient, fearing that would create a further delay, as the soldier slowly, carefully, attended to our batch of documents. Was he expecting a bribe? With a weary wave he let us continue on our way—Alma's long paper chase was finally paying off—and we returned to the car for another worried series of accelerations and decelerations.

The minutes seemed to pass faster than the miles; occasionally I pressed the gas pedal and spurted ahead until the car's rumbling and clanging frightened me. I cursed at the road, every specific inch of it, on and on, until Alma said, "Calm down or let me drive." But I could see from her pinched face that she was equally unsettled. I quieted and cursed silently instead.

Finally we reached pavement, and a small sign announced that M'Bahiakro was only a few kilometers away. Alma and I let out cheers: we were free of the relentless drumming of that rippled road, and our car had held up. As we drove toward the outskirts of town I said, "Hey, I just thought of a name for this lovely little jalopy."

Alma laughed. "I don't know why I thought I had to come to Africa to study animism."

"No, really, I think I've got a name that fits."

"Okay, what?"

"Didadi. Remember? 'The best of the best.'"

Alma agreed, and so our car was christened. It was a name we very much wanted to be a prophecy.

M'Bahiakro was a small town, a patchwork of paved and dirt streets. Market stalls circled a central square, and beside this was another square where small, decrepit buses gathered. The town was located in the region of the Baulé people—one of Côte d'Ivoire's largest ethnic groups—yet certainly some of the people we saw milling about storefronts or sitting stolidly beside large basins of foodstuffs were Beng. Alma and I peered out of the car windows. A man rode by on a bicycle, a stiff, straw mattress balanced on his head; then we passed a woman with a huge enamel basin filled with a pyramid of plantains towering on her head. We gaped, almost forgetting our dilemma—that in less than half an hour our serum would begin to lose its force. We had to find those missionaries.

The first person we asked gave us directions we were able to follow easily, and within minutes we parked outside a long, single-story house with whitewashed walls, iron bars set vertically in place before the windows. But no amount of knocking drew anyone to the door. We couldn't wait for their return. We tried to drive back to the marketplace, but soon we were lost, near what must have been the edge of town. We passed a large, half-built mosque, a line of hairdressing shops and food stalls, until we stopped a few people and learned that there was a Catholic mission nearby, with two *pères* in residence—we were assured that they were in town.

We drove into the mission's courtyard and waited while a young girl in a blue school uniform went to search for one of the priests. Out from the main house came a tall man, his dark hair and well-trimmed beard framing a face that seemed even whiter without a mustache. He walked toward us slowly, with a stiff gait that seemed to signal caution, even suspicion: who were these dusty strangers? We made our introductions, and Alma explained our dilemma in her best French.

Father Denis nodded, motioned us to follow him. "But I cannot guarantee your serum's safety," he said. "Sometimes the electricity in town goes out for hours."

Inside, he led us to a room with a large dining table; in a corner was the refrigerator. He opened the door and we saw stacks of yogurt in plastic cups. We stared at the welcome sight.

"Would you like some?" the father said. "We make it every day." We nodded, and he took out two cups.

Our vial safely ensconced in the cold clutches of the refrigerator, we sat at the table and greedily spooned out the tart, delicious yogurt. Then we all introduced ourselves further, but this conversation between writer, anthropologist, and priest was marked by a strained politeness. I suspected this was because we were in opposing camps: Alma was here to study African culture; Father Denis surely was here to change it.

Then Alma and I remembered that we knew no one in town, had no place to stay, and we asked for directions to a hotel.

Father Denis gave us a thin smile. "There is no hotel in M'Bahiakro." He paused. "Don't you know Mademoiselle Sammet?"

We shook our heads no.

He sighed, with a finality that I assumed was a judgment on our extraordinary lack of preparation. "She is a young American woman who teaches English here at the junior high school. The Peace Corps, I believe. But I think she is gone for the day and won't return to town until tomorrow." He paused and added almost grudgingly, "You can stay here for the night, if you wish."

Alma and I accepted his offer and thanked him again. Though secretly disappointed that we'd have to wait to meet this American woman, we were also surprised at how carefully her movements were tracked. Would our doings soon be so well-known to others? Perhaps assumptions were already being made about the foreign couple whose earliest questions concerned the whereabouts of two sets of missionaries.

Lisa Sammet, it turned out, lived near the Protestant missionaries, in a similarly expansive white stucco house, with three bedrooms and a lovely walled-in grassy courtyard. She was delighted to meet us, two fellow Americans she could gossip with and complain to, her broad, friendly face frequently breaking into laughter as she shook her pale blond hair. During Lisa's first week in M'Bahiakro, the small group of French teachers at the school—working here as an alternative to military duty in France—had quickly made it clear that, socially, she would have to choose between them and the Ivoirian faculty. "You wouldn't believe what the French say about the Africans! That they're lazy and never have to work—if they're hungry, all they do is pluck a mango or banana from a tree."

Lisa had gladly chosen the Ivoirians. Shunned by the French, she found that her decision made her extremely popular with the students, though she spoke with some irritation about the side effects of her popularity: they often came to visit her in droves, sometimes just to stare at her silently, taking in her exotic presence. Now, after three months of living alone, she was hungry to share common cultural assumptions. I could see we were a sort of salve for her; perhaps someday she would be the same for us.

Lisa agreed happily to store our vial of serum in her refrigerator, and all day she spread before us a web of useful advice and news: where to shop, where to eat, how we could rent a post office box, what sort of medical help we might expect from the town's infirmary. She also mentioned a bulletin she'd heard on the radio from the Voice of America: some trouble in Iran, where the American embassy had apparently been attacked and hostages taken.

But what interested us most was the news that the *sous-préfet* was out of town, attending the funeral of a relative; he might be gone for a week. Alma groaned at this unexpected delay. Though she knew the proper procedure would be to officially present her research papers before settling in among the Beng, she couldn't bear to wait. Lisa offered to send a message to us via a bush taxi once the *sous-préfet* returned, and we agreed to her plan. The next day we would drive to Asagbé, the village where Pascal's uncle lived. We would give Pascal's letter to this man we'd never met and hope for hospitality.

2

CHOOSING A HOST

%   %   %

(NOVEMBER 6–NOVEMBER 28, 1979)

Alma: Unpacking

THE DIRT ROAD FROM M'BAHIAKRO WAS CARVED THROUGH A DENSE TANGLE OF FOREST, AND while Philip drove I unrolled an oversize map of the region; it flapped across my knees as I charted our course to Bengland. The map was clear enough, with its washes of green crisscrossed by a winding line for the narrow road that barely allowed oncoming trucks to whiz by, rattling our tiny Renault. But it showed only rivers and streams, main roads and footpaths, of the land we would soon inhabit. I needed a map to the invisible space, the unknown life, we were entering.

For I was about to become an anthropologist. True, I'd studied for years for this moment; but with little published information available about the Beng, I had no way of knowing whether my expectations would correspond to the villages I would soon see, the people I would soon meet. As I contemplated the question marks in our future, and my own failings—shyness, a stubborn streak—my anxieties multiplied. Would I be welcome, make friends, come to understand this new world? And how long would it take me to learn the language? Still, the churning in my stomach was from excitement, too: I was less than an hour away from another set of propositions about how the world worked.

We drove past a series of Baulé villages dotted with square, one-story houses of mud brick. The women, who carried babies on their backs or tended to cooking fires while their children played around them, wore long *pagnes,* the colors now faded to dull prints; the men chatted in groups, sporting old jeans and T-shirts worn from wear. I examined the map: after the last of the Baulé villages, it pictured a ten-mile stretch of forest before the first Beng village—perhaps another twenty minutes until we arrived. I looked out at the thick woods we were passing, then down at the squiggly lines of the map, then up again at the green mass, and I wondered if Beng people were walking along paths hidden in the forest around us.

Finally a road sign announced Bongalo—the first Beng village! Philip slowed the car and said, "I can't believe it. We're actually here."

But what was "here"? The square, mud brick buildings before us looked the same as those we'd just seen in the Baulé villages—though in the limited printed sources on the Beng, I'd read of enormous round houses with thatched roofs shaped like an inverted crown. And the people—they appeared no different from the Baulé villagers we'd just passed. My foreign eyes must have been missing subtle differences, I decided. Before long perhaps I'd come to know some of these people I now saw as strangers.

Soon we came to a second Beng village bisected by an intersection—here, the map indicated, we must turn left. After a mile through a mixture of forest and savanna, the road widened and became a street, with mud brick houses on either side: we were suddenly in Asagbé, the village where Pascal had been born. My heartbeat quickened as Philip braked slowly. Before we could think of what to do next, we were approached by a small crowd. These were Beng people, whose world I had come to study: a few young women with babies on their backs; a boy holding a homemade slingshot; an older woman with a turban around her head; a couple of young men in jeans and untucked shirts. They spoke quickly and animatedly to us, to each other. I strained to catch a familiar syllable, a common root with any of the languages I knew, but of course there was none. Would I ever learn to discern words, find a grammar, in that tangle of sounds?

I looked at the envelope Pascal had given us, then pronounced the name printed on it: *M. KOUASSI André.* Several people pointed across the road, and a few continued to flank the car as they led us slowly up the dirt boulevard. They pointed out a building of pale gray cement with a long concrete porch. A handsome man strode toward us.

"Bonjour," I began tentatively, unsure if the man understood French, *"nous cherchons M. Kouassi André."*

"C'est moi." He greeted us with a cautious handshake, surprise rising in his eyes.

"Ah," I said, "we're so happy to meet you. We saw your nephew Pascal in

Abidjan, and he told us to look for you when we arrived." Philip and I introduced ourselves, and I handed him Pascal's sealed letter.

André studied the note carefully, taking in his relative's explanation of these unexpected visitors. Finally he looked up. "Welcome, welcome. You can stay with us—I hope you'll be comfortable in my home."

Our gratitude somehow left us mute for a few seconds—as if we'd been long awaited, this perfect stranger offered to take us in. Finally I managed, "Thank you, thank you very much," but it felt inadequate to the gift our new host had just bestowed upon us.

André said a few words in Beng to the crowd around us. Suddenly a pack of children ran to our car and started hauling out suitcases, typewriters, bags.

"Please, we can do that ourselves," Philip protested. But André insisted, admonishing the children to be careful. Uneasy, Philip and I whispered to each other in English. Was this special treatment, or was it standard practice for guests?

Soon a boy of about six appeared, his arms filled with two oversize bottles of beer. Our host gestured to the three wooden chairs ranged around a dark wooden table on the porch. "Come," he said firmly, and we sat down. Beside the bottles were two glasses, which André filled and set in front of us.

"What about you—won't you join us?" Philip asked.

"No, this is for you," André insisted, and so we slowly sipped the warm beer, all the while trying as politely as possible to wave away the flies that landed on the wet rims of our glasses. A growing group of women and children crowded the courtyard. A baby cried, and its mother bounced gently, her hands reaching around behind her to support the weight of the infant nestled cozily on her back in a sling made of *pagne* material. The child quieted to her mother's rocking. To my surprise, the baby's face was colored with bright lines and dots. I wondered about the meaning of this adornment, but I didn't dare ask as our audience stared at us intently, murmuring and giggling among themselves what must have been their own ethnographic observations. Were Philip and I creating a first impression we would cringe to hear about later?

When we finished André filled a glass for himself. He tilted it ever so slightly, intentionally spilling a few drops onto the cement floor—perhaps we'd been rude in not doing the same. Then André downed the beer in a few seconds. Another gaffe: we'd sipped our drinks rather than chugging them. My first minutes in a Beng village were starting to feel at once excruciating and exhilarating as I felt all my old patterns of polite behavior suspended— but still at a loss for what to substitute in their place.

André poured two more glasses.

"Won't you join us this time?" Philip asked.

"No, you go ahead," he answered, "I'll drink afterward."

Was turn taking the customary mode of drinking? Pondering what seemed like yet another mistake, I hesitated before taking my first sip. Should I let a drop or two of beer spill from my glass onto the porch floor? No, I'd better wait until I knew what it meant. But when would that be? We hadn't even managed to unpack our own car—how much harder it would be to unpack the significance of the new routines that were already claiming us.

Wordlessly we three downed another round of beer . . . and another . . . and another. A confirmed teetotaler, I couldn't imagine how we'd ever drain those two enormous bottles. And the vacant space that I thought conversation should fill was starting to feel awkward. Was André waiting for us to reveal more about ourselves, or was this a conventional drinking silence?

Finally, the bottles emptied, André broke the quiet and asked me about my research. I explained that I was an anthropology student here to study Beng culture, and André nodded. "I'm glad you've come. You can stay with us for the whole year—my house is large enough. Please be welcome."

Immediately I regretted that I hadn't explained our intentions more clearly: I'd already decided to settle in a smaller village, where I could more easily chart the connections between people's lives. With some regret, I explained my decision. Still, André's generous offer was tempting—who knew if another one would come along?

"Well, you can always reconsider," André said. "But now you should go and meet Pascal's parents. I'll have my son show you the way." He nodded to a boy with a rounded stomach peeking out below his short shirt; the child's intense gaze and smooth, light skin announced him as a miniature version of his father. Philip stood and reached for my hand: we were about to walk through our first Beng village.

Philip: Amwé and Kouadio

The boy beckoned to us with a shy smile, and we gestured back, indicating we were ready to follow. Thus, united by these attempts at a sign language, we three began our walk through the relentless brown of the village: the milk chocolate of single-story mud houses; the dark wooden stilts of granaries, their sloping thatched roofs seeming to flow with motion; and curving mud paths that wove throughout coffee-colored dirt courtyards. I was glad André's son led us so confidently through what—to me—appeared to be a maze.

Villagers gathered to gape at our strangeness, and in turn I was overwhelmed by the poverty and illness of our audience: malnourished children with thin limbs and distended bellies or large, herniated belly buttons; thin old men and women, their eyes clouded by cataracts; an enormous goiter distorting the neck of a young woman; and people of all ages with craterlike sores on their legs, poulticed only by leaves. Aware of being an alien, privileged presence, I wanted to vanish from the gazes of the curious villagers, disappear from this world that had never requested my arrival.

Finally our young escort stopped at a courtyard edged with mud brick buildings, their corrugated tin roofs shining in the late afternoon light. One small house had clearly seen better days: the thatch roof sagged in places, and parts of the mud walls were worn away, exposing the dark interior. Another, larger house was under construction but seemingly arrested midway, a hope gone sour: the walls uneven, no roof, and stacks of unused mud bricks that appeared to be melted into each other, perhaps from years of exposure to the rains. Was this unfinished home an example of the great sacrifices Pascal's family was making to support his university studies?

At the end of the courtyard sat a small group of older men, drinking and talking gaily. They grew quiet when one of them rose to greet us. Short and solid, he wore a Western-style raincoat and a torn woolen cap, though it was neither raining nor cold.

"*Bienvenu,*" he said, smiling. "I'm Bwadi Kouakou, Pascal's father. Welcome to the village. I understand you've met my son."

This man had politely addressed us in French—shouldn't we respond in Beng? Alma and I glanced at each other, and I whispered, "You go first." This was, after all, her fieldwork.

"*Aba . . . ka kwo!*" she managed, and the men in the courtyard roared with delight.

Bwadi Kouakou grinned and said, "Very good! But that's for the afternoon—it's evening now. We'll have to teach you those greetings."

Alma glanced down at her wristwatch. "It's only four," she murmured to me. Frowning, she shook the watch to check if it had broken. That would be a fitting reaction, I thought: our first day in the village, time stopped.

"Unless evening starts earlier for the Beng," she whispered, pleased with this sudden thought, but then she stopped: "*Damn,* I left my notebook at André's."

I stared at Alma's empty hands, surprised at her forgetfulness but relieved she was as overwhelmed as I.

Bwadi Kouakou was waiting patiently, and Alma knew the time had come to begin her formal speech. After introducing us, she began tentatively, "I'm a student of African culture, and I'm here to study your way of life. We'd like to live in a Beng village for about fourteen months."

"*Bon, bon,*" Bwadi Kouakou said, nodding. Alma paused expectantly—the *secrétaire* of Asagbé's first impressions of us would surely influence the other villagers' reactions. Just then a woman emerged from one of the smaller buildings, her smile almost toothless, her withered breasts dangling above a ragged, wraparound skirt that was tucked loosely into a knot at her waist. She shook our hands effusively, saying in Beng what we assumed were the evening greetings. Unable to reply, we smiled and nodded our heads encouragingly.

"Pascal," she said, then added something further in Beng.

"Oui, oui," we replied, "we know Pascal."

She continued speaking in Beng excitedly, at first unaware that we couldn't understand her. Then, with some frustration, she pointed a long finger at herself and said, *"Maman."*

Pascal's mother. We shook her hand again, hoping we hadn't insulted her.

"She's asking for news of Pascal," Bwadi Kouakou said.

Clearly, saying hello involved more than trying to memorize the right words. Chagrined that we hadn't mentioned Pascal earlier, Alma said how helpful he'd been to us, how well he spoke English. Bwadi Kouakou translated this to his wife, who shook our hands yet again. Suddenly a pair of frail metal folding chairs were produced. We were invited to sit, and a young man—who looked as though he might be Pascal's brother—addressed us: "The *secrétaire* says that you should join him and his friends in some palm wine."

"Merci," we replied together. Did this mean he approved of Alma's speech? The *secrétaire* nodded to the young man, who picked up a rectangular plastic container. I glanced at the faded label—the can had once held engine oil. He tipped the spout over a hollowed-out gourd and poured out a bubbly white liquid that, disappointingly, resembled watery milk: was this the magical drink of one of my favorite African novels, Amos Tutuola's *The Palm-Wine Drinkard?* That book's hero loved the concoction so much that he drank 150 kegs of it each day, then topped it off with another 75 kegs at night. Disconsolate when his palm-wine tapster died, he set off to recover the treasured employee from the Town of the Deads, and on his fantastical journey through the rain forest he saved a woman from a husband who was only a skull, discovered an entire village of creatures who looked like human beings but had artificial heads, and encountered a spirit who could kill a victim merely by blinking.

The young man handed me the gourd filled with palm wine. I lifted it to my lips, then stopped. Tipping the edge, I let a little spill to the ground, and the men around us laughed again.

Bwadi Kouakou clapped his hands. *"Voilà!* You're Beng already!"

"But what does spilling the drink mean?" Alma asked, annoying me—she was spoiling my performance. Yet she *had* to ask, I knew—with or without her notebook, Alma was an anthropologist.

"C'est pour la Terre"—For the Earth—he explained. "It's how we show our respect."

"The Earth?" Alma replied. While she and Bwadi Kouakou spoke, I took a cautious sip. My lips pursed at the excessive sweetness, which competed with an underlying bitterness—I couldn't imagine enduring any of the Palm-Wine Drinkard's torments for this unpromising stuff. In my mouth, at least, something was definitely lost in translation. I passed the gourd to Alma.

"*Bon,*" said Bwadi Kouakou, obviously pleased. "If you're going to live among us, you'll need Beng names." Of course—why not? In Beng eyes we were just one day old. In swift order I was dubbed Kouadio, and Alma became Amwé. We continued to pass around the gourd, and I repeated my name silently a few times, trying it on: Kouadio, Kouadio, Kouadio. Perhaps I was already under the growing influence of the palm wine, perhaps not, but Kouadio seemed to fit.

Alma: *Very* Vlong Vlong

We returned to our host's compound, and André chuckled appreciatively when we told him our new names. Then he called over his senior wife, Marie—a tall, stately woman who hurriedly whispered something to a young girl who I supposed was her daughter. She then came over and shook my hand warmly, both of hers enveloping my own.

"Amwé! Kouadio!" She laughed, delighted with the surprise of our sudden appearance and the incongruity of our newly minted Beng names. But there was little more to say: neither of us spoke the other's language. Our muteness stretched before us, an invisible valley over which we couldn't leap.

Perhaps sensing this, André joined in: "My second wife speaks French." He gestured to Maat, a slightly plump woman who sat nearby on a stool, tending to a cooking fire. Glancing up with curiosity to regard her improbable guests, she came over and welcomed us, "*Bonjour et bienvenu.*" Delighted that we could speak together, I happily accepted her invitation to keep her company while she cooked.

On the dirt floor of her small, windowless kitchen, a round-bottomed pot sat on three large hearthstones; between them, three logs burned slowly. Inside the pot thick white chunks—yams, Maat told me—shook in the boiling water. Most of the smoke and steam escaped out the corrugated-tin door, but a few thin curls lingered, leaving a seasoned smell in the hot room. I asked for a knife and joined Maat in slicing okras into another large pot. Poor Philip, I thought—his least favorite vegetable. Maat added green berries to the pot and, to my chagrin, a *handful* of red peppers. Perhaps the berries would add a sweet touch to counter all those fierce chilies.

As Maat continued preparing the meal, she pointed out her children scrambling about the compound with happy energy.

"And your children . . . ?" she asked me.

"None yet," I said.

Maat nodded. *"Eki mi gba lenni."*

I reached for my notebook. "What does that mean?"

"May God give you children."

I thanked Maat, adding lamely that I hoped one day to be a mother, too. I didn't dare mention my techniques for family planning.

With a sigh of sympathy for me, Maat removed the white yams from the cooking pot and, stepping out the door, placed them in an enormous mortar made of a beautiful, mahoganylike wood. From a dark corner in the kitchen she fetched a shoulder-high pestle and then began to pound the chunks in a lovely rhythm—*kathunk* on the soft yams, *kathink* against the inner side of the mortar for a contrasting, hollower sound, *kathunk kathink, kathunk kathink.* I asked Maat if I could have a try.

"Sure." She laughed and handed me the heavy pestle. I managed to mash a few pieces, but I couldn't make that hollow sound or match its rhythms.

"That's very good!" Maat complimented me, but she gently took back the pestle: her hungry family couldn't wait indefinitely for their dinner. She resumed pounding until, miraculously, the yams transformed from a pasty mass into an elastic, round ball about the size of a small cantaloupe: so this was the famed yam *foutou!* Maat completed the task, making two more white balls.

By now the sauce was cooked, and Maat apportioned it into a few colored enamel bowls, then divided the balls of *foutou* into matching plates. I watched silently as she carried out a pair of dishes, setting them on the ground in front of André, who sat on a low stool, chatting with some other men. A pail of water was passed around for hand washing, and the small group plunged into dinner. Why didn't the men wait for André's wives and children to join them? And why weren't these men eating with *their* families? Perplexed, I went into the house to fetch Philip. Ever the tidy one, he was unpacking our belongings and arranging them neatly in our new room.

"Hello, Amwé," he said.

I giggled. "It's dinnertime, but I'm not sure where to eat—actually, I'm not even sure *who* we should eat with. . . ."

"Oh, it can't be that complicated," Philip teased, following me out to the porch. We saw a set of pale blue bowls sitting on the table, two chairs ranged around it expectantly.

Maat walked over. *"Ka ta poblé."*

"Pardon?"

"Allez manger," Maat translated.

Ah, a good phrase to learn—Go eat! Obediently Philip and I sat down, but I was too disappointed to start right away. I'd hoped to dine with the family—but the family itself was divided. In front of the open doors to their adjacent kitchens, Maat and Marie crouched on the ground with their children, and the two groups started in on their separate dinners. I stared at the steaming plates in front of us. "I guess we should stay here by ourselves," I muttered to Philip.

We shot sidelong glances at André to observe how he lopped off a small piece of *foutou* with his thumb and forefinger, dipping it in the sauce. Then I tried, but my bit of yam plunged instantly into the slick sauce, and I cast about for it, hoping I had no audience. Unfortunately André caught sight of me doing battle with the fugitive chunk.

"The sauce is *vlong vlong*, eh?" he sympathized.

"Mmm, very *vlong vlong*," I replied, chuckling silently. "Slippery" seemed a good word to learn on my first day: so far, the rules for all the day's encounters seemed, at best, *vlong vlong*. Eventually I fished out the doughy piece and popped it in my mouth. The peppery gumbo assaulted my taste buds, though it did little to mask the sharply bitter taste of the berries. I chewed the thick yam, then swallowed.

"*Whew,*" I warned Philip quietly, "that's *hot!*"

"Hmmm," he said cautiously. Never a fan of spicy foods, he followed suit nervously. "My dear, you speak the truth," he gasped. Our eyes teared, our noses ran, with each bite of the fiery meal. A glass of water would be just the thing. I glanced around—why wasn't anyone drinking? Sighing, I dipped into the spicy roux again, sniffling and blotting my eyes with each bite. Soon André and his friends finished their meal, and they sipped from a gourdful of water. Ah—now was the time for drinking. I finished hurriedly so I could finally take a large swig of water.

After dinner Maat told me, "*Ta zro*"—Go wash up, she translated to my perplexed expression—and pointed across the courtyard to a tiny, roofless mud brick building; spanning the open doorway was a stick with a colorful *pagne* hanging over it. So this short structure was a bathhouse. Grateful, I walked over and found a bucket of warm water waiting. Then, under a vast black sky dotted by shimmering stars, I discovered the pleasures of a delicious outdoor pail bath. But this luxury was at my hostess's expense, for Maat must have carried the water some distance, perhaps from a pool or well deep in the forest. So I made sure to save Philip enough water in the bucket, which I left in the bathhouse. As I returned to the courtyard, I heard the sound of water splashing: Maat had emptied the pail! I cringed to think how Maat might interpret this new faux pas I'd just made.

Later that night Philip and I settled into the small guest room. In the corner was a straw mattress; our suitcases, cameras, typewriters, books, kerosene lamp—all now arranged carefully by Philip—occupied the remaining space.

"Well, this is it," Philip said as we lay in bed.

"What do you think?" I asked. "Can you handle it?"

"I have no idea, it's all so ... I can't say, it's ... overwhelming." Philip sighed.

"Do you think you'll be able to write about it?"

"Maybe." Philip paused. "Do you really think we'll learn the damn language?"

"We'd better," I answered quickly.

A sudden high-pitched animal cry interrupted us. Then the cry returned, this time longer and louder, again and again, until the shrill, gravelly scream seemed to fill the room around us.

"What's *that?*" I barely whispered.

"Shhhh, let's listen," Philip whispered back.

Slowly the screech receded; in moments it quieted to silence, and the room was again just four walls, no longer enclosed by our fear.

"Do you think it'll come back?" I asked.

"We'll know if it does," Philip said nervously, and we snuggled together into a worried sleep. My muscles ached, my mind was filled with images of mud brick houses, babies with brightly painted faces, gourds of palm wine tumbling over each other—perhaps, in the dark of the room, my dreams could make sense of them.

In the morning we stepped outside and found the family scattered about the compound—the children loitering by their mothers, who were stirring some kind of porridge over their fires, André packing coffee beans into a large burlap bag. We asked our host about last night's eerie concert. He pursed together his lips. "I'm not sure...."

Philip tried his best imitation of the roar. The children all looked up and tittered.

"Oh, that!" André laughed. "It was just a *gbaya,* a tiny animal that lives in the trees—all they eat are fruits and leaves."

So we'd been afraid of something like a squirrel! The forest seemed one shade less dark and looming as I imagined those furry creatures scampering among the trees.

We passed the rest of the morning meeting neighbors, with André or Maat serving as translators. I felt immensely grateful for their efforts and guilty for the time they must have been taking from their own work. But by noon I was exhausted by all those dual-layered conversations—which made it seem as though the villagers' words were spoken from behind a scrim. I knew I needed to begin language lessons, but at the moment I knew of only one possible teacher. After lunch I said to André, "There's a young man who Pascal told us might be a good language tutor, maybe help me in my research. His name is Kona Kofi Jean. Do you know him?"

"Yes, he lives in the village of Bongalo."

"What's he like? Do you think he'd work with me?"

"*Ça, je ne sais pas,* he's the only one who can say," André said.

"Of course," I agreed. "I guess we'll go over to Bongalo to meet him."

"*Bon,* I'll come along, too," André offered graciously, and we all readied for the drive.

I was about to interview someone for a job, a role I'd never played before. Yet in the car I found myself suppressing the urge to prepare a list of questions—for if Jean didn't answer them to my satisfaction, then what? He was an applicant pool of one. Most likely there *were* other Beng who spoke French, were curious about their own culture, and could move to a new village for some fourteen months . . . but I had little idea how to find them.

In Bongalo a curious crowd gathered as André escorted us through the village. In front of a tiny, ramshackle house, André clapped his hands three times rapidly, said, "*Kaw kaw kaw,*" and entered. Philip and I followed a bit hesitantly. Inside the small room, a young man wearing old blue jeans and a striped shirt squatted on the dirt floor. Seeing us, he stood and greeted André in Beng; then, casting us an intense gaze, he greeted Philip and me in a French that was far better than that of most villagers we'd met, who'd clearly just picked up some phrases in the marketplace. At Jean's feet lay an open wooden suitcase of the sort we'd seen in the Abidjan *marchés*—piled neatly inside it were cigarette packs, gold-colored chain necklaces, boxes of matches, individually wrapped candies, schoolchildren's notebooks.

Jean shut the case, explaining apologetically that he'd been arranging the wares of his small business. "Please, have a seat," he said, offering us some wooden stools.

"We bring you greetings from Kouakou Kouadio Pascal," I began. Immediately Jean grasped our hands and thanked us. Then I told Jean that I was an American university student and a longtime admirer of African culture, and that Philip was a writer, now working on his second book, a collection of short stories.

"I've always admired America," Jean responded. "I listen to the Voice of America's French broadcasts twice a day on the radio."

"*Ah, bon,*" I said, encouraged by his cultural curiosity. "We've come to see you," I continued, "because I want to learn your language. I hope to study your rituals, your customs, and people's everyday lives. We'll be moving soon to a smaller village for my research," I added.

Abruptly Jean hopped up from his seat, muttering, "Excuse me a moment."

I worried that I'd said something wrong. Jean rummaged around the room until he found a small stack of papers.

"Please, would you look at these?" he asked nervously. "They're some drawings I've done."

I accepted the sheets and marveled: in pale, colored pencil lines there was a detailed map of Jean's current village, another of his home village, complete with public plazas, chiefs' houses, main roads, and shaded-in trees—it seemed he'd made maps of all the Beng villages. "These are wonderful!" I said, passing them to Philip, a longtime map buff, and I saw that he, too, appreciated the observant eye behind those sketches.

I asked Jean a few questions—as much to get a sense of his French vocabulary as to hear his answers—and as we spoke I noticed Jean's wrinkled brow, a few worry lines around his mouth. He told us he'd converted to Islam some time ago—he no longer drank alcohol, and he prayed four times a day. This was an allegiance I hadn't anticipated.

"I myself am Jewish," I mentioned cautiously.

"Ah, one of the religions of the book," Jean responded immediately. "I have great respect for the Jewish people. But you're the first one I've met."

"*Ah, oui?*" I said, tickled by the exotic space I was occupying in Jean's mind. But I was also somewhat assuaged: with this ecumenical spirit, he'd probably be able to cope with my interest in another set of religious customs that he himself didn't practice. In short, Jean seemed qualified: he had an anthropological imagination, and his French was fine. I leaned forward and continued, "I need someone who can work with me as a language teacher, translator, and research assistant. When I spoke with Pascal, he suggested you. Would you be interested?"

Looking a little dazed, he stammered, "*Merci beaucoup*, it would be a great honor."

Had I really hired Jean, just like that? It seemed somehow too easy. Then, with the delicate help of André, I broached the question of a salary. I wanted to pay a fair wage—and then some—commensurate with Jean's skills. In the car ride over, André had suggested twice the rate customarily paid to day laborers; now I proposed that to Jean.

"*C'est bon*," Jean agreed. "I'll pack up my business and move into Asagbé tonight with some relatives. Once you choose a smaller village, I'll move there with you."

Later that evening Jean joined us on André's porch. While the children lounged quietly around the courtyard near their mothers, who washed the dinner dishes in large basins set on the ground, I asked Jean about his life.

"I loved school, I worked hard, I always received the highest grades in my class," he began. "But my father didn't want me to continue—he wanted me

to help him in his fields." Jean's face twisted into a bitter knot. "I started having terrible headaches. They were so bad I couldn't study anymore—I had to quit. I always wanted to go to the university, but now I'll never be able to. *Ah, mon père"*—he sighed—*"il m'a maltraité.* How could I return to the village and his farm after that? I refused. But without a high school degree, I couldn't get a job in town. That's how I became a trader."

"Oh, Jean, I'm so sorry," I said softly.

"And my father hasn't found a woman for me to marry—you know, *chez nous,* we almost always have arranged marriages. That's why I'm still single."

Contemplating what he had just confided to me, I realized that Jean was by no means the typical villager—whatever that was. Perhaps it was inevitable that I—far more marginal myself—had chosen him as my assistant. But Jean's liminality seemed to gnaw away at him. Was it arrogant to imagine that I might reverse the plunge his life had taken? I wondered if Jean himself expected as much from our collaboration.

"I'd like to hear more about you and Philippe," Jean said. We shared with him our family histories—Philip's Scottish Catholic background, my Eastern European immigrant roots. But it was late—some of the children had gone inside to bed; others were dozing on parents' laps. The next day we'd begin work.

In the late morning a letter arrived by bush taxi: Lisa had written us that the mayor of M'Bahiakro had returned from his relative's funeral. We decided to drive to town immediately. In the car I worried that the mayor might be annoyed because we'd gone to the village before obtaining his authorization. For his part, Jean fretted that his worn clothes weren't appropriate for meeting a high government official. With his first paycheck, he promised, he'd buy a new wardrobe for our work together. I told Jean this wasn't necessary, but he insisted, "Our work together is too important."

The town hall was a long white building with green shuttered windows. After a surprisingly short wait, the secretary pointed us to Monsieur Mory's office, an open doorway at the end of a hallway. Seated behind a desk was a tall man with a strong jawline. He looked up from a pile of papers. *"Bonsoir,* what may I do for you?"

"Bonsoir, Monsieur le Sous-Préfet," I began, then introduced the three of us. I brought out my stamped papers and explained my research. "I'm very sorry we went up to Asagbé before seeing you," I concluded. "We didn't know when you'd return—"

"That's perfectly all right," he interrupted amiably, ' you're here now, aren't you?" He glanced through my papers. *"I'm very intrigued by anthropology.*

I'm from up north myself, and to tell you the truth," he said, leaning forward on his desk, "I know very little about these Beng people. You're probably aware that the constituency of this *sous-préfecture* is mostly Baulé."

I nodded. "Yes, quite a few anthropologists have worked with the Baulé—that's why I've come to live with the Beng, no one's done any research on their culture."

"Ah, that explains why I don't know much about them." Now the mayor turned to Jean. "Young man," he said a bit sternly, "you are in a most important position."

Jean sat straight on his seat, hands folded in his lap, and murmured, *"Oui, Monsieur le Sous-Préfet."*

"This scholar has come from America to study your people—no one has ever done this before—and it's your job to ensure that she understands everything correctly. It's you who will translate for her; Americans will form their opinions and judgments about your people on the basis of your words. Speak wisely. Your country is counting on you."

"Oui, Monsieur le Sous-Préfet," Jean repeated, his head bobbing.

Monsieur Mory went on in this patriotic vein for a while longer with Jean—I was touched, but also chagrined, by how much importance he was ascribing to my research. Soon the meeting was over. As we walked out to the car, Jean's hands fidgeted. The *sous-préfet*'s admonitions had clearly unsettled him.

Philip: *"Thank You for Your Lie"*

Each morning the solid sound and hollow echo of women pounding large wooden pestles into mortars rang through the air, that distinctive *thwonk*ing rhythm marking the new day like the pealing of communal bells. When Alma and I wandered sleepy-eyed onto the porch, the steaming pails of hot water for the morning bath and the smoke of cooking fires already mingled with the morning mist. Maat and Marie swept the dirt courtyard with hand-held brooms made of dried palm leaves, raising curling waves of dust before them. Watching these two co-wives perform their morning chores, I searched for hints of their true feelings for one another. But their easy formality together—very polite yet seemingly with little warmth—could have hid resentments as well as tenderness and resisted my curiosity.

After a breakfast of sweet corn porridge, with Jean's help we entered into the shifting puzzle of Beng greetings. Their complicated rules drew us into a pervasive social nicety, for whenever two people passed each other those elaborate exchanges started up, and even if by the end of the exchange they were sometimes twenty or thirty feet away, they still muttered the end of the greetings to themselves as they continued on their way.

Whenever hailed by a friendly villager, I made hesitant, fitful replies, calculating all the possible combinations I needed to match up, and with my accumulating, awkward silences I felt the need to speak faster. Yet one small mistake collapsed my confidence, and I was unsure of what to say next. Even if I *did* manage to reply correctly, the emboldened villager then chatted away rapidly to my stunned, silent face.

There was nowhere to hide our faltering abilities, for dozens of people surrounded us when we sat on André's front porch, conducting a running commentary in Beng on our peculiar ways. Sometimes the continuous gaze of all those eyes exhausted me—I couldn't see how I'd ever find the solitude necessary to write, but I would simply have to adjust to this aspect of my new life. I thought of a proverb Jean had recently taught us: "If I dislike one finger, should I cut it from my hand?"

Once, while Jean quizzed us on Beng verbs, I silently protested the numbing repetition by letting my eyes wander. Maat stood across the courtyard, pounding peanuts in a mortar for the evening's sauce, and sheep and chickens paced hungrily as close as they dared to the mortar. When a chicken darted forward at an untended morsel, Maat foiled its petty pillage with a well-timed kick.

I watched the villagers return home from their work in the fields, men with machetes in hand, women carrying large basins filled with firewood or yams on their heads. I had long grown used to the exceptional balancing skills of Ivoirians, but I gaped when I noticed a thin woman, her hair slightly graying, who walked past us with only an angular, pinkish stone perched on her head. She stared ahead intently, as if in a tunnel of her own making.

"Alma, look," I whispered.

She followed my gaze. "Jean, who is that?" she asked.

He glanced at the woman and quickly turned away. "I don't know," he said.

"Why is she walking with a stone on her head?"

"I don't know," he repeated, his normally animated face feigning indifference.

Now quite interested, Alma turned to Maat and asked, "Do you know that woman?"

"Oui," Maat answered simply after a quick glance. "She is sick." Then she lifted her wooden pestle and returned to mashing peanuts.

Was Maat saying, as delicately as possible, that the woman was mad? In the embarrassed silence, Alma and I exchanged glances, and she asked no more questions, at least for the moment. We returned to our language lesson with an uncharacteristically subdued Jean. Of course he hadn't spent years honing an anthropological curiosity, as Alma had, yet I suspected that she was as disappointed as I over his uncooperative answers.

With the afternoon meal over, Alma and I washed our hands—stained an orange yellow from the palm-nut sauce—in a communal pail of water. *"E nini"*—Delicious—we called over to Marie, who'd prepared the meal. Then, silently, a boy appeared at André's porch. I dreaded the sight of this child—he was waiting to accompany us to Bwadi Kouakou's compound, where another lunch awaited us. Ever since our first day in the village, we ate first at André's home, then commuted to Bwadi Kouakou's for a second meal: two hosts honoring us. Of course Alma and I couldn't refuse, though we were always presented with more food than we could eat at each compound. So we began pacing our appetites, preparing for the afternoon's landslide of lunches, the evening's dueling dinners.

Pascal's mother was a good cook, but her co-wife, Kla, prepared terrible meals—the sauces watery and bitter, the *foutou* undercooked, pasty. Lately it had been Kla's turn to feed us. We sighed and set off. Jean, who accompanied us on these journeys across the village, set his face in silent suffering.

At Bwadi Kouakou's compound our host led us to one of the small mud houses, and we sat with him inside the entrance, away from the glare of the sun. Another circle of male guests was already gathered in the room, waiting to be served. Jean joined them. Then one of Kla's daughters appeared and set before us on the floor one bowl filled with a roundish ball of *foutou,* another filled with a thin green sauce—Kla's bitter specialty—well stocked with thick pieces of meat.

The meat was spoiled—its fetid smell filled the room.

"We can't eat this," I whispered to Alma.

"I know," Alma whispered back, her nose crinkled, "but how can we insult the *secrétaire?*"

"Ana poblé"—Let's eat—Bwadi Kouakou announced. He broke off a piece of *foutou* with his fingers, then scooped up a chunk of meat.

"What kind of meat is that?" Alma asked, stalling.

"Antelope," he replied, now chewing without complaint.

I turned to Alma and murmured, "Maybe it's not so bad." But the stench was nearly overpowering. My greatest urge was to leave the room as swiftly as possible and not, as I did now, reach down and pluck a bit of *foutou* from the ball, then dip it into the sauce and collect a piece of meat.

Slowly I raised it to my mouth. Eyes closed, I popped it in, then tried not to recoil. I kept chewing, unwilling to swallow. But I couldn't stall with this seemingly meditative mastication forever, so I gulped down the vile mess.

Alma soaked up the sauce with her pinch of *foutou,* but she avoided the meat. Still, she had to stiffen her face to avoid grimacing—even the sauce was permeated with the putrid taste. She managed this tactic for a few minutes until Bwadi Kouakou said, "Don't be shy, eat some meat."

Her mouth a grim line, Alma followed our host's suggestion. "Oh my god," Alma said in English, her voice cheerfully disguising the meaning of her words, "this is absolutely horrible."

Following her example, I replied in a similarly happy tone, "You're right, it's quite monstrously bad. I think I'm going to throw up." We turned to Bwadi Kouakou, smiled, and lied: *"E nini."*

Jean, sitting with the other circle of guests, cast a desperate look over to us, then bowed his head and continued to eat. So it wasn't just us. Then why was Bwadi Kouakou—and everyone else in the room—eating politely? Perhaps the *secrétaire* was too embarrassed to admit what his wife had served. And of course we, as guests, couldn't insult our host. So we all suffered through the meal, making a great pretense that nothing was amiss.

Finally we finished the ball of *foutou,* the last chunk of malodorous meat. "I thought that meal would never, ever end," I said in English, my voice now genuinely cheery. Suddenly Kla's daughter appeared and placed another bowl on the floor: seconds.

"Oh shit!" Alma gasped. Though Bwadi Kouakou didn't understand English, the tone of Alma's voice was clear. Shamed, Alma picked at this new ball of *foutou* and gathered up a few more slices of antelope, and I followed her lead reluctantly.

"Have more," our host urged us quietly as we slowed down, but I'd had enough. *"N kana"*—I'm full—I told him, and Alma said the same.

On our trek back to André's compound, Jean railed against Bwadi Kouakou's reluctance to criticize his wife's meal. "That meat should *never* have been served to anyone," he insisted, his arm sweeping dismissively in the air, "and certainly not to *guests!"* We nodded in agreement, and Alma smiled slightly—Jean's vehemence eased her regret over her involuntary outburst.

The next morning I awoke to Alma's groaning; instantly awake, I turned over and saw my wife clutching her stomach, her face one large wince. One of us was finally sick—but which of the innumerable, exotic illnesses we'd fearfully anticipated did Alma have?

"Ooh, I just know it's from that meat," she gasped.

"Maybe," I replied, stroking her forehead, working hard at a pretense of calm. "But then how come I'm not sick, too?"

She had no answer. I paged through our medical text—with the less than comforting title *Where There Is No Doctor*—and found too many illnesses with symptoms resembling Alma's terrible cramps. Yet there *was* a doctor nearby, at the M'Bahiakro infirmary; Lisa had told us his name—Dr. Yiallo.

"I think it's time to go to M'Bahiakro," I said, and I helped her dress—she could barely move without sharp spasms.

On the trip down, Alma groaned in counterpoint to the rattling bumps in the road, and I drove as carefully as possible. When we finally entered the gates of the infirmary, I couldn't tell at first which of the long, single-story cement buildings bordering the vast courtyard contained the doctor. People wandered about the courtyard, but I wasn't sure if they were patients or visitors.

I parked the car under one of the large trees that formed a shady avenue. "Let's try over there," I said, pointing to one building where a long line waited outside a green shuttered door. There were Dr. Yiallo's patients for the morning: mothers carrying wailing infants on their backs, hunched old men, a young girl who hacked into a colored kerchief, a boy on crutches, another boy in a khaki school uniform who simply stared dully before him, and many more cases of stoic suffering. We stood at the end of the line, Alma's body bent from the pain. I held her by the arm, and slowly, over the course of a long, hot hour, we shuffled our way to the door. When we entered a dimly lit office the doctor rose from behind his desk. On the filing cabinets beside him loomed three large glass jars filled with alcohol and the thick, coiled bodies of snakes. The doctor's dark face filled with curiosity as he greeted us: though we'd come as patients, we were clearly a break in his busy day, a puzzle to be solved.

After Alma introduced us, Dr. Yiallo peppered her with questions about her research. Then he told us he was the only doctor for this entire complex, though there was a head nurse who sometimes doubled for him and occasionally even performed surgery. The doctor spoke so rapidly we could barely follow his words; I wondered if this breathtaking speed was the result of his trying to treat as many patients as possible in the course of a day. But Alma was a patient as well, and soon he asked her, now all business, why we were here to see him.

Alma described her pain, her suspicions about the spoiled meat.

"Amoebas, absolutely," he said, "though I'm sorry we don't have lab facilities here to confirm the diagnosis." He sighed, then swiftly scratched out a prescription.

We thanked him and left. Gaping at the line of new patients, now even longer, I was stunned by Dr. Yiallo's impossible, daily task. I wondered how many more times in the months to come we'd have to return to see him.

Sitting on a stool before a bowlful of one of Maat's violently spicy specialties, I made a brisk pinching motion with three fingers, reached for the ball of starchy *foutou,* and pulled away a pliant, sticky piece. I dipped it in the okra sauce and then deftly gobbled it up: my Beng mealtime mechanics were definitely improving. Yet while I ate with one hand, the other ached: across the base of my thumb and down to my wrist was a thin, pus-filled trench. Apparently some mysterious insect was responsible. None of the antibiotic ointments Dr. Yiallo had given me seemed to help.

After the meal we lounged about André's porch. Alma massaged her stomach cramps as inconspicuously as possible, while my hand continued its determined throbbing, and we cast each other grim smiles. Hoping for a distraction, I asked Jean if he would tell us a traditional Beng story. Realizing that Alma intended to tape his words, he agreed at once.

A small crowd gathered and grew. Jean began, emphasizing every word, his eye on the tape recorder, and André punctuated Jean's pauses with *"Hmm," "e-eh,"* and *"yo"*—an appreciative commentary that seemed to speak for the entire audience. Alma and I understood nothing of what was said, and I found myself concentrating on the listeners' attentive faces, their obvious pleasure echoing Jean's words: they suddenly laughed—a burst of real glee—and then, when Jean began singing in a soft, high voice, the audience repeated the melody after him, an exchange repeated three times. I was surprised at how their impromptu chorus joined in so smoothly. It wasn't only the story they were listening to, I realized, but the *telling,* and this particular telling they obviously enjoyed.

Finally Jean said, *"E nyana"*—It's finished—and I was pleased that I understood at least this. The audience, by way of applause, chanted together, *"A oukwa,"* and Jean thanked them for their appreciation. Then he translated their words—"Thank you for your lie."

"No, a story isn't a lie," I protested, prepared to defend my calling.

Jean and André nodded—out of politeness, not agreement. Cautioned by their response, I kept silent, too, suppressing a speech about the paradox of fiction: though invented, it expressed subtle truths not easily arrived at by other means. Labeling a story a lie denied fiction its essential power. But Alma and I were here to listen, not lecture. "Jean," I asked, "could you translate your lie for us?"

"Of course," he replied with a little laugh. The steadily growing audience waited patiently as he spoke—most villagers didn't speak French—and Alma and I reenacted in our minds the interplay of teller and listeners, the exuberant rhythms of performance.

"Here is one of my stories," he said. "There was this young man who lived with his mother. The mother slept in this room here, and the young man slept in that room there." With his finger he gestured in opposite directions.

"His mother gave him some advice: 'If at any time you see a pretty girl, forgive me for saying this, but don't tell her all your secrets, don't show her everything. It won't be good.' So she told him.

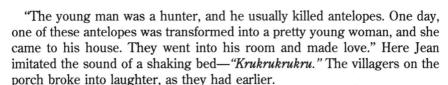

"The young man was a hunter, and he usually killed antelopes. One day, one of these antelopes was transformed into a pretty young woman, and she came to his house. They went into his room and made love." Here Jean imitated the sound of a shaking bed—*"Krukrukrukru."* The villagers on the porch broke into laughter, as they had earlier.

Jean paused, then continued. "Later, his mother told him: 'Hmmm, what I told you the other day, don't you forget it.'

"However, he ignored her. One night he told this woman, who was really an antelope, 'I'm a hunter, and I'm especially good at killing antelopes.'

"So it was like this: that night when they went to sleep, the antelope-woman plucked out his two eyeballs so he could never hunt again. She put them in her turban, and *whoosh,* she was transported to the forest. There she found her fellow antelopes: they were in the middle of a *lolondalé* dance, catching each other in their arms.

"She sang this song: 'Here are the eyes of Mamadou, the antelope killer.' " Again Jean sang that clear, soft melody, and again the audience sang back. Jean translated the lyrics: the dancing antelopes called out, "Give the eyes to me, so I can look at them."

He continued. "Okay. Since the young man had spoken like that to the antelope-woman, well, his mother, she knew some things, too. So *she* was immediately transformed into an antelope and appeared in the forest, *whoosh.* When she arrived, the eyes of her son were being thrown around, thrown around like this." Jean made a tossing motion.

"The mother-antelope joined the dance, and soon her son's eyes fell into her hands—first one, then the other. She put them in her turban and was transported back to the village. She had taken her son's eyes, and now she gave them back to him. She said, 'The other day I warned you about this, but you didn't listen. You must never do that again, never again.'

"Okay, it's finished," Jean said, and even though he hadn't told the story in Beng, the villagers chanted, *"A oukwa."* I refrained from joining in, still mulling over the message of Jean's story: did this eerie paranoia that cautioned against intimacy contain a Beng truth?

But the storytelling session wasn't over. It was André's turn to perform. "Here is one of *my* stories," he announced in Beng, and now it was Jean who supplied the *hmm*'s and *yo*'s. They leaned close to each other, André speaking as though they were alone, and again I found myself relishing the rhythms of the Beng language when spoken by an enthusiastic storyteller. Small children giggled throughout André's performance, and at one point the villagers roared gleefully. I couldn't wait for the translation.

When the crowd once more chanted, *"A oukwa,"* André turned to us and spoke in French. "Here's one of my stories: Mosquito used to be king, but he was big back then, as big as a person. One day, Arm and his companions started a journey on the road. Ear heard something: he heard the footsteps

of their slave, who was running away in the forest. Then Eye saw him. Then Leg caught up with him. Then Arm grabbed him, like *this.*" Reaching out, André grasped an invisible person with his hand.

"Then all the parts of the body started to argue over who had really caught the slave. They argued until finally they said, 'Really, Mosquito is our king, so let's ask him to decide.'

"When they arrived there and told him of their argument, Mosquito said, "The truth: who saw him?'

"Eye said, 'It was me, I saw him.'

"Then Mosquito said, 'Who heard his footsteps?'

" 'It was me, I heard his footsteps,' Ear replied.

"Mosquito said, 'Who chased after him?'

"Leg spoke up: 'Me, I chased after him, and then Arm grabbed him.'

"So Mosquito said, 'In that case, the slave belongs to Arm.'

"Now the others still didn't agree, and they angrily announced: 'It's you who are king, but since you said the slave belongs to Arm, may you shrink and grow small.' Then Mosquito shrank." Here André pursed his lips and said, *"Kokloko!"*—apparently the sound of shrinkage—and his audience again howled delightedly.

"Now, Mosquito stayed teeny-tiny, and he wasn't at all content with this state of affairs. So he decided to apologize to Ear, who had first heard the slave. Mosquito wanted to be big once again. He flew up to Ear and tried to change his decision, but Arm said, 'That's not what you decided before, go away, that's not what you decided before!' " André slapped at the air near his ear, as people do to confound buzzing mosquitoes. Again, everyone hooted with pleasure.

"So, if you see that Mosquito comes buzzing in someone's Ear, that's why the Arm tries to swat it away. *E nyana.*"

"A oukwa," the crowd chanted. Thank you for your lie. Now I joined in too with the required appreciation, but I would never like that phrase. I wondered if someday I might stand among Beng villagers at night, telling a story in this unfamiliar language. And what story would I tell—one of my own or one I'd learned here?

Alma: A Difficult Village

Seated on André's porch, Jean, Philip, and I were working on a new set of "hello" phrases when a woman approached who, after greeting us briefly, asked me if I knew her. I couldn't remember her name, but I knew we'd met, so out of politeness I muttered, "Uh-huh."

My nervousness at being found out must have given me away, for immediately the woman asked me teasingly, *"Ngwo n si paw?"*—What's my name? I was mortified—my bluff had been called.

Another day, after being introduced to a man named Kwamé Kouassi, a distant synapse clicked: I recalled meeting someone else with the same first and last names. I asked Jean if that was unusual.

"Oh, no," he answered casually, "because lots of people are called by day names, and there are only seven, one for each day in the week."

"What?" I blurted out.

"Well, actually there are fourteen," he clarified, "seven for men and seven for women. Take my name: Kona is from my father, because he was born on *Mlan*—Wednesday. Kofi is my day name, because I was born on *Fwé*—Saturday. And Jean is my French name—I got that when I started school." So much information in a simple moniker. Now that I knew the system, it was easy to decode—or so I thought.

One Wednesday morning, on a break from a language lesson, I glanced up and noticed Maat and Marie returning from the fields. They walked along on the narrow path; each balanced a large basin on her head, some logs poking over the edge. When they reached their kitchens, Maat slowly, carefully helped Marie down with her heavy load, then Marie assisted Maat. Their movements were so deft, I was sure they must have helped each other in this task thousands of times before.

I walked over to the two women to try out my new "Welcome back to the village" greetings. They chuckled approval of my progress, then Maat mentioned that she was going over to visit a friend who'd given birth to a baby girl last night. Proud of my new knowledge, I asked if the infant was named Ajua, for *Jowole*—Tuesday. No, she corrected me: the baby was named Amenan, for *Mlan*—Wednesday.

"Mais pourquoi?" I asked, baffled. Maat explained patiently that since today was Wednesday, then the child must be called Amenan.

I was even more confused. "I thought you said she was born last night?"

"Yes, she was."

"But last night was Tuesday!"

"Mais, non"—Maat laughed—"for us, the day begins at dusk. Last night, it was already Wednesday."

Another morning, sitting on André's porch, I worked on constructing an alphabet for this language whose intimate pathways I was just beginning to sense: with the International Phonetic Alphabet as my guide, I asked Jean to pronounce a few select words over and over. This was important, for if we mispronounced a vowel, we might ask a visitor where she shaved from (*baw*) rather than where she came from (*bow*) or ask a hunter if he'd successfully followed his prey's run (*bey*) rather than its tracks (*beh*). The consonants presented no less of a challenge as Philip and I tried to produce little explosions: *kp*'s and *gb*'s that proclaimed irrefutably the alienness of this language. Now it was Jean's turn to drill us, coaxing those bursts of sound from our unwilling lips.

In the middle of this lesson a woman came by to say good morning to Maat. I was happy to give my mouth a rest and eavesdrop on their conversation, listening furtively for diphthongs that had no life in my own language. At well under five feet tall, Maat's very pregnant friend looked almost comically round, but something in her penetrating gaze—a sharp intelligence and curiosity—checked my urge to smile when the woman, done chatting, strode onto the porch to greet Philip and me.

"Je m'appelle Amenan," she said, surprising me—so far, Maat was the only woman in the village I'd met who spoke French. After our introductions Amenan asked me about my research.

"I'm here to study village life," I began. "I'm especially interested in women's experiences."

Amenan nodded. *"Oui, c'est très important de considérer les femmes."*

I couldn't help glancing down at Amenan's large belly. "Actually, one of the things I hope to study is pregnancy and childbirth."

"Ah, that's something we women know much about!" She laughed, then spoke again, lowering her voice. "If you're pregnant, you shouldn't eat large plantains, only small ones—otherwise the baby will be too fat. And you can't eat the striped gazelle we call *kiya,* or the baby's skin will come out striped. Also, never eat the small mongoose we call *kangbo,* which has a long snout and teeth like a dog. If you do, your baby's mouth will be as long as the *kangbo*'s snout! Oh, and you mustn't eat the fish we call *kokofyofyo* that bites people in the water—otherwise your baby will grow up to bite people, too."

Before I could respond, Amenan said, *"Pardon,* I must return to my compound now. I hope we'll meet again." With that we parted, and I walked back to the table. I felt breathless from Amenan's unexpected flood of revelations—and disappointed that she'd vanished as quickly as she'd appeared.

Jean was examining our list of Beng vowels, so I turned to Philip. "My god," I said, "did you hear everything she told me? Too bad we're not staying in Asagbé. . . ." I stopped, caught up in regret—Amenan and I might not have a chance to resume our conversation.

"Mmm. But I bet there'll be lots of others like her, wherever we move," Philip offered. I wanted to believe him.

Philip and I often stayed up late with our two host families, drinking and trading stories. When André asked skeptically about the lunar landings he'd

heard reported on the radio, he listened politely to our answer, but we weren't sure he believed us; and Bwadi Kouakou was shocked on learning that Philip and I weren't related to each other—many Beng couples, he explained, are the grandchildren of two sisters, while most others are related in some other way.

Philip and I both felt so welcome in these two compounds that it was painful to contemplate leaving—but I was anxious to settle into my research site. How to choose the right village? I had certain requirements. A population of less than four hundred would allow me to know everyone personally, charting their genealogies to figure out exactly how everyone was interrelated. I also hoped for a village in which there were few Christians or Muslims, so I could concentrate on the traditional religion of the Beng. And Philip and I both wanted easy access to a decent road even in the rainy season, so that we could drive to town quickly in case of a medical emergency.

This list had seemed reasonable enough when I'd constructed it in consultation with my professors. But now that I was in Bengland, I wondered if any village actually met all these criteria. With Jean we made up a schedule of the smaller ones to visit. Tolégbé, Anzanzangbé, Siaregbé, Gbagbé, Ndogbé, Kosangbé—their names were hard to pronounce, the possible futures they represented even harder to imagine. For each of these villages housed people with their own family histories, and each villager would undoubtedly interpret an uninvited observer in his or her own way. What if I selected the wrong village?

When we arrived in Tolégbé, a crowd of children whooped and ran to inspect this rare vision of a car stopped at their small patch of roadside, though some of the smallest children ran in terror at the sight of us. A small group—some elders, some mothers with babies—ambled over to an enormous tree that dominated a cleared space, and someone offered us chairs. Philip and I tried out the morning greetings, and a few villagers exclaimed *"Yih!"*—a combination of appreciation and surprise. But my paltry attempts only depressed me—so far, saying hello marked the limits of my linguistic competence.

Jean whispered that now was the time to announce why we'd come to visit. Standing next to me, he seemed to relish the public role of translator; indeed, his rendition of my short speech that we'd practiced earlier seemed to have expanded significantly. Just how was Jean embellishing my thoughts?

Then the chief, an elderly man in a toga, announced to Jean that the villagers would be happy if we settled among them. The chief outlined a brief history of Tolégbé—it was a new village, the founders having left Asagbé to start their own village—and he mentioned that according to the last census, the population was ninety-two.

I'd already been told that this was the smallest village, but now I was

disappointed to hear the exact figure, for the village was *too* tiny—not enough families, not enough social ties to chart. Before I could respond, a boy brought some bottles of beer, evidently on the chief's instructions. The older men formed a circle, and we shared the bottles, while Jean sat quietly a few feet away, abstaining from our drinking fest.

A child brought a red-and-black feathered rooster over to the chief, and the old man made a short speech, which Jean translated: "The elder is presenting you with this chicken as a sign of respect for you and your work."

Having already decided that I couldn't live in tiny Tolégbé, how could I accept this generous gift? Yet refusing the chicken would surely be a terrible insult. So after profuse thanks, Philip tucked the rooster under his arm, and we gave the squawking bird what must have been the first car ride of his life—and its last, for once in Asagbé we donated him to André's household for that night's dinner.

The next village, Siaregbé, promised to be a better candidate: it wasn't too small, and we'd heard that most of the residents still practiced the indigenous religion. But well before we reached the village we had to abandon our car because of the narrow dirt road that was pockmarked with huge, gaping craters every few yards—hardened remnants of the rainy season's puddles. As we trekked the rest of the way, we worried: what would happen if one of us became seriously ill or were bitten by a snake? By the time we arrived in Siaregbé we were exhausted and certain that this village would not be our home. We stayed long enough to be polite, then began trudging back to our car.

As Philip started up Didadi, Jean suggested we consider his hometown. I had to demur. While Dezigbé was the right size for my study, two-thirds of its inhabitants were Muslim. Jean continued to press me, but I worried about his motives: given his difficulties with his father, he must have yearned to return in triumph with a new, prestigious position. I wished I could help him, but it might be impossible for him to separate his personal problems from my research.

Out of courtesy to Jean, I agreed to visit the village. The residents were polite enough—even his father, a small, bearded old man with sharp features, put on a good front of civility. But I wasn't swayed; hoping Jean would forgive me, I eliminated Dezigbé from my list.

Over the next few days we continued to visit the other small villages— always leaving with a chicken in tow—but none seemed fitting for my study. Finally only one small village remained. Kosangbé was my last hope—and fortunately it sounded fine: situated on the main road, the size was just right, about 250 people. Even better, almost all the villagers were animists. With a mixture of hope and anxiety, I said to Jean, "I guess it's down to Kosangbé—we haven't been there yet."

Jean frowned. "Those people drink all day. I don't think you'd be happy."

André, sitting nearby, agreed and added, "They don't have much water: their pump is two miles away."

"Oh, really?" Philip asked, then turned to me. "Are you sure you want to bother?"

"But this is the last village on our list! It might not be so bad. Anyway," I said, now lowering my voice, "Jean could be calling them drunkards just because they're not Muslims and drink a gourdful of palm wine once in a while."

When we arrived at Kosangbé, Jean led us to the village's kapok tree, and the elders in the village assembled to meet us. After Jean's standard speech there was an awkward silence. Finally the elders spoke quietly, and the chief, a thick-set man with speckles of gray flecked through his beard, said, "We'll have to talk this over ourselves, and we'll let you know what we decide." In a few minutes the meeting concluded.

We walked back to Didadi, taken aback by our swift dismissal. In the car Philip said, "I guess we can cross that one off the list."

"Well, let's just wait to see if they'll accept us," I said cautiously.

Philip raised an eyebrow and kept on driving. Back in Asagbé, when I told our host of our less-than-enthusiastic welcome in Kosangbé, I also mentioned that I still hadn't given up on the village. André wrinkled his brows. "You know, there's no bus service there to M'Bahiakro. What if your car breaks down?"

Philip cleared his throat conspicuously. Then André's cousin Bertin, who'd been chatting in the courtyard, piped up with another problem: "It's a difficult village. They get into fights all the time." But coming from Bertin, I didn't find this objection particularly compelling, as Bertin was rather cantankerous himself.

While I was awaiting word from Kosangbé, my stomach cramps returned. After seeing Dr. Yiallo in M'Bahiakro, Jean suggested we pay a visit to Blaima, a Beng elder living in town. We found Blaima at home relaxing on a lawn chair while a throng of children played noisily around him in the courtyard. He welcomed us and, after offering us Tip Top sodas, asked how we were getting along in Asagbé.

"We love it, but it's just too large for my study," I explained. "I'm looking for a small village where I can study the traditional Beng religion."

"Have you thought of Kosangbé?" Blaima suggested. "That's the seat of our religion."

"Really? Quite a few people have warned us away. . . ." I stopped.

Blaima smiled mysteriously. "Well, in that case . . ."

But I'd heard all I needed. If Kosangbé was the *center* of indigenous religious practice, my mind was made up, for this easily explained the cautiousness of the villagers: if they were the most traditional Beng, of course they would be reluctant to accept outsiders. I would have to be delicate in my questions in the beginning and just ask about simple things, take a census, collect genealogies. Later I could broach more sensitive topics.

Back in the car, I tried out my decision on Philip. He stared intently at the road, hands hugging the steering wheel. Finally he said, "It would be nice if they wanted us there. Anyway, we've already settled into Asagbé, and André's family is great."

"I know, honey, but it's just too big."

"Then what about Tolégbé? Those people seemed *really* friendly. And we'd still be near Asagbé."

I shook my head. "Too small."

"Oh, maybe you're right—the people in Kosangbé might warm up to us." But Philip didn't seem swayed by his own logic.

I turned to Jean, who was on the backseat gazing out the window, and told him in French that my talk with Blaima had decided me on Kosangbé. "I still think you should try Dezigbé," he muttered, and was silent the rest of the ride.

That evening, on André's porch, I shared my news with our hosts. Marie said simply, *"Ka ka an dé."* André translated: We'll miss you. But other people who'd come to chat with the family trotted out the same objections to Kosangbé that I'd heard before—plus a couple of new ones: the village was divided, they could never agree on anything; the food supply wasn't adequate because the villagers never worked in the fields. So many people were passionately opposing my plan, yet each had a different reason! I had to admit it: my curiosity was more than piqued.

Later that night I composed a letter to San Yao, the chief of Kosangbé, writing that if he and the villagers were willing, we would very much like to live among them. In the morning a messenger biked over with the letter. I eagerly awaited the reply, but the next couple of days brought no return message.

"It's not a very good sign," Philip offered.

"Maybe people have been too busy in the fields to hold their meeting," I replied, trying to believe my own words.

"They gave you *two* chickens in Dezigbé," Jean reminded me.

After another few days of silence, we decided to drive to Kosangbé. The chief greeted us coolly. Soon several elders and a group of young mothers joined us under the large kapok tree; some children brought chairs and stools for the older men and women. Was my future about to be announced? Philip and I sat expectantly; Jean declined a seat.

San Yao addressed us with a short speech. We looked at Jean inquiringly. "The chief says that they've had a meeting about your letter," he translated, his even tone concealing his own reaction, "and he says the three of us may move into the village."

"Ah, *merci!*" I said. I smiled at Philip; he forced a smile back. Then we rose and shook the chief's hand. Though San Yao's unexpectedly firm grip encased my own, his curt welcome speech had done nothing to help me imagine how we might call this village home.

As I regarded the faces around us, wondering who among them might become my first friend, another man in the group, whose trim physique belied the wrinkles on his forehead, came up to introduce himself: he was Wamya Kona, the national government's party representative in the village. But unlike his Asagbé counterpart, Bwadi Kouakou, this *secrétaire* spoke no French. Flashing us a wry smile that I couldn't interpret, Kona addressed us through Jean: "You'll need a place to stay. My cousin Bandé Kouakou François is building a house. Perhaps you could live there."

A line of excited children followed us to the courtyard, where we found a short man sitting outside. François looked at us quizzically, then greeted us in French. What luck—to have a host we could talk with while learning Beng! I was inclined to like the house. François pointed it out—a long, mud brick structure facing the back of his own home. He unlocked the wooden door, and before us was a small but sunny room connected to an inner chamber of the same size.

"We could use the second room as the bedroom," I whispered to Philip, "and this outer room could be a kitchen." He nodded agreement.

"The house belongs to my younger brother, Kossum," François explained. "He's waiting for the harvest money to finish building it. If you want, as rent you could cement over the inner walls."

"Okay, let's take it," Philip whispered to me, and I nodded.

Now the *secrétaire* addressed Jean. "I have an extra room in my compound. You can stay there if you like."

So Jean, too, had just found a new home. But his acceptance barely forced its way through his tightly set lips. He'll just have to adjust, I thought, disappointed by his continued sulking. We all shook hands, then sealed the deal with a large bottle of Ivoirian beer. By now I'd reconciled myself to celebrating each meeting, each decision with alcohol. Even the smallest villages, I discovered, to my teetotaler's regret, had beer: a local middlewoman or -man bought cases from a Lebanese shop owner in M'Bahiakro who toured the area each week in a truck. After we emptied our glasses, Kona spoke through Jean: "I'll be your village father. When you need anything, come to me."

I turned to Philip and flashed him a tipsy smile: we'd been adopted! He returned my grin with a wink: he seemed to want to believe the "Hurrah!" in my eyes.

"How can we finish building Kossum's house?" I asked our new father through Jean.

"You'll need sand for the cement. We can gather it on the riverbank."

"That's very kind," Philip said, "but we can help, too."

"No, you're our guests," François broke in firmly.

Over the following week, there was no news of the sand. Via a messenger, we suggested to François that we fetch the sand ourselves. The return messenger brought us our new landlord's response: this was out of the question. If the villagers would neither fetch the sand nor allow us to do so, what *could* we do? Finally Bwadi Kouakou suggested we contact the *sous-préfet*. We did, and for a small fee he quickly arranged for a load of sand to be delivered to Kosangbé by the M'Bahiakro road crew. Now that we had the sand, the cement must be mixed and the inner walls of the entire house plastered. But no masons offered their services in Kosangbé. I didn't allow myself to examine too closely the Kosangbé villagers' continued stalling, but one thing was certain: it was taking longer and longer for my research to get under way.

Philip: Almost Moving In

No one wanted us to move to Kosangbé, least of all the people of that village. Even though they'd given us permission to live there, it seemed we were always unraveling the latest delay, always *almost* moving in. I still felt Alma had chosen poorly, and I repeatedly expressed my doubts—until I realized that these objections, like those of the Asagbé villagers, only increased her fascination with Kosangbé.

At the time I was reading Laurence Sterne's *Tristram Shandy*. I had brought to Africa a box of various great works of Western literature—books I had neglected over the years—believing that a remote village might be an ideal place to read them. Sterne's novel made an odd fit: Tristram, the procrastinating narrator, spun ambling digressions—small books in themselves—that reminded me of the mysterious postponements we encountered from the Kosangbé villagers. Near the end of the novel, Tristram provided charts depicting the dramatic curve of his narrative: demented loopy lines that resembled curled, abandoned shoelaces. In light of our continuing negotiations with Kosangbé, those convoluted lines seemed like photorealism.

Jean, also dissatisfied with Alma's choice of a village, grew sullen and less forthcoming, even about apparently innocuous details. But was this the only reason? Recently we'd overheard Jean tell André and a few visitors that he would soon be interviewed by the Voice of America, that through his work with Alma he would make the Beng famous around the world. I remembered that long speech the *sous-préfet* in M'Bahiakro gave Jean, telling him that Côte d'Ivoire was proud of him and counting on his good work. Alma and I began to worry that Jean was intent on presenting to the world a Chamber of Commerce view of Beng culture; if this were so, he might feel free to hide whatever didn't present the Beng in a positive light.

As the days passed, whenever Jean resisted Alma's questions she suspected he was hiding something. Once, at one of Asagbé's evening dances, we saw a single old man twirling among the young girls. Curious about this apparent anomaly, Alma pointed and said, "Jean, who's that?"

"He's a man," Jean replied tersely.

"Who is he?"

"He's an old man."

"I know that. But what's his name?"

"I don't know." Jean turned away from her, but she ignored this rudeness. "Will you please find out?"

Reluctantly Jean ambled over to the man, then returned. "His name is Kouassi Kona."

Alma marked this down in her notebook, then looked up. "Why is he there alone among the girls?"

"He's dancing."

"I *know* that. Why?"

"Because he wants to."

Alma sighed. *Was* her curiosity so unreasonable? She looked over the crowd—there was no one else nearby who spoke French, no one else she could appeal to. She bit her lip and said no more. But her resentment was growing.

Another evening a group of girls gathered in front of André's courtyard to perform *lolondalé,* the same dance that Jean had mentioned in his story. The girls formed a tight circle, clapped their hands, and sang in an affecting, ragged harmony. Then the girl who led the song suddenly leapt backward, flinging herself into the waiting arms of the girls across from her—such playful trust!

Alma decided to record the sweet lilt of the children's voices, which delighted Jean. "The *lolondalé* songs are so sweet, the whole world should hear them!" I set a tape in our small machine and checked the batteries.

But before long a minor tussle broke out between two girls who'd come to watch, and as the dance continued they aimed a few insults at each other, setting off a minor ripple of nearby giggles. Suddenly Jean screamed at the two culprits, his arms waving wildly. They clutched each other momentarily, staring up at Jean in fear, and then they fled, joined by some of the dancers. *Lolondalé* was over. To my surprise, Alma—normally so patient—shouted at Jean for his interference. "Don't you *ever* interrupt again!" she hurled at him.

Soon André appeared, trying to calm everyone, and we made our way to the porch for his mediation of the dispute.

"Those girls were swearing, they were spoiling the dance—I had to stop it! You were *recording* them!" Jean insisted.

"I'm an anthropologist, Jean," Alma said. "I have to observe *everything,* even arguments."

"But those girls will break the name of the Beng!"

"Jean, *everyone* swears, all over the world. The Beng would seem odd if they didn't."

Jean knew he couldn't win. After all, he was arguing—with a stubborn bravery—with his employer. Yet he sulked all evening, and the next morning as well, until he finally apologized. But it was tactical, grudging—he didn't agree with Alma's approach. Ashamed over her public anger, Alma let the subject drop, though it was clear that she and Jean wanted to present competing stories about the Beng. If she couldn't convince him, there were bound to be more disputes in the future.

A marriage had recently been arranged between Gaosu, a young man from Asagbé, and Afwé, a young woman who lived in Kosangbé. A large group of women from Gaosu's extended family would soon walk the five miles to Kosangbé and dance their thanks for this arranged marriage. We were invited to come along. I looked forward to the celebration: in Kosangbé we were invariably greeted with only perfunctory hospitality by the wary crowds who gathered to watch us; perhaps at this festive occasion we'd see another side of that reluctant village.

In the early afternoon the Asagbé women began the long walk to Afwé's village, and Alma and I drove ahead with a few women who'd asked us for a ride. We swiftly left the gently sloping terrain of the savanna and entered a forest thick and seething with green. Towering here and there above the dense mass were gigantic trees, their enormous bases fanning out like the flying buttresses of Gothic architecture, their trunks rising up to a huge crest of leaves. Perched here and there at the edge of the dirt road were magnificently large termitaries, some ten to fifteen feet tall, each rising from a broad, brown base to a thin, irregularly shaped spire.

We arrived at Kosangbé long before the rest of the engagement thanking party and waited at the village border, for none of our future neighbors seemed pleased to see us. Standing by our car, I looked back at the road we had driven down, hoping for any sign of the rest of the celebrants. The thick smell of long-haired goats—a smell unlike that of any other Beng village—filled the air. Bored, I watched small herds wander in and out of the compounds, I listened to their harsh bleats; I even examined the broad, dark scar on my hand—that oozing trench had finally healed.

When the Asagbé women finally arrived, they danced in a slow, swinging motion, waving fans and singing, as they formed a circle in an open space in the village. Their hosts gathered slowly to watch, an oddly quiet audience. If Afwé—the center of this grand event—was present in the crowd, even standing next to me, I didn't know. Would I soon learn the names of all these people, would Alma and I learn something of their lives, their personalities? Alma moved among the crowd, taking notes on the dance, and the villagers of Kosangbé eyed her furtively, perhaps seeing in her scribbling an inkling of what they could expect once we lived among them. But I couldn't read welcome in their gazes.

I was happy to return to Asagbé: I felt more at home there and was reluctant to leave. Still, I tried to convince myself that perhaps Alma was right—the Kosangbé villagers' initial resistance would surely ease once they saw that our desire to live among them was respectful, that Alma simply wished to understand and record their lives. Furthermore, she argued cannily, with our own two-room house, we'd be able to close the doors and be alone whenever we wanted. Here in André's compound, we had no choice but to be part of the constant flow of family and neighbors. Now, as I sat in a corner of the busy porch dimly lit by lamplight and tried to reawaken one of my unfinished stories, I thought that setting up our own small household would be—for me—a necessary anchor in this confusingly unfamiliar world.

Still, I *did* enjoy those friendly gatherings on the porch after dinner, always loud with gossip and advice. One evening I carried out of our room on a piece of cardboard the corpse of a spider I'd just killed, a corpse as wide as the span of my hand. Too often I would reach for a shoe, a book, or my eyeglasses and startle one of the nestling monsters; while it swiftly scuttled away I'd try to calm my staggering heart.

"What is that?" André asked as I flung the corpse to the edge of the dark courtyard.

"A spider."

"Did it bite you?"

"No," I replied, suddenly worried. "Do these spiders bite?"

"No," he said.

Alma, her anthropologist's antennae out, snatched up her notebook. "Then why did you ask, André?" she said.

"Chez nous," he began, "we only kill insects that try to bite or sting us— because they have bad characters. Otherwise we leave them alone."

I understood the indirect criticism. By killing a harmless creature—though to me it was frightening—I myself exhibited bad character. Shamed, I vowed silently to restrain myself, and I was grateful for André's words. The lack of privacy in a family certainly had its advantages: even a casual exchange filled me with this new life we were entering, a novel of manners written in a foreign language.

I stood in the bathhouse and stared up at the stars covering the sky: bright clusters surrounding the wide, luminous path of the Milky Way. Lifting full cups of hot water from the pail, then letting that water pour down my hair and the length of my body, I listened to the distant sounds of the village: a children's song, the excited gab of two or three young women passing by, disembodied laughter, a baby's sharp wail. Entranced by the glimmering stars and the insect hum of the forest, I was suddenly aware of how cold the night air was—perhaps the cooling harmattan winds we'd heard about had arrived. I held my arms to my chest and felt a chill run through me, so I filled another cup with hot water, splashed it over my shoulders.

I still felt cold. I stood quietly and tried to feel the evening's thick heat against my face, yet I shivered, a small shudder I couldn't control. Malaria, I thought.

But how? I took my daily malaria pill religiously. I'd grown up fearing the disease, primarily because of an old film, *Monkey on My Back,* that I'd seen on television when I was a child. Made soon after World War II, the movie depicted the inexorable wreckage of a man's life, a man who'd contracted malaria in a mosquito-infested bomb crater on some battle-racked Pacific island. Given morphine for the disease, a growing addiction stalked the man after the war, tightening an increasingly unhappy fate around him.

I quickly finished my bath, returned to the porch. Alma sat with Maat, helping her chop okra.

"Alma, do you feel cool?"

"Cool?" She squinched her face in surprise. "It's boiling!"

"Well, I feel a little chilly."

Alma set down her knife and led me into our small room, where she began flipping through our medical text. I lay under a blanket but still felt shivers race through me. We decided to wait and see if I developed a fever.

Within two hours my blankets were soaked with sweat, so I popped six quinine pills—equivalent to a week's dose. Then we waited and worried until the fever—surprisingly quickly—subsided. In the morning I felt fine, and with a certain jaunty air I swallowed an additional six pills, as prescribed by the medical text. Was *this* malaria, so easily conquered? Already I was composing in my mind letters to friends, filled with contempt for my exotic illness.

Alma insisted on driving me down to the M'Bahiakro infirmary, and after

Dr. Yiallo examined me he agreed that I'd likely contracted malaria. "But you are well now, so who can tell? There are so many different fevers here." He suggested I rest for a few days.

But how could I? The next day we received word that our mud house in Kosangbé had finally been cemented and was ready for our arrival. Now there was so much to do, to prepare for our move.

Alma: Sweeping a Room Good-bye

Our last day in Asagbé we hauled our belongings out to the car. Still tired from his malaria attack, Philip seemed to grow weaker with each lugged suitcase, each carton of books. I insisted he rest while I finished packing.

"I'll check the room one last time," I said. Dust clung to the corners. Hurriedly I grabbed the palm-leaf broom Maat had loaned me and began sweeping out the room. Behind me, André's vehement voice filled my ears: "No, no, you mustn't!"

Turning around, I saw our host facing me, his hand now on the broom. "But why?"

"If you sweep out the room when you're about to leave, you'll never return to stay with us—and we want you to return."

"Oh, André, thank you for telling me," I replied, chagrined at my error. André nodded nonchalantly—no doubt he was inured by now to our mistakes.

We said our sad good-byes to our host and his family. Then Philip, Jean, and I started down the road to Kosangbé. Would our new neighbors share with me tidbits of knowledge such as the one André had just divulged? Or was André's remark a prediction that the people of Kosangbé would refuse to discuss their lives with me? It would be an intense year if what I most wanted to study our new hosts and hostesses most wanted to conceal.

3

TRESPASSING

❧ ❧ ❧

(NOVEMBER 29–DECEMBER 20, 1979)

Philip: Border of Ash

IN KOSANGBE, ALMA AND I WERE NOW EXAMINED BY A WHOLE NEW SET OF NEIGHBORS: while we carried our belongings from Didadi to the two small rooms of our mud house, a score of curiosity seekers marched inside, commenting openly on our singular presence. We tried to ease through our audience patiently, pretending they weren't in our way, when an unshaven man, staggering about and smelling of beer, kept insisting something in a loud voice.

"What's he saying?" Alma asked Jean.

Jean's face filled with self-righteous misery—this drunk was further proof that we should never have moved to Kosangbé. "He's saying that he doesn't care what anyone else tells you, he's the real chief of the village, not San Yao."

"Is that true?" she asked.

Jean laughed bitterly and Alma said nothing more, for now a few hands were reaching out and touching our hair, our arms, apparently admiring the smoothness. Such behavior would never have been tolerated in André's compound; belatedly we realized how much he and his family had shielded us from scrutiny.

But now we were setting up our own household, and that evening, when we finally closed our door and found ourselves alone, we looked over our little sanctuary. In the first room a narrow table supported our small camping stove and its gas canister, wooden shelves held rows of canned goods—mostly sardines—and against a wall stood our writing desk and chairs.

In the inner room two more sets of shelves held medicines and—for me, a particularly satisfying pillar of domesticity—books. Our suitcases, lying in a corner, became our dresser, while a chair served as a night table. Over the bed we hung mosquito netting, attaching it to the ceiling rafters and tucking it down under the mattress, until we'd created what looked like a giant bassinet. We also pinned mosquito netting over the square opening in the mud wall that served as a window, and over this I attached a piece of cloth that we could roll up and down as a curtain.

"At last, privacy!" I said, a bit guiltily, for I suspected that the villagers surely felt invaded, too, by this pair of strangers who had arrived to observe them.

In the morning Alma and I were awakened by the crowing of roosters; the snorting goats that banged their horns together on the huge termitary behind our house; and the multiple, rhythmic clunks of wooden mortars and pestles. We crawled out from under the mosquito netting and dressed. I rolled up the curtain over our bedroom window: a knot of inquisitive children peered back at me. *"C'mon,"* I moaned, and they laughed and swiftly scattered. How long had they been waiting?

We concentrated on a language lesson that first day, our small room continuously crowded with spectators. By the afternoon, when our neighbors left for their own compounds—only a few children loitering near the doorway—Jean suggested nervously that if we remained in our house too much during the day, the villagers might suspect us of witchcraft.

"Witches stay in their homes and plan who they'll bewitch," he said. Jean almost never offered such information, so we took it seriously. While Alma and I knew we were exotic creatures of the highest order, this was not the sort of typecasting we wanted. We decided to have an *akpa*—a free-standing veranda—built a few feet from our doorway, with a roof of palm leaves to protect us from the sun. Each morning we could bring out our desk and a panoply of gadgets—two typewriters, a battery-operated clock, a tape recorder—and work in the shade.

I was bitterly disappointed by Jean's advice, however well meant: what I had assumed would be a small stronghold of privacy had just vanished. My best hope was that when we worked outside, available to all interested eyes, our strangeness might become part of everyday village life and the crowds would thin out accordingly.

That evening I awoke in the dark, alert to some change that at first I couldn't identify. I lay there listening, and through the mud walls I could just make out distant laughter and singing.

I woke Alma. "Listen," I whispered.

"Let's go see," she said, slipping under the mosquito netting. Though still quite tired from my recent attack of malaria, I followed. After opening the door, we peered out into the darkness and heard, clearly now, the happy shouts of children.

"Well, well," I said, "what might this be?"

We quickly set off, following those wild, joyful cries. By the side of the road dividing the village, a virtual mob of children elatedly played games under the light of an almost full moon and the watchful eyes of a few adults. As if performing in a multiringed circus, the children were divided into various groups: a few girls held on to each other's *pagnes,* tied around the waist as if they were tails, and they ran in a circle, faster and faster; beside them a group of boys stretched their arms toward the center of their own circle, hands moving swiftly in complicated, interlocking rhythms while they sang a song in unison.

Alma wrote furiously in her notebook, trying to capture all that we saw. Every three or four minutes one or more of the games broke off, the patterns of play metamorphosing into another game, which in turn transformed into something else by an offhand gesture. At times the air was full of dust, and Alma and I felt some of the children's exhilaration as we wandered among them.

"Alma, look," I said, pointing to five boys engaged in a sort of leapfrog: one boy leaped over a crouching boy, then a third leaped over the first two, a fourth over them, until a fifth boy failed to clear the long line and they all tumbled down, laughing. Nearby a boy balanced a stick across his head, pulled a *pagne* over it, and became a monster, hopping up and down and rushing at a growing ring of children until he fell down, his *pagne* and the stick torn from him by a girl. Quickly a semicircle of girls formed around her, and she leaned on the stick, her bottom stuck out, her arm on a thigh: wiggling her knees, she feigned the halting walk of an old woman while her companions sang a mocking song. Then the girls formed a piggy-backed line, each rider holding the shoulders of the rider before her in a counterclockwise shuffle, singing a new song. Beside them a tug-of-war broke out, each child holding on to the waist of a teammate, boys pulling against girls and laughing until the lines split apart, neither side winning. Alma and I watched for over two hours, dazzled by such joyful transmutations.

Two nights later another evening surprise awaited me. Just before going to bed I walked behind our mud house toward the termitary on the edge of the forest, which had become my usual late night place to pee. Though I carried a flashlight, I didn't use it because of the full moon's glow. In that half-light the ground seemed almost to seethe, and as I continued toward the termitary I felt an eerie tickling up my ankle.

I stopped and flashed a spotlight at my feet: all around me were hordes of ants. I whooped with alarm and jumped up, streaking back toward our house, where I frantically beat off the ants that crawled up my calves and bit me. I peered back with my flashlight toward the termitary and saw a thick, rippling carpet of ants, stretching all the way back to the forest: they were heading straight for the village. I ran to François's compound, trying to decide how I would communicate the danger in Beng. I didn't know the word for "ant" yet, so the word for "insect"—*kaka*—would have to suffice. This, coupled with *e bling*—"many"—should do the trick.

François, his brother Kossum, and their wives were sitting beside a dimming fire. *"Kaka e bling!"* I shouted, bursting into their quiet circle.

Kossum chuckled, and his wife, Afwé Ba, joined in, gently bouncing a daughter on her lap. My struggles with the language were a source of local amusement, and my loud insistence and mangled pronunciation must have been a rare comic treat. But I kept repeating, *"Kaka e bling, kaka e bling!"* and motioning with my hand for François to follow. Finally he began to catch some of my excitement, and together we returned to the edge of the village.

François grunted in shock at the sight of the teeming multitude. He called out to his brother, and soon there were shouts throughout the neighboring compounds: men and women came running, lugging pots of ash and hot cinders from hearth fires. Quickly we made a line along the edge of the village, and the first thick surge of insects wriggled and twisted from the hot embers, their antennae dusted with the fine ash. The horde slowly turned at a right angle to this barrier, and the villagers continued arranging a border of ash and cinders to deflect the foraging ants. The dry season was just beginning, François explained, and this was a vast, collective search for food.

Long after our neighbors satisfied themselves that their improvised line would hold and that the marching army was slowly skirting the village, I stood at the ashy, smoldering border and stared at the waves of insects: huge-jawed warriors, compact workers, and, scuttling among them, even the tiniest of ants.

"Philip, are you coming in?" Alma called from our window.

"I'll be back soon," I replied, though I found it difficult to break away. I was fascinated by the collective, roiling motion, which, like my memory of those children's games, seemed to echo my excited, unsettled response to our new home.

The children of the village loved to play near us, their songs and laughter a steady sound track to our days. I enjoyed their playful stunts, my patience perhaps influenced by the children's own patience with our baby steps in their language. One morning, as I was making coffee inside our house, a crowd of young admirers elbowed each other for a better look at my strange doings. They chattered in excited waves, and I murmured, "Uh-huh," in counterpoint, forgetting that it was almost identical to the Beng "yes."

At one point I thought I heard the Beng words for "car" and "road." "Uh-huh," I murmured, spooning instant coffee into two mugs, thinking I was grunting acknowledgment that Alma and I would be driving somewhere that day. The children cheered and tore out of the room. Surprised, I watched briefly their excited scattering and then went back to our pot of boiling water.

Before long I heard their voices again, laughing and arguing just behind our house. I looked out the window and saw a troop of children scrambling in and out of our car, happily wiping any surface they could reach with torn pieces of cloth. Realizing I'd mixed up the Beng words for "road"—*zreh*—and "wash"—*zra*—I hurried outside and almost collided with two boys lugging a pail of water. When I reached the car I saw that the kids were essentially just rearranging the dirt of the road—no harm done. They were in heaven, exploring the dust-lined mysteries of an exotic wonder, so I laughed and thanked them and went back to breakfast.

Perhaps another measure of our popularity with the village children was that Alma and I thanked them for favors done. Simple words of gratitude, I had already begun to notice, were not bestowed on children. Adults ordered them around with an offhand curtness that was never questioned: *lo kro,* the Beng word for "children," literally meant "little slave." My politeness was a quiet critique of this attitude.

One afternoon Kona—our village host—came to our compound for a visit; hoping to encourage his friendliness, I decided to buy him a beer. *"Maa,"* I said to a boy loitering in our courtyard, "go buy a beer for me. Here's the money." Then, proud of myself, I added a Beng phrase I'd just learned, *"Ngwo mi popolo"*—please.

The boy giggled, took the coins, and hurried off. Behind me Kona laughed quietly, and I turned to see Jean grimacing in embarrassment.

"What did I do wrong?" I asked.

"You shouldn't have said *'Ngwo mi popolo'* to that boy," Jean said almost under his breath.

"But doesn't it mean 'please'?"

"Yes, but you never say it to a child."

"Only to adults?" Alma asked, always ready with her notebook.

"Well, truly, only to a king, and only if you're asking a very large favor."

Kona was still chuckling, and now I understood why I'd inspired such mirth—I'd addressed a little slave as if he were a king. Still, when the boy returned I made sure I said, "Thank you."

As in Asagbé, many people in our new village came to us for medicine, and Alma and I treated pus-filled wounds, infected sores, rashes, headaches, and malarial chills. I was never entirely comfortable with my role as doctor, yet in the face of such clear need I suppressed my squeamishness, keeping within the boundaries of my amateur abilities. Though we asked for no payment for the help we gave, the villagers, once cured, thanked and presented us with gifts: a small sack of rice; a live chicken, ripe for slaughtering; dozens of oranges; huge yams—all of which we accepted gratefully.

One of our neighbors, Komena Kouassikro, came to us one evening with a stinking cloth wrapped around his hand. A large, hulking man in his sixties, he spoke in a disjointed slur apparent even to us. When he unraveled the bandage we saw a terrible gash at the crook of his thumb—a few days before, he had accidentally slashed himself with his machete while farming. The wound was horribly infected, and I washed it carefully with antiseptic while Kouassikro's face twisted with pain. After slathering antibiotic cream over the raw skin and then dressing it, I asked him to return the next morning. I worried that his hand might turn gangrenous—if there was no improvement, I would drive him to the M'Bahiakro infirmary.

The next morning Kouassikro's wound looked better, and he said the pain had gone down. But he returned with a dirty bandage—through Jean, I told him that he should keep it clean, and he must wash his hand with water that had been boiled. Kouassikro nodded and thanked me, and I asked him to come by again in the evening.

He returned that night with another soiled dressing, and as I treated his hand—now healing nicely—I began to lecture him again about proper bandage cleanliness. Jean translated Kouassikro's reply. "He wants to know why."

"Because," I said, but then stopped. How to explain bacteria? "Well," I started again with Jean's help, "there are these little animals, so tiny that you can't see them without a . . ." I paused: what would "microscope" mean to

Kouassikro? "Without a special machine. But these little creatures are so dangerous they can kill you if you don't keep your wound clean."

I watched Kouassikro's face slowly harden into a deeper and deeper skepticism. "Little animals?"

"Yes. Very, very tiny ones."

Clearly this was one of the most ridiculous stories he'd ever been told, but as I was kind enough to give him medicine, Kouassikro nodded politely, thanked me again, and returned to his compound. How could I blame him? Murderous, infinitesimally small animals and special detection machines sounded implausible even to me.

Not long after, I gave a villager quinine tablets for one of his wives who was suffering from malaria. After I explained the dosage—proud of my new proficiency in Beng numbers—I suggested that he buy mosquito netting, to prevent a return of the disease.

"No," he said through Jean's translation, "she just needs to stay out of the sun."

"The sun?" I asked, counting out the pills.

"Too much sun causes malaria," Jean said matter-of-factly.

"No, that's not true. It's the bite of a mosquito that causes malaria."

Jean, nodding, said nothing.

"Please tell him," I insisted, anticipating another argument. Since our arrival in Kosangbé, Jean had become less and less cooperative: just the day before, he had angrily insisted, despite Alma's skepticism, that the Beng had no word for "prayer"; then, when he'd finally admitted there was such a word, he'd refused to tell her what it was. Now I waited for Jean's objections, but to my surprise he translated my explanation, however grudgingly.

The man laughed. "A mosquito?" Chuckling again at the thought that a mere buzzing nuisance could cause a deadly fever, he ambled off to his compound.

I decided simply to dispense medicine without lectures. Obviously my explanations weren't going to win any converts: the Beng were as confident in their own beliefs about disease as I was in mine. Though they sought out Western medicines from us, they clearly had their own ideas about what caused a sickness and what was being cured. Already Alma had learned that the images painted on the faces of Beng babies by their mothers—a tiny, orange crescent moon or a white radiating sun—were protections against illnesses, though no one would tell her yet what those illnesses were.

While I didn't have to agree with what the Beng believed—whether it was how malaria was caused or how children should be treated—I couldn't allow my skepticism to cut me off from this new world I was living in. I worried that my cultural preconceptions were another border of ash, a barrier I could too easily carry within me. Somehow I had to cross my own defenses. Only then would I, unlike the ants, be able to enter the village of Kosangbé.

Alma: Standing Clear of a Corpse

I placed our chopping block on the table, alongside a knife and a large yam. Then I looked over to Moya, Kona's twelve-year-old daughter, who was playing with her baby sister on a bark cloth mat; she pursed her lips into a string of nonsense words that made the infant squeal and giggle. We'd just hired Moya to cook and wash laundry—though with misgivings: how could I easily enter into the lives of my neighbors while serving as a village employer? And Moya was still a child herself; perhaps she was too young to work for us. Still, it would be pleasant to have a companion in our courtyard for a few hours each day, and along the way I might pick up some new vocabulary: learning to say "that smells delicious" and "not too spicy" should be useful. Moya might even tell me about the world of adolescent Beng girls.

When I called to her she settled the baby on the mat, and as she approached I thought I saw hints of her mother Sunu's austere beauty, her father's sparkly eyes.

Standing next to the table, Moya regarded the cutting board with curiosity. "I'll show you how to use it," I offered. Moya stood silent as I tried to hold the foot-and-a-half-long yam steady against the slab of wood and endeavored to cut away its thick, hairy skin.

"*Ihh,*" Moya said skeptically, her voice rising as she stared at my clumsy attempts to master the rolling tuber. Finally she stuttered, "*N-n—n-n gba*"— Give it to me—and extended her hand. Sighing, I agreed. Holding the yam a few inches out from her body, Moya made quick slicing motions, the knife moving rapidly away from herself. In a few moments she had ably skinned and chunked the enormous yam, with no help from my chopping board or my slicing techniques. Then she set the yams to boil, all the while keeping close watch on her sister.

Moya would certainly do well, releasing me from chores that would otherwise take hours out of my workdays. However, she seemed to stutter even more around me than she did with her friends—I made her nervous. I suspected I would have to look elsewhere for a confidante.

But how could I hope to make a friend while I was still struggling with the names of even our closest neighbors? When I regarded the packs of children scurrying playfully from courtyard to courtyard, I had little idea who their parents were. Perhaps now was a good time to begin a census—this might help me see invisible contours of village life. I might even ask about clan affiliations—I knew from the French colonialists' reports I'd read that membership in Beng clans was passed down through the mother.

On a bookshelf in our room, I dug around in my stack of papers until I found a stray sheet that I'd brought with me from America. On it I'd copied from my advisor's own field notebooks the format he'd used in taking down census material:

NAME: _____

AGE: _____

PLACE OF BIRTH: _____

CLAN: _____

CHILDREN: _____

SPOUSE: _____

SPOUSE'S CLAN: _____

I was excited; up until now all my notes had been impressionistic, even random. At last I could begin to collect information in an orderly fashion.

I went out and sat at the desk to arrange my cards and notebook. Soon Jean came by to work, and before he sat down I said, "I have a plan! I'd like to start on a census, maybe even ask clan names."

Jean nodded and mumbled, *"Bon."* Though I was insulted by his lack of enthusiasm, I said nothing.

Philip sat on a reclining chair made of palm tree ribs, reading Rilke's *Duino Elegies,* and he had that dreamy look about him that I knew so well. I hesitated to interrupt but finally said quietly, "I'm going to start the census."

"Okay, honey," Philip replied, looking up, "I think I'll just stay, maybe get some writing done."

"Great!" Then I asked Jean, "Where shall we begin?"

"How about over there?" he said, gesturing a few houses away.

The first person we encountered was a woman sitting on a low stool tending her fire.

"Good morning, little aunt," I said.

She glanced up, smiled, and returned my greetings, then invited us to sit on two nearby stools. We gratefully accepted. I opened my notebook and asked Jean to tell the woman that I'd like to ask her a few questions, beginning with her name. With a little embarrassment, Jean said something and the woman responded quickly, without looking up from her work.

"What did she say?" I asked Jean.

With obvious unhappiness, Jean answered, "She said she doesn't know her name."

"Why would she say *that?*" I asked. "Maybe she doesn't know why I'm

here—maybe she wasn't at the meeting when we told everyone about the work I'd be doing."

"She knows," Jean said. "Even if she wasn't at the meeting, the chief has told everyone about your work."

"Let's just explain anyway. It couldn't hurt," I said.

So Jean offered another summary of my reasons for living in the village.

"My name is Akissi," the woman said after Jean had finished.

"Ah, wonderful," I said, jotting down the name in my notebook. "Now let's ask how many children she has, and what their names are."

"I don't think she'll tell you," Jean said, looking away.

"Please," I said.

Jean capitulated, and the woman said something brief. Perhaps she didn't have any children.

Shifting position on his stool, Jean said, "She said she doesn't know the names of her children."

I felt like crying. If I encountered such resistance to what seemed innocuous information, who would agree to say a word about the more complex issues I had come to study? "Well, let's go to the next house," I said forlornly. "Could you thank Akissi for me?"

Walking along the thin path, I wondered if I had somehow offended Akissi, even frightened her. But how could I possibly allay her worries, whatever they were, if I couldn't speak to her directly? I vowed to work harder learning the language.

We approached the next compound, where a young woman sat nursing a baby.

"Good morning, big sister," I said, trying to muster as much enthusiasm as I could.

"Good morning," she responded, shifting the baby on her lap so she could see me—a good sign—as we proceeded to complete our greetings.

Then, staring at the ground, Jean mumbled something quickly, and the woman responded.

"She says her name is Au," Jean said.

Thank goodness, I thought. "And how about her husband's name?" I asked Jean.

Au said something that made Jean wrinkle his brows. "She says you should ask her husband," he muttered in a barely audible voice.

I didn't feel I had the stamina to risk another rebuff. We thanked Au and walked back in silence to my compound. I couldn't understand these declarations of impossible ignorance. Then I recalled that the British anthropologist Edward Evans-Pritchard wrote back in 1940 how the Nuer people of the Sudan, who had just recently been conquered by England, refused to tell him their names, driving him to "nuer-osis." The Nuer had, of course, good reasons for remaining aloof from their British visitor—after all, Evans-Pritchard had been sent to the Sudan by the colonial government to study Nuer customs, the better to "pacify" them. But Côte d'Ivoire had been independent from France for almost twenty years, and in any case, I was an American—so the Beng had no similar reason to fear me.

Then I thought of another motive. The French anthropologist Claude Lévi-Strauss once described how the Nambikwara Indians of Brazil kept from him their names because it was taboo to utter them aloud. Could I be encountering something similar? But I had already learned many people's names in casual conversations. I couldn't understand why they wouldn't tell me them now, when I wanted to write them down. Lévi-Strauss had resorted to coaxing children into whispering people's names to him; would I be tempted into such tricks?

I glanced at the dozen or so index cards I'd tucked into my notebook—optimistically I'd planned to transfer my census information onto them as soon as I'd collected it. Made in France, the four-by-six-inch cards were a bit thicker and stiffer than the American index cards I was used to, and they were printed with a grid of boxes rather than with lines. Now, still blank, those cards looked as alien as they had when I'd first seen them piled in stacks on an Abidjan store shelf.

Approaching our compound, I longed for Philip's sympathy, but I found him surrounded by a small crowd. Women with crying children were obviously there with cuts to be treated. Others, peering over Philip's shoulder as he bandaged a wound, murmured quietly to each other, punctuating their comments with little cries of *"Yih!"* that showed they had come just for the amusement of observing the stranger's antics: they were doing their own anthropology.

"What are all of you doing here?" Jean barked to the bystanders. "Don't you see Kouadio's busy? Stop bothering the man!"

"No, it's okay," Philip said gently, "I'm happy to take care of the cuts, and the others can watch if they want to." But because of Jean's harangue, the crowd thinned out. I wanted to rebuke him for his rudeness but feared further alienating the few visitors who remained. I glanced at Jean, who sat on a chair and pouted. How could I possibly continue to depend on an assistant who regularly offended people?

And Jean often concealed as much as he revealed. One day, in the middle of morning greetings, our hostess, Makola, said, *"Ka ma gbria."*

"That means, 'Thank you for yesterday,' " Jean translated.

We were baffled until Philip said, "I washed a lot of cuts yesterday, I'd forgotten about hers—it was so tiny. It was sweet of her to remember."

"But she *must* say that!" Jean said. "Whenever someone gives you a gift or does something nice for you, the next day you should always thank them."

I thought of all the lovely small presents people in the village had given Philip and me since we'd moved in—sometimes for having treated their wounds, sometimes just to be friendly. We'd always thanked them at the time, but not again the next morning. Did the villagers realize that our rudeness was inadvertent, or had they condemned us as barbarians who couldn't manage even the simplest acts of politeness?

"Why haven't you ever told me this?" I asked Jean, deflecting my own shame all too easily onto him.

"Well, you never asked," he answered.

Seated at our desk with Philip and Jean, I was grateful for the thatched canopy we'd had built. At midmorning the hot sun of the dry season was already relentless.

"I am sick, you are sick, he is sick, she is sick," I intoned like an incantation, "we are sick, you are all sick, they are sick."

"Bon," said Jean in a noticeably lackluster voice. My attention was elsewhere as well: my dysentery and stomach cramps were back, and Philip had developed a bad cough. As Jean drilled me on pronoun conjugations—past tense for "I," past tense for "you," past tense for "we"—we heard a loud chorus of what sounded like wailing.

"What's that?" Philip and I asked Jean almost at once.

"A village elder died this morning," Jean explained. "The funeral has just been announced, and the women are starting to mourn."

"We've just been working on verbs when there's been a death in the village?" I asked. "Why didn't you tell us earlier?"

Ignoring the anger in my voice, Jean said, "You didn't ask."

"Let's go!" I told Philip.

With Jean lagging behind, we ran in the direction of the keening voices coming from the other side of the village—near the chief's compound, where we were rarely welcomed. Hesitant to approach the mourners, Philip and I paused until Jean caught up and pointed out the widow: the door to her kitchen open, she sat hunched over, looking haggard and shriveled, giving voice to a lament I wished I could understand.

Without warning, the women of the village approached in a long, winding line, slowly, wordlessly filing toward the widow's courtyard, appearing so serene I almost forgot they were at a funeral. But when the first woman reached the door frame of the widow's kitchen, suddenly they all wailed, *"Weeeeeey, weeeeeey"*—that same chant we'd heard from across the village. One after another, each woman stopped at the doorway to give condolences to the widow while the others around her continued their mourning cries.

Finally, after the last woman had greeted the widow, the chorus of wailing ceased: abruptly, silence reigned.

Had this been just a performance? My anthropological imagination was sparked by dozens of questions, and I looked to Jean for guidance. "Why did everyone wail all together? And why did they stop?" I began. Before he could answer, I saw a group of children marching up and down the road, laughing.

"Why are they doing *that?*" I added.

"Too many things happening at once," Jean said curtly. "I can't explain it all."

"Just tell me the gist of what's going on—or a little bit at a time," I pleaded.

"No, I can't."

Then I saw a new stream of visiting men file into a house near the widow, each person emerging only seconds after they'd entered.

"Who are *they* going to see?" I asked.

Jean's eyes twitched, as they often did when he felt tense, and he was silent a moment. Finally he said, "The corpse is in that house."

"Ah." I too fell silent, then I suggested, "I think I'd like to see the corpse, too. Would you come along so I know what to say?"

"Oh, I couldn't do that, I might die if I saw the corpse!"

"You'd die?" I asked incredulously. "Why?"

"I just would."

I couldn't understand Jean's anxiety, since other people weren't making efforts to stand clear of the corpse. Yet his determined look seemed planted on his face forever.

"All right," I said, sighing, "let's just talk about who's come to the funeral. Do you know which guests were relatives of the man who died, and which were his friends?"

"They're all relatives," Jean answered curtly.

I strode off, determined to observe as much as I could on my own. Feeling courageous, I peeked into the corpse room. There indeed lay the body on a thick, handwoven cloth. Suddenly I felt giddy: I'd never been so close to death before. A few men brushed by me and rapidly undressed the body, which seemed frail and defenseless, subject to the gaze of any who cared to look—even an uninvited anthropologist. I wondered at the emotional entanglements he'd left behind, this man I would never have an opportunity to know.

The men carried the corpse outside. Was it time for the burial? Cautiously I followed, but they stopped only yards away, at a bathhouse. Ah, it must be time for his last bath. I peered in and watched the men sponge down the stiff limbs and torso—efficiently yet with obvious care. Then they carried the body back to the corpse room and proceeded to remove all the objects: some stools, an animal skin, a kerosene lantern. A woman began to sweep the floor, sweep out the life of the man, sweep out the dust from the room in which he had lived that life. Finally a mourner gently spread a new, richly patterned cloth over the corpse. All the while I wrote quickly in my notebook, trying to capture what I saw. Everyone taking part in this funeral seemed to know exactly what to do. But when had they memorized the script, and with no apparent director, how did they know which part to play? And what was my own role?

Suddenly I was aware of a presence behind me. I turned and found myself face to face with the chief. His red print cap perched jauntily on his head, San Yao nevertheless stared coldly. He addressed me: "Amwé, *ka ta wala*"—Go home.

I smiled, pretending I didn't understand.

"*Ka ta wala,*" San Yao repeated in such clear Beng that I couldn't possibly keep up my charade of stupidity. I nodded and obeyed this curt dismissal, which echoed my own sense of trespassing.

Back at our house, I was surprised to find Philip sleeping. When had he returned? I looked down and gently blotted the sweat off his forehead with a cloth, listened to him breathing noisily through his congested chest. The sound of drumming intruded on my preoccupation. Was it announcing a speech, another dance, the burial? I wanted to investigate, but with Philip sick, the least I could do was be at his bedside if he awoke in need of medicine or just a familiar face.

The drums beat faster; I stepped outside and saw that my neighbors were hurriedly leaving their courtyards. How could I stay home while the rest of the village tended collectively to this death? I took a last peek in on my husband, then headed back guiltily toward the funeral, determined this time to ask the chief for permission to observe: perhaps acknowledging his authority would relax his hardened posture toward me.

But when I found San Yao, he waved me away from the corpse room and said nothing more. Then Kona, sitting on a bench in the shade of the enormous kapok tree, called me over. Gratified by his reprieve, I took a seat next to him—perhaps I wasn't such an unwanted guest. Still, why had he decided to rescue me? Was it out of sympathy, or was he using me in some rivalry of his own with the chief? I hoped I wasn't caught in another battle—this time one in a small village—between a very different pair of "ministers."

Standing a few yards before us was a thin, gray-haired man, his *pagne* wrapped around him toga style, delivering a formal speech to all the elders. At the same time, new lines of visiting women, some with babies strapped on their backs, wound through the village, while nearby, young men tied up chickens and a bleating sheep—perhaps for an impending sacrifice. Then the mood turned celebratory as the drummers started up again, first quietly, then furiously—this time to accompany dancers.

Impatient to understand the meaning of all I was watching, I turned to Kona. But his French was as bad as my Beng, and besides, he was a terrible mumbler, hard to understand even when I suspected he was uttering words I knew. Where was Jean? *He* should be here, translating for me. Finally, frustrated, I returned home and typed up my notes. But they were little more than a disembodied list of actions performed by people I didn't know, for reasons I couldn't yet begin to fathom.

In the evening Philip revived slightly. Dismayed at having slept through so much of the day, he wanted to return to the funeral with me. Approaching the chief's compound, we heard an oddly tinny guitar music ringing out: tucked in the crook of the kapok tree's enormous flying buttress was a small, battery-operated record player, wired to a pair of small speakers. A few young people swayed slowly in place in the cool night air. What had happened to the funeral—had I missed the burial?

"Come over and join us," called out Kwamé, the son of our neighbor Ché Kofi, "it's disco!"

We thanked him for his invitation but continued on our way. The lilting music ringing quietly in our ears, we peered into the corpse room: the body lay on the floor, still wrapped in cloth and now fanned by a few women. The room was filled with the pungent-sweet fragrance of lemons. Was this to cover up the stench of the corpse? I took a step inside, but the women shooed me away.

Philip and I trudged home to bed. After a full day and despite my best efforts, I, too, like Jean, had stayed clear of the corpse.

The next morning Philip's cough was throatier, more insistent.

"How about some chamomile tea, love?" I asked.

"Mmmm."

I put some water on to boil, but Philip said, "I can finish that. You go on over to the funeral." So I walked across the village, hoping to blend in with a small group of mourners. But the chief hardly needed radar to find me.

"Amwé," he said in a tone that I recognized, "go home."

I sighed. Then, to my chagrin, he added, "You can come back when the visitors from the other villages have arrived." I understood his point: I could participate in this funeral only by greeting the villagers of Kosangbé as if I lived elsewhere.

I needed to find Jean—even if we had to keep our distance from the corpse, there was much else he could help me to understand. But he was certainly avoiding me, and as I searched for him I grew increasingly annoyed. Finally I found him alone on a mat, crouched in the shade of a bathhouse. Only a few

feet away, two men I didn't recognize stood dangerously close to each other, shouting.

"What are they arguing about?" I asked Jean.

"I don't know, they're talking too fast."

I remained silent while the men shook fists at each other and their voices grew louder.

"Do you know if they're related to each other?"

"No, they're not."

"But do you even know them? Aren't they from another village?" I persisted. "Why don't you ask someone?"

Jean looked away, utterly disinterested in my curiosity. As if the men's anger were contagious, suddenly I felt my accumulated frustrations burst out. "You're supposed to help me *understand* what goes on in the village," I shouted, "but you don't explain things even when I ask you!"

He said nothing, which further fueled my anger. Curious villagers gathered to watch, yet even through my embarrassment more words tumbled out, louder than the first. "You're not even *interested* in my questions. What do you think I've hired you for?"

Kona strode over and quickly herded us toward his compound. I walked along meekly, ashamed that I'd lost control, but when we reached Kona's courtyard I couldn't help reviving my litany of complaints in the face of Jean's sullen silence.

Finally I blurted out, "This arrangement isn't working! Let's forget about you being my assistant—it's obvious you don't like that part of the job. Why don't you just give me language lessons three times a week, and nothing more?" Immediately regretting my impetuous outburst, I stopped.

"Bon," Jean said quietly. His swift acceptance caught me off guard: he even smiled at me, as if relieved by this demotion. I couldn't take back my words now. But how would I be able to replace him? In Kosangbé only a handful of men—and no women—spoke even a smattering of French. If I didn't find another assistant, how could I carry out my research? I glanced over at Kona: his eyes focused on us carefully, and somehow I felt he knew more than he revealed.

Philip: Visitations

On the second night of the funeral, we heard that a young musician named Kouakou Ba had just arrived from the nearby village of Manigbé. I could sense the excitement created by his presence: a relative of the dead man, Kouakou Ba was here to perform his own music.

Although weary from a cough that shook my chest until it ached, I was eager to meet this man, and Alma and I walked to the compound where Kouakou Ba was resting before his concert. I easily made him out in the dim lantern light: he wore a skirt made of colorfully patterned towels sewn together, with fringes reaching just above his knees; below them were Western-style socks and shoes. Suspenders divided a white T-shirt depicting the map of Côte d'Ivoire, and his narrow red hat was decorated with cowrie shells on the sides and a flourish of goat hair hanging from the top. The unlikely combinations of his costume seemed somehow elegant in their individuality.

We greeted the musician, and he returned our greetings in a soft voice, his intense eyes looking out above sharp cheekbones. Beside him sat his father, a man with the same sharply defined features. Kouakou Ba knew a little French and agreed to speak with us before his concert. I asked him how he'd become a musician, and he hesitated thoughtfully before answering.

"I'd heard some guitar playing on the radio and seen pictures of guitars in newspapers and magazines. A friend of mine gave me a banjo as a present. When it broke, I carved a guitar for myself, by copying the pictures I'd seen. Last year, I bought a new guitar.

"At first I sang songs in Baulé," he continued, "but then I began writing my own songs in Beng." He had been composing for over four years now, he said, first thinking of the words—mainly short, proverblike lyrics—and then adding the music. I was so pleased to meet this original creator of traditional music that I could have talked with him for hours, but he needed to prepare for his concert.

"Could we speak again?" I asked.

"Yes," his father broke in, adding that we must send his son a letter a few days before we wanted to conduct the interview. Alma and I agreed, thanked the two men, and said good-bye, though as we left the compound I wondered why Kouakou Ba's father had demanded such formality.

Alma and I joined a large crowd that waited in a nearby courtyard for the musician's arrival. A single kerosene lamp lit the open space, casting stark shadows against the house where the widow sat mourning beside her husband's corpse. Finally Kouakou Ba stood before us, guitar in hand. Behind him were three young men holding various small rhythm instruments. When he began to strum his guitar I turned on our tape recorder. His voice, like his guitar playing, was plaintive and increasingly rhythmic. The young men behind him, sometimes singing in chorus, shook gourds and struck thin metal sticks together, creating a gritty roll layered with high-pitched ringing.

In a whisper Alma asked François to translate this first song. Impatient with her interruption, he murmured quickly, " 'Death isn't only for one person, it belongs to everyone.' "

I touched Alma's arm. "Maybe we should just sit and listen. We can always ask Jean to transcribe everything later."

She nodded, and we watched Kouakou Ba take small dance steps while he sang: his toes in place, he clicked his heels together, then he stood on one foot and gracefully twisted the other in the air. After a few songs he took small scuffling steps along the edge of the audience. At times someone near us sang along quietly, apparently enjoying a personal favorite; others threw coins at his feet; and in the brief pauses between songs people spoke freely among themselves, perhaps commenting on the message of the lyrics. Kouakou Ba seemed so sure in his performance, his audience so happily familiar with his work, that I envied him the comfort of his creative world. Alma and I listened far into the night.

Though I slept late the next morning, I was too tired to do more than sit back and read—I set about finishing *Njál's Saga,* another of those Great Books I'd brought with me to Africa. A medieval saga of Iceland, it depicted a grim world of blood feuds that lasted generations, entire families gripped by a carefully nurtured desire for revenge that was eventually carried out by men with names like Thorgeir, Mord, and Sigurd. The fatalism of the characters and the inexorable logic of retribution gripped me until late afternoon.

At last I set the saga down and sighed. How easy to enter another, distant culture through a book, how difficult to actually live in one. Still tired, I decided to type a letter to a friend. But before I finished the first paragraph a familiar shivering wave swept through me.

By the evening, though I'd taken extra quinine pills for a cure, my body seemed to radiate heat; when Alma took my temperature she discovered it was a ferocious 106 degrees. Her face strained, she rubbed down my body with a cloth drenched in rubbing alcohol. Then she tried to make me drink some freshly squeezed orange juice, even water, but I was so dehydrated from the fever that I threw up whatever she offered.

When I wasn't coughing I lay back in bed, less and less able to move my arms and legs or even turn my head. As the long hours passed I lay still, in a kind of sickbed floating, and felt somehow apart from the burning that was my body.

"I think I'm dying," I whispered, surprised by my words as I said them. This couldn't be true at all, yet once again I heard myself say, "I think I'm dying."

"Don't be silly," Alma replied quietly. "But you have to drink something."

"Can't," I moaned softly. She sat beside me and stroked my hair, felt my forehead. Again she took my temperature.

"No change," she said grimly. She returned to the chair by the side of the bed and pored through our medical text.

I closed my eyes and listened to the swift turning of pages, which fluttered into a strange echo. When I opened my eyes, Alma's anxious figure seemed to wobble and waver in the dim light of the room, as if she were stuck in a fun house mirror. She said something, but her voice seemed terribly distant.

I nodded, and when Alma stood, the mosquito netting between us sparkled in the lamplight, creating such bright patterns as she moved that I closed my eyes again and tried to steady the dizziness inside me.

Then I heard Alma, so far away, stirring something in the kitchen: the faintest sound of a spoon scraping rhythmically inside an enamel cup. It went on and on forever, until I felt it would pull me out of myself. Struggling with the heavy weight of my lids, I finally opened my eyes.

I saw, just outside the mosquito netting, two huge armored and bearded warriors, the outlines of their bodies faint, like ghosts. They were Vikings, visions straight out of my Icelandic saga. They pulled out their swords and slashed away at each other, and the odd, almost dispassionate sweep of their blades temporarily distracted me from my fever and the terrible dryness in my throat. I gaped at this slow-motion battle and listened to the Vikings' shields echoing from each blow like footsteps.

"Alma," I called out, and there she was, alone before me.

"Shhh," she whispered when I tried to speak. "I made a rehydration drink. You should be able to keep this down—try it." After pulling away the mosquito netting, she helped me sit up and held the cup to my lips.

I cautiously sampled a bit of the salty, unpleasant concoction, waited, then drank more, sip by sip, until the cup was finally empty. I settled back on the bed, felt Alma's hand stroke my cheek. There was my wife before me, undistorted by feverish eyes.

"That was good," I said. "Thank you, love." We were alone: no ghostly Vikings battled beside us, and only the dark insect drone of the forest intruded on our quiet moment of relief.

"You feel cooler," Alma said, her smile only slightly strained. "Let me take your temperature."

Soon after I returned from the M'Bahiakro infirmary, weak but well, Alma and I heard the excited village news: in two days Côte d'Ivoire would host an international Grand Prix featuring some of the leading European and African drivers, and the race was due to pass by on the narrow dirt road that divided Kosangbé.

No one planned to work in the fields that day. In the early morning some villagers moved chairs and stools to the edge of the road for a first-row look. Others sat under the shade of nearby thatched canopies. When a small prop plane flew over the village, the children cheered and raced about: apparently the radio had announced a plane would be following the course of the drivers. I stared up at the noisy silver thing, which seemed so out of place.

Soon enough a dull, grinding roar could be heard. Anticipating the sight of the first sports car, we all stared down to where the road curved into the forest. Suddenly there it was: a low-slung, brightly colored roadster speeding through our small village at nearly one hundred miles an hour. Gone in moments, it left behind an enormous dust cloud that settled slowly on all of us as we waited for the next racing car.

At ten-minute intervals we heard another approaching rumble, watched each racing car appear and vanish in seconds, and felt another layer of dust rain on our almost comically covered bodies. I wondered what the drivers thought of the split-second blurs of people and mud houses they passed so quickly. Already I knew that Kosangbé was far more than a momentary break in the overhanging tropical rain forest: it was a complex world that was slowly beginning to reveal itself to Alma and me.

Certainly the unfamiliar faces of our neighbors were already beginning to assert personalities, histories. Amina, Kona's daughter-in-law, often sat beside Alma and tried to chat, coaxing out Alma's stumbling Beng. Her husband was a tailor in Bouaké, almost seventy miles away: he was there to make money without having to support a family in the city; eventually he would return to the village. Perhaps longing for that day, Amina sometimes just sat quietly, nursing her infant daughter and thinking her own thoughts as Alma typed up field notes.

Another frequent visitor to our compound was Yapi Yao, a thin, soft-spoken young man who'd learned some French while serving in the army. He was less wary of us than were most villagers, and he liked to stroll by and ask questions about America, his gentle face tinged slightly with melancholy. He didn't even mind discussing Beng beliefs—Alma wondered if he might one day replace Jean, whose transition from field assistant to part-time language teacher was awkward for us all.

Jean showed his impatience more easily now; our hours with him were a necessary drudgery, whether it was memorizing Beng numbers into the thousands or repeating again and again the names of body parts: hard work to begin with, made more so by an unwilling instructor.

Once, to lighten the time, I watched the children playing in our compound, gleefully hurling at one another what were clearly insults. Soon the children crowded around us, tossing out their favorites, and Jean finally gave in to their increasingly inventive competition, translating such choice invective as "You have tiny eyes," "You have stubby toes," "You have monkey ears," "You smell like a goat," "You shit like a chicken," "You're the child of dogs."

Enjoying this rare, relaxed moment, I tried to convince myself that maybe our new relationship with Jean would succeed. Yet often, alone at night, Alma and I expressed doubts about him. He still argued over even trivial matters with my normally mild-mannered wife, and she worried about the conclusions the villagers might be making about her. But without Jean, how would we learn Beng?

Despite these concerns, we found ourselves slowly establishing a daily routine. Each morning two pails of hot water, left by Moya, waited for us beside the bathhouse. Alma washed first while I cooked breakfast on our little gas stove: oatmeal flavored with fresh bananas or imported dates and cups of hot Ovaltine. When Alma returned, I took my turn in the bathhouse and she finished preparing the meal.

Sometimes, instead of cooking, we walked over to the Jula quarter, where a woman had set up a small morning trade: for a few CFAs we could buy *boflotos:* little balls of flour fried in a pan as you watched. Crunchy on the outside, soft on the inside, they tasted a bit like French toast when dipped in sugar. She also sold us freshly picked oranges, which we learned to eat the local way. Making a circuit from top to bottom, I'd peel off long, thin coils of rind with a knife, taking care not to cut through the pulp. When the orange was finally skinned, I sliced an edge off the top, exposing the juicy interior. Holding the orange with two hands, my mouth against the opening, I squeezed: instant orange juice.

As we ate breakfast, neighbors came by and greeted us, and then we walked about the village, reciting the required morning greetings and thanking those who had given us gifts the day before—a gourd filled with roasted peanuts or a bowl of dried okra powder for a sauce. When we returned to our courtyard, I boiled pots of water: once cooled, this would be our drinking water for the day. Then we carried our table and chairs outside and set them under the shade of our thatched canopy. The villagers who marched off to work in the fields waved to us and called out in Beng, "I'm going to the fields today"—the beginning of another specialized greeting.

"*Ka ma!*" we'd call back, which meant "courage," adding, "*Ka nu batwa*"— Come back quickly.

While Alma worked with Jean on the language or typed her field notes, I would tend to whoever came by for medicine. Then I joined the day's language lesson, long hours that grew increasingly tense. Each day we paused in these trials when Moya came by to cook lunch—usually rice with some of our canned sardines in a tomato sauce. After the meal I'd either return to the mysteries of Beng verbs or write a letter, read a book, attempt to scratch away at a story.

When the sun began to set, the villagers returned from their hard day of work: the men with hoes slung over their shoulders, the women carrying on their heads huge piles of firewood and yams for the evening's dinner. Moya arrived with two pails of hot water for our evening bath, and Jean returned to Kona's compound for his own ablutions. While we washed, Moya cooked dinner: perhaps *foutou* with peanut sauce or fried yams with a sauce of okra and dried fish. Though Alma and I had adjusted to much of the local cuisine, we still suffered from its mouth-numbing spiciness. Once our neighbor Ajua overheard us instruct Moya to put only two chili peppers in the sauce, and she chortled at the thought of such an impossibly bland meal. Now we refrained from any culinary suggestions and endured whatever fiery seasoning Moya served.

After dinner, unless there was a dance or a village meeting, Alma and I worked by lamplight in our compound. Flying insects buzzed our heads as they circled the lantern, and neighbors dropped by to watch and comment on our unusual doings. When the last of our visitors finally departed for the night, saying, *"Eki mi gba dring"*—May God give you tomorrow—Alma and I carried the desk into our mud house and locked the door. We were finally alone, and it was a blessing to be our private American selves, speaking to each other in our own language. I still felt overwhelmed by how public all my actions were, how difficult it was to find a moment for reflection. I had few new ideas for my stories, a writer's dry spell in this dry season, and I could only wait for the beginning of both rainy seasons.

Yet recently a sudden, anomalous storm had swept over Kosangbé. The rainwater rushed in patterns through the village, skirting all the compounds, revealing that what I had assumed were merely cracks and fissures in the dry ground were actually a web of carefully planned rain gutters. This system, until now hidden to my eyes, gave me comfort, for it reminded me that often some of my best writing was done during my own dry spells, quietly and invisibly inside, waiting to become words.

As we slowly eased into the foreign rhythms of the village, our progress was interrupted by a vivid remembrance of home. One day in M'Bahiakro, when Alma and I searched in our postal box for news of her delayed grant money, we found instead two cassettes from a friend: a recording of the last game of the 1979 World Series.

I had no idea who'd won, the Orioles—those despicable crushers of Yankee dreams—or the Pirates. I'd been desperately curious for over a month and now couldn't wait to return to Kosangbé and our tape recorder. Once there, I settled into one of our palm wood lounge chairs and sent a child off to buy me a large bottle of Ivoirian beer. Then I sipped with lazy pleasure, watching the sun go down as I listened to three hours of the exotic play-by-play of a distant, long-ago-decided game. While goats bleated and the steady hum of insects rose from the darkening forest, I saw in my mind's eye three-and-two pitches, pop flies, improbable catches, and I cheered at Willie Stargell's game-winning home run: an elated, foreign whoop that rang through our corner of Kosangbé.

But the dramas of village life were never far away. One afternoon a group of excited children pulled at our sleeves and led us hurriedly toward the Jula quarter, where a girl was sitting at the edge of a compound, blood streaming from her foot. Beside her knelt a young man, dressed in a long, flowing, Muslim-style *bubu*. He spoke Beng to the children, then French to us. "She slashed her foot with an ax while chopping wood," he said. "Can you help?"

"*Oui,*" I said, but when I looked closer and saw the gaping wound between her big toe and the rest of her foot, I was afraid this emergency was beyond our abilities. Still, we fetched our first-aid kit, and soon Alma and I lifted the girl's leg and applied compresses on the gash. The girl shook her head and whimpered from the pain, her eyes staring out at the encircling forest, while the young man murmured a steady flow of calming words. He also kept the children from crowding in too closely, using only a word or two. I regarded his unremarkable square face and close-cropped hair, trying to detect what radiated such quiet authority.

Blood continued to soak through the bandages, and I worried that we'd made a mistake by not immediately driving the girl down to M'Bahiakro. But gradually the flow ebbed, then stopped. I applied a final dressing on the girl's foot, and Alma gave the man instructions on how to care for the wound. He translated this into Jula for the girl's parents, who we only now realized had been hovering nearby. They thanked us and carried their daughter into one of the small houses of their compound.

Alma and I exchanged Beng expressions of gratitude with the young man. Was he Beng? If so, why was he living in the Jula quarter? Before we left I asked him his name.

"Yacouba," he said. It was a name I was determined to remember.

Alma: Singing with Bells, Dancing with Talc

Eager to continue his talk with Kouakou Ba, Philip sent him a letter by messenger, as the singer's father had instructed. That evening we received the reply: an invitation to meet in his village, Manigbé, in three days. For the long interview we envisioned we'd need a translator. With some embarrassment I asked Jean if he would accompany us; to my relief he brightened at the suggestion. Kouakou Ba perfectly fit Jean's boosterism: a model Beng to present to the outside world.

When we arrived in Manigbé, Jean escorted us to Kouakou Ba's compound. We were surprised to see the musician sporting the elaborate costume he'd worn at the Kosangbé funeral. Even more unexpected, a large crowd was gathered in his courtyard.

We greeted Kouakou Ba and his parents, then Philip whispered to Jean, "What's going on? Why so many people?"

"They're here for the concert," he answered.

"What concert?" I said, stunned. Jean quickly led us to a corner of the compound, and we asked him to tell Kouakou Ba's father that we'd merely come for a private conversation with his son. Jean shook his head in discontent—already he regretted coming along—but he crossed the courtyard with our message.

More villagers arrived, and they shifted about restlessly, looking back and forth between us and Kouakou Ba's family. Finally Jean returned, his face pinched with concern. "The old man says you should pay six thousand CFAs for the concert."

Philip and I cast each other looks of alarm. "But we don't even have six thousand CFAs!" I said. Jean knew this was true—with my second grant installment overdue, we owed him his salary for this week's language lessons.

Then Philip whispered, "Like it or not, we seem to be the sponsors of a show—the whole village is waiting for it to start."

I looked at the expectant faces surrounding us. He was right. "But we're almost broke," I began.

"We can spare one thousand CFAs," Philip calculated quickly, "and we'd just better hope that your grant money comes in the next few days."

I nodded and turned to Jean. "Please tell Kouakou Ba's father that we can't pay him what he's asked—we just don't have the money."

He frowned and crossed the courtyard, where another animated discussion ensued. When Jean returned he reported, "He says four thousand is the least he can accept."

"Oh god," I said to Philip, "he thinks we're *bargaining.*" Yet why shouldn't he doubt our claim of poverty and try to charge us as much as he could? We had, after all, arrived in a car, toting a tape recorder and a camera. I turned to Jean. "Please, tell him it's true—we really can't pay more than one thousand CFAs."

Jean sighed and crossed the courtyard once again for more haggling. Soon he returned and whispered, "He's come down to three thousand."

I groaned with embarrassment, and Philip said, "We can't go up. He has to understand this."

Jean set off to relay this seemingly heartless message, and as the negotiating continued, the crowd in the courtyard murmured impatiently.

Finally Jean returned. *"Bon*—he's accepted one thousand CFAs."

Kouakou Ba strode over, shook our hands, and smiled generously, as if hard-nosed negotiations hadn't just taken place. Trying to salvage our hope for a simple conversation, Philip asked Kouakou Ba if he would talk briefly before the concert about the source of his inspiration.

"It's better for me to sing than to talk to you about singing," he replied quietly. Abashed, Philip nodded.

Kouakou Ba motioned to the other side of the courtyard. A few young men stepped out, maracas and metal sticks in hand. The villagers spread out in a circle, settling on stools, leaning against mud walls. When Kouakou Ba began to sing in his high, insistent voice, I turned on the tape recorder. But I'd already listened to a concert with little sense of what I'd heard, so at the end of the song I asked him to talk about his lyrics.

His guitar poised, Kouakou Ba said patiently, "A bride complains to her mother that her new husband is too poor to buy her earrings and new clothes." But he offered no further commentary and, strumming his guitar, began a new song.

Again I asked for a translation, and Kouakou Ba said, "If you want to have children, don't be surprised if you end up having twins."

During these awkward interludes the audience shifted restlessly, and I decided to simply listen—I could translate from the tape some other day. Resuming the performance, the band members rang their bells, and Kouakou Ba sang and swayed while his mother sprinkled talcum powder on his sweaty forehead. Song after song, the audience threw coins at his feet—though we'd seen this happen at the Kosangbé funeral as well, Philip and I felt humiliated, convinced that the coins were a critique of our inadequate offering.

Our visit couldn't have been further from what we'd planned—a private interview recast into a public concert. Perhaps this was as it should be: if I was here to understand Beng society, why should I alone decide how to gain that understanding? Yet I stopped listening to the music and brooded over my latest failure. How many more mistakes could I make before the Beng gave up on me?

4

ADRIFT

𝕐   𝕐   𝕐

(DECEMBER 21, 1979–FEBRUARY 19, 1980)

Alma: Missionary Meat

THE DUST OF THE DRY SEASON BLEW IN THROUGH THE CAR'S OPEN WINDOWS, ADDING A FINE brown layer to our clothes. While Philip drove, I kneaded my stomach. We were off to M'Bahiakro, but not to the infirmary—we couldn't afford whatever medicines Dr. Yiallo might prescribe.

When we reached town we went straight to the post office, keeper of the town's only public phone, and called our bank in Bouaké. Bad news: they hadn't received any funds into our account. We had no choice, we'd have to borrow money—but from whom? Perhaps our Peace Corps friend Lisa might loan us some. We rode the dusty road to her home, but yards from her white stucco house we moaned at the sight of the locked gate: Lisa must have left for Christmas vacation.

We went through a very short list of all the people we knew in town. The only possible moneylenders we could think of were the two Protestant missionaries from Ohio, Barbara and Jane. We'd had a few lunches with those women on occasion—after almost two months of fiery okra sauce and yam *foutou* for lunch and dinner day in and day out, their American-style meals were too seductive to refuse. But borrowing money from them was far more problematic. Already we regretted our weakness in regularly frequenting the Catholic *pères'* house for their delicious, homemade yogurt—the Africans who saw our car parked beside the church called out to us, *"Mon père! Ma soeur!"* How could I possibly conduct my research if I was seen as a missionary?

"No, we just can't ask them for money," I protested to Philip. "It's too compromising."

"I know," Philip said. "But what's the alternative? You can barely get up some days. We've *got* to get you some medicine." From the impatience in his voice, I knew this was an argument I wouldn't win. I sighed and silently contemplated Philip's point: I didn't know how much longer I could endure these cramps. Racked with misgivings, I said quietly, "All right," and we drove to Barbara and Jane's house.

The women were not only happy to loan us $125, they cheerfully invited us to dinner on Christmas Eve. Could we decline this further generosity? Still, we hesitated.

"Oh, don't worry, it won't be any trouble," Barbara said, "we have lots of food." She led us to an enormous freezer and opened the door. We stared shamelessly at the dozens of bags of frozen meats, vegetables, fruits, even pizzas, all imported from the States—surprising, considering how thin both women were.

"Yes," Jane said, filing through the bounty before us, "there's a turkey here that's just the right size." She turned to us, smiling. "Barbara's right—no trouble at all."

Christmas Eve was still a few days off, I reflected—perhaps my grant money would be in by then and we could repay the two women before the dinner. "Thank you." I smiled back, ashamed of my hypocrisy.

We sat before Barbara and Jane's lavish dinner and murmured politely as they said grace. Another phone call to the Bouaké bank that morning had confirmed that no funds had been cabled into our account. Now we passed the plate of turkey, the bowls of green beans and salad, and Barbara took advantage of the occasion to ask me about Beng religion.

"I haven't found out much yet," I answered, "but I know they worship the Earth."

"That sounds like devil worship," Barbara said, passing the mashed potatoes.

"No, I don't think so," I said quickly.

"Well, dear, we *do* know the signs." Jane sighed. "They're practicing pure idolatry."

"Idolatry?" Before I could continue, Philip nudged my leg under the table. Staring down at the meat piled on my plate, slathered in brown gravy, I realized he was right: it would be rude to engage in a theological argument with these women as we ate their food. Surely I should use my anthropological training and try to respect their point of view. But I was too partisan to do this in good faith: ironically, I couldn't help condemning *their* condemnation of another religious tradition.

The two women continued what seemed like a planned speech, raising the specter of human sacrifices and other pagan horrors. Philip and I demurred as politely as possible, yet with growing resentment—we were a captive audience, beholden to these women for the money they'd lent us. We finished our dinner as quickly as possible and excused ourselves. I vowed silently to repay their loan as soon as possible and never return to their home again.

That night back in Kosangbé I developed a 102-degree fever. It lasted through the next day until finally Philip declared that we had to drive to Abidjan and find a doctor. I remember nothing of that feverish journey except our arrival, uninvited, at the doorstep of a charming and witty middle-aged American couple, connected with the American embassy, whom we'd met during our initial stay in the capital. Al and Eszti invited us in, clearly unsure what to do with us. But in the course of recounting our past two months to them, Philip waved his arm in an offhand gesture and his wedding ring sailed across the living room—a striking example of the four belt holes' worth of weight he'd lost from his two attacks of malaria. Al and Eszti took pity on us and offered us the keys to the apartment of mutual friends who were away for the holidays.

We settled into the spacious apartment, and I stumbled to the bedroom, hot and exhausted, ready for a long sleep. But, lying on the bed, I suddenly felt an itch on my arm . . . then another running up my leg . . . then another spreading across my back. As I scratched, I inspected my skin: no signs of bites. I rubbed and rubbed ever more furiously, but new tingly waves announced themselves faster than I could scratch. I called Philip, but even four frantic hands couldn't keep up with this feverish, insistent prickle. I tore off my clothes, I wanted to jump out of my body—perhaps a freezing cold shower could wash off the maddening sensation.

Philip beside me, I hurried into the bathroom and stood under a stream of water, hopping from one foot to the other, slapping at my wet skin. But the itch was relentless. Finally, after nearly an hour of torment, the seizure disappeared as mysteriously as it had arrived. I dried off and lay down again, even more exhausted, and tried to make sense of that strange attack. If I couldn't sweat off my recent anxieties through fever, maybe I was trying to scratch them off. My terrible stomach pains and excruciatingly slow progress in the Beng language, my inability to make any friends in Kosangbé, our humiliating indebtedness to missionaries—fieldwork had literally gotten under my skin.

The next day Philip and I drove to a clinic Al and Eszti had recommended, but I was told I'd have to wait two days for an examination. I resigned myself to facing the mysterious world of electronic international banking in the interim. Though my fever had eased a bit, I felt too weak to drive all over town, so we decided to call the banks instead. We drove to the Hotel Ivoire, which had a cluster of public telephones.

Well-dressed Europeans and Africans strolled past us in the air-conditioned lobby, their designer suitcases carried by porters in crisp, double-breasted white uniforms decorated with golden buttons and braids. We made our way to the wall of pay phones, but after depositing my coins, I heard nothing. We tried each telephone in succession—not one worked. I felt sweaty—my forehead was hot again. Philip led me across the expansive lobby to a plush sofa near the indoor cafe. I collapsed onto the soft cushions, then looked around at the wealthy hotel patrons savoring chocolate sundaes, croissants, iced tea; nearby, shoppers browsed in the hotel's record store, while across from them tourists exclaimed over thick ivory bracelets and malachite earrings shimmering in the illuminated glass cases lining a lobby wall. This place felt utterly alien. All I wanted to do was return to . . . where? The thought of Kosangbé reminded me of all my failures.

"If only they'd *talk* to me," I moaned, "but everybody in the village is so damned suspicious."

Philip put his arm around my shoulder. "Of course they're suspicious," he said, comforting me, "they barely know us."

"They'll *always* be suspicious. I can't get along with Jean, I can't learn Beng—even if I could, no one would answer any of my questions!"

"It takes time to learn a language," Philip said quietly. "God knows you're doing better than I am."

But Philip's soothing words did nothing to console me, and I felt tears beginning to roll down my cheeks. I hid my face against his shoulder. "This has been one big mistake," I whispered. "I want to go home."

Philip: Happy New Year

Alma surely meant this—she wasn't someone who indulged in false dramatics. Holding my wife, her face pressed against my chest, I secretly worried

that I'd added to her misery by undermining her confidence: though I'd shared the difficulties of the past months as well as I could, I'd also complained too often, questioning the move to Kosangbé and openly longing for home.

Before we'd left for Africa I'd read a fieldwork account by the anthropologist Robert Dentan in which his wife, Ruth, declared that if she'd known what difficulties they were going to encounter, she never would have accompanied him to Malaysia, but once fieldwork was done she wanted to go back. I'd been struck by her words, and now, considering what Alma and I had already been through, I understood them far better. Yet if we left today, would we want to return?

I regarded the overpriced tourist shops around us and their glossy, palatable images: a travel agent's Platonic ideal of Africa and a betrayal of the complex Beng world we'd just begun to enter. I sighed—if I'd accompanied my wife to give her my support, then that was what I was going to do. Sitting on that luxuriously cushioned couch in my sweaty clothes, homesick, hungry, and nearly broke, I tried to talk Alma out of leaving.

"No," I said, stroking her hair, "you have to stick it out or you'll never forgive yourself."

Alma was crying openly by now, releasing the tensions and disappointments of the past months. Though her sobs were lost in that vast, air-conditioned lobby, one of the hotel staff eased nearby us, silently offering the possibility of assistance. I smiled thanks and shook my head no. Then, murmuring comforting words in Alma's ear, I planned my strategy. When she finally sat up and wiped at her teary face, I said, "You say no one will talk to you. But what about that woman in Asagbé, the one who rattled off those weird pregnancy taboos? She speaks French, and she asked you to visit her. What was her name?"

"I can't even remember. Maybe it's Amenan," Alma said unhappily. "But she doesn't live in our village."

"So? We have a car."

"You think—"

"If she wants you to visit, then what's the problem?"

Alma hesitated. "But what if she turns out to be just as secretive as everyone else?"

I had no good answer. "We'll worry about that if it happens."

The next morning Alma—still feverish—began a long acquaintance with the foreign exchange clerks in the Abidjan branch of our bank in Bouaké. She should have been resting in bed, but my French simply wasn't good enough to negotiate the complexities of lost telexes. I drove around the block again and again, unable to find a parking space. All the cars were parked tight against the curbs in this downtown business district, and I imagined circling the bank for hours, wasting four-dollar-a-gallon gas that we couldn't afford to replace. Suddenly I saw, near a corner, a slight space between two cars, and I half nosed Didadi in until the tail end poked out only slightly. I had already set off for the bank across the street when I heard a gruff voice behind me shout, *"Monsieur!"*

A gendarme motioned with his finger for me to return. I glanced over at the car—it wasn't, as far as I could see, parked illegally. But apparently the gendarme disagreed. He chastised me in a rapid flood of French that I could barely follow. *"Pardon,"* I attempted, *"je suis américain."*

This seemed to make him angrier. Perhaps he thought I was invoking some sort of colonial immunity. To highlight my ignorance, I shook my head and pointed at my ear. *"Américain. Comprend pas."*

He let out an exasperated sigh. Taking out a pad, he asked me my name. I couldn't afford to pay a traffic fine at this point. But in that case, what would he do—impound the car? I recalled how a year earlier, in my hometown in New York, I had been pulled over by a traffic cop after having driven through a stop sign. Because I was living in Virginia at the time, I took advantage of my out-of-state plates and affected a southern accent, claiming I was lost. No ticket was served. Perhaps some playacting would help me again, so I decided to further heighten my wobbly French. *"Nom?"* I repeated, trying to affect the broadest possible air of stupidity. *"Quoi?"*

This only produced a further stream of abuse. I leaned toward him, pretending I was sincerely trying to understand. I shrugged my shoulders, admitting defeat. Then I set about to butcher what little French I knew. *"Je ne pas comprendez vous bien la français,"* I eked out painfully.

His face filled with anguish as he listened to this tortured sentence, but I didn't mind. I hadn't much respect for the gendarmes in Côte d'Ivoire: their main function, from what I had seen, was squeezing bribes from bus drivers. As far as I knew, he was trying to squeeze one out of me.

He tried again, slowly—expressing some wonder, I guessed, at how I could manage in Abidjan if I really couldn't speak French.

"Oh, *monsieur,*" I said, *"ma femme, il dit la français, beaucoup bon. Mais elle*—oh, what's the word," I muttered in English, "but she's . . . *ici.* No, *loin, peut-être . . .*" I motioned vaguely across the street, grimacing from the struggle with words I supposedly couldn't find, and I tried to hide my secret exhilaration, for I was exacting a bit of revenge against this language that so often defeated me.

By now a small crowd had gathered to watch our ridiculous exchange. The gendarme sighed, glancing up at the sky as if in supplication. Then he tapped on his pad, trying to decide what to do.

I decided to push my luck. "Ohhh, you want me to give you money?" I said in English. I took out my wallet. *"Argent?"* I glanced at the people around us, as if seeking their approval for my interpretation. The crowd murmured with nervous amusement.

"Non, monsieur, c'est fini," the gendarme said, his face wide with alarm at this idiot so openly offering him a bribe. *"C'est fini. Au revoir!"*

I reached forward and shook his hand. *"Merci très!"* I thanked him, smiling the grin of a moron who had no true conception of his good fortune. He waved me away. I thanked him again and hurried across the street to the bank, desperately hoping that Alma's grant money had arrived—I was certain I'd never be able to pull off another stunt like that.

We spent more days searching unsuccessfully. Then, on the morning of New Year's Eve, Alma's fever finally broke, and we happily lounged the day away, relieved that her health was finally improving. Alma felt so much better that we decided to celebrate the new decade with a dinner out, and as if daring a turn in our luck, we counted our remaining money and estimated just what we could afford to spend. That evening we wandered through the neighborhood in search of a place to eat. Soon we were examining the prices on the menu displayed outside a restaurant named Hanoi: even a bottle of cheap wine was possible, along with a decent tip.

The restaurant was a long, narrow room crowded with small tables. In one corner the black-and-white glow of a television offered "Flipper," dubbed in French. At least the evening news wasn't on—the continuing Iranian hostage crisis and the Soviet invasion of Afghanistan were more than we could manage tonight. By the bar sat a tiny, ancient Vietnamese woman, ordering the Ivoirian waiters about with little nods of her head: a specialized sign language they all seemed to understand. I tried to decipher the woman's subtle gestures but was distracted by Flipper—Alma and I glanced over at him whenever he poked his nose up from the water and squeaked. The service was quite slow, which suited us fine, since we wanted to savor our night out. Finally we clinked glasses, wishing ourselves good luck for 1980—a year filled with more unknowns than we dared dwell upon.

Alma: Bestowing Gifts

At last, a sympathetic bank manager tracked down our funds—which had been sent through the regular mails, rather than telexed—and we finally said good-bye to the city. Back in the car heading upcountry, Philip and I tried to serve as a mutual cheerleading squad. I told him that he'd surely begin writing soon; in turn, he assured me that the villagers would confide in me and that my new medicines would finally work.

Once in Kosangbé, I plunged back into language lessons with Jean, vowing to be more patient. But on our first day back, he refused to translate what a tipsy but friendly villager mumbled to me, claiming the man was so drunk that no one could understand a word ... though others in the courtyard seemed to have no such trouble. I regarded Jean's face, stiff with stubborn rage, and thought silently: It's time to visit Amenan.

The following day I drove to Asagbé and found Amenan in her compound, pounding together herbs in a small mortar. Now eight months pregnant, and even shorter than I'd remembered, she looked quite the butterball. Her feet tired easily these days, she said, so she wasn't working much in the fields: she had plenty of time to chat.

"I'd like to know about being pregnant," I began after our greetings. "I'm not a mother yet, myself," I added, trying to draw her out by evoking my own inexperience.

"May God give you children," Amenan said quietly.

"Thank you," I replied, embarrassed as usual. Then I asked, "Are there other pregnant women in the village who might talk to me?"

"Oh, yes," Amenan said with an openness that surprised me.

"Maybe we could all meet some time?" I suggested diffidently.

"Tuesday would be a good day," Amenan offered. I beamed.

On the next market day, I bought some *pagne* material. I'd been living among the Beng for three months now: it was time to dress like a Beng woman. I asked Kona's daughter-in-law, Amina, if she'd show me how to wear my new clothes. An elegant young woman with prominent cheekbones, whose high forehead was always crowned with elaborately plaited hair, Amina had a fine sense of local fashion. I was flattered when she agreed to my request, and we retreated to my bedroom. With sure hands Amina moved me this way and that, chuckling at my awkwardness and wrapping the *pagne* around me, then readjusting and folding it here and there. As she did so, she ran her hand up and down my arm.

"So smooth," she said.

Beneath Amina's admiration was, perhaps, envy, for unlike the farmwork that the villagers performed, *my* work didn't produce weekly gashes and bruises. But I suspected she also felt more than a touch of disdain for my unblemished skin: in her eyes I probably did no "work" at all.

Finally the cloth sat right, and Amina tucked the ends neatly into the waistband. We left the room, and Philip admired my new look, then Amina escorted me around the village, a debutante at a coming-out party, gathering warm words of admiration from the women, even teasing marriage offers from some older men. One woman murmured graciously, *"Eki a kiki a man"*—May god let it never rip on you. Later that evening I took out our tiny rectangular mirror and propped it on a nearby chair, then stood back to see my new image. Turning slowly and bending low to see every angle, I frowned at my reflection. I'd always be a white woman wearing a *pagne.*

On Tuesday I dressed quickly in my *pagne* and said good-bye to Philip, who had decided to stay home and try to write. Navigating Didadi over the dry, rutty roads, I was filled with anticipation of my first group interview and once again went through some of the questions I'd planned. Did these women count the months of their pregnancies? Did they have any methods for predicting the gender of the fetus? Were they permitted—or even required—to have sex during pregnancy? I hoped I'd manage to overcome my shyness and ask these embarrassing questions . . . and that the women would consent to answer them.

When I reached Asagbé I saw Amenan sitting with three other women, all with large, round bellies, under the shade of the elevated, thatched granary in the center of the courtyard. Seeing my dusty car pulling slowly into the compound, they looked up, surprised at the unusual sight.

I greeted Amenan warmly, and she introduced me to her companions. "Thank you for coming," I began in French, my notebook out. "I guess Amenan's told you that I was hoping to talk to you about pregnancy and childbirth."

Amenan translated, and the women nodded and smiled. I took out my notebook and posed my first question. "Is it better to get pregnant right after marrying or to wait a bit?"

"I wanted to get pregnant right away," said Aya.

"I did, too," said Au.

"That's because both Aya and Au had arranged marriages," Amenan whispered to me, "so they were *supposed* to have children right away."

"Ah," I said, grateful for this explanation. Then I asked, "What happens if you have twins?"

"It's best to have a boy and a girl," Amenan said. "If you have two girls, they'll gang up and try to kill their father. If you have two boys, they'll gang up and try to kill their mother—it's by witchcraft."

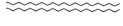

Trying to conceal my astonishment, I encouraged Amenan to go on. "If you have a boy and a girl twin," she continued, "the boy will stop the girl from killing their father, and the girl will stop the boy from killing their mother— though they might end up by killing each other."

"Really?" I managed.

"Yes. My brother has twins. The girl is walking now, but the boy doesn't even have his teeth in yet, and he isn't walking at all. His twin sister has bewitched him."

Amenan stopped for a moment to let me write down this latest information, then concluded, "I'm afraid of twins. I wouldn't want them myself."

I wanted to hug this woman, who so casually illuminated what had seemed a world hidden in shadows. But the other women in the courtyard had fallen silent, no doubt impatient with having to wait for their words and mine to be translated. Amenan and I were soon left alone, and for the rest of the afternoon we chatted—or rather, I listened as Amenan continued to recount for me the knowledge of Beng women: a pregnant woman must not eat eggs; nor should she steal anything, or the baby will become a thief as well; and if a woman bewitches someone while pregnant, her child, too, is destined to be a witch.

Speaking of witches reminded Amenan once again of twins. She mentioned that twins were given special names: boy twins were called Zi; girls, Klingo. This last sounded familiar; I remembered there was a young woman in Kosangbé named Klingo. She'd seemed pleasant enough—now I knew her neighbors must think her a witch. But where was her double? Quite possibly the villagers believed she'd killed her twin.

As I took notes on this unexpected news, Amenan continued to bestow on me her gifts. Another set of names, she continued expansively, also revealed personal misfortune. If a couple suffered the tragedy of having two children die one after the other, she explained, the next child born was named Wamya if a boy, Sunu if a girl. Such a newborn would have three small lines incised on the face. I thought of all the faces we'd seen sporting what Philip and I had playfully described as etched cats' whiskers around their mouths: these people must all have been Wamyas or Sunus. Radiating out forever their family tragedy from the corners of the mouth, the lines engraved Africa's horrible infant mortality rate on the cheeks of the luckier babies.

"Are these people witches, too?" I asked, venturing a guess.

"No," Amenan said, "they're just sad. The day before someone will die, they cry all night because they foresee the death. As adults, they won't go to the fields on those days, and a woman won't cook at all. A Wamya and a Sunu shouldn't marry each other, because what would happen to their children on the days when they're both sad? Neither parent would go to the farm, nothing would get done."

I reflected on our village mother back in Kosangbé: Kona's wife, who was named Sunu. She was often rather serious, and sometimes sharp, with those around her; now I wondered if this was because she could predict deaths on those days. I thought ruefully: I had to come to Asagbé to begin to understand the village I was living in.

On my next visit to Asagbé, Amenan led me to the shade of some coffee trees adjoining her courtyard, where we settled onto a large, brown mat—it was so softened with wear that I was surprised to learn it was made from pounded tree bark. From here Amenan could keep an eye on her children playing nearby, while the grove, which bordered the surrounding forest, afforded us an intimate space. This afternoon I hoped to find out what made Amenan so willing to talk about her culture with me, and I began by asking about her life.

Stretched out on her side, her large belly resting heavily on the mat, Amenan said, "I'm the oldest in my family, and I was my father's favorite."

"Ah, *bon*," I said, intrigued already.

"I went to the primary school right here in Asagbé," she continued. "There weren't many girls in school then, just Maat and I and a few others. When I graduated, I continued in M'Bahiakro through fifth grade. After that I joined a Rural Development Program for two and a half years in Bouaké, organized by a group of French nuns. We went around to small villages and taught the women nutrition and housekeeping skills." She paused for a moment, then said quietly, "But I had to return to the village when my father died." She paused again, caught up in painful reflection.

During the awkward silence, I thought about Amenan's unusual life. Curious about the outside world, Amenan had worked in rural villages far from home, as I was doing. Then she'd returned to her native land to live as she'd been brought up, as I would do as well. The two of us seemed filled with both a restless spirit and an urge toward the familiar—perhaps parallel ambivalences were what had drawn us to each other.

Amenan continued matter-of-factly, "My father's brother is the king of the Beng. And on my mother's side, my uncle Kokla Kouassi is the village priest for the Earth that we worship."

I tried to conceal my surprise: I'd had no idea that the Beng had a king. I felt blessed to have met this woman: fluent in French and knowledgeable about Western customs, yet centrally placed in her own society and eager to discuss its customs, she seemed the perfect informant.

Amenan's two-and-a-half-year-old son interrupted my reverie, complaining tearfully that his older sister, Bea, had insulted him. Amenan soothed little Kouadio, then said to me, "He cries so easily. He should spend more time

working in the fields with his father—but my husband doesn't go to the fields every day."

I realized I hadn't yet met Amenan's husband and asked her about him. "I was first married to someone else," she said, "but he never gave me so much as five francs! He wasn't at all interested in our daughters. Even now, three months can go by without him seeing them—and he still lives here in the village! My present husband, Kofi, is much better," she continued. "He loves all the children. When they're sick he buys them medicine, and he buys clothes for all of us. At first my mother was very angry with me, because she didn't want me to marry someone who doesn't speak our language."

I stopped writing, looked up from my notebook.

"Kofi is Ghanaian," Amenan explained. "We speak Baulé to each other. Anyway, now that my mother sees what a good man he is, she's forgiven me and is kind to him."

My mind wandered to the troubles my own mother had accepting an ex-Catholic son-in-law early in my marriage. Considering the complex nature of such troubles, I wondered: What dramas were contained in Amenan's brief summary, and were they really resolved as neatly as she suggested? Perhaps sometime soon I'd overcome my natural reticence and share my own family trials with Amenan—for I had begun to make a friend.

Philip: A Homeopathic Cure

One late afternoon Kona asked us to accompany him into the forest to tap palm wine. Delighted by his invitation, Alma and I quickly gathered cameras and notebooks, though not without some secret anxiety: this would be our first time entering the forest, for we'd always been intimidated by the lush green world that encircled Kosangbé.

We followed Kona down a narrow dirt path. He held a *bidon*—a plastic gas can—in one hand and a machete in the other, and a bark-cloth sack hung from his shoulder, swinging lightly by his side. Occasionally he stopped to examine freshly cut notches made on a tree—signs, he told us, that two of his tapping partners had already come by. Kona set a good pace through the large shadows of the forest, sunlight flashing through in rippling patterns. But soon Alma interrupted our progress.

"What's this?" she asked, pointing to a bright red insect scuttling along a leaf. "And what's the name of this?" she continued, indicating a tree, a tangle of vines, a flower. With a quick glance, Kona named them all. Emboldened, Alma posed still more questions, and I joined in, pointing out a distant bird on a branch, a dark-leaved bush. Amused at our persistence, Kona answered as he marched along. What had started as a short trip to his palm trees had now become a naturalist's tour: slowly the forest around us ceased to be an undifferentiated mass—it seemed that everything had a name.

Finally we arrived—but not to what I'd expected. From my readings of African novels, I had an idyllic vision of tall, thin palm trees growing in rows or clusters and a tapster carefully climbing nearly to the treetop and collecting palm wine from a siphon: a tropical version of maple syrup collection in New England. But Kona led us to a small clearing where a short, squat palm tree lay uprooted on its side, its fanning, spiky branches chopped down to stubs. A few of those branches lay cast about on the ground, and I noticed that the woody stems were studded with sharp thorns—no romantic palm tree climbing possible with these! Instead the tree had to be toppled, its death an exchange for a heady drink.

"What's the name of those?" Alma asked, pointing to the sharp spikes on the branches.

Kona laughed—he could see she'd give him no relief. *"Leleng,"* he said, and as Alma wrote it down he reached over to the side of the tree, where there was a thick patch of dark, oval leaves. He pulled it away, revealing a squarish hole not much larger than the size of a fist. I looked inside at the raw bark, moist with what seemed to be watery sap—it was the palm wine, collecting at the bottom of the hole, and in the shallow, sticky pool floated a dark, winged insect and a few long-dead ants—accidental flavoring.

Kona pointed out a thin, hollow reed sticking out from the side of the tree, just below the hole—it filled a tiny tunnel carved through the tree, and from here the palm wine dripped into a ceramic pot. The pot's narrow mouth was stuffed with more leaves—further protection against any more insects spiking the drink. Kona pulled off the leafy stopper, gave the pot a slight shake, and listened with satisfaction to the deep-toned sloshing inside—the palm wine was almost up to the ceramic lip. He poured it into his *bidon.*

Then Kona took from his bark-cloth sack a small, thin-bladed knife and a bundle of reeds tied together with lianas. He bent over the hole in the tree and cut away at the raw, leaking walls inside, making fresh wounds from which new sap would drip. With the flick of a match, he set one end of the reed bundle on fire and placed it in the hole. Then he blew through a single hollow reed at the smoking bundle, stoking the fire—further inducement for sap to flow. Finally he covered the hole again with the mesh of leaves and set the ceramic pot back in place. I knelt beside Kona, fascinated by this complicated process—he was a one-man assembly line for his own private brewery—yet saddened that the making of this popular drink seemed to be a form of deforestation.

Kona motioned for us to sit down. After filling a gourd with some of the fizzy brew, he passed it over to me. I tipped the edge, spilling a few drops on the ground—a libation to the Earth. But I was also stalling, because a large army ant floated on the surface of the palm wine. Would it be impolite to pick it out before drinking? I decided to sip carefully, making sure not to draw the ant too close to my lips. The palm wine was sweet and tart at the same time—the best I'd tried so far—and I managed to savor the taste in spite of the drowned guest that circled among the bubbles on the surface. I handed the gourd to Alma, my raised eyebrows a silent warning.

She paused, then made her own libation, tipping the gourd away from Kona as she quickly flicked the ant from the drink. Still, he caught sight of her trick and chuckled lightly as he took his turn. Apparently no faux pas had been committed—he was merely amused at our fastidiousness.

We walked to another small clearing and found Kona's two partners there, seated by the toppled tree and sipping from gourds. They laughed at the sight of us—unexpected foreign helpers, for now I joined in, holding the bundle of leaves while Kona blew on the flames. I poured palm wine from collecting pot to *bidon* and even helped cut away at the inner walls of the trunk's hole. Meanwhile Alma continued to collect new Beng words: "bubble," "slice," "palm tree leaf," "palm wine foam."

We proceeded from palm tree to palm tree, sampling a respectable proportion of the day's take. By now I was an aficionado of the drink's carbonated fizz, its pleasant tartness and slowly gathering kick. Unlike Amos Tutuola's hero, I still wasn't willing to travel to the Dead's Town for a gourdful, but this slowly winding tour of the forest was quite an acceptable alternative. Then, as the sky quickly darkened, we set off for the village, dizzy with palm wine. Not wanting to travel through the forest at night, Alma and I asked no more questions on our return—any further, hidden knowledge could wait for another time.

We didn't have long to wait, for after a few days Kona invited us to his farm. We marched a mile or two through the forest to a spot where his two wives, Sunu and Busu Amla, were harvesting *jimisan,* those bitter berries that had spoiled many a sauce for me. I was surprised to see that their "fields" weren't my idea of fields at all, but an area in the forest that had been partially slashed and burned. We stood in the center of a large circle of dead, still standing trees—a terrible waste, I thought, though I could also see the local logic: with their leaves long gone, the trees allowed the light of the tropical sun to beat down on the flourishing crops below.

Dotted among thick plantings of tomatoes and eggplants were what I at first thought were termite mounds or anthills: pyramids of dirt over three feet tall. But then Kona bent over one and, probing with his machete, dug out a fat, gray-skinned yam, then another. So this was where our daily allotment of starch came from! I scanned the farm again and with new eyes saw more

clearly how those mounds extended in all directions to the edge of the uncleared forest, silent guardians of hidden booty.

Alma continued to visit Asagbé, and I often came along, hungry for more of Amenan's stories. One afternoon I listened, rapt, as Amenan recounted the names of various Beng diviners and their special methods: one stared into a mirror, another threw cowrie shells on the ground, another scribbled on paper and interpreted the marks. Alma wrote as quickly as she could, trying to keep up. I looked down at my own notepad: nothing yet. Though I shared my wife's excitement, to what use could I put my wonder? Perhaps this strange world would seep into little corners inside me and someday sprout into stories.

Sighing, I glanced about the compound and counted heads: eighteen people, fourteen of them children. One girl washed the pots from the afternoon meal; two girls dressed each other's hair while a few other children commented on the patterns; a boy lazed under the shade of a thatched *akpa,* where two of Amenan's daughters helped their grandmother flatten a new mud floor for the cooking area; the rest of the children watched two older sisters loudly half joke, half argue with each other.

Within minutes a few girls gathered to shell palm nuts, two more began to play in a hammock, three boys threw stones at each other. In an American home or even a backyard, all this activity would be an impossible hubbub. Yet here it seemed almost silent, despite the tiffs of the children, one bubbling up almost as soon as the last quieted down. No child seemed to win or lose, and the adults were less than interested beyond an occasional lazy shout.

When we left Amenan's compound that day we noticed a spirited gathering of men sitting under Asagbé's large, thatched canopy on the edge of the public plaza. There seemed to be two sides arguing, each represented by a small group of male elders. One side was led by our Asagbé father, Bwadi Kouakou.

The two clutches of elders spoke heatedly—long, contrapuntal bursts of words we couldn't possibly follow without help. Then, without warning, the meeting ended and the two sides mingled together, shaking fists at each other, shouting, *"Voleur! Voleur!"*—Thief! Thief!—and, inexplicably, *laughing.* By now we dearly wanted to know the source of all this commotion. Alma approached Kouakou, who beamed at the sight of us and shook our hands in greeting.

"Aba, could you tell me about this meeting?" she asked.

"Of course," he said. "Wait a moment, and then we'll go to my compound." Then he returned to that odd mixture of abuse and amusement.

Back at Kouakou's compound, we sat on wooden stools in a small circle and Alma repeated her question. He chuckled. "The meeting was about the people of Sangbé stealing chickens from our village."

"Who stole the chickens?" Alma asked, ready to write down the names of the culprits.

"Everyone."

"Everyone?"

Kouakou nodded.

Alma paused, worried that perhaps she had misunderstood. "But why do all the people of Sangbé steal your chickens?"

"Because they're allowed to."

Alma crinkled her face in puzzlement. Amused by her surprise, Kouakou added, "But they can steal chickens only during one of our funerals. And we steal their chickens during their funerals."

According to Bwadi Kouakou, the villages of Asagbé and Sangbé had a joking relationship that was only in effect during funerals, when chickens could be stolen at any time, no limit on the number. But during the last Asagbé funeral too many chickens were pilfered: Kouakou alone lost eleven. The joke had gone too far, so today's meeting had been arranged. Since the two villages' traditional joking relationship could not be abolished, it had to be modified, and the elders decided that in the future, when a funeral was held at Asagbé, the villagers would donate a male goat to the visiting Sangbé mourners; Sangbé would in turn do the same.

Alma wrote and wrote, then asked, "Do only your two villages have this sort of joking relationship?"

Kouakou smiled, perhaps realizing that he would not soon be free of her curiosity. "No, all the Beng villages do."

As Kouakou answered her continuing questions, Alma worked up a diagram of two columns, with lines connecting those villages that had special relationships. He peered at the page, impressed with her industry, and I couldn't help staring, too, for I realized that some version of Alma's thin, crisscrossing lines on the page were also within every Beng, invisibly connecting their villages together.

As the days passed, Alma delved with increased confidence into the hubbub of Beng life. Perhaps her brief crisis back in Abidjan and its seemingly successful resolution now brought on my own crisis. Increasingly I yearned for a solitude that I could no longer successfully imagine. The Beng didn't understand why I sat so quietly, rubbing my chin, pulling at my mustache, and intermittently scribbling marks on a piece of paper, and I didn't know how to tell them that with each interruption I felt the budding characters on the page lose their outlines, their words becoming inaudible and my latest sentence evaporating, until the world I was trying to create was gone.

Though I continued each morning to treat villagers for fevers, infected cuts, and other illnesses with our small supply of medicines and my limited knowledge, I still felt I had no identity my neighbors could easily categorize. "I'm a storyteller," was the best I could manage whenever I tried to explain myself, but in Beng culture stories are for *telling*, and I still made the simplest errors in daily conversation.

How could I translate the world of the Beng into *my* stories? With my usual faith in the power of fiction, I turned to the books I'd brought with me to the village, hoping they would help make sense of my dilemma. My greatest disappointment was Conrad's Africa in *Heart of Darkness*. Despite its psychological acuity, I found the novel guilty of an appalling cultural arrogance: European actors on a stage cluttered with cardboard African props. To Conrad, through his mouthpiece Marlow, Africans were "simple people" whose faces were "grotesque masks" and who spoke a language consisting of "short, grunting phrases." Despite its anticolonialist ardor, the book seemed like an inadvertent template for every stereotypical depiction of Africans I had ever read or seen.

But I was most surprised and chagrined to read that Kurtz simply entered the rain forest and dominated a tribespeople with an ease that implied there was a cultural and linguistic vacuum he had no trouble filling. This was as far as possible from our own experience. Our continued faltering in the local system of common sense placed us closer to the category of children than adults. After three months among the Beng, we still struggled with the difficulties of conjugating pronouns along with verbs in this tonal language, and in even the simplest sentence little affixes like *ni* and *lo* seemed to crop up confusingly out of nowhere. Often Alma and I lay in bed in the mornings, listening to the heavy echoing throughout the village of women pounding yams with mortars and pestles, and we were reluctant to get up, knowing that before the day was over we would make fools of ourselves many times over.

Heart of Darkness was not a model I could follow. Perhaps V. S. Naipaul's *Miguel Street*—a series of stories depicting the interrelated lives of a poor neighborhood in Port of Spain, Trinidad—offered another possibility. One sentence in particular I read again and again: "A stranger could drive through Miguel Street and just say 'Slum!' because he could see no more. But we, who lived there, saw our street as a world, where everybody was quite different from everybody else." The truth of this rang inside me as I remembered the racing cars that had sped through Kosangbé months ago. Yet I still didn't see how I could write stories about village life, because already I knew enough to understand how ignorant I was of its complexities.

I still didn't know how this unfamiliar culture might engage my imagination or what within me might be drawn to it. I found myself less and less able to write, and the quiet keys of my typewriter presented a silent, untranslatable reproach. I needed a rite of passage, but what ceremonies were available for a homesick writer in this culture?

One evening in Kosangbé, while I pecked out words for a possible story, words with no life in them, Alma sat across from me, typing her recent field notes and occasionally reading out to me Amenan's tales of local diviners. Listening to the excitement in Alma's voice, I suddenly realized it made sense to ask the very culture that afflicted me for help: a sort of homeopathic cure.

Quietly I asked, "Do you think it might be possible for me to see a diviner, for my writer's block?"

"Really?" she said, surprised. "What an idea! Do you think it might work?"

"Who knows? A Beng ceremony might be just the thing to patch me up. At least you'll be able to come along and take notes."

But who would take us to a diviner? We decided to ask Kona and at once marched over to his compound. Alma and I approached him in our best Beng and told him that "Kouadio's work isn't going well," which was the best translation we could come up with to describe my writing malady. Kona's polite face, always so patient during our awkward struggles with his language, stiffened when we mentioned a diviner. But as our host he couldn't—at least overtly—deny our request. Kona replied that he would consider how best to go about this.

The next day he was gone from the village, off to a distant corner of his farm deep in the forest. I was annoyed that he'd left without deciding on our request; days passed, and still he didn't return.

"I don't think Kona will ever agree to take us," I told Alma one night. "I think he'll keep putting us off and hope we just give up. In this village, religion is just too touchy a subject."

"Maybe we should ask Amenan for advice," Alma suggested.

I agreed. On our next trip to Asagbé we explained our dilemma to her, and she suggested that we ask Bwadi Kouakou to sponsor my visit. I thought this was a marvelous idea, and later that day Amenan accompanied us to his compound.

He was just back from working in the fields, and as he greeted us his friendly face was lined with exhaustion. I gave some coins to one of Kouakou's children, who ran off to a nearby compound for a large bottle of beer. After our gift was poured and libations made, Amenan put forward our request.

Kouakou nodded carefully as he listened, seemingly unfazed by the thought of an outsider entering into the Beng system of healing. He recommended one of the diviners Amenan had mentioned to Alma weeks before:

Akissi, who lived in the distant village of Bondékro. "She's very powerful," Bwadi Kouakou said in a confiding tone. "A few years ago, when Pascal was having trouble in school, I consulted Akissi. After I performed the sacrifice she recommended, my son's grades improved."

"Then that's who I'll consult," I replied. "Thank you, Father."

Kouakou nodded. "If you wish, I can accompany you."

We accepted his offer, agreeing to travel to Akissi's village the next day.

Back in Kosangbé, we discovered that Kona had returned from his hidden encampment, and I reproached myself for my impatience. Still, if Bwadi Kouakou was willing to help us, it might not be so bad if a friendly rivalry developed between our two village fathers. We decided to make a formal presentation to Kona, with Jean translating. But since Alma suspected that Jean might refuse to discuss a religious subject, she asked Yapi Yao to come along, too—a secret test to see if Yao had fewer compunctions about sensitive subjects.

In Kona's compound, after welcoming him back to the village with a gift of beer, we announced our plans for the following day. This was news to Jean, but he translated without complaint—perhaps he guessed the reason for Yao's presence.

Kona nodded as Jean spoke, giving no hint of surprise or displeasure.

"I felt I had to see a diviner immediately, and because we weren't sure when you might return," I apologized, now turning to Yao so he could translate, "we asked Bwadi Kouakou for his help. But we would be honored if you came, too."

Kona paused for a long moment before replying. In that brief, tense silence I was aware of the insistent insect buzz emanating from the surrounding forest. *"Bon,"* Kona finally said, which needed no translation. He would accompany us the next day, he said, "God willing."

The following morning we drove to Akissi's distant village, both Kona and Kouakou sitting in the backseat. They were both dressed formally—matching pants and shirts, the sort of attire usually reserved for special events. I was secretly touched that they saw my divination as such an occasion.

Bondékro was on the edge of Beng territory, and we traveled through long stretches of savanna, the occasional huge kapok tree looming over the landscape. The night before there had been a sudden rain, rare for the dry season, and often we had to stop before gaping stretches of mud. Alma and I collected thick bunches of reeds and grasses and laid them across the mud to improve Didadi's traction, then I pushed while Alma guided the car over our frail construction. Kona and Kouakou remained comfortably seated in the car, seemingly unaware of our difficulties. After a few more swampy stretches, my sandals and pants sloppy with mud, I had a sense of what a young Beng man must feel, on the wrong end of the culture's gerontocracy.

Finally I asked our two fathers to step out of the car a moment so it would be easier to push. I also hoped they might help, but they stood at the edge of the road, commenting to each other about my tactics as I pushed through to dry ground. Minutes later I idled the car before yet another barely navigable bog. Wondering if we would ever arrive at Bondékro—the village seemed as distant as my writerly inspiration—I sighed deeply. Perhaps Kona and Kouakou heard my despair in that slow release of breath, because they immediately volunteered to push.

With their help we made quicker progress, and soon we approached the village. A curious crowd was already gathered for our unusual presence— Kouakou had sent one of his relatives to Akissi the day before, alerting her to our eventual arrival. Alma and I had never been to this village before, and as we made our way through the winding mud alleys, a number of children fled from us, a few adults laughing at their terror.

We entered Akissi's compound and found her waiting for us. I wasn't sure what I'd expected, but I was surprised that Akissi looked no different from any other village woman—simple blouse and wrapped-cloth skirt, her hair bound by a scarf—and her compound was no different from any other in the village. Yet what did *she* make of *us*—the *secrétaires* of two villages accompanying a white woman wearing a *pagne* and a white man with dried splashes of mud crusting his pants up to the knees?

Akissi led us quickly through the doorway of her main house, and we all sat in a circle on the floor. A crowd of villagers gaped and jostled at the doorway, which was kept open, I suspected, because Akissi wanted to advertise her unusual clients. Between us, on an animal skin, I placed a copy of my first book, a slim volume of prose poems, and a recent, unfinished manuscript—Akissi examined them, her face unreadable, while Kouakou translated my reasons for consulting her. She then picked up a brass pan that contained a few black pebbles and a small amount of water made milky by the addition of white powder. Turning the bowl in her hands, she watched how the pebbles settled.

Akissi sometimes shook her head slightly from side to side, as if displeased with what she saw. Then she noticed that Kouakou was smoking a homemade cigarette—quietly but firmly, she asked him to put it out. He did so, and she returned to her examination of the milky water.

Finally she spoke, and Kouakou translated. "She says that no one in Bengland is the cause of your problems," he reported with quiet confidence. "You're being bewitched by a jealous writer in your own country, someone who wishes harm to come to you."

Though surprised by Akissi's divination—as far as I knew, I had no enemies to speak of—I nodded politely, but not without a quizzical side glance to Alma. Still, I was struck by Akissi's apt intuition—sometimes writers' jealousies *were* akin to witchcraft.

She turned her gaze back to the bowl, once again shifting the pebbles in the white water, stopping only to push away a puppy that had wandered into the room. After a few minutes Akissi enumerated what steps I must take to undo the harm directed at me: if I sacrificed a white hen on a sacred rest day, then a goat once I began to write, I would be safe. I agreed to the sacrifices, pleased to hear that Akissi had prescribed a public ritual: what I sought from her wasn't so much spiritual guidance as social acceptance.

Alma asked Kouakou if she could observe the sacrifices.

"No, women can't attend sacrifices in the forest. But Kouadio can go if he wants."

Alma simply nodded, hiding her disappointment very well. Then Akissi said that before any of these sacrifices could be performed, we had to properly honor the sacred Earth in our own country.

Alma and I conferred together. "How can I possibly honor the Earth in America?" I whispered.

"Why not send a donation to some environmentalists?" she replied.

I whistled softly. "That's a terrific idea. How about the Sierra Club?"

We told Akissi that we would give money to a group in America that respected the Earth, and she nodded, pleased by our suggestion. Once we received a letter from home reporting that the donation had been made, the sacrifices could proceed and then I would be cured.

"Great," I whispered to Alma, "I'll write to my father tomorrow."

We thanked and paid Akissi her standard fee: one hundred CFAs, plus, at Kouakou's suggestion, another three hundred for a large bottle of beer she could buy later. Then we drank sweet and heady palm wine with her before leaving.

Back in Asagbé, we formally offered gifts to Kouakou for his assistance—two bottles of beer and two rolled packets of locally grown tobacco—and when we returned to Kosangbé we did the same for Kona in his compound, with Jean and Yapi Yao participating. Slowly we were learning the relaxed pace of Beng thanks on important occasions: long speeches, gifts, expressions of gratitude back and forth, drinking and toasts. The formality of it all was oddly comforting—a social dignity practiced daily.

We walked back to our compound, looking forward to our evening baths and a meal cooked by Moya. But before we settled in, Kona visited us. *"Boyena,"* he said, which was the Beng request for news from returning travelers. At first Alma and I were confused—Kona had, after all, accompanied us. But apparently he wanted a summary of Akissi's divination in our own words.

Kona listened quietly, nodding, as Jean translated Alma's description of the day.

"Everything you have said is true," he said, "except for one mistake: the sacrifices will not be done in the forest."

We thanked him for his correction, though we felt sure that Kouakou had mentioned the forest as the place for the sacrifice. Alma and I whispered to each other our uneasiness but decided not to press the point, since the subject of Kosangbé's sacred Earth always seemed to create nervousness— perhaps the day's events had skirted forbidden territory.

Later that evening Alma and I lay in bed in our mud house and whispered about the mysterious "jealous writer" Akissi had mentioned, idly gossiping our way through a list of possible culprits.

"So, do you feel any different now?" Alma asked.

I stared for a while at the honeycomb patterns of the mosquito netting above our heads and considered her question. "No," I said, "not yet." If anything, I felt a bit of a fraud for consulting Akissi when I had limited faith in her mystical abilities. Still, I suspected that a public ritual might aid my artistic self-healing, and I was determined to go through with the recommended cure.

My introduction to the Beng method of curing emboldened Alma, whose stomach ills were back in full force, and she asked Amenan to recommend an herbal medicine.

"Yes, certainly," Amenan replied. "Kofi is going to see a healer for me—I need special medicines for my pregnancy. He can ask for you, too."

I offered to accompany her husband, and the next day Kofi and I drove through long stretches of dry savanna to the distant village of Siaregbé. I still had to struggle to understand Kofi's thickly inflected Ghanaian English as he spoke in vague terms about his past life. He was evasive about why he no longer lived in Ghana, though I gathered that he'd once lost an office job of some sort.

"Politics is *no* good," he said, shaking his head. He quickly turned the conversation around, asking about America, laughing when I disagreed with his assertion that everyone in my country was rich. The grin on his broad, handsome face exposed a gap of two lost front teeth. When I asked him how he'd lost those teeth, he laughed louder. "Oh, trouble, for sure, some kind of trouble!"

At Siaregbé we were told that the healer was in the forest, collecting medicines, and a young man offered to guide us. We trudged along a dusty path for a few miles, into a thick world of competing birdsongs. Finally we halted at a tiny clearing—we'd have to wait there. Kofi explained our wives' ailments, and the young man continued on in search of the healer.

Leaning against the roots of a kapok tree, Kofi and I waited over an hour, sharing sips of water from a bottle in my backpack, reveling in the shade.

Then an extraordinarily old man—his face a maze of furrows and wrinkles—appeared, our young guide behind him. The elder gave me a long, steady look before responding to our greetings.

Kofi chuckled lightly, surprised to see this healer who rarely revealed himself. "For certain, the chap wants to see you with his *own* two eyes!" But I must have been staring as well at that ancient face—this man had lived a long life I could barely imagine.

The healer held out to Kofi a large glossy leaf folded into a bundle. They spoke for a few moments, apparently going over the dosage. Then the old man handed me my own shiny bundle. I couldn't help peeking. Inside was a ball of twigs and bark bits—not a particularly promising mix of ingredients, but then Alma's rigorous course of antibiotics hadn't managed to work many wonders. *Something* had to finally work.

"What should we do with this?" I asked Kofi, who questioned the healer.

Kofi lowered his voice, as if imparting a secret. "He says your wife must make a tea with this medicine and keep drinking it, every day. Soon, she will be all right."

Kofi and I both thanked this frail old man and paid for his remedies. Then we trekked the long miles back to Siaregbé.

When I finally returned to Kosangbé, Alma carefully unraveled the leaf, peeked inside, and smelled the pungent, barky aroma. "Thanks so much for going, love," she said. "What am I supposed to do?"

I repeated the healer's instructions, and Alma set a pot of water on the gas stove.

"Great. I sure hope it works," she said.

While we waited for the water to boil, our neighbor Afwé Ba came by to greet us, and she caught sight of the little pack. *"Yih,"* she said incredulously, "is that for you?"

"Yes, why not?" Alma said, pleased that her first experiment with Beng medicine had been so quickly discovered. Casually she put some of the woody ingredients into a cup and poured in boiling water.

Alma took a sip of the tea, and her face scrunched up from the taste. When Afwé Ba stopped giggling she taught us the word for "bitter"—*chéché*. Alma thanked Afwé and slowly drank the whole cupful, muttering this new Beng word.

That evening, as we toured the village with our greetings, a villager asked us, "So, Kouadio and Amwé, are you going to M'Bahiakro tomorrow?"

"No, we hadn't planned on it," Alma answered. "Why do you ask?"

"Ah leh paw doi"—No reason—the woman replied, using the all-purpose sentence with which the villagers usually deflected Alma's questions.

At the next household an elder asked me, "Will you be going to Bouaké tomorrow?"

"No, we were just there recently," I answered, adding, "Why do you ask?" *"Ah leh paw doi."* He turned away, our conversation suddenly over. Variations of this exchange were repeated often that evening. Either the people of Kosangbé mistakenly thought we'd be gone from the village, or they very much wanted us to be. Later that night as we lay in bed, Alma laughed ruefully at her latest effort to be accepted—apparently her herbal tea had counted for nothing. "It's back to suspicion as usual," she said with a sigh.

The next morning we settled in our courtyard and worked on prepositions with Jean, who seemed more withdrawn and tense than usual. There seemed to be quite a few visitors in the village, but whenever anyone approached us, Jean fended them off, at one point angrily proclaiming that we were busy. Alma found herself in yet another argument with Jean when the children who had been playing in our courtyard suddenly whispered excitedly among themselves and rushed off together toward a neighboring compound.

"What's *that* all about?" I wondered aloud.

Though I'd spoken in English, Jean understood. *"Nothing,"* he said too forcefully, "there's *nothing* happening there."

That decided me—I chased after the children. When I reached the large public space on our side of the village, I saw a solemn line of some thirty or so people, all dressed in white, their dark faces covered with white powder. I stared in astonishment as the visitors marched in a stately circle, addressing the gathered crowd with rehearsed greetings. So this was why everyone had hoped we'd be gone today.

I hurried back to our compound and told Alma what I'd seen. She turned to Jean. "What's this ritual all about?"

"I don't know," Jean answered, looking away.

"Of course you know," Alma said, infuriated. "How could you have kept this from me?"

"I didn't know anything about it," he repeated.

"I don't believe you," she countered.

Jean said nothing.

"Forget him," I said, grabbing our camera, "let's go!"

We hurried toward the procession, but when people saw the camera and Alma's notebook, they waved us away with such fury that we stopped, stunned.

"No means no," I said to Alma. "I'll put all this away."

I rushed back to our compound. Jean had vanished, and I suspected we wouldn't see him again for quite some time. When I caught up with Alma the procession was under the kapok tree near the chief's house. We joined the gathering, but whoever we greeted didn't respond—a terrible Beng insult. I saw the pain and indecision on Alma's face—the people of Kosangbé clearly

felt violated by our presence, yet with her interest in traditional religion, how could she leave what was certainly an important ritual?

"I just don't know what to do," Alma whispered. I knew she was ready to give up, when first one, then another villager standing nearby cast us quick, surreptitious smiles. We decided to remain and hovered uneasily at the edge of the crowd, watching male elders deliver long, formal speeches. One stocky man whom we didn't recognize spoke in a deep, gravelly voice, his brusque gestures filled with authority. Though he was dressed plainly, Alma and I suspected he might be the leader of the ritual. "If only they'd let me tape this," she murmured. Just then we heard shouting nearby. We turned to see a few villagers berating two shamefaced young men—one of whom was holding a tape recorder. It was taken away, and without complaint the men skulked off.

Alma heeded the warning and simply watched as carefully as she could, then she hurried back to our house to scribble down whatever she remembered. Throughout the afternoon Alma reappeared, vanished quietly, and then reappeared again. I tried to fill her in on what she'd missed, but there was little I could say besides "The elders are still giving speeches, and I can't understand a word they're saying."

When the ceremony finally ended, the villagers broke into small groups and set off for their various compounds, and Alma and I discovered we were still anathema: no one who passed by would greet us.

Alma: The Spy

I tackled my scrawled notes, attempting to type some sense into them—an exercise in frustration. And where was Jean, that traitor? I bristled at the thought of how he'd done all he could to conceal this key ritual from me.

The blowing of an antelope horn announced some new phase, yet I hesitated to investigate, fearing another round of angry stares. All around us our neighbors were leaving their courtyards.

"What do you think?" I asked Philip. "Shall we—"

"Let's give it a try," he replied with forced enthusiasm. So we too walked over to the dusty public plaza, where four villagers had set up their drums in the shade of the kapok tree—no sign of the earlier formal speeches, no line of visitors staring at us coldly. The drummers began to beat out a slow rhythm, then the pace quickened and a few men led off the dancing with exuberant twists and turns. The women around them threw scarves over the dancing men's shoulders, bedecking them with bursts of color, and some of the women slipped into the circle with their own slower, shuffling steps.

Philip and I watched admiringly, and people on either side urged us, *"Foto kun!"*—Catch some pictures! Apparently the most secret moments of the ritual had passed, but I'd deliberately left my usual gear behind, so I ran back to the house, trailed by a chorus of *"Batu, batu!"*—Quick, quick! Inside, I grabbed the camera and caught sight of my notebook, started to bring that, too, then thought better of it: why push my luck? I hurried back to the open plaza and took my place next to our neighbor Afwé Ba, always giggly, who pointed out the best dancers to me: "Catch a picture of Kofi. And just look at Yaokro, catch his, too!"

Then Afwé Ba turned to Philip and me and, with a sly smile, said, "Amwé, Kouadio: *Ka ta bewo!"*—Go dance! Surprised by the sudden invitation, I worried I might mangle the graceful steps of the dancing women. Then I cast aside my doubts: I wasn't going to miss this opportunity to join the celebration. Tentatively Philip and I entered the dance space and imitated the dancing steps around us. People cheered at the spectacle, but after a few moments a succession of men's exuberant solos claimed the space, and with the other women I retreated to the outer ring of spectators. Philip remained and took his turn, twirling and leaping with abandon as the crowd whooped and women draped brightly colored scarves around his shoulders. Proud of my husband, I snapped picture after picture of his dancing debut.

The next morning we awoke and were astonished to find the courtyards nearly deserted: where could everyone be? We asked the few remaining villagers about their neighbors. No one seemed in a mood to divulge much: they were back to yesterday morning's wariness. But one woman, sorting through a large pile of dirty clothes in her courtyard, betrayed hidden sympathy. "My husband said he was going to Manigbé," she whispered, "and my brother-in-law said *he* was on his way to Ndogbé." Then she turned to her large basins of cloudy water. I thanked her for her information, at once touched and disturbed, wondering if Sam Spade would have approved of me. I hadn't brought any of Dashiell Hammett's novels to Africa—maybe I should have. After all, detectives were masters of subterfuge, underground questioning. But had I really come to Africa to spy?

Still, I thought wearily, having obtained this tip, I couldn't ignore it. Philip and I prepared several water bottles for the long trip, settled ourselves on Didadi's dusty seats, and started off down the road.

Soon we saw a small group of Beng men walking on the road to Ndogbé. We slowed down to greet them . . . but they mumbled the most perfunctory of replies. Philip looked at me expectantly; I had no plan. Sighing, he pressed on the gas pedal and we passed more groups of villagers. A few yards down the road we recognized yesterday's leader—that stocky man who'd delivered his speeches so eloquently—walking slowly alongside his companions.

"I'll bet he's tired," Philip said. "I have an idea. . . ." He stopped the car and began to exchange greetings with the leader of this mysterious ritual, then pointed to our empty backseat and asked him if he'd like to ride with us. He pumped our hands and immediately introduced himself in his deep and gravelly voice: "My name is Yoma Kouassi." He laughed to hear we had Beng names.

"Il y a place pour . . . plang plus," Philip said in a mixture of French and Beng, holding up two fingers. Yoma Kouassi nodded again, and he and two others squeezed onto the backseat, talking in low tones.

Finally we were close to Ndogbé. We approached an almost continuous line of Beng people walking along the sloping roadside, and Philip slowed the car. Many glared at us until they spotted Yoma Kouassi on the backseat, and then they gaped, astonished. Suddenly a tall, bony old woman dressed all in white, her hands waving wildly, ran onto the middle of the road just yards in front of our moving car: a huge goiter hung from her neck, a side of her face was frozen, perhaps from an ancient stroke, and one eye socket was a red hole. She stretched out her long, thin arms to block our passage, and Philip slammed on the brakes. Then the screaming woman threw her lanky body over the hood of our car, her face, speckled with white powder, inches from our windshield. I stared back at her, terrified.

Immediately Yoma Kouassi leaned out the window, his deep voice firm as if rebuking a child. Reluctantly the woman backed off Didadi's hood and retreated to the side of the road, her face still a twisted scowl. But Yoma Kouassi said quietly to Philip, *"Ana"*—Let's go.

I looked at Philip helplessly. Nothing in my graduate training had prepared me for such a moment. How could we defy that woman's desperate opposition and simply continue past her? But Yoma Kouassi wasn't about to relinquish his chauffeured entry into Ndogbé.

"Ana," he repeated.

Once in Ndogbé, this leader of the ritual was our talisman: people welcomed us and offered gourds of palm wine and shot glasses of clear, potent *kutuku*. A woman named Amwé, on being introduced to me, was so delighted by the oddity of meeting a white woman who bore her name that she immediately pressed a coin in my hand, instructing me to buy a bottle of beer with it.

In a short while the formal part of the ritual started up, with more speeches and collective offerings of thanks back and forth. Emboldened with all that we'd been given to drink, Philip moved two free stools to the central plaza, where the main participants in the ritual sat. Wearing elegant *pagne* outfits and necklaces with chunks of gold and coral dangling from them, the women seated there made room for us and, even more shocking, assured me I could take notes. Philip and I watched the ritual unfold before our uncomprehending eyes and ears while I wondered if I would ever understand the speeches and actions that must mean so much to all those around us. So many of the anthropology books I'd read had presented information as if it had been offered by data machines that merely needed to be switched on. Yet the past two days had made it clearer than ever that no amount of coaxing or meddling would convince people to share with me that which they fervently wished to keep secret.

But what of Jean? Though I no longer relied on him exclusively to interpret the Beng world, how could I continue to work with any assistant who'd tried to conceal from me a major ritual occurring in my own village? Tomorrow morning I would fire Jean. It could hardly come as a surprise; I suspected he'd even be relieved to return to his stall in the Bongalo *marché*.

I'd be on my own. I tried to convince myself that I had few misgivings or regrets.

5

THE ELUSIVE EPIPHANY

𝕰 𝕰 𝕰

(FEBRUARY 20–APRIL 30, 1980)

Philip: Two Very Distant Places

JEAN APPROACHED OUR COMPOUND SLOWLY—HE CERTAINLY SUSPECTED WHY ALMA HAD summoned him this morning. If only he'd hurry, I thought, for I wanted our final, painful moments together to end as quickly as possible. I had come to deeply dislike this man who undermined the very research he'd been hired to assist, but of course we were a great disappointment to him as well—*we'd* undermined his fantasy of fame on the Voice of America, his chance to reclaim the dignity his father had denied him.

Finally Jean stood before us, his sleekly tailored pants and shirt wrinkled and dusty—a stark contrast to the usual care he took with his appearance. After greeting us in a monotone, we went through the most perfunctory of exchanges. Then he sat down at our table, his eyes settling on a space between us.

In the awkward silence, Alma spoke. "I'm sorry, Jean, but you haven't helped me very much lately. I can't keep you as an assistant if you won't answer my questions or if you try to keep secrets from me."

Jean nodded tersely, preparing for one last lecture. Alma paused—if he didn't want to hear it, and she didn't want to deliver it, why go on?

"So," she continued in almost a whisper, "I don't think we should work together any longer."

Jean nodded again, a grim bobbing of the head that seemed to respond as much to an inner voice as to Alma's words.

"Here," she continued, offering him a thick packet of CFAs. "This is last week's pay, plus something to help you start up your trading again."

"Bon, merci," he murmured, tucking the money in his shirt pocket. Then, for the first time, he looked at us. Jean's farewell face was complicated with the happiness of release—for he wouldn't miss either Alma or me—and regret at the loss of what his association with us had promised. And there was something more, I felt, some secret that enabled him to regard us now with barely concealed disdain even in his moment of defeat.

Alma blushed, then said something about perhaps seeing each other again, and Jean mumbled a few words in agreement. I said nothing, filled with an odd mixture of sadness and relief. Then Jean stood: it was time to collect his belongings at Kona's compound and leave. We said our good-byes. I watched Jean walk off, a sad, solitary figure. Yet surely he wasn't alone—Alma and I must still be with him, sharing interior territory with his father as betrayers of his destiny.

With Jean's departure we were now quite on our own. When Alma asked Yapi Yao if he would consider replacing Jean, Yao's father quickly intervened and declined the offer for him. We let it be known, in a number of villages, that Alma was looking for an assistant, but no one came forward.

Still, we were beginning to make a friend in Kosangbé. Yacouba, the man who'd helped us treat a young girl's machete wound, now often dropped by our compound. He had picked up some French while serving in the Ivoirian army, and so we managed to speak together in an improvised mixture of Beng and French. "I didn't know a word of French when I was drafted," he told us. "But we weren't allowed to speak our own languages—not one word, or we were beaten. So I learned by listening—I was afraid to say anything for six months!"

I liked Yacouba—he had an easy laugh, and he wasn't shy about introducing us to social niceties. "Why do you leave all your belongings alone when you leave your compound?" he once asked us. He gestured toward our desk—cluttered with typewriters, tape recorders, and our short-wave radio— and the perpetually open door to our mud house.

"Why shouldn't we?" Alma answered. "We want to show that we trust everyone in the village."

Yacouba nodded. "*I* believe you. But some villagers think there's another reason."

"What's that?" I asked, not sure I wanted to hear his answer—some young men in the village, having seen a few American action films in Bouaké, were certain that I knew karate, and they wanted lessons. I still hadn't been able to convince them otherwise.

Yacouba hesitated, then said, "Some people think that only witches would leave their valuables alone—they're afraid of the protective spells you've cast on your things."

"Witches? We're not witches!" I protested.

"I know," Yacouba replied. "You're ordinary people, just like us. But others aren't so sure."

Alma sighed heavily; I understood the despair in her voice. We'd purposely decided to show trust, hoping our behavior would induce the same in our neighbors. But we had frightened them instead—for what sort of people, living among strangers, wouldn't closely guard their belongings?

Over the next few days Alma and I hauled our desk and its contents back into our house whenever we left the compound, then back out again when we returned. But eventually we abandoned this extra, far too frequent task—half out of laziness, half out of resignation. After all, the damage had already been done.

Though the cooler weather of the rainy season was due in a month, I couldn't imagine it ever arriving. Even a nap was unthinkable, because the tin roof of our mud house absorbed and intensified the heat quite efficiently. The week before, I'd bought a head of cabbage at the market—an unusual find, a reminder of home—and stowed it in a plastic bag inside our house, where it promptly cooked itself. At bedtime Alma and I stopped rolling down the curtain of our little window, hoping for any breeze, yet almost every night we awoke sweating, just a degree or two shy of being toasted.

I thought ruefully of the government's decision to ban new homes from having thatched roofs: an attempt to project a Western modernity that disregarded the effect it would have on the daily lives of villagers. If only I could get my hands on a postcard of an English cottage, I'd send it to the housing minister. Alma and I had stayed in such a cottage briefly during our honeymoon and had marveled at the elaborate sculpting of its thatched roof, its welcome coolness.

Yet one night the heat bestowed an unexpected gift. Once again awakening in the seething air, I was startled to see a square of bright light suspended in midair in the middle of the room. As my eyes focused I realized it was the light from a late-rising full moon, framed by the open window and reflected on the mosquito netting, otherwise invisible in the dark of the night. It hovered there like a little beckoning door, an entrance—or exit?—that shivered when I tapped the netting.

I awakened Alma. "What is it?" she asked, still half-asleep. "What?"

"Look at the mosquito netting."

"Where? At what?"

Alma could barely see anything without her glasses. But I didn't want to spoil her surprise, so I said, "Wait," and reached for them beside her pillow.

"Now look," I said, slipping the glasses on her face.

"Oooooh," she murmured, and we shared this private, floating vision until we slowly fell back to sleep.

I sat at the desk in the center of our compound, a few small children idling by my chair and causing lazy clouds of dust to rise and settle slowly over the typewriter, my small stack of papers, me. Alma was in Asagbé to interview Amenan, and I'd decided to stay behind, in the hope of eking out something on the typewriter. But the heat was an extra, stifling skin that kept me from concentrating. I regarded the page in the typewriter—less than a paragraph of lifeless words. I'd placed two characters, a man and a woman, together at a hibachi table. They were strangers, and I'd been waiting for something to happen between them, but they just sat there, their inner lives tongue-tied by my lack of invention. In disgust I pulled out the offending sheet and crumpled it, feeling an odd pleasure at how it offered no resistance to my frustration. Holding the ball of paper in my hand, I examined its strange enfoldings, a few typed words staring out from a twisted ridge like eyes. Setting it down on the table, I imagined it was an origami sculpture.

An *idea*—the woman was an artist. I slipped another page in the typewriter and tapped out a sentence or two. Then, fingers poised above the keyboard, I waited for another entry into my story, but nothing came.

François bounded into our compound, speaking so fast I could only make out something about Kona falling. But François didn't have time to be patient with my struggles with his language. He pointed to his eye and, with a mixture of Beng and French, managed to tell me that Kona had fallen off his bicycle while riding on a forest trail to his fields and his sunglasses had ripped into his face.

I rushed with our first-aid kit to Kona's compound. He sat on a stool in the center of a small crowd, strips of flesh dangling from his cheek and just below his left eye. My own eyes teared at the sight, and for the first time I hesitated before cleaning and dressing a wound. Kona regarded my reaction calmly. Then, wearily waving me aside, he reached for the scissors in the kit and cut a bleeding strip from his cheek while François held a mirror. I knew that Kona, despite his age, regularly hunted large game with a shotgun that even some young men could barely lift, and weeks ago I'd watched him efficiently scramble up an orange tree with a wooden hook, snagging clusters of oranges for waiting baskets below: now here was another reflection of our host's strength.

But I knew that Kona's stoic self-treatment, no matter how brave, would not be sufficient: I was afraid he might lose that eye. He would have to be taken to the infirmary in M'Bahiakro, but at the moment Alma was in Asagbé with the car. Luckily Karimu, Kona's younger half brother and the owner of one of two motorbikes in the village, was among the small crowd: I asked him to drive to Asagbé and tell Alma to return. He agreed, but not, I thought, very graciously.

Karimu roared off. Meanwhile I fashioned a bandage swabbed with antibiotic cream over Kona's torn cheek. He sat silently, the very picture of suffering patience, and I kept thinking of my earlier hesitation, his reaching for those scissors. Then we waited. I estimated that a round trip by Mobylette should take thirty minutes, but after an hour had passed Karimu still hadn't returned. Finally, too anxious to wait any longer, I borrowed the only bike available: the old, shaky affair that Kona had just fallen from. I pedaled off as quickly as I dared, trying to avoid ruts in the dirt road.

As I rode along, impressed as always by the overhanging forest trees that cast huge shadows across my path, I wondered why Karimu and Alma were taking so long to return. Had my wife gone to the fields with Amenan or to another village to record some ceremony? I hoped not, and I tried to imagine them back in Amenan's compound: notebook in hand, Alma would be stretched out on a large bark-cloth mat with Amenan, under the coffee trees at the village's edge, and Amenan's face would be filled with the pleasures of recent village gossip. This was indeed the scene I found when I finally pedaled into Amenan's compound, yet my relief at finding Alma was now mixed with anger.

"Why are you still here? Where's Karimu?" I said, stepping down from the bike.

"Karimu?" Alma asked, clearly surprised by my sudden appearance.

She hadn't heard. I began to tell her of Kona's accident, and before I could finish she was packing her gear. I stuffed the bicycle into the car trunk and as we drove to Kosangbé we couldn't fathom Karimu's failure to find Alma. Even in relatively large Asagbé everyone knew everyone else's business, particularly when it concerned visitors. And white visitors were anything but invisible.

Back in our village we quickly helped Kona—now holding a bloody cloth over his bandage—into the car. Sunu, his senior wife, sat beside him. I raced

over the sudden gaping traps of the dirt road, hoping to arrive at the infirmary before noon, when the three-hour siesta would begin. But we arrived minutes late: except for a few patients fanning themselves beneath the trees, the long courtyard was deserted and the doctor wasn't to be found. We would have a long wait before he returned. Kona sat on the concrete entrance steps, ready to endure the delay stoically. Though no one spoke of Karimu, Alma and I—and perhaps Kona and Sunu as well—silently blamed him.

When the doctor finally returned, Kona was led to the operating room. Sitting beside us, Sunu didn't seem to need our presence: her stiff waiting face turned inward. We decided to walk off our worry by wandering about the town. As we passed the post office, I decided to check our postal box. Today I was especially hungry for the distractions of mail: any letter from a friend, even another package of nutritional gifts—dried soups and Japanese seaweed—from Alma's perpetually worried mother.

I opened the combination lock and discovered one slim envelope. It was a letter from a New York literary agent: she had read a story of mine in *The New Yorker* last September and was now proposing to represent me. I read it again quickly, barely believing that I held in my hand this offering from another world, and on such a day.

"Let me see, let me see," Alma said, and she read through the letter excitedly. She was deeply worried about the isolation I felt, and I knew that this unexpected news was a relief for both of us. She waved the letter over her head and cheered. "I can't believe you're so calm!" she said.

I was anything but, yet I couldn't quite accept the promise of this little piece of paper. The anxious spell of the day's events was briefly broken, and standing in the sunny courtyard of the post office, I suddenly realized I was famished. "Let's get something to eat," I said.

In a nearby stall we drank coffee thickened by sweetened condensed milk—the Côte d'Ivoire fashion—accompanied by long slabs of French bread spread generously with butter. This served as our informal, somber celebration—our concern for Kona kept returning as we read and reread the letter. Then I noticed the date on the envelope: October 18. Forwarded by *The New Yorker,* the letter had taken almost five months to arrive. How would the agent have interpreted my prolonged silence? Had she by now forgotten her interest in my work?

Our minds in two very distant places, Alma and I bought fried fish snacks in the market for ourselves and Sunu, and then we hurried back to the infirmary. Sunu accepted the fish with the friendliest nod she could manage. She still didn't like us much, and I could see she wasn't going to let our assistance today change her opinion too quickly. And why should it? We were strangers with peculiar ways, and our presence had exacerbated the rivalry between her husband and the village chief. We ate together in silence.

Soon Kona emerged from the operating room, half his face hidden by a gauze bandage. The doctor assured us that Kona wouldn't lose his eye, but he would have to receive antibiotic shots daily to avoid infection. He and Sunu decided to stay in M'Bahiakro for at least a week. Obviously in pain, Kona managed to smile at us as we said good-bye.

When we arrived in Kosangbé, we were greeted with relief and thanks and, from François, offerings of palm wine. We enjoyed this extended moment of warmth, sipping from gourds and accepting grateful toasts, but gradually our neighbors left for their own compounds—there was evening bathwater to warm, dinner to be cooked. As François poured the last round of palm wine, he mentioned that my riding off to fetch Alma had surprised everyone.

"Why should anyone be surprised?" she asked.

"We didn't know white people could ride bicycles."

"Really? Why would anyone think that?" Alma set down her gourd and reached for her notebook. But a familiar, nervous evasiveness crept into François's eyes, so she didn't pursue the question.

Later in the evening our friend Yapi Yao confessed to us in our compound—and without embarrassment, for of course *he* didn't believe such a thing—that some villagers thought white people were spirits who happened to have bodies, which made physical exertion of any kind out of the question. We three laughed together and drank more palm wine. But I had the sense that Yao was telling us this as a kind of test—that if we had said, "Yes, that's right, we're spirits," he wouldn't have been shocked. Hadn't Yacouba confided that some villagers suspected we were witches? Didn't some young men still imagine I was a karate expert? It was exhilarating to be the center of such fantastic speculation, yet I was disturbed to think how easily we could become fictional characters in a language we barely understood.

Alma: From Nurse to Healer's Apprentice

Karimu had not been among our greeting party, and by evening he still hadn't returned to the village. While sitting at our lamplit desk trying to copy my latest collection of Beng words onto index cards, I kept returning to one of the unfinished stories of the day: as Philip had rushed into her compound Amenan had just begun recounting for me a dispute over a stolen hat that had degenerated into name calling, one woman shouting, "Dead arm!" at the accused thief's clan elder—who indeed had a permanently paralyzed left arm. Then I thought about Karimu and his mysterious failure to find me: might he have misunderstood where I was or asked for another Amenan? Then I heard the drone of Karimu's motorbike and quickly made my way to his compound to welcome him back to the village.

We exchanged greetings politely, and then, trying to conceal my annoyance with him and appear merely curious, I asked casually, "What happened? Are you all right?"

"Well," he said, meticulously brushing the dust off his shirt, "when I got to Asagbé, people told me you'd gone to Totogbé, so I went there to look for you."

Bewildered, I said, "But everyone knew I was still in Asagbé."

"Oh, yes, they told me you'd gone to Dezigbé," he then asserted, now dusting off his pants.

"But everyone knew I was staying in Asagbé," I repeated.

Karimu tried again. "Oh, no, they told me you hadn't arrived yet."

Frustrated, and sensing that there was far more to this episode than I could possibly understand that evening, I decided to drop the subject. Later that night our friend Yacouba told me that just a year ago Kona had fallen off his bike and, oddly enough, had also received an eye injury from sunglasses, for which he had gone down to M'Bahiakro to be treated. This coincidence—a term that does not exist in the Beng language—made the day's events look very suspicious. Given that witchcraft appeared to be the common local explanation of accidents, I wondered if Karimu's still unexplained absence would cause people to believe he had bewitched his half brother.

Our help during Kona's accident was a small repayment to him and his family for hosting us in the village: we were beginning to enter the African world of favors and obligations. Some of Kona's grateful relatives gave us live chickens as thanks, and over the next few days Philip and I had several meals of chicken stew with onions, rice, and a palm nut sauce—thick, red, and slightly sweet—which we shared with neighboring families. We even began to gain back some of the weight we had lost in the early months from malaria and amoebic dysentery.

We received so many chickens as gifts that we decided to raise them. Our neighbor Bani wove us a small basketry coop from thick vines. In the mornings Philip let out our rooster, and it flapped and crowed about our compound while our single hen huddled over her eggs. In the evenings it was the job of young boys to round up each family's chickens, and François's sons were happy to do so for us. It was always a good game of chase, as the pursued often created sharp turns where there had been only air.

Our rooster had been donated to us by Yoma Kouassi, the leader of the secret ritual that we had struggled to see the previous month: he had made all the formal speeches with deft flourishes of his hands and a strong, fluid Beng that seemed extraordinarily eloquent even to our still ignorant ears.

Ever since then, whenever Philip and I met Yoma Kouassi he shook our hands extravagantly and thanked us for the privilege. He presented us with chickens and palm wine, he told us stories, and we in turn gave him bottles of red wine, sacks of salt, and rides home—while he had been born in Kosangbé, he and his wife lived in a farming camp about three miles to the north.

Though I wasn't certain why Yoma Kouassi was so enthusiastic about us, I hoped it had to do with our tact once we had finally been allowed to view last month's ritual, and our discretion about it since then. As our friendship developed I wondered if it would ever lead to what was, for me, the ultimate prize: knowledge. One day he might agree to explain the ritual to me. At the same time I worried if the chauffeur service that we were soon offering Yoma Kouassi regularly was approaching bribery.

I felt more confident about the terms of my relationship with my friend Amenan—at least for the moment. Recently I had promised to do all I could to help in her next childbirth. Despite having been trained by French nuns in the city as a rural health worker, Amenan had given birth to five children in the village, and this was where she would soon have her sixth. But as the time neared, she increasingly confided to me how worried she was. The birth of her last baby had been very difficult, and she was uncertain whether to believe one or another explanation that different people had proposed.

During much of her last pregnancy, Amenan had been angry with her husband for having inexplicably left the village for several months. The Beng think that anger—which they describe with the phrase, *mi zu e bina*—"your chest is lit"—can cause sickness if it is ignored. Her mother, Akissikro, was certain that Amenan's anger had brought on the difficulties in her last labor; Amenan wanted to believe this, for she was no longer angry with her husband, who had since returned to the village. But a diviner had proposed another explanation. According to him, the difficulties of Amenan's last childbirth were due to a jealous former lover who hadn't wanted her to marry Kofi and so had bewitched her. Fearing this was true, Amenan was nervous that he might try to harm her again.

I started anxiously reading and rereading the frustratingly short chapter on childbirth in our dusty medical text. The drawings and instructions made a "normal" birth—whatever that was—sound so easy. But complications, the author suggested, might require injections of medicines: preparations we didn't have and wouldn't even know how to administer. In truly difficult cases the village midwife was instructed to give up and take the laboring woman to a doctor. But could a laboring Amenan and an unborn baby in fetal distress withstand the bumpy, hour long ride to M'Bahiakro? Not knowing exactly when Amenan was due to give birth made these uncertainties worse—perhaps I might be in another village when the time came and I would miss the event altogether. I didn't permit myself to imagine the worst scenario.

One day I drove to Asagbé for the Sunday market, where Amenan's uncle, Kokla Kouassi, greeted me and mentioned casually, "Amenan has a stomachache." I thought my friend probably had diarrhea—a common complaint—and was sorry to hear it, but I finished buying the chili peppers, onions, and okra I had come for before walking over to Amenan's compound. There I found Amenan in the middle of an obviously painful contraction and only then realized that "stomachache" was a euphemism for being in labor.

But I didn't have time to be depressed that I had misunderstood such an obvious expression, for the immediacy of the scene overwhelmed me. Amenan was sitting on the dirt floor, legs extended, moaning. Her mother was mopping her sweaty forehead, and another old woman, whom I did not recognize, sat behind Amenan, rubbing her back. Of two other elderly women present, one, Pono Nguessan, was a specialist in coaxing out afterbirths. I greeted all the women and prepared to take notes in my usual obsessive manner, but when Amenan managed to say quietly in fine French, *"Je souffre un peu,"* I immediately remembered that the Western medical supplies I had promised were back in Kosangbé. So I ran out to the car, then crept with infuriating slowness through the village, its paths crowded from the shoppers at the Sunday market.

Out on the road I longed to be back in Amenan's room, and I chided myself for not having brought the planned birth supplies to her weeks earlier, to avoid this emergency trip. Finally arrived in Kosangbé, I gathered up rubbing alcohol, gauze, and new razor blades and explained quickly to Philip that I would probably stay over in Asagbé that night. Back in the car, I contemplated the seemingly endless stretch of road ahead of me and pondered how much of my seeming altruism was really my own simple craving for gratitude from a good friend and reliable informant.

By the time I returned to Amenan's room the baby had just been born, happily without complications, and mother and daughter lay on a dirt floor puddled with blood. I was able to contribute a razor for cutting the umbilical cord in sterile fashion, but I was crushed that I had missed the delivery.

After a gentle stomach massage by Pono Nguessan, the placenta came out, and all the women in the room said tenderly to Amenan, "God bless you," and then to each other, "God bless the woman."

Within minutes news of the birth was out, and Amenan's husband, Kofi, entered the room, saying softly to her, "God bless you," then asking, "What have you given me?"

Amenan answered, "A girl."

"Thank you," said Kofi.

This exchange was then repeated word for word perhaps a hundred times as a stream of visitors started filing into the room and giving small change as gifts to Amenan. It seemed that someone from nearly every household had come to congratulate her.

Finally alone, Amenan casually stood up, walked out to the bathhouse unassisted, and washed. Her mother swept out the room and sprinkled dirt over the floor to absorb the blood of the birth. The two older women held the baby over an enamel basin and ritually washed her with ash and homemade black soap. Then mother and baby were reunited in the bedroom, where they finally nursed. Amenan lay next to a burning fire to help the remaining blood in her womb come out; she was too tired and the others were too busy to answer my annoying questions. ("Where was the placenta thrown?" "How often will the baby nurse?") Amenan put papaya leaves in the fire and on her stomach to ease her postpartum cramps, and she ate a bowl of corn mush cooked by one of the women to harden her flabby stomach.

Amenan glanced up from gazing tenderly at her sleeping new baby when she heard singing coming from a clearing a few yards into the forest. The three enormous Ghanaian prostitutes of the village were dancing gaily and singing a birth song from their home country. The Beng women of the compound ignored them. Amenan couldn't chase the prostitutes because they were compatriots of her Ghanaian husband, yet she too looked away, embarrassed.

Amenan's uncle, Kokla Kouassi, lived next door, and he came over to congratulate his niece, then asked me for a ride to a stretch of savanna some eight miles away, so that he could collect herbs that were good for helping postpartum women heal quickly. I was happy to oblige: here was my second chance to contribute something that Amenan would surely appreciate, and we set out for the savanna. Arriving at a meadow still parched from the end of the dry season, Kokla Kouassi spotted two young boys coming back from the fields. He described to them the plant he was seeking, and though strangers to Kouassi, they went off obediently to look for it.

We returned to Asagbé with the valuable plant, and I felt intrigued that I had converted successfully from Western nurse to healer's apprentice in a scant few hours. Amenan, tired but pleased, made herself a tea of the herbs.

I slept over, and the next day, after watching the baby's grandmother apply an herbal medicine to the raw umbilical cord to hasten its drying, I returned to Kosangbé: exhausted, exhilarated, and somehow disappointed all at once. I had managed to help, but in the most peripheral of ways: it was the village that had orchestrated this birth and taken responsibility for it, the village that took over care of mother and baby. I couldn't help but feel a little irrelevant.

Yet Amenan's childbirth was to take on wider significance in my life. My relationship with Amenan deepened considerably: I was no longer just an inquisitive foreigner, but a friend who had shared in an intimate moment. Moreover, the baby, like all girls born on Monday, was named Amwé—my own adopted Beng name. And though Amenan herself was only nominally Catholic—she never went to church and regularly sacrificed chickens and attended animist dances—her husband, Kofi, was considering baptizing their little daughter "Alma." Amenan and her family began referring to me as Amwé's "real mother."

Soon after Amenan's childbirth, Philip and I drove down to M'Bahiakro to pick up Kona, who had been staying with friends in town while receiving further treatment from the doctors. His wound was now thoroughly healed, but the lower eyelid, patched together expertly from raw strips of flesh, was noticeably drooping, and he appeared a bit sad even when he smiled at Sunu.

Back in the car, the engine began to sputter before we were halfway to Kosangbé, and we stopped outside a small farming encampment on the edge of the road. There, in an example of the little kernel of good luck that often hides in the bad, we found a young man who had once worked as a mechanic in town. Relieved when he immediately opened the hood and began poking away, we didn't question why he was now working as a farmer. It took him until evening to manage some makeshift solution, and as we prepared to drive off, we noticed Kona and Sunu's nervousness. Perhaps they had less faith than we did in the young man's mechanical abilities.

As we approached Kosangbé we saw that a huge crowd was gathered near the roadside, illuminated by the swaying light of hand-held lanterns. We heard shouting, and as we parked the car we saw a sudden burst of pushing and shoving among a few men, the people near them either joining in the fray or trying to stop it. The entire village seemed to be a cluster of furious knots. I took advantage of the pandemonium—the angry men and women were more than eager to elaborate their grievances—and I managed to discover that the dispute was about a niece who had refused to cook dinner for her bachelor uncle. How could this uproar be caused by what seemed such a trivial incident? Whatever the underlying tension might be, this was not the time to probe for festering grudges.

In the middle of all this hubbub, our next-door neighbor Komena Kouassikro, who was considered not quite right since serving in the French army during World War II, decided that this was the perfect time to publicly announce his daughter Akissi's engagement as a second wife to Karimu. She immediately began wailing, as she was ritually expected to do:

I'll cut my throat
I'll run away into the forest
I won't marry him.

And indeed, she started running—to any place as long as her father was not there—and a troop of children followed her, laughing and cheering. As Akissi stalked past pockets of still angry villagers, some women began singing, "The groom is beautiful, the bride is beautiful." Before long, in celebration of Kouassikro's announcement, almost everyone in our part of the village was drinking palm wine and beer, while a few older boys drummed to accompany the women's songs.

Delighted to be up so late, the village children added to the celebration in their own ways. Some combined their evening robes to form a long, flowing cloth rectangle, which they proclaimed a bus, while others packed in the middle as passengers. Still others made wild, flutelike sounds from palm reeds as their little orchestras marched through the reveling compounds.

As the prospective bride's father, Kouassikro was already quite drunk when, tipsy myself, I asked him about his daughter's engagement. He explained that he should have proposed the marriage to the prospective groom's father, but Karimu's father had died long ago, so he had instead negotiated with Karimu's much older half brother—our host, Kona. I realized that Kouassi had been waiting impatiently for Kona's successful recuperation and return to the village so that he could publicly announce the engagement.

Presumably Karimu had agreed to this match, but all evening he was noticeably absent. Later that night Philip and I wondered if Karimu was at all enthusiastic. With a square block of a face, Akissi was generally considered the least attractive young woman in the village. By contrast, Karimu was one of the handsomest men; indeed, he was the most openly vain Beng man we had yet met. While his first wife usually wore torn clothes, he himself always sported clean new robes and pants; often we found him gazing admiringly in the mirror when he shaved in the morning. Could he really be content with this proposed union? Then I realized that the marriage negotiations must have been conducted before Kona's bicycle accident—three days before, I soon found out.

The next morning, when we drove to Asagbé to visit Amenan, our car leaked oil and overheated. We knew that we needed to travel to Bouaké, where Philip hoped he could find an able mechanic for our ailing Renault and where funds from my grant should already have been cabled to our bank.

The ninety-mile drive to Bouaké was, thankfully, uneventful. Once there we settled into the apartment of Marcel, a Peace Corps friend, and set out to meet Kona's son Kouassi, who now lived in the city, working as a tailor. Kouassi's village wife had entrusted me with fabric for him to sew into a blouse. Kouassi was quite friendly, but he sometimes smiled as if he knew more about us than we knew ourselves.

Our next order of business was repairing the car, but at the moment this proved impossible: my expected grant installment had once again taken a mysterious detour in the telex system. Twice a day Philip and I set out anxiously for the bank, hoping for news, and twice a day we returned glumly down streets lined with mango trees, the leaves green and lush, the fruits ripening but too high for passersby to pick. The city children, as ingenious and ambitious as those of the village, used long crooked sticks to pull down the fruits, which they sold on the sidewalks at three for ten cents.

Beset by the failures of Western technology—a car that didn't work and a money order lost in the electronic mail—I settled into an enforced vacation of sorts, a frustrating week of waiting. After a few days of longed-for rest, I occupied myself by typing field notes. I remembered that Margaret Mead, in her field memoirs, had cautioned young anthropologists never to lag more than a day in this endless task, but with all the events of the past few weeks, I had fallen hopelessly behind.

Rather than wonder about the practicality of Mead's advice, I doubted myself. I worried continually that I was not asking the right questions and that people were not offering me the right answers; that car and money troubles were increasingly taking up my time; that I was deciphering the difficulties of the Beng language too slowly; that I was spending too much time typing up field notes. And I worried that I had made a mistake in choosing to live in a village where people could be so secretive.

Perhaps my expectations were unrealistic, my frustrations more a result of my own impatience than intransigence on the part of the villagers. More than once I had tried a time-honored anthropological technique: quietly making known the fact that I had already learned some preliminary information about such-and-such, so that anyone else might feel comfortable discussing it further with me. But on hearing that I already knew, say, the name of a shrine or the reason for a certain ritual, many in the village would immediately and indignantly ask, *"Dih a pey mi ni?"*—Who told you that? Of course I felt I had to protect my sources, so I always answered, "I can't remember," and the discussion ended. From this I learned something valuable about Beng notions of knowledge: it was always social. If something was told as a secret, it was never to be repeated; conversely, if a bit of information was repeated, the original speaker's identity must be revealed. But understanding these unspoken rules hardly made fieldwork less difficult.

Philip: *The Parting Curtain*

I had hoped that our days in Bouaké would be a welcome release from the unpredictable round of emergencies and interruptions in the village; but, ironically, the long-sought-after peace of the city served to remind me of my isolation. I'd written back to the literary agent, indicating that I would be quite happy to have her represent my work, and now, as I awaited her reply, I longed for home and what home had to offer: a community of writers with their sometimes conflicting but often common enthusiasms.

I sat for hours on the balcony of Marcel's apartment, pen and notebook in hand. I had managed to write a bit since the divination for my writer's block, though the prescribed chicken sacrifice still hadn't been performed. I suspected that this remaining ritual, which I hoped would publicly bestow upon me a recognizable identity, might be the cathartic release I needed.

Or would it? So far, whatever I had reached out for among the Beng often seemed to slip away, yet the frustrations of my life in the village had their own attractions. I recalled a recent morning back in Kosangbé: Alma and I were working at our desk when I noticed that tiny, gray-green butterflies were flitting about us in increasing numbers. By noon there were fluttering clouds throughout Kosangbé, the swarms so thick we could barely see through them. All day, whenever a cluster settled, hungry chickens chased after them, and ecstatic children churned their arms and tore through the compounds, trying to create maximum butterfly turbulence. Then, as dusk approached, the dense formations steadily thinned out and finally disappeared. But the next morning the butterflies returned, and this cycle was repeated for nearly a week, each day yet another extended, fantastical moment. I often wandered through the village just for the eerie experience of seeing the multitudes of butterflies parting before me like some ever-transforming, ever-receding curtain. The villagers were surprised by my wonder—though an adult, I reacted like the children. For our neighbors, the flying creatures were simply a sign that the rainy season would soon arrive, that it was time to take out hoes and prepare for the coming hard work of planting.

Near the end of that Week of Butterflies, I was summoned across the village to treat the severe abdominal pain of Wuru San, the father of the village chief. He groaned and rocked back and forth on a curved wooden stool while I quickly flipped back and forth through the pages of my medical book, but I wasn't sure what caused his distress; perhaps it was a bladder stone blocking the urinary tract. Once again our car was unavailable: Alma was in Asagbé interviewing Amenan. I gave Wuru San two strong aspirins with codeine to cut the pain until Alma returned and we could take him to the infirmary in M'Bahiakro. I sat beside the old man on one of the stools in his compound and waited among the dwindling clouds of afternoon butterflies.

But Alma was later than usual in returning to the village, and Wuru San's wrinkled face had become so puckered up in distress that I decided again to borrow a bicycle and ride off to fetch her. I hadn't gone more than a half mile when I saw the distant dust cloud of Alma's approaching car. Once more I packed the bike into the back of the car and headed back to Kosangbé— where the old man claimed he felt much better, no need to go to the infirmary. His hands grasped his cane firmly, as if to plant himself to the ground to prevent me from leading him off. Had the aspirin cured him, or was the prospect of going to the infirmary—where most old people went only to die—terrifying enough to shock him into health, or the pretense of health? Perhaps he saw my friendly gestures, in offering to help him to the car, as the beginning of the end of his life. But I might never really know; like so much else that occurred in Kosangbé, this story clung tenaciously to its ambiguous ending.

Now, as I glanced down from time to time at the distant street life of Bouaké, I felt that here, as in the village, I was just a pair of eyes watching a strange culture go by; perhaps that was why I kept thinking back to the swarms of butterflies, those shimmering curtains that always retreated as I approached. Or was I retreating? I was working on a new story set in America, and slowly I entered a fictional world far removed from Africa: an artist and a lawyer first meet at a hibachi table in a Japanese restaurant; she fashions his profile in origami from her empty cigarette pack, and he reveals that he files suits against toy manufacturers for the parents of maimed children. No matter how I stared at the scribbled words on my notepad, I couldn't connect them to my recent experiences. As usual, though I couldn't anticipate where this story might take me, I had little choice but to follow myself into it.

And soon Alma and I would return to the beckoning uncertainties of village life. Her cabled grant money finally arrived, and Kona's son Kouassi introduced us to his friend Dramane, an ace mechanic who specialized in repairing battered taxis. Though we were in Bouaké, the second largest city in Côte d'Ivoire, we were never far from tiny Kosangbé and its complex net of kinship ties, for Dramane treated us as if we were Kouassi's relatives. In the large yard that was his garage, littered with the hulks of cars and their scattered parts, he quickly set to work on our car. In the center of this yard stood a particularly lush mango tree with ritually powerful amulets—animal horns, tortoise shells, plastic beads—hanging from almost every branch. This tree, under which Dramane and his young apprentices worked, protected from the sun and witchcraft alike, was a good reminder that Africa was a palimpsest. Dramane's technical skills were Western, but supporting them—and his Muslim prayers—was the animist African village.

This was the world I missed. When we finally returned to Kosangbé the children of the village chased happily after our car; our strange language and bizarre habits were always a source of entertainment. Our neighbors welcomed us home, and the village seemed comfortingly familiar: the busy courtyards of the interlocking compounds; herds of noisy goats ranging through the narrow paths; lines of farmers marching back from the fields in the late afternoon; Moya coming by to cook for us; the evening bath; quiet talks with Yacouba and other neighbors by lamplight; the Milky Way an arching canopy above our courtyard.

Alma: Two Cows

Our pleasure at returning to Bengland was short-lived. Through a very surreptitious grapevine I discovered that just before we'd moved into Kosangbé back in November, the villagers had held a meeting during which they'd resolved not to tell me anything significant. The price for breaking this rule had apparently been fixed at two cows. I was stunned by the news and especially by the size of the fine, for the Beng did not themselves raise cattle: on the local market, a single cow cost about $250, easily equivalent to a struggling farmer's annual salary. What information could be so secret, so "significant," as to warrant such a fine?

I remembered an encounter I'd had recently with our landlord, François. He'd invited me into his house for the first time, and my observational energy had gone into fifth gear. Who slept where? All five children slept with their parents, François told me readily. What were the other rooms used for? Guests, storage, he replied. And what was that dusty knot of fabric, lianas, shells, and gourd pieces hanging over a doorway? I suspected that it was a religious icon, but I was not prepared for the look of panic that crossed François's face, followed immediately by some mumbled syllables as he quickly ushered me outside. Knowing now about the two cow fine, I realized how unanswerable my question had been.

Yet there was more: according to my source, a few days after our arrival the elders had met with Jean, instructing him that he too was forbidden to discuss any important matters with me. Immediately I understood many of my troubles with Jean, particularly his infuriating, feigned ignorance, his refusal to translate. Of course I'd encountered difficulties with him long before moving to Kosangbé, but with the advent of his truly inexplicable behavior I'd failed to question what wider forces might be constraining him—I had forgotten to be an anthropologist with Jean.

How unfair I'd been. Jean had been stuck in an impossible situation, risking at any given moment either the punishment of powerful elders or the anger of his employer. Then I remembered the day I'd demoted him, with Kona officiating. Kona had known Jean's dilemma but had said nothing to me about it, for he too was subject to the two cow fine. My own village "father"! What other relationships in this village were founded on deceit?

Amenan was appalled when she heard of the fine, and she urged me to come to live in her own, more enlightened village, where, she assured me, we would be welcome and people would be happy to talk about anything that interested me. Philip and I spent the next few evenings whispering about my dilemma inside our mud house, the door locked.

Finally, one night in bed, Philip declared, "We have to make a decision." The surrounding mosquito netting, which usually seemed a comforting protection, now felt imprisoning. "I feel stuck," I said. "I don't know what to do."

"Well, if you want to know my opinion, I think we should move back to Asagbé. Life will be a lot easier. Kosangbé is just too secret crazy."

But I had chosen Kosangbé because it was the most traditional of the Beng villages, and now I had to accept that this very quality was responsible for my current difficulties. My reluctance to leave was surely based on my own stubbornness as well. The more the villagers resisted my research, the more I felt challenged to win them over, to prove that I was living among them for honorable aims. I was determined to stay, and I said so.

Concealing well what I knew to be his disappointment, Philip said, "Okay, but I think that if we stay here, we have to tell people that we know about the two cow fine."

I dreaded any possible confrontation, yet I had to agree that the success of my fieldwork rested on a forthright airing of the problem. We decided to request a meeting with the Kosangbé elders over a "serious matter," leaving the reason for the meeting vague—otherwise the elders might refuse to speak with us at all. "Surely," Philip argued, "we can have our own secrets, too."

The next morning Kona agreed to the meeting but said he needed to consult with the other elders to choose a day. Kona had always been a master of the silent response, and now, with his droopy eyelid, it was even more difficult to read his expression. If he knew this, he used it to his advantage.

While we waited for this meeting to take place, a drama was unfolding in the village that no one bothered to conceal from me. Afwé, a young woman of the village, had become engaged to a distant cousin in Asagbé, but now she was firmly resisting Gaosu, who had been chosen for her by her father. A few months ago, before moving to Kosangbé, Philip and I had witnessed the celebration of the engagement—though we'd had no sense of the match's hidden tensions. Now, rumor had it that Afwé wanted to marry Kouassi Ba, her village boyfriend. But the complex arranged marriage rules of the Beng—which I still hadn't deciphered—were far too stringent to accommodate such youthful attachments. So, against Afwé's wishes, the wedding ceremony was held in the groom's village: the bride refused to dance at her own wedding. The next day she ran off, first into the forest, then back home to Kosangbé.

Finally a number of elders were summoned. They agreed that, like it or not, Afwé must wed Gaosu. In turn, she asserted that if forced to marry him, she would commit suicide. While this was the standard ritual refusal, Afwé's unusual vehemence, along with her reputation of childhood rebelliousness, was convincing. It was tentatively decided that the marriage might be annulled, even though Afwé's maternal uncle had already provided a number of expensive wedding gifts. He lived eight miles up the road and needed to be told of the news, so a few elders of the village asked Philip and me for a ride in our car. We agreed, delighted to be included. On learning of the recent events, the uncle called Afwé's father, Zang, a "bad man" and blamed him for the situation. "And don't expect me to contribute gifts to her next wedding," he added, visibly disgusted.

The next day the Kosangbé elders held another meeting about the problem under the village's huge kapok tree. People from a number of villages came for the well-publicized event. Already tense from an earlier screaming match with her older sister, who insisted that she go through with the marriage, Afwé now sat facing the men, who did the formal judging, while the women stood behind them, peppering the trial with their comments and opinions. She repeated her refusal before the entire village until her father, Zang, howling from his disgrace, approached her with a whip. Some elders quickly disarmed him, but he broke away and began slapping his daughter. She ran off into the forest again, and the meeting broke up.

Soon Zang walked over to Karimu's house. It was there that Afwé had had her trysts with her boyfriend, Kouassi Ba, and Zang had heard that she had left a skirt of hers in the house. Rumors were circulating that Kouassi Ba had cast a spell with the skirt, bewitching Afwé to refuse the marriage to Gaosu. Zang now wanted his daughter's skirt back, but Karimu's wife refused to hand it over. She chased Zang out of her yard, shouting, "Why don't you just let Afwé marry Kouassi Ba?" He went home, defeated again.

Later Afwé returned to the village to sit in the house of the "President of the Youths," which in this case served as a kind of sanctuary. The children gathered around her were unusually solemn. Perhaps they feared that a similar drama might someday be repeated for them.

A few days later I was in Asagbé with Philip, enjoying the shade of Amenan's coffee trees. Amenan was telling me that toddler boys must stop nursing if they wanted to eat chickens that have been sacrificed to the sacred Earth of the village. She pointed with exasperation to her two-year-old son, Kouadio. He had recently weaned himself in favor of Earth chickens, but Amenan complained that he often played with her breasts, half trying to nurse, "just to annoy me." Listening to his mother, little Kouadio pouted and started to approach her just as San Komenan, a young man from Kosangbé, bicycled into the compound. Breathlessly he told us that his sister-in-law, Nguessan, was having a very difficult birth, and could Philip and I please drive her down to the M'Bahiakro infirmary? Of course we agreed, and as Philip struggled to fit Komenan's bicycle into the trunk, he smiled at me. "Déjà-vu, huh?"

On the drive back to Kosangbé, I realized that I barely knew Nguessan, who lived in the chief's compound. It was there that I was often met with a close-lipped suspiciousness when I dropped by to deliver morning greetings; I wasn't surprised that no one from the compound had mentioned that Nguessan was so close to delivering.

Arriving in the village, we found a large, quiet crowd gathered outside Nguessan's door and listening to her screams. While Philip and I slowly led her to the car, Nguessan's face twisted in pain: she stepped as though the ground burned her feet. Nguessan sat in the backseat with her panicking husband, Yaokro, and an aunt who was prepared to help with the childbirth. By now familiar with the various potholes and ruts, Philip tried to give Nguessan as smooth a ride as possible as he sped along, but the road, as always, rattled the car. Nguessan kicked the seat behind Philip in rhythm to her contractions; sometimes her screams were so high-pitched that I thought the baby had just been born and was crying.

When we finally reached the infirmary, an indifferent attendant coolly told us that the doctor was in Abidjan and the midwife was away on a lunch break. The midwife's assistant nervously confessed that she had never delivered a baby on her own, but then she quickly ushered Nguessan and me into the labor room.

Weak with pain, Nguessan lay flat on her back on the delivery table. Standing over her, the assistant began to massage Nguessan's bulging stomach, and she asked me to help. In those tense minutes, while Nguessan gasped and howled, I merely carried out the assistant's instructions as best I could: I pushed up on the perineum, and soon I saw the baby's head crowning. Then out came the rest of the body. This happened far more quickly than I had expected, and I wondered if all that jostling on the road had helped move the baby down the birth canal. "A girl," I heard the assistant whisper. But the baby's head was badly misshapen, and she was covered in a slimy meconium, a sign of fetal distress. Worse, she was not breathing. In increasing desperation the assistant suctioned out mucus from the baby's nose and mouth, rubbed her with alcohol, and then gave her a shot. Finally the tiny infant started breathing.

After a few long moments of relief, I timidly asked the assistant about the baby's elongated head and was relieved to hear that this was just a temporary effect of the soft skull bones having squeezed through the birth canal. The woman added that the newborn—weighing only 5½ pounds and her skin almost transparent—would undoubtedly have died if she had been born in the village not breathing. I felt blessed that I had been able to help, and once again I was relieved to think how easily Amenan's labor had gone.

The midwife's assistant told Nguessan that she should remain in the infirmary for several days until the baby's umbilical cord fell off. Though her aunt would stay with her, I thought Nguessan would be quite lonely: no line of neighbors congratulating her, none of the familiar, elaborate village care that Amenan had enjoyed.

Now that the birth was over, Yaokro was quite irrelevant: even in the infirmary the care of babies was a woman's domain. We took him to a nearby bar to celebrate, and then he returned to the village with us.

On the drive up, Philip and I spoke in English to conceal from Yaokro our nakedly selfish thoughts about the medical emergencies of the past month. The combination of Kona's earlier accident and Nguessan's difficult labor might have given me an unintended boon in the village. From our modest role of chauffeur in these two crises, the two main political factions of the village—the chief and his family and Kona and his family—had become indebted to us. Considering this, I hoped that I might be able to negotiate the divisions and suspicions of the village with more grace.

When we arrived in Kosangbé we found no less than half the village—the side where Yaokro and Nguessan lived—waiting uneasily by the roadside for our return. Soon we had the unexpected pleasure of joining the palm wine celebration convened by Yaokro's much older brother, San Yao, who so distrusted us. He toasted us again and again, but above his salt-and-pepper beard was that familiar, ambiguous smile.

Philip: The Snake Child

One afternoon Kona and San Yao, ambling about the village separately, found themselves alone in the center of an open courtyard near our mud house. I

was listening to our short-wave radio—another Voice of America broadcast about the endless Iranian hostage crisis—and I turned down the sound to watch this rare private encounter. They stood stiffly across from each other, Kona's arms crossed, San Yao's hands clasped before him, the half-circle of thatched houses in the background serving almost as an arena.

They spoke briefly—neither a friendly chat nor the usual formal African address—and I was too far away to hear. What was it they spoke of, I wondered: trivialities masking their rivalry? I couldn't help thinking how aptly they were dressed: as the village representative of the country's single political party, Kona wore a modern shirt and pair of pants; Yao, the chief and caretaker of religious values, wore the more traditional men's toga. They had known each other all their lives, and now, both in late middle age, they embodied opposing forces in the village.

Yet their true positions were not so simple. Alma had discovered that many villagers considered San Yao a stand-in for the "real" chief, a man who lived in another village entirely and who had abdicated the chiefship because he did not want to return to Kosangbé. In fact, San Yao held his position by virtue of a double default: after the abdicated chief, the next man in line had been the village drunk. As for Kona, he was our host and protector, but I wasn't sure how willingly he had taken on this role. Had he volunteered to be our village father because he thought he might thereby advance his own prestige in the village, or had he felt compelled to take responsibility for us because of his local position in the national party? I took a photo of their brief encounter, though I doubted that, once the film was finally developed, I'd have much success in reading the respectful wariness of these main actors in a competition of which we were somehow a part.

The rainy season had finally arrived, and day after day huge columns of clouds approached slowly and darkly before bursting upon the village. But although the rains brought cooler weather, they also brought winds so strong that I sometimes wondered how some of the frailer mud brick homes managed to remain standing. Recently a woman in Asagbé had walked through the forest on a Monday—a day when it was forbidden to do so—and on her way back home through turbulent winds, a tree had fallen on her. The wind was so terrifying that all the Beng villages organized a collective propitiatory goat sacrifice.

At night the stormy approaches were marked by spectacular lightning accompanied by surprisingly little thunder; yet when the rain slammed down on the tin roof of our house, it sounded like thousands of percussion orchestras. During the dry season, as Alma and I had lain in bed at night and stared up at the enveloping mosquito netting, we'd often indulged in the pastime of lazily murmuring memories of what we most missed from home. But now, as the rain battered our roof, we had to shout into each other's ears.

"Felix the Cat and his Magic Bag!" I began, and Alma countered with, "The Metropolitan Museum of Art!"

"Trisha's veal with artichokes!" I replied, and once I mentioned food we had to continue with a shouted string of delicacies: "Ann's Cornish hens! Manhattan clam chowder! Cold sesame noodles! Pizza, with everything on it!"

Perhaps my increased longings for food from home was spurred by the new exotic foods that now made their appearance. Huge forest snails, creeping along the edge of the forest in shells of brown, swirling designs, were caught and eaten, as were turtles, which were baked in their own shells. Our favorite new delicacy was the giant, fanning white mushrooms that grew in the forest around our village and apparently nowhere else; they were considered a great treat, and with good reason: after frying in oil, they tasted like a very tender veal.

We also had dreams of omelets for breakfast and frequent chicken stews, for our hen's eggs had finally hatched, and five tiny chirping feather balls scrambled about our compound. But within a week one chick was crushed by a wooden mortar as a neighbor pounded yams for dinner; three others were crushed under the wheels of our own car as we set off one day; and the last was seen being eaten by a snake at the edge of the forest.

Still, I wasn't entirely disappointed by these little tragedies, because if those chicks had grown up, I would have had to take on the distasteful role of butcher—among the Beng, a traditional male task. Whenever a neighbor gave us a gift of a chicken, I was the one who carried the squawking bird behind our mud house, followed by a crowd of children, and I thought longingly of those plucked, packaged wonders of the American supermarket. Knife in hand and my foot pressing the wings of the struggling chicken to the ground, I always felt sympathy for the terrified creature and wondered if I was really hungry. In one particularly unfortunate case, I slit the throat too high, above the esophagus, and its head dropped off entirely, a breach of local butchering etiquette. In embarrassment I let go, and the headless body jumped up and ran, squawking with a grotesque gurgle, its blood shooting into the air, a gang of whooping children chasing after it. Yacouba teased me about this for a week, but I didn't mind. I always enjoyed his laughter, even when it was directed at me.

I finally received in the mail the means to carry out my writer's block sacrifice: a Xerox copy of a check my father had sent to the Sierra Club as part of my cure for writer's block. During the weeks of impatient waiting for the slow

international mails to deliver my father's response, I came to regret my translation of Akissi's request to make an offering to the Earth in the American way. Now I could finally sacrifice the necessary chicken.

On the next rest day we held a sacrifice under the giant kapok tree in the center of the village. With the village's four Masters of the Earth present, San Yao sprinkled water from a gourd onto a small sacrificial stone that was caked with layers of dried blood. Curious children huddled as close as the adults would allow them; then Wuru San cut the chicken's throat and, as he must have done thousands of times before, dripped its blood on the stone and over the exposed roots of the sacred tree. All the while he whispered prayers that Alma strained to hear as she took careful notes. I stood nearby, waiting for a magical transformation that didn't come, and I felt slightly irrelevant. After gutting the chicken, the old man handed it over to San Yao, who inspected the insides. He pointed out two small, round organs—the ovaries—and nodded approvingly: they were white, a sign that the spirits had accepted the sacrifice.

Following the ritual I still felt no immediate surge of empowerment, no irresistible force drawing me immediately to the typewriter. Yet as the days passed I did feel that with this public ritual I had crossed some uncharted boundary: even if the Beng may not have known exactly what troubled me, at least they understood that I'd needed to be cured. Now, as I worked at my typewriter in the mornings, a line of men walking to the fields, hoes in hand, shouted, "Kouadio! Come with us!" I pointed to my typewriter and called back, "This is my field." We laughed at what was becoming a common, daily joke. While I thought I had made my point, I was still interrupted again and again each day, as a farmer working in the fields would never be: somehow my metaphor of the typewriter as farm didn't really address what was important to the Beng.

At least the villagers' laughter did acknowledge that I was doing something at the typewriter. In turn, I was able to resist tagging along to the fields in hopes of gaining an ethnographic tidbit for Alma. I was beginning to realize that I need no longer be torn between my writing and helping Alma in her research: I could simply be at hand whenever she needed me and otherwise concentrate on writing. And so that long anticipated surge finally came, an interior release that was its own form of magic.

And just in time, for I had received a reply from that distant literary agent. She was still interested in representing my work and was intrigued by my current circumstances; I began revising a number of manuscripts from my story collection in progress to send to her. The rainy season was my secret ally: whenever those storm clouds approached, Alma and I scrambled to drag our table, chairs, and typewriters into our house before the first lashing wave of rain. Inside, I was able to work for hours without interruption, and this helped me make steady progress on a new, still untitled story that would not let me go. Because one of the main characters was a conceptual artist, I painstakingly—and with surprising pleasure—invented her creations: pairs of shoes nailed to a parquet board and arranged in a series of dance steps, the laces and straps lacquered into the poses of arms softly brushing together; a collage of her lover's sleeping figure, filled with paragraphs of his dreamy confessions when he talked in his sleep. I still couldn't imagine how I could write a story so remote from my new life. But one of the stories I was revising, though written before coming to Africa, now seemed oddly apt: a young woman viewed her entire life through a pair of binoculars, obsessively turning the knobs and trying to focus and draw closer what stubbornly remained distant.

At the same time that my imagination was happily renewed and repopulated, our village seemed surrounded by a startling profusion of forest life. After a heavy rain at night thousands of bats began a high-pitched chirping that resembled radio static, and in a nearby pond caused by the rains, innumerable frogs started their deep-throated cries. It was surely from the mosquitoes breeding in this stagnant water that I was stricken with my third attack of malaria—though it was mild, and I enjoyed my few days of enforced rest. Yet our encounters weren't always so relatively benign. One evening Alma walked across our compound unaware that she was approaching a large scorpion: our neighbor Yaa shouted a warning and leapt past her with a wooden club.

Soon after this incident, we were entertaining San Kofi, the chief's younger brother, in our compound at night. He was trying to teach us, without success, the various birdcalls of the forest when we heard the excited squawkings of distant chickens. "Kofi, maybe the chickens are asking you to go over there and teach them, too," I said, teasing him for his disappointed grimaces at our awkward attempts.

Then a gun went off. We all hurried in the direction of the sound, to a large circle of people, in the center of which was a spitting cobra, wounded and angry. A Jula migrant farmer had shot it when he'd caught it raiding his chicken coop. Everyone kept just out of range of the cobra's venom, which it could spit at a person's eyes with great accuracy. While the Jula man struggled to reload his ancient gun, our human circle continually changed shape as the wounded cobra slithered about. Finally the anticipated shot came, and after the snake's twisting death throes settled down, everyone approached its still body cautiously. Close up, I was startled by the elegance of its markings: broad orange stripes that contrasted sharply with the slate gray neck.

How chilling and typical, I thought, that something so dangerous could be so beautiful. But the fluid world of appearances among the Beng held more disturbing surprises. I had often noticed a young girl in Kosangbé who had an odd, bony forehead and a smile that never conveyed pleasure, and she seemed too old to be wearing only a child's loincloth. Her name was Amlakro—little Amla—and she was the younger sister of poor, benighted Afwé. Her eyes and movements awkward, wild, Amlakro often rushed randomly through the village, laughing while adults spoke, interrupting families while they ate together.

Once in passing we mentioned her to Amenan. "That girl is really a snake," she said, and proceeded to tell us that a pregnant woman was forbidden to eat anything while walking on a forest path to or from her fields, for should she violate this taboo she might inadvertently drop crumbs along the way. If a snake was nearby—and when was this not so?—it would eat the crumbs and become filled with an overwhelming desire for human food. The snake's soul would enter the woman's womb, possess her unborn child, and then be born into the human world. But this snake child, unused to four limbs and language, would forever struggle through its new existence. I listened, rapt. Amlakro had always seemed mildly retarded to me, and this must have been the Beng explanation for such a condition. But it was also a damned good story.

Amenan paused, then smiled and said, "There's a snake person now." A young man whom we had never seen before was making his way awkwardly across Amenan's compound. "He hasn't come by in months," she whispered.

We exchanged greetings with difficulty, finding it hard to understand his garbled words, and then the man simply stood there, his eyes roaming across the compound, settling on nothing. We waited for him to say something, but he raked his peculiar eyes past us—they were filled with such intense unhappiness—and then he began to walk away. We watched his halting movements until he was gone.

"He must have known we were talking about snake people," Amenan said with some satisfaction. I was shocked by her callousness—how could that man's sadness be invisible to her? Yet to her he wasn't a man, he was a snake.

Amenan continued, saying that one way to definitively identify—and permanently exile—a suspected snake person was to take one to a diviner, who would put a specially prepared dish of cooked yam, egg, and palm oil in a secluded spot in the forest. If the snake person refused the dish—which was understood by the Beng to be a favorite of snakes—that person's true humanity would be revealed and no further treatment would be offered.

But more often, Amenan claimed, the suspect would begin to devour the food ravenously. As he or she did so, the head and then the whole body would start spinning until it finally twisted itself into the snake that it really was and slithered off into the forest, never to be seen again. When Alma and I glanced at each other, Amenan asserted that many people, including her, had witnessed such an event. Seeing greater disbelief on our faces, she said—rather smugly, I thought—that should such a ritual occur during our stay, she would make sure we would attend, so we could take photos and document the transformation.

In Kosangbé I watched Amlakro more closely; it wasn't long before I saw her cousin pelt stones at her while shouting, "Snake! Snake!" She crouched away from the speeding stones but never fought back, and when hit she didn't allow herself to cry out. I remembered Amenan saying anyone could strike Amlakro capriciously because snakes "felt no pain." Amenan had also said that the girl would never marry. "Who would marry a snake?" she had said, laughing. Snake people might be a good story, I thought, but unfortunately for Amlakro it was a story she would have to live in for the rest of her life.

Alma: Public Airings

As appreciative as I was of Amenan's willingness to share Beng culture with me, especially in the face of the two cow fine presumably still operative in my own village, her account of a snake child's ritual transformation to a real snake shook my faith in her reliability as an informant: how could Amenan claim actually to have seen such an event?

We returned to Asagbé a few days later to see Ajua, a young Beng diviner who danced a Baulé-style possession dance that she had been taught by Akissi, the same diviner whom Philip had consulted for his writer's block. For her performance, Ajua cut a striking figure: she wore a white cotton robe that left her shoulders bare; a red felt hat perched archly on her head, topped by a thick fringe of white goat hair; and iron rings circled her ankles. Though it was known that she had a husband, I heard many men around me whispering that they would love to marry her. Next to Ajua stood two small wooden statues—one male, one female—themselves wrapped in white cloth. Ché Ba, a village sculptor, had just carved these statues for her, and she was dancing to thank him and also to give them their debut. The statues, Amenan explained to me as we waited for Ajua to begin, could be brought outside only for this dance. At all other times they must remain inside, in complete darkness; anyone who shone a light on them would be rewarded with terrible eye pains.

Now the statues seemed to be watching approvingly as their new owner paid them homage. Backed by a group of drummers, Ajua slowly began warming up for a quiet but intense solo dance as members of the large audience tossed her coins, which she then tossed to her female assistants. But before she had really abandoned herself to her dance, Ajua angrily called the drummers to a halt and left the dance circle while one of her assistants carried off the statues. I was baffled. Amenan explained that Ajua was disgusted because the drummers' interlocking patterns hadn't been properly coordinated: undoubtedly pleased with his work, Ché Ba had been drinking heavily for the past two days, and now as a drummer his shaky hand and awkward timing were ruining the dance.

At first this seemed to me an unnecessarily fussy reason to cancel the public performance. But when I considered the interruption from Ajua's perspective, I understood that the steady drumming enabled the diviner to transport herself to another state of consciousness, in which she could hear the forest spirits whispering their secrets; if the accompanying drumming didn't initiate this spiritual journey, then divination simply could not take place.

Surely Ajua could hear the revelations of forest spirits because she—and the others of her society—believed she could. As for Amenan's assertions to me about snake people, I didn't know what she might have seen during a snake-transformation ritual, but whether or not a person was "really" a snake or "really" turned back into one by eating certain food were not issues I wanted to prove. What interested me was that Amenan's claims were windows—however unverifiable—into her consciousness, itself shaped by her culture.

Our own village snake child, so used to being tormented, seemed satisfied these days at seeing her rebellious older sister, Afwé, as the object of family harangues. After three weeks of marital standoff, Afwé's conjugal drama was revived when Gaosu came to Kosangbé one evening to sleep with her. In the middle of the night Philip and I were awakened by her shouts, and, still sleepy, we hurried over to the scene. A small crowd was gathered outside the open door of her uncle's house. Inside, Afwé was screaming at her husband, who sat nearby, miserable but quiet for the moment.

Then her uncle Kofi came in and began threatening her. "Tomorrow I'm going to take you to the fields and just leave you there! Or maybe I'll tie you to a tree in the village!"

Afwé continued screaming above these threats. I felt doubly embarrassed: first for listening to this public airing of what my culture told me was a terribly private affair, then at my own dutiful efforts in taking notes on the scene. Finally her uncle threw a bucket of water over her; this surprised and quieted her, and the audience began to go home, muttering, "Now she'll sleep with him."

But the next morning nearly everyone in the village offered their own opinion of the previous night's outcome. Most—including Afwé—maintained that she had managed not to sleep with Gaosu, but others—including Gaosu himself—insisted that she had capitulated.

A few days later Afwé returned with resignation to Gaosu in Asagbé, but she soon came back to Kosangbé, this time with a black eye. And she discovered that in her home village she was no longer Afwé—everyone now called her Nakoyan, the new name given her by her Muslim husband. She accepted this change with surprising cheerfulness, unaware of the troubles that would soon face her.

I was disturbed by the inequities in the arranged marriage system. Women were not allowed to spurn the men who were offered to them, though in the case of strong, independent women such as Afwé—now Nakoyan—they often tried to. In contrast, men rarely rejected the women who were offered to them as arranged brides. But they were legally permitted to do so.

Karimu was now taking advantage of this privilege and was trying to break his engagement to Akissi, as negotiated by his half brother, Kona. Long ago he should have asked some of his kinswomen to ritually thank Akissi's relatives in other villages for having agreed to the match. But he was stalling noticeably in taking this next step, and finally he announced that he didn't want to marry Akissi at all.

The reason he offered was that on the night of their engagement, Akissi had proclaimed repeatedly that she did not wish to marry him. It didn't matter that she was ritually expected to say this, Karimu asserted—he knew that she'd really meant it. So Karimu's cancellation of the engagement was based on a technicality, which was suspicious enough for people to say that he must have other motivations. Whatever they were, he clearly resented his older half brother's attempt to force him to marry Akissi. Karimu was permitted by his culture to exit from his engagement, but this did not stop Kona from being furious. I wondered how he would exact his revenge.

One morning when Philip and I strolled through Kona's compound to offer the ritual greetings, we found him bent over a small stone mortar, grinding tobacco leaves into a fine powder. Without looking up from his task, Kona told me that the meeting with the elders that I had requested a few weeks ago would finally take place.

"When?" I asked.

"Tonight," he replied.

I thanked him and, immediately starting to plan my speech, walked through the rest of the village. As we gave morning greetings to everyone we met, I wondered uneasily if they knew about the planned meeting for that night and suspected what I wanted to speak about.

All that day I anticipated the coming meeting with some optimism but also much wariness. By now many people in the village had come to feel affection for Philip and me, and they offered us food and numerous other daily kindnesses; some felt indebted to us. Hadn't our help in the recent medical emergencies proved our good intentions? But the Beng were a small minority ethnic group, and they had managed to survive as a people only by resisting the incursions of outsiders. I couldn't expect them to overcome the value of secrecy that their culture had taught them to respect. Sometimes I even suspected that the sacrifice we had recently done for Philip's writer's block wasn't an authentic ritual. Why had I, a woman, been allowed to observe the village sacrifice when I knew—from Amenan—that women were forbidden to witness forest sacrifices? Was the entire ritual a sham, a performance done just to humor nosy, uninvited guests, or were there different levels of prohibition for certain sacrifices? I hadn't allowed myself to confess these worries to Philip.

I thought back to an article by the anthropologist Clifford Geertz that I had read in graduate school, one that had become a model for young fieldworkers. In it Geertz chronicled the pervasive suspicions he and his wife had endured on the part of their Balinese hosts, suspicions that reminded me of my own frustrations. One day early in their research the Geertzes were watching an illegal outdoor cockfight when the Indonesian police staged a raid. Everyone in the audience turned and ran, including the Geertzes, who took refuge in a courtyard of strangers. The fact that the foreign anthropologists had not shown their authorization papers to the police, but had instead appeared as vulnerable as everyone else, spread quickly throughout the community. "It was the turning point," Clifford Geertz wrote, "and we were quite literally 'in.' The whole village opened up to us." I longed for such a moment.

That night, with François serving as translator and Philip by my side whispering suggestions, I tried to present my best case to a small group of elders. As light from the kerosene lantern on the ground projected stark shadows on the faces of the men who listened to me, I tentatively introduced the subject by declaring formally that I had come to live in Kosangbé to record and thereby help preserve Beng culture, not undermine it.

"Yes," the chief said, "we now understand what your work is about."

"Well," I asked, speaking quickly rather than put off what needed to be said, "does that mean that no one will be fined two cows for talking to me about important matters?"

François's face was unreadable, and he was silent for a long moment before translating. Then there was another long pause, followed by San Yao's inevitable *"Dih a pey mi ni?"*—Who told you that?

"Oh, nobody . . ." I began. Someone laughed softly, and then there was further silence. Here was that familiar bind again.

"Well," Kona said finally, "nobody was ever fined two cows, and nobody will have to pay two cows in the future."

I wanted to feel relieved, but I didn't know if San Yao's silence was agreement. And Kona's words, I reflected as palm wine was brought out, were neither a confession nor a denial. Perhaps nobody had paid a fine because no one had yet told me about any of those mysterious "significant matters," and if any of the elders had admitted to the prohibition, would that itself be a violation of it, bringing with it the heavy penalty?

The brimming gourds were passed around again and again, though the elders seemed curiously quiet. But at the end of the meeting, to my surprise, Kona spontaneously launched into a detailed explanation of the family structure of the village, the first time he had spoken of such things. I scribbled excitedly in my notebook by flashlight while I asked questions through François. Yet why did I doubt that this was the moment I had been waiting for?

6

BEDAZZLED, BELEAGUERED

🌀　　🌀　　🌀

(MAY 1–JUNE 30, 1980)

Philip: Hairline Cracks

ALMA AND I WERE TYPING OUR WAY THROUGH A QUIET MORNING IN THE VILLAGE: WHILE I concocted a sanitized version of recent events for a letter to my anxious family, Alma tapped out a new batch of field notes from her notebook scrawl. I stopped in the middle of a sentence to watch a group of children speeding after each other in a neighboring compound—some game with its own intricate rules. I always admired their inventiveness. A few days ago a band of girls—none over five years old—had gathered for a cooking party, and they'd made a series of tiny hearths, using sticks for logs, rocks for boulders, and abandoned sardine tins for pots. After setting the sticks on fire, they'd placed little mud balls into the tins—imitation *foutou,* perhaps—and they'd poured in a bit of water for a nice, muddy sauce. All the while they'd giggled and screamed with pleasure—a sharp contrast to the silent concentration of their overworked mothers and older sisters.

Suddenly I saw an odd sight over Alma's shoulder: Fotié, a Jimini man married to a Beng woman in the village, was returning from the fields with Apu, his eight-year-old son, but they walked too quickly, in a strange lockstep, and Fotié's hand firmly grasped Apu's arm. Then I noticed the boy's face: a blank stare, his mouth slightly twisted. There was a rag tied around his knee.

"Alma, look," I said, gesturing to the two. As she turned to them they passed by the children, who immediately shouted, *"Mleh! Mleh!"*—the Beng word for snake. Then I understood. I ran into our house and grabbed our snakebite kit. When we had bought this in America I'd hoped we'd never have to use it; though I'd read the instructions over and over again, now they seemed a jumble in my memory. Alma snatched our book on West African snakes off the shelf. Together we hurried to Fotié's compound, but he met us on the way—coming to ask for help.

Apu lay on the ground, a small crowd hovering about him. I quickly made two incisions at the tiny fang points: a bloody X intersecting those two deadly dots.

"How did it happen?" Alma asked as I applied the suction cup to the wounds. From the conflicting rush of voices we managed to learn that Fotié and his son were hunting birds in the forest when Apu, barefoot, ran through the underbrush after a fallen bird and stepped on a snake.

Alma opened our book. "What did it look like?"

Fotié described it in Jimini to the children, who then pored through the pages with Alma. They stopped at a drawing of a snake with a triangular head, its thick body a multicolored pattern of rectangles and lozengelike spots.

"Oh god, a Gabon viper," Alma moaned, "the worst possible snake." She read aloud that the viper's venom cóntained both a blood and a neurological toxin. I looked down at Apu—his body was covered with a sheen of sweat and his eyes were dull and glazed. I told his parents we'd have to drive him to the infirmary immediately; secretly I feared he might die before we arrived.

His parents rushed about their compound, gathering whatever they felt they needed for the trip. Sété, a Jimini friend of the family, picked up Apu and carried him to the car, and they sat in the backseat together while we waited for the boy's parents to finish their frantic search. I couldn't understand their obsession with packing during these crucial moments—perhaps this trivial difficulty was easier to confront than their child's terrible condition.

"Here," his father said, pushing a child's *pagne* in the window.

"Here," said Mokro, his mother, handing us Apu's sandals.

But we couldn't calm them down and coax them into the car, so I started the engine and Alma told Fotié to follow us on the next bus that passed by Kosangbé. He nodded and watched, anguished, as we roared out of the village.

I drove faster than I'd ever driven before down that familiar road, barely slowing for curves or the gaping trenches eroded by the rains, hoping we wouldn't have one of our all-too-frequent flat tires or blowouts. Alma leaned over the backseat every few minutes, easing the tourniquet, then tightening it again, making sure the suction cup was in place. Apu stared off blankly, but before we were halfway to M'Bahiakro, his eyes started to close. Alma was afraid he might be going into a coma. "Don't let them close, keep him awake!" she urged Sété.

He shook Apu. "What's your name! What's your name!" he kept repeating.

"Apu," the boy managed to mumble, his eyes now open.

But almost immediately his lids lowered again, and again Sété shouted, "What's your name!"

This desperate quiz continued as I sped into M'Bahiakro. When we arrived at the infirmary Sété and I quickly hauled Apu's limp body into the main building. Immediately the staff led us to a bed. The boy looked barely alive. "I'll go fetch his sister," Sété said, "she lives in town."

The head nurse, who wore the deep scarification lines of the Ando people cut across his forehead and cheeks, entered the room and asked what happened.

"This child has been bitten by a Gabon viper," Alma said. "He needs snake serum immediately."

"But we have none here."

"*None?*"

"No, we can't afford to stock it. But the pharmacy in town has serum. Here," he said, scrawling a quick note, "take this."

Alma and I drove off to the nearest pharmacy: a small, weather-worn wooden building a few blocks away. When we arrived the double doors were shut and locked, and we slammed on them until they opened.

It was the pharmacist's wife. "My husband isn't here," she said, annoyed by our banging but trying to be polite.

Alma handed her the nurse's note. "We need to buy serum—a boy is dying."

"I'm sorry," she said, her face suddenly filled with regret. "The door to the refrigerator is locked. Only my husband has the key."

"Where is he?" I asked. "We'll go get him."

"I'm sorry," she repeated, clearly distressed, "I don't know where he is."

We thanked the woman and left, but we knew that we couldn't afford to search through the neighborhood for the pharmacist. How much time did Apu have left? "We have to go to Lisa's," I said, "and get our own serum."

Once again we raced down the streets of M'Bahiakro, past Jula traders with their stacks of *pagne* material, past market women sitting beside large bowls of *attieké* and fried fish.

"What if Lisa's not in?" Alma asked. Considering our luck so far, we knew this possibility wasn't out of the question. Alma and I went through a desperate scenario: we'd shatter the front door's glass pane, reach in through the iron grill for the latch, and somehow force open the door.

Our planned break-in wasn't necessary. Lisa's moped leaned against the front stairs, her door open for any breeze. We ran inside, surprising Lisa, who pushed back from the table and her class preparations.

"Snake serum!" I managed to blurt out, heading for her refrigerator.

"It's in the back, behind the butter," she said. "What happened?"

I had the vial. I turned and ran out the door.

Following me, Alma called back breathlessly, "A boy, a snake, we'll tell you later!"

From Lisa's, I sped down a shortcut to the infirmary, wondering if Apu was still alive. All our assumptions had been wrong—that the infirmary would have serum, that the pharmacy would be open. If only we'd gone straight to Lisa's, we wouldn't have wasted so much time.

Apu's sister Yengé was already at his bedside. Her dark round face turned to us expectantly, and I held up the large vial of serum. The head nurse opened it swiftly and prepared the syringe. Saying that Apu had little time left to live, he injected the serum directly into a vein in the boy's arm, then injected the rest into a vein in his other arm.

We waited for some sign from Apu's still body. Suddenly his eyes opened, as if he'd been awakened abruptly. A surge of relief swept through us all. Yengé moaned happily, Sété grinned, Alma and I shook hands with everyone. Then the nurse took over, shooing us out of the room.

In the infirmary courtyard Sété decided to wait for Apu's parents to arrive, while Yengé asked us to accompany her to her uncle's shop with the good news. Her uncle, Kouadio Honoré, had moved from our village years ago and was now a successful tailor. He liked to wear his success— whenever he returned to the village he sported gaudy, expensive outfits with lots of embroidered filigree. In the same grandiose spirit, he was now having a house built in Kosangbé for his extended family: a spacious mud brick house, cemented inside and out, with a tin roof and a large front porch. There was even a room inside for bathing, supplied with its own drainage system. Though not yet completed, this house was considered the finest in Kosangbé; a few village trials had already been held on the front porch.

We all drove to Honoré's small tailor shop on the edge of the M'Bahiakro *marché*. Inside, Honoré held court behind his foot-powered sewing machine as his assistants snipped fabric to his instructions. Everything stopped when we entered, and Yengé described what happened to Apu. Honoré nodded and punctuated his niece's speech with the usual Beng *eh*s, then he stood and shook our hands, thanking us formally for helping his nephew. A tailor of men's fashions, Honoré offered to make me a suit in the local style. I accepted, pleased that we were entering into another Beng relationship of favors and obligations.

From Honoré's shop we returned to Lisa, giving her both an explanation for our mad dash through her house and thanks for her months of baby-sitting our serum. Lisa loved to listen to our tales of the village—in a way, we were a form of home entertainment for her—and she offered us lunch. Famished, we tore into her specialty: a thick sauce made from dried okra powder, ladled over rice and dried fish. Often, when Alma and I dropped by, we came with fresh fish or recently butchered meat from the *marché*: our own American version of favors and obligations.

On the drive back to Kosangbé Alma and I, still shaken, mulled over the morning's drama again and again. As we spoke, a logging truck roared by from the other direction; suddenly we heard a sharp report, and our windshield blossomed with hairline cracks. We both cried out. Unable to see, I stopped the car, while behind us the truck disappeared around a corner. A small stone on the road must have careened off one of the truck's tires, and the result faced us: our windshield was now a crazy pattern of cracks. I groaned and rested my head against the steering wheel. This seemed like an inappropriate reward for our good deed.

"What are we going to do?" Alma gasped.

"Well, we'll have to replace it, that's for sure. Hello, Bouaké."

"Not again! These car repairs are taking up too much time—can't we wait just a bit?"

I examined the windshield—it was still in place, though the view was what an insect with a compound eye might see if it could drive. We could get around well enough if we drove slowly. "Sure," I replied, "I'm in no rush to leave the village."

I understood Alma's frustration. Didadi was slowly succumbing to the hazardous roads: in the past few months the chassis had cracked and we'd had it soldered at a makeshift garage in M'Bahiakro; the engine had failed from the accumulating dust, and we'd had it air- and water-blasted; and we'd gone through more tires than we cared to count. Each disaster took us away from the village. Yet we'd also helped save lives with our car—how could we do without it?

The last miles of our return to Kosangbé were far different from our headlong rush in the morning: we crept along the road, taking some of the deeper ruts as carefully as possible, and the greenery of the forest shifted strangely through the web of cracks.

When we arrived back at our compound in the village, we stared at our desk. It was as if we hadn't been gone for hours; the pages were still in the typewriter's rollers, my coffee cup was still half-full. Perhaps if we sat down on our chairs, the morning might start over again and conform to our initial expectation of a lazy, quiet day. But there was little time to contemplate such tricks. Already villagers were greeting us, ready with questions, and when we told our story more and more people came by to thank us for helping save Apu's life. Alma and I basked in our neighbors' praise, yet we felt increasingly embarrassed by so much gratitude; we seemed to have become, however inadvertently, professional rescuers.

Yacouba stayed to chat, as he often did now. I had envied Alma's relationship with Amenan; now I enjoyed my own new friendship. He and I liked to tease each other. "What's the name of this? And this?" he liked to ask me in rapid-fire fashion, knowing I lagged behind Alma in Beng, trying to expand my vocabulary and trip me up at the same time. When I mangled his name in revenge, pretending I'd never pronounced it before, he laughed his easy laugh.

With friendship came confidences, and I now knew of the troubles in Yacouba's life. His father was a drunkard and so, in this extremely traditional animist village, Yacouba had converted to Islam because it forbade alcohol. Though there were a few other Muslim converts in Kosangbé, Yacouba had chosen to live in the Jula quarter, apart from his relatives. Even his marriage history was atypical. He hadn't officially married his first wife, Dongi, since theirs was a "love match" not sanctioned by his family. A few years later his father arranged a marriage with Sramatan, a young woman in Yacouba's matriclan, and Yacouba had given in to his parents' pressure. Yet Dongi, first married to Yacouba, considered herself the senior co-wife, while Sramatan, his "official" wife, was certain that *she* was senior, and the two women squabbled frequently. They were at peace now, but my friend wondered how long this would last.

Before long our cracked windshield caved in—during a short drive to another village, a multitude of tiny pieces of glass scattered over the dashboard, the front seat, our laps. Back in Kosangbé I spread a sheet of plastic over the front of the car in case of rain, but I knew we wouldn't be able to put off the trip to Bouaké much longer.

The next day a diviner from the Baulé region came to Kosangbé, offering consultations to any interested villagers. He stayed in the house Kouadio Honoré was building, as a guest of Ché Kofi, Honoré's older brother. Ready for any opportunity to enter into the belief system, Alma and I decided to ask the diviner why our windshield had shattered.

Ché Kofi and Na Kouadio, the diviner, were huddled together in a room that was nearly empty except for a straw mattress and a burlap bag of the diviner's belongings, and the newly cemented walls and floor were shockingly bright in the lamplight. Na Kouadio had a wild look about him. His hair slightly unkempt and his staring eyes bulging, he seemed like an eerie, animated version of the small statue that stood beside him; it too had bulging eyes, and its hands reached out so they could hold an egg offered by a supplicant.

"He's very good," Ché Kofi confided, clearly amazed at Na Kouadio's secret knowledge. "Before you came he told me about something that happened to me long ago, something I've never told anyone." Shaking his head, Ché Kofi kept repeating, "I've never told anyone."

I hurried back to our compound for an egg. When I returned Alma asked our question, and Ché Kofi added another: Why had a snake bitten his nephew Apu?

We placed the egg in the statue's hands. The diviner took a whip of leather thongs, to which were attached various charms: a gold weight, a bone, part of an animal horn. Then he slapped the whip against an animal skin that lay on the floor before him, and we sat silently, waiting.

Finally he spoke in Baulé to Ché Kofi, who then translated for us. "He says that Apu was bitten because his father is a Jimini and hasn't yet sacrificed a chicken to the Earth of our village. And your windshield was broken because you haven't offered a chicken sacrifice to the chief as a sign of respect."

This last explanation seemed a bit unfair—Alma and I hadn't known such a sacrifice was expected of us, so why should we have been punished? Still, we agreed readily to the sacrifice, pleased with this opportunity to make a peace offering to San Yao. Na Kouadio recommended the next rest day, five days off.

We couldn't put off repairing our shattered windshield any longer, particularly if we didn't want to miss the date set for our sacrifice to the chief, so the next morning we drove to Bouaké, the wind in our faces. While there, we also bought *two* new vials of snake serum: one for Lisa's refrigerator, another for our house, to be kept sealed in a mason jar under cool water at the bottom of a ceramic pot—our own improvised cooling system. Apu's accident had sobered us.

Our return was uneventful until we passed M'Bahiakro and turned onto the long dirt road leading to the Beng area. Dark storm clouds gathered behind us, and a strong wind swept through the forest trees.

"This looks nasty. Maybe we should have stayed over at Lisa's tonight," I said, staring anxiously at the rearview mirror.

"*Please,* no," Alma replied, "we've already wasted enough time. It's just a rainstorm."

"You're probably right," I said, gunning the engine. But before long the storm caught up with us, rain lashing over the car so brutally that I had to slow to a crawl.

"My god, look!" Alma cried out. Through the largely ineffective windshield wipers I saw a tree lying across the road ahead of us: how terrifying that the huge trees of the forest could be toppled so easily. The trunk seemed to block our way, but as I edged Didadi closer I saw there was just enough space to skirt around it.

"I was definitely *wrong,*" Alma moaned. "Let's turn back to Lisa's."

"Well, we're more than halfway to Bengland," I said. "Who knows what's fallen behind us? I think we should keep going."

With Alma's assent, I edged past the twisted branches. But less than a mile later we saw another tree lying on the road and, a few hundred yards off, yet another. We were able to pass both, but we grew increasingly frightened of what might face us ahead, and the road was so flooded that I worried that we might get stuck in the mud. The trees of the forest swayed alarmingly in the terrible wind—what if one tumbled down on us? As I drove, Alma tried to peer out every window through the insistent sheets of rain, on the lookout for falling trees.

Slowly we neared home—by now I had virtually memorized this road, and I knew we weren't far from a long rise of a hill that crested just before Bongalo, the first Beng village. But as we turned a corner, there was an enormous kapok tree, its overturned trunk taller than our car, completely blocking the way. We were less than a quarter of a mile from Bengland.

"Now *I* was definitely wrong," I said.

"Oh, we were so close. What should we do?"

We didn't dare venture into the storm and slog through the mud to Bongalo, leaving Didadi exposed to another falling tree, and we certainly couldn't stay in the car ourselves, hoping for eventual rescue from the M'Bahiakro road crew: our vial of snake serum would spoil. Our best choice was to return along the route we'd come and hope that no other trees had fallen to block our way to M'Bahiakro.

So we turned around to face more muddy miles of storm, repeating our journey through a rainswept landscape of destruction. Eventually we arrived safely in M'Bahiakro, yet I felt little relief: twice now, in trying to return to Bengland, we had met with disaster. What further calamity might await us?

Alma: Skirting Disaster

The morning brought clear skies, and we returned to the village, passing the evidence of yesterday's frightening devastation: branches and small trees were strewn about at virtually every turn, and the huge tree that had barricaded our way was now shoved to the side of the road, courtesy of the M'Bahiakro road crew. In Kosangbé we settled in quickly, and the next morning we prepared to sacrifice our chicken to the chief. Philip tied the white hen's feet together to make a neat bundle he could carry across the village. She squawked and flapped her wings ineffectually as we waited for Yacouba, who had agreed to translate for us.

Yacouba approached slowly, his usual jaunty gait gone. "There's bad news in Bongalo," he said quietly after we exchanged greetings. "A woman named Aya just died in childbirth."

I gasped, and Philip's face distorted with concern. Turning to me, Yacouba added, "You should go to the funeral, there'll be a special women's dance that only women can see."

"Thank you for telling me," I managed to whisper. I knew few people in Bongalo and doubted I'd be allowed to watch the dance, yet with my interest in women's lives, how could I stay home? But first we had that sacrifice to offer. In silence we three walked across the village to the chief's compound. His *pagne* wrapped around him toga style, the chief nodded solemnly when we greeted him. Then he called over his aged father, Wuru San, who sat on a small stool on the other side of the courtyard. The old man leaned on his crooked mahogany cane, rose with some difficulty, and accompanied us to the nearby shade of the lush kapok tree. There, Ali Kouakou—the village drunk—was waiting for us, looking rather dapper in a pressed black pants suit.

Wuru San seemed to take on new life as he presided over the ceremony, huskily intoning his prayers over the hen. Then he gave the doomed fowl to his son, who slit its neck and dripped the flowing blood over the same stone that had received the blood of our last sacrifice. I was relieved: Philip's sacrifice for writer's block *had* been authentic, as Amenan had assured me. I glanced at the chief. I hoped this ritual might somehow appease his concerns about us, but as usual his face betrayed nothing. He handed the dead bird to Ali Kouakou, who'd once been passed over as village chief. Today he singed off the feathers from our sacrificed chicken, then carved it up. Everyone received a piece—even San Yao's four-year-old granddaughter, Madeleine, bounded off with the liver and the intestines. However, I kept thinking of the woman who had died in labor. Had she left behind other children or her own mother? And what about others who might be pregnant now? How panicked the news of Aya's death must make them.

When I arrived in Bongalo, I saw only men near the roadside. I wandered through the village until facing me was a small dancing circle of virtually nude, pregnant women. Their enormous bellies, bared for women's eyes alone, rose and fell slowly, over a strip of bark cloth worn as underwear—what the French call a *cache-sexe*. They alternately crouched low to beat their short rhythm sticks on the ground, then straightened up one by one and circled around the dusty plaza. From Amenan I knew that an expectant mother ordinarily concealed her breasts for fear that another woman—perhaps barren and jealous—might bewitch her, spoiling her milk. Once born, the infant would quickly die. Were these women risking their babies' lives to engage in this dance? Or perhaps they believed that not even the witches were callous enough to contemplate sorcery on such a day.

I heard loud wailing and turned to see an older woman in the center of a group of women of her age: neither pregnant nor dancing, they simply stood in place, keening. "The one in the middle is Aya's mother," someone standing nearby whispered to me. As she wailed, arms outstretched, face turned to the sky, her sadness seemed to be groping for a way both to express and to contain itself. Gently her companions encircled her and inched their way to the room housing the cadaver.

Inside her daughter's kitchen, the unfortunate woman fell to her hands and knees and began crawling around the room, crawling and wailing, crawling and wailing, until one of her companions quietly led her away. Meanwhile another woman went outside with the three large stones that Aya had used for her hearth and there started up a fire. She placed a large iron pot over the flames and heated some water. I didn't know what she planned to do with the hot water; all I saw in the pot was an empty calabash, bobbing up and down like a boat whose sailors had drowned.

I felt everyone's grief, but, neither a mother nor a Beng, I didn't know why it took the shape it did. When the dancers forbade me to take photos, I knew that this was not a day to pretend that I was, or could be, one of them. Soon I drove back to Kosangbé, filled with the vision of the dancing women's bulging bellies, filled with grief-laden life, heaving slowly above bark-cloth belts, in rhythm to their sticks clacking mournfully on the dusty ground. Exhausted, I turned in early to bed.

That night Philip and I were awakened by screams. Half dreaming, I thought I was back in Bongalo, Aya's mother wailing her sorrow, and the painful memory roused me. Philip and I dressed and hurried out anxiously. We recognized the voice: it was Nakoyan's.

We followed the sound of her cries. Already there was a small gathering

outside the house in her family's compound. From inside a room came the howls of a woman in near hysteria.

"What could they be doing to Nakoyan now?" I asked Philip.

"Poor thing," he said, "god only knows."

Nakoyan's aunt Asaw joined us. "That little black cunt," she said, "she's really rotten. She should just sleep with her husband and that would be the end of that."

"But she says she doesn't like him," I couldn't help but say.

"That's not why you marry someone," Asaw snapped back. "Gaosu is her cousin, he's in the family. He's the perfect man for her to marry. Why doesn't Nakoyan see that?"

I liked Asaw and couldn't help feeling disappointment at her elevation of duty over love. The romantic in me wasn't living up to the demands of cultural relativity that had originally attracted me to my discipline. The moral ground of anthropology never seemed shakier.

The screams started up again. "What are they doing in there?" I asked, dreading the answer.

"They're forcing her to sleep with Gaosu," Asaw said.

Philip's shocked face must have reflected my own. I felt the urge to vomit, faint, flee, anything to distance myself from this news, these screams, this procrustean system of marriage that brooked no dissent.

"Who's forcing her?" I made myself ask.

"Andama and some other relatives of hers," she answered brusquely.

A fresh batch of cries pierced the starry night. The door opened and Ché Kofi—Asaw's husband—came out, cursing and sweating. Those around us flocked to the door and peeked into the room. I forced myself to look at that which I dreaded most.

On an iron bed lay Nakoyan on her back, naked and wriggling like a trapped antelope, both defiant and defeated, her left leg chained to a nearby window bar, her hands tied behind her back with the black strips of rubber I'd seen men use to secure packages on their bicycles. Screaming, she was trying with all her force to break free of her bonds. The other men in the room struggled to hold down her one free leg as Gaosu, naked himself, approached her.

I wanted to run in and unknot those rubber strips, release Nakoyan's hands, and carry her out of the room. But before I could move, Ché Kofi went back inside and shut the door.

"Philip," I said, "shouldn't we drive down to M'Bahiakro to tell the police?" Surely rape was illegal in this country, and the whole gang—rapist, accomplices, and approving onlookers—would be punished. Nakoyan would be allowed to marry the man of her choice.

Before Philip could reply, Nakoyan's mother and older sister began to curse her. "She should just marry him," the old woman hissed, her face a knot of fury, "otherwise she should leave the village. If she finds good luck or bad somewhere else, that'll be her affair. Meanwhile, if I die, she'll hear about it and she'll die, too!"

Was this the sweet, meek woman whom Philip and I greeted every day on our morning rounds—the woman who frequently clasped my hands to her chest, who once had led me into her house to show me some herbal remedies for her worsening cataracts? Hearing Nakoyan's own mother condemn her, I felt less sure of my position.

In any case, even if Philip and I did inform the police of the rape, the gendarmes might just shrug off the event as local village custom and laugh at our intrusion. Nor was I confident that Nakoyan herself would be grateful to me for interfering. Just last week Gaosu had told me that his father had consulted the diviner Lamine, who had pronounced that Nakoyan was possessed by a male spirit of her clan who was especially jealous of human rivals: if the spirit-husband were propitiated with a chicken sacrifice, he would release Nakoyan to Gaosu. Had she accepted this explanation? If so, perhaps tonight's rape was also an exorcism. Contemplating such questions—unanswerable for the moment—sapped my will to take action. I turned to Philip and said, "I hate to say it, but I think we have to stay."

Philip nodded unhappily, unwilling to interfere in this crucial decision in my fieldwork. I forced myself to take out my notebook.

Now every few minutes another man—Nakoyan's great-uncle Andama, her cousin Kwamé, her would-be husband, Gaosu—entered or exited the room, and the door was left slightly ajar, inviting all those gathered outside to peer inside once again. Philip and I squatted on the ground, miserable, waiting for the ordeal to end.

Across the courtyard, Lanzé Afwé stood alone. A sensitive and delicate older woman who spoke very deliberately, with an obvious love for her language, Lanzé Afwé seemed to me a paragon of reasonableness. I asked her what she thought.

"Nakoyan should just sleep with Gaosu of her own free will," she said, shaking her head, "without having to be tied up."

At least she wasn't urging the men to beat Nakoyan even more brutally. But enmeshed as she was in her culture, even Lanzé Afwé didn't feel that Nakoyan should be permitted to renounce this marriage.

Finally all the men stumbled out, wiping sweat off their foreheads and muttering, but Nakoyan remained inside. The door was now fully open, but no one around me thought to enter. After handing my notebook to Philip, I ventured in. Nakoyan was still tied down, still writhing. I tried to say something soothing—something to let her know I was on her side—but her movements were so wild that I doubted she even saw me.

I left the room. A few men reentered, untied Nakoyan, and brought her outside to wash in the bathhouse. Then, to my dismay, they led her back into the room and tied her up again. In went Gaosu, and once again the door shut firmly. We heard Nakoyan whining feebly. But conversation was now the men's aim.

"Why are you putting up such a fuss?" I heard Ché Kofi ask.

"A spirit is forcing me," Nakoyan answered, "he's bad, he's rotten, no good." She concluded in a voice that I supposed must be ironic, "Come tie me up again, come hit me."

The men had no rejoinder to this, and after untying Nakoyan, they left the room, not bothering to close the door. But Nakoyan remained in bed, staring at a private vision. Her cousin Kwamé, a young man of about twenty who was serving in the Ivoirian army, came out and caught sight of us. A quick look of shame, I thought, crossed his face, then he sauntered over to Philip.

"Hey, Kouadio, are you here, too?"

"Yes," Philip said, restraining himself. I sensed that Kwamé was testing to see if we revealed any disapproval of what we had just witnessed.

"Well, it's late, eh?" Kwamé said with a sigh. "Let's all go to bed."

"Ah-heh," we agreed.

Everyone wandered off to their own houses, with their own thoughts of what they had just witnessed. As for Philip and me, we spent much of the hot night awake, deeply disturbed. Intellectually I could justify my reaction—why was I left feeling confused and exhausted? I suspected my decision not to go to the police was motivated more by fear than ethics: denouncing the villagers might well have ended my fieldwork—an extreme price I wasn't willing to pay. I thought back to the photos of maimed peasants and their children I'd seen during the Vietnam War and remembered questioning the moral stance of the photographers who'd taken those pictures without intervening in the atrocities occurring a few feet from their cameras. Was tonight any different—would my younger self endorse my not having interfered, could she endorse the triumph of the anthropologist in me?

In the morning I found Nakoyan aimlessly wandering the village, eyes puffy, her short hair untressed. Hoping she sensed my sympathy, I greeted her, received her mechanical response, and then I asked why she continued to resist Gaosu.

"A spirit possessed me," she explained in a monotone, as if merely describing a day of work in the fields.

"Ah-heh," I said. If Nakoyan was satisfied with the diviner's explanation, I didn't want to question her belief—at the very least, the story enabled her to

save face. She turned to leave, explaining she had to help her mother cook lunch.

Later I noticed Gaosu walking through our *quartier;* he was headed toward our compound. I felt an urge to turn away, then another to shout at him for his odious performance the night before. But I did neither—I resolved to interview him as I would anyone else. Gaosu himself began the conversation.

"You know, Amwé," he declared unhappily, "I wish Nakoyan would just go away. I already have a wife and children, what do I need her for? She's just trouble."

This was news indeed: did Gaosu truly believe his words, or was he just eager to vindicate himself? "What about last night?" I asked.

"I didn't want to do that," he said quietly, "I was *forced* to. It's my father who asked me to marry Nakoyan, who made all the arrangements, so I have to go through with it for him. How can I refuse?" He clapped his hands once, then opened them, palms up, to show his helplessness.

Gaosu's claim unsettled me. While I still loathed him for what he'd done, I understood that he was suffering, too: like Nakoyan, he'd been born into a system that dictated to young people whom they must marry. Gaosu was certainly a villain; but, much as it pained me to admit it, he was also a victim.

"Anyway," he concluded wearily, "once we do a sacrifice to the spirit, I think she'll agree to sleep with me on her own."

"Mm-hmm," I said, quite sure that he would be proven wrong. Then I returned to the house to take care of Philip, who'd awakened that morning with a fever and the first signs of a skin fungus that would soon dot his chest and face.

The next evening I paid a visit to Asaw and her husband—those enthusiastic supporters of their niece's rape. They had similar, intense personalities: both quick to laugh and quick to anger. Once Asaw and I had spent a giggly afternoon together with our neighbor Komena Kouassikro, the World War II veteran, who had told us bawdy stories that Asaw had tried to explain to me. But when Kouassikro had asked me if I enjoyed sex and I'd feigned incomprehension, Asaw had protected me from my embarrassment and immediately changed the subject.

In their courtyard I found Ché Kofi sitting on a stool, sharpening the blunt edge of his hoe. We exchanged greetings, and I asked after his wife.

"She's gone to greet people," he said. "She should be back soon—do you need her?"

"I wanted to ask her . . ." But I stopped, vocabulary failing me: how to say "gender roles" and "male dominance" in Beng?

Sensing my frustration, Ché Kofi rescued me. "Why don't you ask me?" "Well, okay," I said hesitantly; then I began, "Can you tell me which things belong to men and which belong to women?"

"Sure," he said, chuckling. He noticed a kola nut lying on the ground nearby and split it open, offering me half. "We could start with these. Men own kola nut trees, and also coffee trees, cocoa trees, and cotton plants."

These were all the cash crops of the Beng—I wondered how women made money.

"Men own manioc," Ché Kofi continued, "and all the fruit trees: banana trees, palm nut trees, mango trees, and orange trees."

"Wait a minute," I heard behind us—Asaw had entered the courtyard. "Women own orange trees, too!" she said, winking at me.

"Orange trees? *Mm-mm,*" said her husband. Then he looked over at me, smiled, and said, "She's lying."

"Hah! Not only that," Asaw added, "women can own banana trees, palm nut trees, and mango trees, too. They can even own manioc plants! And women own the kitchen, and everything in it—pots, fire, water, even matches."

For the rest of the list that we constructed, Ché Kofi and Asaw agreed with each other—no more teasing dissensions. I wondered if their marriage had been arranged. If it had been, could it have begun on as stormy a footing as Nakoyan and Gaosu's?

It was a workday, and Kosangbé was almost deserted. At the kapok tree I found old Wuru San sitting on a low stool, head on hand, hand on cane, snoring lightly.

"Amwé, is that you?" the chief's old father suddenly asked, squinting through the sun and his cataract-glazed eyes.

"Yes, *Duti,* it's me," I said, using the Jula term for "chief" I'd heard others call him. "Maybe we can talk some?"

"Ngwo blo"—I'm here—he said woefully.

But my Beng was still so shaky, I might have trouble understanding the long, involved reminiscing of an old man. Discouraged, I was about to turn away when I noticed a young man sharpening a knife against a stone in a neighboring courtyard. It was Bandé, who knew some French—better yet, he was related to Wuru San. He agreed to serve as pro tem interpreter.

Speaking through Bandé, I said, "You've lived a long time. I thought you could tell me some stories from long ago, when you were young."

"When I was a boy," Wuru San began, "the *blofwés"*—white people—"had just come. They didn't allow anyone to sit around—even the small children had to work all day in the fields."

He smacked his lips lightly, muttering, *"Mh, mh, mh,"* then continued, "If anyone was caught in the village by the *blofwés,* three men would come right away: one to hold down his arms, one to hold down his legs, and a third to beat his back and chest, like this"—Wuru San bent over, reached around toward his back, and slapped himself—"until he was almost crippled." He paused a moment, then resumed, "All the roads around here were made by manual labor, from Dabakala to Bouaké and up to Ferkessédougou. Even the tallest trees were chopped down with machetes. We worked thirty days, then we'd be replaced by a new crew. We were supposed to rest for a month, but we just walked all the way back to our villages and worked in the fields, or hunted. But there wasn't enough time to do all the work that needed to be done—it was a time of hunger."

"Duti, who did the work on the roads?" I asked.

"Everyone!" he said. "Young girls fetched sand to fill up the holes; women and older girls tapped the sand in place with flat, wooden tapping sticks. Some boys and men were taken to other parts of the country to work. Me, I spent two years at Dabou, building the roads. I already had two wives and two sons, but I was forced to leave my family to do the *blofwés'* work." He stopped and looked at me intently. What could he be thinking when he saw me? Then he went on: "While we were building their roads, they also made us pay them tribute. We had to grow cotton and palm nuts in special fields for the *blofwés,* and every few months we had to walk to M'Bahiakro to bring them the crops, which we carried on our heads." He sighed. "They really made us work." Then he fell silent.

"Duti," I began, "thank you for telling all this to me. I had no idea that you had to do so much for the *blofwés.* Truly, it was a hard time." In speaking of the *blofwés,* I meant to distance myself from the contemptible French colonialists, but I couldn't help realizing the irony of my position: like it or not, I too was a *blofwé.*

"Amwé," the old chief concluded, "we still worry that forced labor will come back one day."

Later that morning I drove to Asagbé to work with Amenan under her coffee trees. I found her nursing little Amwé and brushing flies from the baby's face. Suddenly Amwé turned away from the nipple and began wailing.

"What's the matter?" I asked. "Is she still hungry?"

"No, it's not that," Amenan said. "She wants her necklace."

Taken aback, I asked, "Which necklace?"

"A very special necklace with a lot of things on it," Amenan said. "I took her to Lamine to find out why she was crying so much."

"Who's Lamine?"

"You forget? He's the diviner who said Nakoyan was being possessed. . . ."

"Oh, yes!" I said, embarrassed at my bad memory.

"Anyway," Amenan continued, "Lamine said there are a lot of things that Amwé longs for, and she'll keep crying until she gets them." She laughed. "It's going to cost me!"

"But how can Lamine know what her desires are?" I asked. "She's only a baby. . . ."

"Babies are like spirits, so diviners can talk to them," Amenan explained. "After Lamine threw his cowrie shells, he heard Amwé telling him what she wants: a white dress; a copper ring put on the waist beads that she wears; and a silver ring put on her necklace. Plus she wants a new necklace with two small animal horns hanging from it, and inside the horns must be a certain kind of black leaf; some pieces of bark from two trees that have been blown toward each other by the wind and attached to one another; and the wing feathers of the *pelo* bird, which lives in the savanna but is very rare—it'll be a while before I can find one of those. But until Amwé gets all these, she won't stop crying."

Amenan was now rocking her daughter in her arms. "Also, she doesn't like the small *kpesekpese* chili peppers we cook with—I'll have to stop eating those as long as I'm nursing." I knew this would be a sacrifice: Amenan liked spicy food.

"Plus, she doesn't want to be touched by women who are menstruating," Amenan continued. "Whenever I have my period, I'll have to give her ten CFAs to apologize for touching her."

"And what will she do with the money?" I asked with a slight smile.

"I'll put it aside for her," Amenan answered, "and when there's enough, I'll buy her something nice with it—maybe some new clothes."

I looked in amazement at the chubby, two-month-old infant facing me and was struck by the strength of her desires—and by her mother's efforts to understand them. Back home the only explanations I'd ever heard for baby cries were hunger and gas pains. Here babies were listened to far more attentively than I had imagined possible.

"At least she doesn't have *galee*," Amenan said, interrupting my reverie. "Then she wouldn't be crying, she'd just have no energy at all."

"That sounds terrible," I said. "How does a baby get it?"

"In the womb," Amenan explained. "If a woman goes to a funeral when she is pregnant, *galee* might catch the fetus. As soon as the baby's born, it doesn't want to do anything, even nurse. It just lies there."

"A bit like a . . . corpse!" I mused aloud, suddenly remembering the Beng word: *galee*.

"Older children can have corpse, too," Amenan continued, "if a mother takes her children to a funeral and they get close to the cadaver."

Suddenly I recalled Jean's worries during that Kosangbé funeral back in December. "Can adults catch *galee?*" I asked.

"They're not as vulnerable as children are, but it *can* catch them," she said. "That's why I always protect myself when I go to a funeral."

"Ah, bon?" I said.

"If you bring along a short branch from a lemon tree and chew on it during the funeral," Amenan explained, "you should be safe. Or you can just tie up a whole lemon into the waistline of your skirt," she said. Then she looked at me: I was wearing pants. "Or put a whole lemon in your pocket," she added.

So that was why I'd smelled lemons all around me that night in the corpse room in Kosangbé! And it was fear of corpse that made Jean refuse to approach the cadaver: perhaps because he was a Muslim, Jean was unwilling to use lemons as a magical talisman—but as a Beng he still felt vulnerable. Even worse, because of the two cow fine, Jean couldn't tell me the reason for his fears.

Amenan interrupted my rueful thoughts. "I forgot to mention that dead dogs can also give people corpse," she was saying.

"Oh?" I said. "Why is that?"

"It's because dogs are like people," she said. "That's why we never eat them." Then she thought for a moment. "Well, there is *one* time when a dog is eaten," she said. "If a woman dies in childbirth, a powerful healer kills a dog and eats it, as part of the funeral."

I thought of the funeral dance I had seen in Bongalo only three days ago. That healer must have been in the village, eating his dog feast—but like so much that happened that day, I'd missed that, too.

Later, driving back home between forest trees that sprouted new shoots from the first rains, I thought about all I had learned. Why wasn't I living in Asagbé, nearer to Amenan? True, Kosangbé was the center of traditional Beng religion—my main interest—but I hadn't yet found an Amenan in my village; maybe I never would. My refusal to move, I worried, might be based on little more than a mixture of blind hope and stubbornness.

The following morning I awoke with a swollen, achy ankle, and before long I could barely walk, limping along like an old woman with rheumatism—the knob of pain had opened to reveal a pus-filled hole. By the third day the hole was larger, deeper—as if an acid were eating away my ankle—and Philip insisted that we drive down to the M'Bahiakro infirmary. When Dr. Yiallo examined me, my infection perplexed him. Perhaps it was from an insect whose bite acted like a poison on me—Africans must have been immune. He gave me a ten-day dose of tetracycline pills, and medicine in hand, we returned to Kosangbé.

But the next morning there was no improvement. When Yacouba came by, he winced at the sight of my foot, now too swollen for the straps of my sandals—I had to wear rubber flip-flops. "Anzoumena's a good healer," he said, "he should be able to do something."

When the middle-aged Jimini man arrived, he brought half a lemon and a small black animal horn. He held out the horn: inside was a thick, black gel.

"That looks horrible," Philip said to me sotto voce. "You're not going to let him put it on your foot, are you?"

"I'm taking tetracycline anyway," I said. "What harm could it do?"

Philip's eyes widened with possibilities. We'd already argued that morning about my reluctance to return to the infirmary: how could I leave the village with Nakoyan back in Kosangbé, having just run away from Gaosu once again? And I'd taken the pills for only two days—surely they needed more time to work; but Philip, citing all the weight I'd lost from dysentery, worried that I might not have the strength to withstand the infection. Now, almost defiantly, I agreed to the healer's treatment. Anzoumena scooped out a small handful of the gel, then squeezed some lemon juice into it and rubbed the gooey substance all around my left ankle.

"Keep this medicine on your foot all night," he said through Yacouba, "and in the morning I'll come back to put more on."

"Ka niché," I said in thanks—one of the few Jula phrases I'd picked up—and held out my hand to shake his. But immediately he drew back.

A bit hurt, I asked Yacouba why Anzoumena had recoiled from me.

"It's taboo, because you're a woman."

"That doesn't seem fair," I said.

"But it works the other way, too," Yacouba added. "If a male patient goes to a female healer among the Jimini, they can't shake hands, either."

"Ah," I said. "Well, please thank him for me."

The following morning the hole in my ankle was wider, my foot swollen further. When my friend Lanzé Afwé came to greet me in the morning, she murmured, *"Eki mi bo a o"*—May god get you out of this—then suggested, "Why don't I tell Amani to come over and massage it?"

"Really? Do you think that would help?"

"He's very good at that, because he's a third twin."

" 'Third twin'—what's that?" I asked, reaching for my pen.

"The children before him were twins, so we say he's like a twin, too," she explained. "They're always good at massaging—they learn it from their mothers, because mothers of twins are good at it themselves. I taught Amani."

"Well, okay, he can have a try," I said.

Amani came by and proceeded gently to rub my ailing foot, pulling it forward and sideways. It felt pleasant enough, given my pain.

But the next day, when we heard the drone of a motorbike engine and wanted to see who'd arrived, I had to lean on Philip for a cane as I hobbled, and we slowly made our way to the roadside. We found Gaosu, newly arrived, with a cousin. Then, suddenly, there was Nakoyan—dashing wildly in the other direction. Immediately Gaosu raced after in close, silent chase; a trail of children followed, hooting and collecting adults in their path. Philip and I started to follow, but I couldn't possibly keep up. Without a warning, he scooped me up in his arms—all ninety-two pounds of me. "Hold on!" he said, and off we hurried in pursuit, creating our own spectacle as, folded up in the moving perch of my devoted husband's arms, I scrawled a bouncing record of it all in my red notebook.

Gaosu tackled Nakoyan and wrestled her to the ground, and immediately the scattered laughter stopped. He and his cousin quickly tied Nakoyan's hands together with some strips of black rubber. But Nakoyan practiced her own form of passive resistance by letting her body go limp, and they had to drag her to the waiting moped. Finally loaded onto the back of the bike, she wiggled like a loosely packed sack of yams, rolling this way and that. Gaosu walked the bike out of the village, and striding alongside, his cousin propped up the unwilling passenger. In morbid curiosity we all stood by the road and watched.

A few yards from the village, Nakoyan, ever determined, managed to fall off the bike. Her hands still tied, she rolled about the dirt road as Gaosu braked and jumped off. He and his cousin loaded her back on. When they approached the hill that lay just beyond the village, Gaosu turned on the motor. His companion stepped quickly to keep up, but Nakoyan wriggled off again. Once more the two men lifted her limp body onto the back of the bike, and finally the trio disappeared beyond the rise of the hill. How many more such stops would there be before they reached Asagbé?

Nakoyan's stubbornness alarmed me. Though privately I cheered her on in rejecting a husband she surely abhorred, I worried that her resistance might eventually destroy her. When Philip carried me back to our compound, my foot still ached sharply, and suddenly I understood I was no less stubborn: I'd moved to Kosangbé despite everyone's warnings, and now I was resisting a return to the infirmary for my worsening foot—ironically, so I could remain in the village to observe poor Nakoyan's trials. What might befall me for my own obstinacy?

By the next morning my foot throbbed terribly and had taken on a greenish tinge. I could no longer even hobble. Philip's patience with me was exhausted. "Alma, we're going down to M'Bahiakro," he announced. *"Period."*
This time I didn't disagree.

At the hospital, Dr. Yiallo was shocked when he saw how my foot had worsened after four days of medicine. "I'm going to give you nine antibiotic treatments a day, shots *and* pills," he said. "You could lose that foot."

I gasped, and Philip reached for my hand, his lips closed tight with worry. "This time," Dr. Yiallo said slowly, his voice quiet with concern, "you *must* stay in town until it's obviously better."

Our friend Lisa graciously offered us her guestroom. Three times a day Philip drove me to the infirmary for my shots, then back to Lisa's, where he applied a steaming, medicated cloth to my foot while I wriggled and cried. But these first few days of grueling treatments produced no improvement, and we began to worry about gangrene. Lisa tried to cheer me by reading aloud from her old *Newsweek* magazines, but the news from home was all horrible: the failed American mission to rescue the Iranian hostages, race riots in Miami, Mount Saint Helens's eruption.

Finally the throbbing eased: my foot was slowly healing. "Thank god we came down," I said to Philip, leaning against him as we made a slow, tentative circuit around Lisa's living room. Soon I'd be able to walk again. And then we could return to Kosangbé.

Philip: Foreign Fictions

One evening Yacouba lounged on one of our palm-rib chairs and talked with Alma about the recent lack of rain and the coming hard work of building yam mounds in the fields. During a lull in their conversation, Alma walked over to the desk where I sat typing and scribbling, and she reached for a notebook. I smiled at her, silently thankful once again that her foot had finally healed.

Yacouba expressed curiosity about what I was doing.

"It's a new story he's working on," Alma said, trying to head him off from interrupting me.

"Kouadio," he called to me teasingly, "we tell you our stories, why don't you tell us one of yours?"

Two neighbors, Asaw and Kouassikro, were also lingering in our courtyard, and they murmured their approval of Yacouba's request.

I looked at the page curled in the typewriter roller. I'd finished a first draft of my story, I even knew the title—"Waiting for the Right Moment." But there was still much to work on, much I wasn't sure of. Even if it were done, how could I explain its list of dangerous toys—a motorized jumping rope, Home Graffiti, Little Behaviorist, a doll that grew sharpened fingernails? How to explain hibachi restaurants, superrealism, dental X-rays?

"It's not finished," I said.

"Then tell us another."

I considered the manuscripts I had with me and decided that a short piece titled "Shadows" might work. Half prose poem, half story, it was fresh in my mind because I had recently mailed off a revised version to a small literary magazine in New York that had accepted it many months before.

Still, I knew this would be a difficult enterprise, and not only because Alma and I would have to translate from English to French, and Yacouba would then translate our French into proper Beng. I recalled the anthropologist Laura Bohannan's famous account of her difficulties telling the story of Hamlet to the Tiv people of Nigeria. The Tiv don't believe in ghosts, so Bohannan's audience declared that the "ghost" of Hamlet's father must have been a zombie. Also, the Tiv practice the levirate, which requires a man to marry his widowed sister-in-law, so Claudius and Gertrude's behavior was considered highly appropriate. To the Tiv, Hamlet was an inexplicably disruptive son.

"My story," I began, looking at the expectant faces lit by our lantern, "is about a man whose shadow left him."

As I listened to Yacouba translate, I realized that the Beng word for "shadow"—*nining*—was also the word for "soul." But before I could wonder what emphasis Yacouba was giving, I noticed that Kouassikro and Yacouba spoke intently in low tones back and forth. Feeling forgotten, I asked Yacouba what they were discussing, and he said, "Kouassikro wants to know if this was the work of spirits."

"No," I replied in Beng, a bit startled. My small audience remained quiet, not entirely convinced, I suspected. Then I continued, telling Yacouba that the man had stayed in his house for days, struggling with his fluid shadow.

When he translated, Asaw now interrupted, murmuring rapidly with a wicked grin much like her husband's, "If he stayed inside all day, then he must be a witch."

Then Kouassikro spoke with his usual mangled pronunciation, and Yacouba translated: "So the spirits did punish the witch, by taking away his shadow."

I paused and regarded my audience. Here I was in a muddle similar to Bohannan's: simply by being good listeners, the Beng were deconstructing and reconstructing my story, drawing me into their own foreign fiction.

We continued with my story, though the tedious process of translation and interruptions didn't make for compelling storytelling—even simple details such as a rocking chair or double dating provoked elaborate discussions. I suspected we were all relieved when my story was done.

Still, I was pleased that people spoke to us so freely in public about spirits—it made me feel less like an outsider. By this time Alma and I had discovered there were different types of spirits, each type with its own traits and personalities that even the smallest children knew. One evening a month or so earlier, Alma and I had noticed Kofikro, a precocious two-year-old boy, walking along the edge of our compound from behind our house. He was one of our favorite children in the village, and I called out to him.

"Kofikro!"

He stopped and turned to us, his face miserable. Then I noticed he was holding something.

"What's that?" I asked.

He walked toward us sheepishly and held it out: an empty sardine tin. Immediately I felt ashamed. I still had trouble remembering not to throw out certain things that the Beng considered valuable. Sardine tins in particular made excellent toys, as did the keys. The children must have long ago realized that there were goodies to be salvaged in the trash heap behind our house, and this is what Kofikro had been up to.

Mistaking my brief silence for disapproval, Kofikro blurted out, "A spirit gave this to me."

"A spirit?" I said, glad to give weight to his excuse. "What did it look like?"

"It was white, and it had long hair."

Alma reached for her notebook. "What else?" she asked.

"It hissed," Kofikro said, demonstrating dramatically, happy to be taken seriously by adults.

"Does it have a name?"

"*Alufyé.*"

Since then we'd learned more about this type of spirit. Some were men, some were women, and they could be seen by humans when they swooped into villages late at night, their thick, uncombed hair waving in the air. These spirits raided the Beng farms, having a weakness for bananas and yams. And they were *white*. I recalled how, when we'd first arrived in Bengland, some children had run from us in terror while the adults had chuckled. To those children, we must have been *alufyé;* to their parents, convenient disciplinary tools.

Included in the Beng spirit pantheon were the tall *gagon* spirits, who could only be seen in the day, by hunters in the forest. These spirits were dangerous, capable of killing people, but they were afraid of guns and hunting dogs. And then there were spirits called *bonzo* who couldn't be seen, though their noises were audible. Anyone passing close by a *bonzo* would suddenly stiffen and go blind momentarily.

They were all creatures of the imagination, but this made them no less real, for they were creatures who affected the lives of our neighbors. Ché Kofi wore copper rings designed to ward off any spirit: he had seen an *alufyé* when he was young and since then never went into the forest unprotected. When

Yacouba hunted he always brought along his dog, and if it barked, he knew it was warning off nearby spirits. The entire village believed Nakoyan was possessed by a spirit, and even she agreed. For months now I had been filled with these local dramas and beliefs, which fit into a world of such strangeness that I felt I was actually living in a novel written by the Beng. But I was a subsidiary character, however disturbed or bedazzled.

As I tried to polish a final draft of my short story, I found that my budding sense of the Beng language left me and my struggling French vanished—in the last few days of intense writing, my mind had room only for the resources of my own language. I was rendered practically mute to all but Alma: when neighbors strolled by with greetings, she had to reply for me as I sat by the typewriter, my mouth open but the words gone. Yacouba was particularly annoyed by my silent gaping. "You *have* to greet me," he said, explaining with a proverb: "Once you see the spoon, you should taste the sauce!"

After a few days of this oddly selective muteness, I typed what I hoped was the final draft. Gathering all the pages together, I regarded my manuscript with something like disbelief: in the face of the tumultuous past few months I was surprised I'd finished anything at all. Yet secretly I felt ashamed of my preoccupation. Around me, after all, were far greater troubles—Nakoyan's public rape, the poverty of our neighbors, the sicknesses I treated every day.

But I was stuck with my own imagination and its imperatives: in much the same way the villagers had to work in the fields, I had to write. This was, I suspected, the secret, psychic action of my story, which told of a conceptual artist who devotes her work to her new lover—a cubist origami version of his face, made from a cigarette wrapper; a silk screen of their fingerprints together, "joined in a series of increasingly acrobatic positions"; a soft sculpture of his Social Security card. Flattered by her artistic vision, he feels multiplied into versions of himself he didn't know existed. Yet with her increasing success in selling her works, he begins to feel taken apart, with no control over where he might be displayed.

Her lover grows ever more troubled until one evening he returns home to see her latest work: a life-size shadow painted on the wooden floorboards by the window. It's a painting of his shadow, titled "Waiting for the Right Moment"—she tells him that one day, given the identical lighting, moment, and gesture, his real shadow will match, even if only for an instant, her painted one. Although the details of this story seemed far removed from the village of Kosangbé, I believed they echoed my unease at being engulfed by Beng culture and Alma's fieldwork—I was a writer, not an anthropologist, and I had

to forge my own identity out of our new life. In beginning and then finishing
my story, I avoided the shadowy fate of my fictional character.

In early June Alma had to return to Abidjan briefly for various bureaucratic
annoyances, and I was anxious to see a doctor about the fungus that was
slowly eating away little circles of skin on my chest, neck, and forehead. So
we set off for the capital, after a five-month absence. On the way we stopped
briefly in Bouaké, where I phoned my brother on the day before his wedding
to wish him luck. Listening to his New York accent on the crackling line, I
didn't feel the familiar sense of place that I'd expected, and though we gabbed
about his tuxedo, the band he'd chosen, the caterer's plans, the details of this
imminent ceremony sounded strange, even arbitrary: America seemed far
away in more than miles. I was shocked to realize how immersed I'd become
in Beng culture.

But I didn't understand how deeply immersed until our second night in
Abidjan, when we attended a special showing of a film at the American
embassy: *Mother, Jugs, & Speed,* starring Bill Cosby and Raquel Welch. We
sat in a large room filled with folding chairs, surrounded by perhaps a hundred people speaking English: Alma and I marveled at so many easily deci-
pherable words and the nearly forgotten, overlapping rhythms of our
language. Then the lights went out and the film projector clacked away,
sending an expanding pyramid of light through the darkness.

Huge figures filled the screen, moving through rooms that gleamed in
bright colors. I had forgotten how to watch a movie—at first it seemed like
a *thing,* not a story, and I had to adjust my eyes, my attention, as scenes
changed rapidly and the camera's angle sometimes shifted unpredictably. I
felt uncomfortable, sitting in the dark among so many people, listening to
their laughter without laughing myself. The movie—a low-budget, morbid-
humored embarrassment—was about two paramedic crews that competed
for accident victims. The sight of ambulances careening down streets, of
stretchers on wheels rolling down hills, reminded me of the village emergencies of the past few months and made me cringe.

Soon I ignored the predictable plot complications, the car chases, and the
casual, slapstick violence and instead soaked in the scenes of ordinary American life: the source of my bouts of homesickness. There were linoleum tiles,
a jukebox, bowling trophies, a golf course with its alternation of greens and
sand traps, a professional wrestling match, a ceramic Buddha resting on a
television—things I hadn't thought of or seen in months. But the images
didn't quite fit my longing: how peculiar, to spritz breath spray into one's
mouth or to drive up to a restaurant and be served food through the window.

As though in a dream sequence, I felt that I was staring into an interior at once familiar and disturbingly alien.

I had felt this way once before a few years earlier, when reading one of the great works of modern African literature, the book-length poem *Song of Lawino* by the Ugandan writer Okot p'Bitek. The poem's narrator, Lawino, is a traditional Acholi woman who berates her husband Ocol for choosing a younger, Westernized second wife. Lawino praises Acholi culture and castigates the "modern" ways with which Ocol is now so infatuated. When he brings a grandfather clock to their home, Lawino regards its discordant presence:

> *On the face of the clock*
> *There are writings*
> *And its large single testicle*
> *Dangles below*
> *It goes this way and that way*
> *Like a sausage-fruit*
> *In a windy storm*

For Lawino, Western nightclub dancing is horrific, for people

> *dance silently like wizards*
> *. . . inside a house*
> *And there is no light. . . .*
> *It is hot inside the house*
> *It is hot like inside a cave*
> *Like inside a hyena's den!*
> *And the women move like fish*
> *That have been poisoned*

When I first read Okot's poem, the images of Lawino unsettled my sense of a world I thought I knew, and I began to understand how Third World peoples saw us. Now, in the American embassy, *I* was in a dark room beset by Western images. Though they were the images of my own culture, they no longer fit so easily inside me.

Alma: Forest Sex

When we returned to Bengland, I started visiting Amenan more regularly. Though her house lay at the farthest corner of Asagbé and our own shady spot was tucked away at the forest edge, Amenan's compound was often filled with visitors: mothers flocked to her for advice about their ailing children—my friend was known as an herbalist; men strolled by for a shot glass or two of the *kutuku* she sometimes sold; girls skipped over to play with her four daughters; and women gathered to complain about their husbands' excesses, their mothers-in-law's threats, or an aunt's acts of sorcery, for Amenan was a good listener and offered sage advice. With all this activity around me, I gave up my own agenda: no more typed lists of questions, not even scribbled ideas for topics to investigate. Between guests, Amenan endlessly recounted stories of village life.

One day I arrived and found my friend sitting quietly by herself, slicing okra. Baby Amwé slept on a cloth laid on the ground, little Kouadio had gone to the fields with his father, and the older girls were off playing with friends or helping their grandmother on the farm. Amenan put away the okra for a daughter to finish later, and we two settled ourselves on either side of the baby—Amenan lying on her side, propped up on an elbow, one breast positioned near Amwé's mouth for when she awoke, while I sat cross-legged, notebook on lap. Above us the trees swayed gently in the breeze as if searching for the overdue rains.

"Any news from the village?" I asked.

Without pausing, as if she'd been saving up this story all week, Amenan replied, "Poor Busu, they took him down to the hospital." She paused.

"What happened?" I asked.

"His penis was bleeding."

"Oh my god! What did the doctor do?"

"He circumcised him," Amenan answered.

It was my turn to pause. Finally I said, "Did the doctor say what the problem was?"

"Oh, we don't need him to tell us that!" Amenan declared. She adjusted her breast—it was filling with milk, for Amwé had been sleeping for some time—then began her story. While Busu was in the hospital in M'Bahiakro, his father accused him of sleeping in the forest with a woman. Busu denied it, explaining that he'd slept with one of the Ghanaian prostitutes of the village, but his father didn't believe the story, insisting that he'd caught sight of his son walking on a forest path with his girlfriend, Akissi. Finally Busu confessed that one day, while collecting mangoes, he and his girlfriend indeed made love. Though he claimed she seduced him, he admitted that soon they made love again under another mango tree. Shortly after, the bleeding began.

"But what's wrong with making love in the forest?" I asked Amenan.

"That's our biggest taboo—it offends the spirits of our Earth," Amenan said calmly. "Didn't you know?"

"No one ever told us! It's a good thing we're still terrified of snakes," I joked.

Amenan nodded. "I'm glad I told you now—you wouldn't want the punishment!"

"Oh?"

"Poor Busu and Akissi don't know what it is, either, they're too young—if they did, they never would have gone off to the forest!" Amenan slapped at a mosquito on her chest, then continued, "They'll have to go back to the spot where they made love, but this time a lot of male elders will come along. The men will make the couple undress and repeat their crime right there, in front of everyone."

I stopped writing to look up, aghast.

"And this is the worst part," Amenan continued, "the old men will set fire to branches and they'll beat and burn those poor kids while they're having sex."

"That's awful! No one to save them," I said, imagining the scene.

"Actually, there *will* be one old woman there for Akissi. But how will she protect the girl against all those men?" She sighed. "And no one will protect Busu. Then, after it's over, they'll sacrifice a cow—and you know how much *that* costs. Amwé, it's very serious."

"Yes, I see! What would happen if they weren't punished?"

"The rains would *never* come—and we'd all starve. It's because of them that the rains have stopped for the past few weeks."

My eyes widened—I was too surprised to speak. Amenan continued, "Actually, some people are blaming you and Kouadio for the dry—"

"*What?*" I blurted out.

"It's just a few people," Amenan said, ever calm. "You know, we've never had white people living with us. Some people are afraid. . . ."

"Oh, Amenan," I moaned, "what can we do?"

"You shouldn't worry about it," she said soothingly. "Anyway, once Busu and Akissi are punished, the rains will come and everyone will forget about you two."

Philip: Our Own Un-Eden

I woke from a light sleep in the middle of the night to the sound of our small digital clock clattering on the cement floor—but how had it fallen off the chair we used as a night table? The resident geckos usually kept to the ceiling and upper walls of our rooms, scuttering out of reach. Maybe a mouse was responsible—occasionally one or two invaded our home, scrounging for food.

I lay still and listened but heard no scratching of tiny feet. Perhaps a large spider or one of the huge cockroaches that appeared from time to time had knocked over the clock.

I reached under my pillow for the flashlight that I used for reading in bed at night. I flipped on the beam, cast it on the floor, and stared through the mosquito netting at the clock, facedown. Then I sensed movement in the darkness to my right and flashed the light there, where I saw the rippling body of a snake slithering up the straight back of our chair.

"Oh my god!" I exclaimed, waking Alma.

"What is it?" she murmured, searching for her glasses.

"A snake." Its head poked out from behind the chair, its thin tongue extended and vibrating. Framed by the circle of light, its shining eyes stared straight at me.

"What?" Now her flashlight was on, and she trained it on the chair. "Oh god, it can't be."

Attracted by the beams of light, the snake slithered off of the chair toward us, onto the headboard of our bed. Separated from the creature by the mosquito netting, Alma and I, naked in bed, sat transfixed by its slow approach—our own distorted tableau of Adam and Eve, our own un-Eden.

Quickly we devised a strategy: Alma kept her light on and pointed at the snake while I turned mine off and prepared to smash its head against the wooden headboard. When the snake was close enough, I slammed the flashlight on its head, though at the last moment I held back a bit, afraid I might tear through the mosquito netting. But the netting held, and the snake's head reeled from the blow. I struck again, and it tumbled to the floor behind our bed.

"Is it dead?" Alma asked, but before I could answer we heard it hissing under the bed.

"Wonderful," I whispered hoarsely, "now what do we do?"

Alma had no answer, nor did I, except to check the borders of our bed to make sure the flimsy mosquito netting was tucked in securely. The snake hissed for a long time, and we listened in the darkness.

Eventually the room grew silent. "Maybe you killed it," Alma whispered hopefully. "Maybe the snake was hissing because it was dying."

"There's one way to check." I sat up and shook the bed frame. Again that disembodied hissing started up. "Nope, he's just hurt and pissed off."

When the frightening noise died down I tried an experiment: I pointed the flashlight on the ground by the side of the bed. Again, hissing. "Hear that?" I whispered to Alma. "We can't run out of here in the dark, but we can't get out with a flashlight, either: the snake was looking at your light when I hit it, and the damned thing probably thinks that's what gave it a nasty headache."

She groaned. "We're going to have to wait until morning!"

I sighed. "I guess so."

We lay down, with no idea how long we'd have to wait—the clock on the floor was facedown, and neither of us had any intention of reaching out of the mosquito netting to turn it over. But we were afraid to fall asleep, too, so I shook the bed occasionally for another sibilant antilullaby. Eventually the snake stopped responding to these provocations, but we were too tired to wonder why, and then, suddenly, we were asleep.

Hours later I woke to the echoing sound of women pounding wooden mortars and pestles and the competing squawks of roosters, and I turned to face the faint light streaming through the thin cloth of our curtain: the usual morning, except that there was a snake in our house. I rocked my body back and forth to shake the bed. The snake made no sound, but Alma woke up.

"What? Did we *fall asleep?*"

"Believe it or not," I answered grimly. Now I could distinguish the voices of our neighbors as they went through the morning greetings. But they were all so far away—how could we ever get to them? We could call for help, but our door was locked, the key on our desk in the kitchen.

"Let's make some noise to see if we can get the snake to give away where it is," I suggested, and together Alma and I shook the bed. Alma even pounded on the cement wall through the mosquito netting: no snakish protest. We tried again and again, with the same result.

Summoning our courage, we decided to make a break for the door. We gathered the bedsheets around us for makeshift clothes, pulled up a corner of the mosquito netting, and slipped out. Our eyes to the ground for any sudden movement, we raced to the kitchen. There, we grabbed the key and, unlocking the door, ran to François's compound, together blurting out, *"Mleh o shuwé!"*

François stared at us, unable to understand our excited Beng, but as we repeated our words he finally understood. "A snake in your house?" He began calling to our neighbors, "Karimu, Bani, Kossum!" Soon I was among a posse of about six men, carrying clubs and machetes, as I tried to explain the events of the night before.

It was eerily quiet inside. We searched under the bed, the desk, the stand for the gas burners, behind the shelves of books and medicines, but we found no sign of a snake. Had it slithered out of the house moments after Alma and I escaped? The men began drifting away, no longer interested, until only my next-door neighbor Bani was left with me.

Then I poked my club behind our suitcases at the base of the bed and heard hissing. Bani quickly pulled them forward, and there was the snake, rearing up at us. I lifted my club, but Bani held my arm—knowing about my ineffectual aim the night before—and with three swift, accurate strokes he

broke the serpent's neck and knocked out its intestines. Then I gave it a whack, just to be able to say I'd helped.

We carried it outside, and the villagers crowded around for a look. Alma and I returned to our bedroom to dress, then we joined the gathering with our snake book, hoping to identify our intruder. We couldn't quite find anything that fit the look of the dead creature on the ground—the closest we came to a match was a Blanding's tree snake. Our neighbors asserted that what Bani killed was poisonous, and that was enough for us.

"Let's take a picture," I suggested, and Bani and I dangled the serpent between us—like two fishermen with an exotic catch—and Alma snapped the shot. Then Bani flung it into the forest behind our house, a treat for the army ants.

Our audience dispersed quickly—encounters with snakes were, after all, a rather ordinary occurrence in the village. Alma and I made breakfast, and before the morning was over she was typing her field notes and I returned to reading a collection of Gogol short stories I'd begun a day earlier. We'd largely forgotten our small adventure—a telling comment on our adjustment to the pace of life in Kosangbé.

That same day I began a new short story: in the possessing, peculiar moment when an initial image suddenly appears, in my mind I saw an American family—grandfather, grandmother, husband, wife, and two sons—running one by one out of a house, angrily chasing one another. Swiftly I wrote down a long first sentence. Then I realized that just as Alma and I had run out of our house, so did this budding fictional family run out of theirs, though not in fear, but fury. I was certain this would be the story's beginning, yet try as I might, I couldn't imagine what these people, now outside their home, would do next.

I put this problem aside for the moment, because the hard work of building yam mounds was now under way and I finally accepted an invitation to help work in the fields. In the morning I took with me a *kpalé*—a small hand hoe—and marched in a line down the forest paths with François, Bani, Yacouba, and a number of other villagers. We stopped at a desiccated area in the forest, where the underbrush had been slashed and burned. The dead trees had shed their greenery, and now the women of our work party formed a line and bent over with their short-handled brooms to sweep away the leaves. I joined the men in forming a line, and we followed the women, scraping the exposed soil with *kpalés*. Each man drew the topsoil about him into a pyramid—a two- to three-foot-tall mound of dirt—in which the yams would eventually be planted. It was all an act of faith, considering the recent dry spell. I wondered if any of my companions secretly blamed me.

I bent down and gathered the earth in a pile, sometimes using my *kpalé* as a machete to cut through the roots of lianas. When I was done with one mound, I moved forward and began another. François started up a song, its rhythms a counterpoint to the swinging of our *kpalés,* and the other men joined in. I wanted to sing, too, but I didn't know the words, couldn't follow the intricate tune.

The sun beat down on my back through the empty branches of the trees. I stopped often to wipe the sweat from my forehead, but still it dribbled onto my glasses as I bent down. I was beginning to fall behind the slowly advancing line of men.

Yacouba sauntered over to me. "Tired already, Kouadio?" he teased.

"No," I replied, trying to hide my annoyance. I thought Yacouba was secretly pleased at my faltering: too often when he visited our compound I was typing at the desk, settled into a world of written words he couldn't enter. But here in the forest he was the expert, attuned to work he'd done most of his life. I swung my *kpalé* again and again, trying to fit into the rhythms of those around me. But my hands were soft—typing is not physically demanding labor—and as I continued working, blisters rose and broke on my palms and fingers.

I was so far behind now that Bani, then Kossum, broke from their places in line and began building mounds ahead of me, casting me sympathetic smiles. "Kouadio, *ka ma!*"—courage—they said, which I appreciated—after all, only a few months earlier they had wondered if I might be a spirit, incapable of human labor. I scraped faster, creating more blisters, and as I wiped my sweat the saltiness stung the sores on my hands.

When the women were done sweeping, they set up temporary hearths— three large rocks to balance a pot, a few small logs underneath for the fire— and began to cook the afternoon meal. Though I enjoyed the camaraderie of our work crew—the singing, the joking—I saw that resentments and rivalries could still flourish here. Afwé Ba, Kossum's wife, was cooking today, with her hated junior co-wife, Amla. They sat with their backs to each other as they sliced the rough skin off yams, then chopped okra and set it in the pot.

By the end of the day I had managed to produce a small fraction of the yam mounds of the men around me, and my hands ached from all the blisters. Still, my friends seemed pleased by my presence and generously praised my meager production. We walked back to the village together, and I looked forward to my evening bath and a drink of palm wine. I always knew my neighbors worked incredibly hard; now I could feel it in my muscles.

That evening I could barely type a letter. I begged off returning to the fields for a few days, until my blisters healed. In the meantime I tried to coax that angry, fictional family to do something else, now that they had chased each other out of the house. But no one would budge, and I was stuck with my first, single sentence. Perhaps it wasn't the beginning of the story, as I'd first imagined.

7

DIVINATION AND TRIAL

❦   ❦   ❦

(JULY 1–AUGUST 2, 1980)

Alma: "It Wasn't a Dream"

I HAD AN APPOINTMENT WITH LAMINE, THE DIVINER OF ASAGBE WHO HAD DIAGNOSED Nakoyan's marital troubles and baby Amwé's colic. Now, driving to Asagbé, I thought to ask Lamine how he had learned to talk with spirits. What portion of his talents was due to a shrewd grasp of his clients' personalities, and was he ever stumped by their problems and illnesses? But, rehearsing my list, I worried if Lamine would even talk about such things with a foreigner.

Arrived in Asagbé, I greeted Amenan and we settled onto a bark cloth mat that she spread out under her uncle Kouassi's coffee trees. Lamine approached: a short man with a kind-looking face; from his lined forehead, I guessed he must have had years of divining behind him. After we exchanged greetings I asked Lamine how he'd become a diviner.

"One day, a long time ago," he began, "well, it wasn't that long ago—I was already a married man, with children—I had just come back from the fields, and as soon as I stepped into my house, I saw three cowries lying on the floor. I asked an old diviner in the village what to do with the shells. She told me to hold on to them—which I did."

"*Ah-heh,*" I replied.

"About a month later," he continued, "I got up to piss one night, and when I returned to the house, I saw fifteen more cowries lying on the floor, just inside the door. Someone said something, but I didn't see anyone: I didn't even know if it was a man's or a woman's voice. I wasn't sleeping, Amwé—it wasn't a dream." Lamine glanced at me, and I nodded. "The voice told me what each cowrie means; then it taught me herbal remedy after herbal remedy. Everything I know about divining and healing, I learned that one night."

"*Ihh,*" I intoned, amazed. Finally I asked, "What are the diseases you learned that night to cure?"

"Let's see," Lamine said, his eyes taking on a faraway look. Then he spoke so rapidly, he seemed almost in a trance: was he hearing that voice in the night? "I can treat aching feet; women who can't get pregnant, even though they're menstruating; a headache in the middle of the forehead, right above the nose—"

"Wait, you're going too fast!" I said, trying to write it all down.

"Uh, there was foot ache. . . ." He hesitated. Then he picked up a small stick lying on the ground and traced patterns on the bark cloth with it.

"It's as if he's reading the cowries," Amenan whispered to me. With the twig as his guide, Lamine's memory returned, and he continued to tell me all the illnesses he could treat with herbs: waist ache, stomachache, corpse, one swollen testicle, gonorrhea, snakebite, listlessness and fatigue due to witchcraft—in short, a wide and impressive list of maladies.

"What's in the cowries that tells you the remedies?"

Lamine laughed. "It's not only the cowries! Before I throw them, I sprinkle water over them that's been infused with some leaves. This helps the cowries talk."

I asked, "What are the leaves you use for watering the shells?"

Lamine shifted position on the bark cloth. "Amwé, there are four people waiting at my house for divinations. Anyway, it's very difficult for me to talk about this without the cowries. The next time you come, I'll bring them along—then I'll tell you everything."

With that, he rose and we parted: Lamine to meet his clients, I to mull over the extraordinary bit of autobiography he'd revealed to me. Amenan offered to fill me in on some of the gaps he'd left—the two were members of the same matriclan, and Amenan knew much about Lamine's life. Considering him highly reliable, she consulted him regularly for all her own and her children's illnesses.

"Is he training anyone as an assistant?" I asked her.

"No, he doesn't have an apprentice," Amenan said. "Since he was taught everything in a vision, he can't teach anyone what he knows. But when he dies, God will choose a replacement for him: the heir will be called by a vision, just as Lamine was." She paused. "The other day, little Kouadio"—her

two-year-old son—"did a divination with some cowries he found somewhere. When I told Lamine about it, he laughed and said, 'Maybe little Kouadio will be my replacement when I die.'"

Nakoyan seemed resigned to her husband: in Asagbé rumor had it that she'd slept with Gaosu three times that week before getting her period on Wednesday. Still, her earlier resistance must have inspired a fellow villager. Another young woman, Mo'kissi, had recently left her arranged marriage husband, Domolo, in his village of Ndogbé and returned unexpectedly to her own village of Kosangbé. Her spunk surprised me. Unlike Nakoyan, she was quiet and always spoke carefully, measuring her words—not the sort, I thought, to be flamboyantly possessed by a jealous spirit; nevertheless, she demanded rights that her society didn't accord her.

I thought back to the day Mo'kissi's marriage had been announced. It was evening, and she'd sat in a small, darkened room with her cousins and friends. One girl brought a *bundingyéké*—a handmade wooden rasp that she played by rhythmically grating a tiny palm tree rib against its ridges—and the other girls sang in chorus. The music was lovely, though between songs Mo'kissi cried, lamenting that she didn't like her groom. The other girls responded with more songs. Now, the morning after Mo'kissi ran away from her husband, I realized that her protest that evening had been far more than the enactment of a ritual requirement—in her case she'd really meant it.

In the morning her husband and his relatives came to reclaim her, and a trial was held on the recently cemented patio of Gba Apo's new house, with most of the village assembled in front of the building. On the porch sat a group of elders—some uncles, and the matriarch of Mo'kissi's family, a frail-looking old woman who'd walked a long way for the meeting. Among the group I spotted Kouakou Kala: as her maternal uncle, it had been his job to arrange Mo'kissi's marriage. Like his niece, he was a rather gentle person who spoke calmly in the most heated discussions, and I hoped he would rescind his decision. Around the courtyard stood younger men and women, chatting quietly among themselves.

In one corner sat Mo'kissi. Everyone seemed to think the trial would serve as a brief rebuke to the young woman, who would capitulate easily. Yet at only nineteen, Mo'kissi looked far more composed than I imagined I'd be in her place: her broad face was serene and beautiful as she sat on a low stool, arms folded in her lap. I smiled at her cautiously, and she smiled back.

Soon a furious Gba Apo came upon the scene. Wearing a handwoven, black-and-white-striped *pagne* around her waist, her bare breasts sagging with time and babies nursed long ago, she stood firmly in front of her sparkling white house surrounded by mud brick huts on either side. "This is *my house!*" she screamed. "Everyone has to leave!" Gba Apo was a strong-willed old woman who called Mo'kissi her granddaughter: perhaps she felt protective of the girl, even secretly sympathized with her . . . or was she just trying to keep her beautiful new house to herself? Still, no one moved from their places, and Apo, grumbling to herself, stomped away.

Sitting up straight on his wooden chair on the porch, her grown son, Ché Kofi, sporting a purple print shirt beautifully embroidered by his brother, Honoré, opened the meeting by addressing Domolo's male relatives: "Elder brothers, forgive us. Our part, it wasn't sweet, wasn't sweet. Pass over it, we beg you."

One of the men readjusted his green wool cap and, shaking his head, said, "The woman should just marry her husband, marry her husband. He's her *husband,* she should just marry him."

"Forgive us, elder brother," repeated Ché Kofi, "pass over it."

Mo'kissi said nothing but looked more and more miserable as others in the audience enjoined her to return to Domolo. Even our friend Yacouba chastised Mo'kissi: "You're shaming us all!" Though I couldn't expect our friend not to be Beng, I was secretly disappointed in him. In the past few months I'd begun to do some tough genealogical work, so I knew that Domolo was Mo'kissi's mother's mother's mother's sister's daughter's son—an uncle of sorts, and so considered a good match; but why had he, and not some other, more congenial relative, been chosen as her husband? I wished I had a roll of butcher paper, for Beng marriage ties were so dense and overlapping, I needed long stretches of paper to diagram them all.

Now Mo'kissi's relatives argued that she must return to Domolo and give the marriage a chance to solidify. Not only that, but she and Domolo should do everything possible to have children, in the hopes that this would draw them together. This advice shocked me, for it contradicted what my own culture declared as common sense—that a troubled couple should remain childless until their marital difficulties were resolved. How could both strategies be right?

The sun high overhead, the trial drew to its stalemated close: all the couple's relatives on both sides agreed that the marriage must endure, while Mo'kissi said softly, "I refuse." Her usually sparkly eyes now burdened with unhappiness, Mo'kissi was among the first to walk away, and I followed her.

"My sides hurt," Mo'kissi complained. Noticing Amani sitting nearby, she called to him, "Come over and rub my sides."

"Yo." He nodded and sat down next to her. Mo'kissi pulled up her blouse, and Amani rubbed her rib cage, the same kneading hands that had rubbed my infected foot. I hoped Mo'kissi had better results. Perhaps her malady, a sort of migraine located on her sides, would be more suited to his treatment.

Meanwhile I asked her, "Why don't you want to be married to Domolo?" "Because he has a rotten face." When I compared Mo'kissi's own beauty with her groom's short stature and his squished-in facial features, I couldn't help but agree. But was her statement a deeper indictment of Domolo? Once, I'd shown a photo of my overweight parents to our musician friend Kwamla Chakro. Immediately he'd commented, "I can see they're important people: look how big they are!" If a large physique was a sign of power in the world, then perhaps a "rotten" face was, conversely, the sign of a deficient character. And perhaps this equation was simply obvious to any Beng.

Or perhaps I'd never know Mo'kissi's motivations—perhaps no one would. In any case, later in the afternoon Domolo and his family led the unwilling bride away from the village. Unlike Nakoyan, she wasn't bound by rope, but as they neared the top of the hill leading south from the village, I heard Mo'kissi's sobs echoing in the air before the trees on the other side of the hill claimed them.

Philip: Declining an Invitation

While we drove to Asagbé for that village's weekly *marché,* Alma revealed to me that she'd just learned a new complication in Mo'kissi's continuing defiance: the young woman had recently miscarried. "But the father's not her husband," Alma said.

"No? Then who is?"

"Kofi Ba."

"Jeez." He was the son of San Kofi, our bird-whistling instructor and one of the elders who sat in judgment of Mo'kissi's fate.

"And San Kofi is pissed," Alma continued, "because now he has to sacrifice a goat to the Earth to apologize for his son's affair."

"That's enough, please, I can't stand to hear any more," I said, afraid that Mo'kissi's increasingly complex marriage difficulties might lead to a repeat of Nakoyan's fate—another nuptial rape.

At the Asagbé *marché* we temporarily banished these worries and set about the mundane task of stocking up on groceries, filling our basket with a thick yam, fresh okra, bananas, and onions.

"Amwé! Kouadio!"

We turned to see Nakoyan hurrying toward us, a metal basin balanced on her head. She very nearly laughed out her greetings to us, for we were from Kosangbé, the village she missed so much. How typical of the young woman —volatile in everything, including this mixture of happiness and sadness.

"Mi kené?"—Are you well?—I asked carefully, hoping she would understand that I was concerned about more than her health.

She nodded less than enthusiastically, then added, "Please send my parents my greetings."

"Yes, we will," I began, and Alma added quickly, "And they send their greetings to you." A lie—for all the times we'd traveled to Asagbé recently, they'd never said a word to us about their daughter.

"Thank them," Nakoyan said, now grinning again, "and give them these." She set her basin on the ground, plucked out a pair of onions, and dropped them in our basket, and we accepted these gifts for her undeserving parents.

Alma and I said good-bye and moved on through the market crowds, subdued by Nakoyan's misplaced goodwill. Then we approached the women selling their stock of dried fish laid out in long, pungent rows. I looked at those fish longingly: they could be stored for a long time, were quite tasty in sauces, and made fine gifts for our village neighbors.

But we didn't dare buy any. Last week, at the M'Bahiakro *marché,* I had walked over to the small wooden stall of our dried-fish merchant, where he sat idly waving away the turbulent cloud of flies hovering above his wares. Not noticing my approach, he reached down under his rickety counter and pulled up a 1950s-style bug spray: it was the size of a machine gun, with a long-handled pump to push out the poison. But instead of aiming it at the flies' careering trajectories, he trained his weapon on the rows of fish and pressed out a hissing spray. I stopped, stunned: we'd been eating this man's fish for months. The flies quickly scattered away from the noxious fumes. I left, too, frightened at what might be lodged in the lining of my stomach and bitter that a reliable source of protein was now closed. For how could Alma and I trust any dried fish we came upon, in any market?

Now the Asagbé fish merchants looked up at me inquiringly; I shook my head and moved on. But there were still treats to be had: *attieké* piled high in cones made of palm leaves and topped with a piece of fresh fish grilled in a hot sauce. We bought enough for us, Amenan and her children, and Pascal, who we knew was waiting for us in her compound. With the university closed for the summer, Pascal had recently returned to Asagbé to prepare for his October examinations. He'd also agreed to help Alma transcribe and translate some of the Beng storytelling sessions we'd recorded. Today we'd begin work.

As usual, Pascal was dressed nattily—sharply pressed pants, an immaculate shirt, dark, highly polished shoes. He shared in the snacks we passed around, thanking us, but he gingerly gathered the *attieké* in his hand, covertly casting a distasteful glance at his greasy fingers.

"Well, shall we begin?" Pascal said once lunch was done, anxious to leave. The three of us set off for his summer accommodations: a one-room house that bordered his father's compound. Inside was a hammock for sleeping and a small desk cluttered with notebooks, pens and pencils, a tape recorder, and a small stack of books—among them Richard Wright's *Native Son,* Chinua Achebe's *Things Fall Apart,* a selection of English poetry, a dictionary. Pascal obviously lived here alone, and I was surprised at his family's acknowledgment that he had a need for privacy.

We hunched over a tape recorder and red notebook, agreeing on a work pattern: first transcribe the Beng words—using the International Phonetic Alphabet—then translate them into both French and English. Alma returned to Amenan's compound for an afternoon of interviews, and I stayed with Pascal to oversee his initial efforts with "When Mosquito was King," the story André had told our first week in Asagbé. André's tinny, recorded voice brought back memories of Bengland's initial strangeness and my fears that anything I said or did would be a terrible faux pas. Now, months later, I'd become inured to the countless mistakes I made, knowing that each one led me a little closer to socially acceptable behavior. I peeked over Pascal's shoulder, saw him turning André's lilting voice into words on the notebook's lined page—his handwriting gave an architecture, a visual reality, to the particular leaps of Beng grammatical logic. As the hours passed and the separate strands of Beng, French, and English were written down, I realized that Pascal was constructing a kind of Rosetta stone that might help us better understand the language of our friends and neighbors.

At the end of the afternoon Amenan accompanied Alma and me to Didadi. Near our parked car, a procession of old men passed by, an occurrence unusual enough for me to watch with more than casual curiosity. Then I noticed a young couple, nervous and bewildered, being led along by a clutch of men with switches, and at the end of the line was a cow, lazily following the pull of its tether. Amenan whispered something to Alma, and I knew what she was saying: the forest sex exorcism was about to take place.

One of the elders—a distant relative of Amenan's—waved to me: an invitation to join the procession. I waved back but didn't move. The mere knowledge of this ritual already oppressed me—I had imagined the dreadful scene more than once; actually seeing it was more than I could bear.

"Aren't you going?" Alma whispered.

I hesitated, then said, "I'd rather not."

"I'm not allowed to go, you know," she replied quietly.

"I know."

Alma said nothing, waited. The last of the old men were now entering the forest.

"I just can't go," I finally said. "It was bad enough having to sit through Nakoyan's rape." I turned and headed for our car.

We drove back to Kosangbé in silence. I knew that Alma was both disappointed and unwilling to express her disappointment, and that was fine with me, as I was filled with my own conflicts. For months I'd entered into the Beng world as much as I could, yet today I'd reached my limit. Now, perhaps inspired by our recent meeting with Nakoyan and my admiration of Mo'kissi's resistance, I was able simply to refuse.

But my decision couldn't prevent the ritual, even as we drove back to Kosangbé, from entering me and violating my imagination. Were the old men at this moment beating the couple perfunctorily or with real rage? How could anyone make love under such circumstances? I wanted to squeeze this scene from my mind, make it go away, and then I caught myself hoping for the rains to come soon, so that the young couple would be confirmed as the cause of the drought and Alma and I would no longer be suspected. I shivered with self-loathing.

Alma: Our Enforced Duet

The next day I returned to Asagbé to work with Lamine, with high hopes for his cowrie-inspired revelations. As usual, when I arrived I went straight to Amenan's compound.

"Kouadio sends his regrets," I told her, "his stomach hurts today."

"May god let him out of it," Amenan murmured.

"Thank you."

Then Amenan and I settled on our bark cloth mat under the coffee trees: I sat cross-legged, notebook in lap, and Amenan lay down on her side to nurse baby Amwé, now four months old. As we awaited Lamine, I asked Amenan what had happened yesterday in the forest.

"Those poor children," Amenan said, "they really suffered. The king said they shouldn't be beaten and burnt because they're so young. But the old men from other villages whipped them anyway, then they set fire to the branches and burned the couple. The three old women tried to protect Akissi, but it was hopeless. My two uncles also tried, but they only got hit, too: Uncle Kouassi returned to the village with bruises!

"Today, Busu's walking around the village as if nothing had happened. Boys have no shame! But Akissi's in her compound, too ashamed to walk around—she's been crying, crying, crying. And her mother's pregnant now, but for the past few weeks she's barely eaten anything—she's lost a lot of weight. She's crying all the time, too."

"The poor family," I said. "Does anyone know why Busu and Akissi did it?"

"*Nn-hnn,*" Amenan said in that low voice of hers that signaled a revelation about to follow. "They consulted Lamine. He said someone bewitched Busu's

father to make *him* sleep with a woman in the forest. Since he's middle-aged and married, that would be *really* shameful. The Earth changed the spell, making his son Busu commit the sin."

"Mon vieux!" I said.

Lamine entered the compound, this time carrying a large burlap sack under his arm. After exchanging greetings, he spread the sack on the ground next to our bark cloth mat and sat down. Then he took a handful of cowrie shells out of his pocket: the size of a shelled pecan, the white, oval-shaped shells had tiny ridges that ran the length of a slit, appearing like a mouth baring its teeth. The shells came from the Indian Ocean: they'd journeyed overland across the width of Africa. Immediately Lamine tossed them onto his burlap bag and said, "I see Kouadio has a stomachache."

My eyes widened at this unexpected diagnosis—Lamine was nowhere in sight when I'd mentioned Philip's ailment to Amenan. Now Amenan's sly smile seemed to say *You see, I told you that Lamine's powers are from the spirits.*

"It's because you and Kouadio haven't been introduced to the Earth of Kosangbé," Lamine continued. "Give a white chicken to your chief and he'll sacrifice it to the Earth. Then you'll both stay healthy."

I longed to see the chief's reaction to Lamine's directive: if he believed we'd offended his Earth, I thought, that might easily account for his hostility toward us.

Lamine continued: "Kosangbé has a lot of taboos. Without knowing it, you may have violated some. That chicken sacrifice will also serve as an apology to the Earth. And the chief should tell you those taboos so you can observe them now."

What could those taboos be? But already Lamine was returning to the shells: "I see something else in the cowries for you and Kouadio." He pointed to some shells in the corner. "Your taboo time for sex is Friday night and Saturday morning—at those times, you shouldn't sleep together. If you do, some time soon you'll have a big fight."

I blushed at this unexpected advice. Should we really follow it? Perhaps it wasn't a bad idea: to be sure, it would be a rather unusual experiment—even by anthropological standards—but it might give us a more intimate sense of the restrictions a person had to observe in this culture. I wondered if I could talk Philip into it.

"Father, thank you very much for all this information," I said. "Kouadio and I will try to follow all your instructions."

"Nn-hnnn," Lamine said with evident satisfaction.

"I'm wondering how you know all this from the cowries."

"I'll show you." Again he tossed the cowries onto the burlap bag. Leaning over, he stared intently at the patterns formed by the shells. "Do you see that purplish shell by itself?" he asked. "That's a sign of good luck."

"Ah-heh."

Lamine gathered up the shells and tossed them again. "Here are two that landed together, apart from the rest: if a woman can't get pregnant and isn't menstruating, it's because of twins in her family."

After translating his remarks, Amenan whispered to me, "That's because the twins are bewitching her."

"But if the woman apologizes to the twins," Lamine added, "she'll start menstruating."

He tossed the shells again. "Here's one alone, with several grouped around it. They show that the person who's come to me will have a serious illness, and his family will gather round him. Then he'll recover."

Lamine's system intrigued me: each configuration presented a visual metaphor of a social or medical dilemma. Still, the configurations of the shells thrown randomly on a burlap bag seemed arbitrary. But later Amenan explained, "It's the bush spirits who make the cowries fall that way. That's why Lamine waters the shells each morning: for the spirits."

I didn't have to believe in those spirits to see their effectiveness. Lamine had a large and faithful clientele, and people could always explain that if one of the healer's cures failed, the patient must have offered the sacrifice on the wrong day or perhaps skipped a required herbal treatment. The system was self-enclosed—much like Western medical science, I mused. But this realization shook me. With my continuing stomach ailments, I took plenty of pills, capsules, and shots that had no effect, yet I persisted in trying other tablets, consulting other doctors. Was my own tradition's medical system equally predicated on the shared faith of doctor and patient?

That evening, back in Kosangbé, Philip and I told François that we needed to meet with the chief. He agreed to translate. After dinner François told us that the meeting would be held in the *secrétaire*'s courtyard. We three went over, where we found Kona, the chief, and a few other elders already awaiting us. We exchanged greetings and took our seats. Then I turned to the chief.

"Father," I said, "today I saw Lamine, and he told me that Kouadio and I have been sick because we haven't been introduced to the Earth of the village. He said we must sacrifice a white chicken at a certain spot in the forest, and—"

Just then skinny old Andama reeled into the courtyard, reeking of palm wine. "Hey, why didn't you tell me about this meeting?" he yelled, "I'm an elder, too!"

François frowned and said, "Uncle, forgive me, but I'm here representing the family—that's enough. Tomorrow I'll tell you what happened."

"No, I should be here, too!" roared Andama, staggering from *kutuku*.

"Ah, you're just an old drunk," François shouted, "you wouldn't contribute anything useful anyway!"

Philip and I looked at each other, surprised. François's outburst defied the respect he owed the maternal uncle who had raised him.

"Don't you call me an old drunk!" Andama hissed. The two men proceeded to hurl insults at each other until the meeting dissolved in chaos.

The next evening François, Philip, and I walked to the chief's courtyard to reconvene the meeting. It was just after dinner, but the chief was already in bed, his wife told us; we'd have to wait until tomorrow. Philip shot me a look of doubt. The chief seemed to be avoiding us.

The following evening we trekked over to the chief's courtyard even earlier. This time he was indeed awake, but also drunk. "Sorry, I've been to a funeral in Sangbé today," he mumbled, the funeral's accumulated palm wine evident on his breath. "Come back another day."

"François," I suggested, "why don't you just talk to the chief yourself sometime, then tell me what he said?"

"Fine." He looked only somewhat relieved. We all walked back in silence.

A few more days passed with no word. On Sunday Philip and I drove to Asagbé for the market. Soon after arriving, we met Amenan.

"Listen," she said in an urgent tone, "San Yao and Kona are in the village this morning. They came to have a trial about Lamine's divination!"

"What? Why would they do *that?*" I asked.

"I don't know," she answered. "But the trial will be held in our chief's courtyard soon. Go finish buying your things and come back in ten minutes—then we'll go to the trial."

"Okay." As we walked quickly to the marketplace, Philip said, "I *knew* something was up."

In the market I practically ran from trader to trader, collecting tomatoes, onions, and oranges hurriedly, while at the same time contemplating this startling news. Once done, Philip and I started back on the path—where we nearly bumped into Amenan, who was hurrying toward us.

"We're too late," she said, dispensing with the usual formalities. "Uncle Kouassi and I went over to see what was happening, but by the time we got there, the trial was just ending—they must have rushed to keep us from seeing it!"

"But what could it be about?" I asked.

"Let's go back to my courtyard," Amenan replied. "We'll hear about it there."

So we three settled in under Amenan's granary. Soon enough people came to visit: ostensibly for some herbal medicines or a drink of brew, but mainly to share what they'd heard of our chief's meeting.

It seemed that when I'd told San Yao about Lamine's divination, the chief had understood that we must sacrifice our chicken at the most sacred, secret, and powerful of the Beng shrines. Enraged, he'd claimed that Lamine himself shouldn't even know about the shrine, let alone prescribe an offering there by foreigners. Today the elders of Asagbé had agreed on a modification to Lamine's divination: our sacrifice would not be held at that sacred shrine, but elsewhere. In addition, Lamine—or anyone else, for that matter—should think carefully before talking to outsiders.

Hearing this, I slumped down over my knees. If San Yao could intimidate a powerful diviner into changing his divination, what ordinary person would agree to talk to me about *anything?* Despairing, I asked Amenan for advice.

"What I think," she said, brushing away some flies from baby Amwé, asleep on the mat beside her, "is that the people of your village are really upset about another affair—an old vendetta they have with us. About a year ago, a young Beng soldier from Kosangbé died in Bouaké—he was killed in an accident on the base. The soldier was Zang's only son."

I'd long ago condemned Zang for ruthlessly persecuting his daughter, Nakoyan. Now, for the first time, I sympathized with that nasty drunk: between his dead son and his snake daughter, he too had suffered much. But how was his tragedy connected to my own dilemma?

"Since Zang's family is from Asagbé," Amenan explained, "a lot of his relatives from our village went to his son's funeral in Kosangbé. A few days later, a girl in Kosangbé died suddenly. Her relatives accused Ndri, a woman from our village, of bewitching the girl—Ndri had been at the funeral. The Kosangbé elders took the case to court."

"Who was the girl who died?"

"It was San Kofi's oldest daughter," Amenan said.

I sighed. San Kofi, our friend whose heavy-lidded eyes often looked downward or far in the distance even as he was teaching us birdcalls or patiently correcting our pronunciation of new Beng words—he too lived with tragedy.

Now I saw Amenan's point. San Kofi's older brother was the village chief. As the uncle of the girl who died, San Yao must be out to avenge a death he saw as caused by someone from Asagbé. I asked Amenan if I'd reasoned correctly.

"Not exactly," Amenan said. "At the trial, our village elders judged that the girl wasn't bewitched by Ndri at all. The Kosangbé elders had to pay a whole case of red wine as a penalty for falsely accusing the woman. They paid it, but grudgingly. Ever since then, they've been looking to even the score. When San Yao heard about your divination with Lamine, he must have thought this was his big opportunity to win a trial in Asagbé, and get back that case of wine."

"Mon vieux!" I said. "This is all so complicated."

I had to admit that I was somewhat relieved to know that San Yao's anger wasn't directed toward me alone. Still, if there was a longstanding dispute behind our own recent troubles, how could I hope to navigate them? I thought bitterly of my early decision to divide my time between two villages that, I knew now, were enmeshed in a feud.

I turned to Philip. "What do you think we should do?"

"Let's go back to Kosangbé," he replied. "We've got a lot to talk about."

"We sure do." I sighed.

In the car I moaned, "This is a total disaster! I can't believe the chief held a trial about the divination without telling us. Or that Kona was in on it. How could he do that to us?" I stopped, overwhelmed by the enormity of our village father's betrayal.

"When we get back," Philip responded, "we'll have to tell Kona that we know what he did." I dreaded the encounter.

After finishing a quick dinner, we asked François if he'd accompany us to Kona's compound to translate for us. A questioning look flashed on his face, but we remained mysterious, and he agreed to come along. We found Kona sitting on a low stool beside a pile of long pink strips of tree bark.

"We've heard that you and San Yao had a secret trial about our divination today at Asagbé," I began. "We're very upset, especially since it was done without us."

Immediately the *secrétaire* responded, "Did you yourselves see me in Asagbé today?"

"No, but people told us you were at the trial."

"Dih a pey mi ni?" he grilled us.

"Several people at the market," I answered evasively.

"It's true I was in Asagbé today," Kona said, "but I just went to buy some things at the *marché*." As he spoke his face hardened to reveal an anger I'd never seen. "Since my host there is the chief of Asagbé, I went to his court-yard to greet him, and I found San Yao there, holding a trial! I had nothing to do with it. But since you've accused me of participating, we'll return to Asagbé tomorrow with San Yao for another trial to see if I'm lying."

I looked at Philip: his astonished face surely matched my own. If Kona was telling the truth, then Amenan had misled me—a painful thought.

"Very well," I said stiffly. *"Ka n gba zreh"*—Give me the road.

Kona gave us permission to leave, and we returned to our compound. Once there, we immediately closed the door and curtains in our house. Philip began, "I guess if we're going to have a new trial tomorrow, we'll have to challenge San Yao, too."

"Oh god, not that," I said. I hated confrontations of any kind: a formal one such as this seemed a nightmare. Furthermore, the chief was surely powerful in both political savvy and occult knowledge. He'd lived by the rules of his culture for some sixty years—how could we possibly expect to win this case? But if we didn't, it could mean the end of my fieldwork. For if San Yao successfully harassed Lamine, I feared that others might be too terrified to talk with me at all.

And what about Amenan? I thought. Could she . . . ? I stopped, unable to complete my thought.

"That's it, then," I said, suddenly decisive. We had one tiny basis for hope, I consoled myself: we knew San Yao had acted inappropriately in holding the Asagbé meeting without us. But could I convince the villagers to find a chief guilty?

I recalled Jean Briggs' memoir of her fieldwork among a group of Alaskan Eskimos. In typing her field notes inside an igloo, Briggs described, even several layers of gloves didn't prevent her fingers from becoming frostbitten. After reading this daunting scene I'd vowed never to choose a northern climate for my fieldwork. Now I thought: If only the pitfalls and dangers of my fieldwork could be as manageable as frostbite.

For we were locked, the Beng and I, in a pas de deux of power. What I offered were mostly material rewards: cash to regular informants and small presents of locally coveted objects to friends and neighbors, interspersed with the promise that a future generation of urban, literate Beng would learn the ways of their grandparents from reading my work. For their part, the Beng controlled me by using the means of power available to them: knowledge of occult arts and cultural secrets that they knew I coveted and knew they would share with me only at times and in places of their choosing. For the moment, it seemed, we danced with and around each other, each trying to lead, improvising according to the circumstances of the moment. I wondered if, at tomorrow's meeting, there would be another turn in our enforced duet.

Philip: What Can Be Said

That night few villagers came by our compound, and those who did—Yacouba, Yapi Yao, Asaw—were uncharacteristically subdued. After an hour or so of listless conversation, we bade our friends good night, then carried our desk back into the house and locked the door. Once we were alone Alma moaned, "How can I possibly go to trial against the chief of the village?"

"I think it's suicidal not to. If San Yao gets away with this, then no Beng will ever talk to you again—they won't want the trouble. Your fieldwork will be ruined."

Alma slumped over the desk, head in her hands. "It'll be ruined *if* we go to trial."

I sat down beside her. "I don't think so. At least we'll have a fighting chance to reverse today's judgment." She stared at me skeptically. I looked away rather than betray my own doubts, for Alma's fieldwork seemed to be collapsing around her. I forced myself to continue. "Anyway, we don't really have a choice. Kona wants this thing to happen tomorrow. Or do you want to go to trial with him about not having a trial?"

Alma chuckled grimly, and we set about planning a strategy: we'd mention how San Yao had broken the rules of his own culture in arranging a secret trial; how he'd showed disrespect to his own religion by trying to change a divination; how we'd proved the goodness of our intentions among the Beng by the lives we'd helped save.

Alma and I had to agree that we had a pretty decent case. "Actually," I said with an exaggerated frown, "the worst part of this whole mess is that we can't make love on Fridays. But," I added, "*this* part of the divination has no jurisdiction outside of Bengland."

"Ha!" Alma managed to laugh. "You're as bad as San Yao, trying to undermine poor Lamine."

We finally relaxed a little as we took notes for the next day's presentation. I kept thinking of the traditional court scenes in the African novels I'd read for years, where the power of words often carried the day. One of my favorites was Elechi Amadi's *The Great Ponds,* in which two villages suffered a disastrous feud over the water rights to a pond. I liked it so much that I'd brought it along to Côte d'Ivoire. Before Alma and I went to bed, I took the book from our shelf and paged through it, hoping to bone up on African legal rhetoric. Petitioners' speeches were seasoned with incisive proverbs: "Things cannot always go as planned. Even a drum can sound differently from what the maker intended" and "Fighting does not solve anything. Pepper can never be one of the ingredients of a soothing balm." What I read only caused me to worry more: how could either of us come up with such eloquence tomorrow? Certainly not in Beng! Amenan would have to translate for us. But when I recalled the awkward pauses and cultural gaps when Yacouba had helped translate my story, I worried that however we made our case, we'd be swamped.

I kept my doubts to myself as we quietly prepared for bed and listened to the *gbaya* screech its piercing mating call somewhere deep in the forest. After hours of anxious restlessness in the dark, we finally slipped into a troubled sleep.

The next morning a very nervous François accompanied us across the village to San Yao's compound. As we walked I listened to the multiple rhythms of mortar and pestle ringing out across the village, watched women returning from the forest pump with huge pots of water balanced on their heads, their necks stiff with the strain—familiar sights and sounds that now seemed threatened, for if the decision went against us today, how could we possibly stay? Even the forest birds' morning exchanges seemed filled with leaving—just recently San Kofi had corrected me when I'd commented on the birds' singing. "Birds don't *sing*," he frowned, shaking his head, "they *cry*." I'd paused, surprised at what Kofi had inadvertently told me. Music was my culture's metaphor for what birds produced, but to the Beng those same sounds were an extended form of weeping. Birds neither sing nor cry unless we say they do. I had developed a hunger for these unexpected revelations, but perhaps they would soon be denied us.

When we arrived in San Yao's compound we found him relaxing on a Jula lounge chair, still sleepy-eyed. After a stiff exchange of morning greetings, we all sat down, and Alma and I announced formally through François that we knew about yesterday's secret trial, that his behavior was contrary to Beng custom, and that we wanted a retrial.

San Yao listened to all this quietly—in such a small village it was old news by now. *"Bon,"* he said wearily, agreeing to our request. Then he surprised us. "It's true," he said, "that I went to Asagbé alone, without Kona."

He stood up—our brief meeting was over.

We arranged to meet by the side of the road for the drive to Asagbé. As Alma and I prepared for the trip, we thought we finally understood Kona's vehemence in wanting the retrial—a chance to make points in his continuing rivalry with San Yao. The chief had tried our case not only behind our backs, but behind Kona's as well, and this was yet another power struggle between the two men. Just last week there had been a village election for the position of *secrétaire*. Though no one had challenged Kona, he'd used the occasion to complain to the visiting *sous-préfet* that the chief never listened to his advice and was trying to take over his role of collecting donations for a regional infirmary. The *sous-préfet* had managed diplomatically to resolve their differences, but of course this was only temporary. Perhaps San Yao thought that as village guests of Kona, our requesting an Earth sacrifice encroached upon his domain.

Within an hour we drove away from Kosangbé, with Kona and San Yao on the backseat. Such a complicated nest of rivalries, I thought: yesterday Alma and I had been unknowing defendants, today we were plaintiffs; San Yao, yesterday's plaintiff, was now defendant; this morning Kona would be a combination of the two. And there we were, all together in the car, silently plotting our separate cases as we sped past the huge forest trees.

Alma: To Mend, Not Wound

Arrived in Asagbé, we found a meeting in progress under the public veranda. Some government officials from M'Bahiakro had been sent by the *sous-préfet* to discuss a regional affair, so our small group sat down to watch the proceedings. But Philip and I were too preoccupied with our own troubles to pay much attention, so we continued on to Amenan's courtyard.

We found our friend sitting under her granary, chatting quietly with Pascal. They both stared at us in surprise—back so soon? they must have thought. We explained a bit breathlessly that on Kona's insistence we'd returned for a retrial. For one thing, our village father wanted his name cleared: he claimed he wasn't involved in yesterday's trial at all.

"But I saw Kona there with my own two eyes." Amenan frowned, touching an index finger to her temple. She was silent for a few seconds. "Maybe I made a mistake. I'll go ask my uncle what he thinks." She walked next door. While we waited for her to return, Philip and I filled in Pascal on the details of our debacle.

Amenan returned. "My uncle says Kona must be right—he wasn't involved in the trial."

"Well," Philip said to me, "we sure owe him an apology, don't we?"

"I suppose so. But I'm still annoyed at him," I persisted. "Why didn't he stop the trial so we could participate? He knew we were in the village. . . . At least he should've told us about it later."

"All true," Philip agreed. "Still, during this trial I think we should focus on what San Yao did yesterday."

"Okay. And let's keep Lamine out of it altogether," I added. "He's probably furious with me for getting him into this mess." Besides, I thought, my naked self-interest rising up like a phoenix, if he gets involved in the trial, he may never talk to me again. And just when he was beginning to trust me. . . .

"I'm sure Lamine doesn't blame you," Philip said unconvincingly. "But what are we going to say about the sacrifice itself?"

"How could we talk about a shrine whose name we don't even know?" I laughed bitterly.

Soon we all headed over. Amenan, still barefoot, led the way, baby Amwé lodged cozily on her back; Pascal followed, walking crisply in his city shoes; and Philip and I tagged behind, trying to squeeze side by side on the narrow path to continue our worried strategizing in these last minutes before the trial.

Back at the public veranda, we found the *sous-préfet*'s meeting just breaking up—but we didn't see Kona or San Yao.

"Let's walk over to the chief's courtyard," suggested Amenan. "Maybe they're already there."

Soon we heard a group of voices talking. We neared the Asagbé chief's compound and were startled: crowded all around the courtyard sat a group of perhaps thirty or forty solemn, graying men. All eyes glanced at us as we entered the space.

"What are they all doing here?" I whispered in alarm to Amenan.

"They must be here for your trial," she whispered back.

"Oh god, this is a nightmare."

"You can go sit over there." Amenan gestured across the courtyard. There was a free space between two elders that looked large enough to accommodate the three of us. Philip and I turned to walk over, but Amenan remained in place.

"What about you?" I asked my friend nervously. "Will you sit next to us?"

Amenan glanced around at the assembly. Her eyes seemed to focus on San Yao, who was speaking quietly with an elder seated next to him. "It's too sunny there," Amenan said, "Amwé would cry."

Undoubtedly Amenan feared that the baby might catch malaria if she were exposed to the sun for too long; but at the moment Amwé was sleeping, and Amenan could easily drape a cloth over the infant's head, as she often did on sunny days. I understood my friend's unstated reason: she didn't wish to become further involved in these public proceedings. How could I blame her? Our problem wasn't her affair—at least not enough for her to risk falling into the disfavor of the assembled crowd. If she did, our relationship might never be the same again. Philip and I walked across the courtyard to take our seats next to the Asagbé elders.

But with Amenan unavailable to translate for us, and my skills in the elusive Beng language feeling shakier by the minute, how could we possibly state our case? I looked over at Pascal. His French was fluent, and the shyness we'd discerned in Abidjan had disappeared in his home village. He must have sensed my anxiety, for immediately he strode toward us.

"Amenan can't sit with us," I whispered. "Do you think you could translate if we need help?"

"Of course."

"Merci," I said to him, *"merci beaucoup!"*

The elders' murmurings died down, and the chief of Asagbé turned to us. It was time to speak. Hoping that my trembling hand wasn't visible to the old men, I said, "Elders, we're grateful to you for coming to this meeting. We understand that yesterday the chief of Kosangbé had a meeting about the sacrifice we must offer. But the chief didn't tell us beforehand about it, and we weren't allowed to participate."

As Pascal translated this opening statement, I tried to compose my next one. Before I could continue, one of the elders asked, "Who told you about the trial?"

Philip and I glanced at each other knowingly—*Dih a pey mi ni* again, I thought.

"There were many people in the marketplace who told me—I didn't ask all their names," I lied to protect my friend. Betraying neither approval nor disapproval of this perjury, Pascal translated in businesslike fashion my response.

The elder nodded, then replied briskly, "If you can't name one person who told you of the trial, there's no reason to discuss the matter any further."

Had I understood Pascal's translation correctly? Surely the elder couldn't be dismissing our case so abruptly. I turned to Philip, hoping he could think of a rebuttal. He stroked his mustache a few times, then said, "*Who* told us is completely inconsequential. The point is, the trial was held."

I held my breath as Pascal translated: would this line of reasoning persuade anyone in the courtyard?

A few elders around us muttered softly, then one said aloud, "What the man says is true. You can proceed."

"Good going," I whispered to Philip in English, then continued in French to Pascal: "What troubles us is this: San Yao came to Asagbé to formally discuss an affair that concerns my husband and me, yet he didn't include us. How can he explain this?"

The men around us murmured comments—none of which we understood. Then San Yao, who sat across the courtyard from us, spoke for a long time. I caught some phrases of his impassioned response—"what the diviner said," "our strangers"—but the gist escaped me.

"*Ah-heh,*" I heard elders around me mutter in assent.

Finally Pascal translated: "I was just confused about the sacrifice the diviner said you must offer. I came for more information." This abbreviated version of the chief's speech undoubtedly left out the rhetorical flourishes that make any African trial sparkle. But how could we compete with the chief's eloquence when it eluded translation? In any case, I knew San Yao's statement wasn't true . . . but I didn't dare accuse a village chief publicly of lying.

"Since the 'information' the chief sought concerned *us,*" I replied, "we should have been notified of the meeting he planned."

More murmurs. Again San Yao responded at length.

"*Voilà!*" more than one man exclaimed as he continued. Would the chief's eloquence carry the day? This fear heightened my audacity, for when Pascal translated that long speech as simply, "I didn't go for evil purposes," I responded immediately.

"How could we know this if you acted secretly?"

Before the chief could answer, Philip joined in. "We've done many things to help the villagers of Kosangbé. We freely give out medicines and treat illnesses every day; we saved little Apu's life when he was bitten by a snake; we drove San Yao's own sister-in-law to M'Bahiakro when she was in grave danger from childbirth; we drove Wamya Kona down to the hospital after he fell off his bicycle. We've done all this because we care about the people of the village. So we feel we should be shown respect, too: we should know when people are discussing our affairs."

The elders buzzed with comments to each other—I longed to understand them all. Finally one of them addressed us: "Yes, you're right. San Yao didn't mean you any harm, but he should have told you his intentions beforehand—he understands this now. In any case, you'll hold the sacrifice at the spot where the chief indicates. Have we finished?" The elder shifted position.

I couldn't imagine that the trial was over so abruptly. True, my main point had been publicly conceded, but the chief's position was not thereby invalidated—indeed, neither of us had been declared guilty.

But now Kona addressed us. "I have something to say. You accused me of participating in yesterday's trial, but the chief of Asagbé can confirm that I didn't participate at all."

The elder nodded his head and said, *"Mm-hmm,"* with satisfaction.

Now Kona turned to us. "In the future, if you come to me with information, you should be honest in telling me who told it to you, otherwise you shouldn't bother to mention it."

"What our village father says is correct," Philip responded immediately. "As he'll always answer our questions, so we'll answer his." There was scattered laughter throughout the courtyard. Perhaps they understood Philip's irony: if our village father indeed shared things with us openly, we wouldn't be commuting regularly to Asagbé in our search to understand Beng culture.

Now San Yao wanted to speak. "I just want to say," he declared, "that to avoid misunderstandings in the future, whenever Amwé plans to talk with someone, she should tell me first, and I'll come along."

To my horror, the audience murmured assent. San Yao was still trying to intimidate my potential informants. If his declaration were accepted, he might undo all we'd achieved in the trial, for who would agree to talk to me?

Suddenly inspired, Philip said, through Pascal, "Father, we can't allow you to do this, because we care so much for your family. If you come to all of Amwé's interviews, you'll never have time to work in the fields. Your yams would rot, and your wife and children would starve!"

Once again the jury laughed, and even San Yao smiled ruefully at how his cunning suggestion had been turned against him. I was proud of Philip: he'd studied traditional Nigerian legal rhetoric the night before to good advantage.

Pascal whispered to us, "Usually at the end of a trial, the plaintiff buys beer for the elders."

Philip nodded and sent a boy off to the boutique across the road. As the elders conversed among themselves, I realized their model for this trial must have been very different from my own: rather than announcing a victor and a loser, their aim was for *both* sides to come out satisfied. And how could this be otherwise? There were good reasons why neither San Yao nor I could lose this case: he, because of the ancestors and forest spirits that protected him; I, because of the stamped government papers that protected *me*, though in a very different way. Considering our various sources of power, the point of the trial could only be to mend, not wound.

So, a few minutes later, our unlikely small group—two rival village officials, a nursing village mother, a university student, a writer, and an anthropologist—filed down the path to Amenan's compound. There we sat on low stools in the open courtyard and shared several warm beers, talking about the soil, the drought, and the yam harvest, endeavoring to convince ourselves that we could now trust one another.

Philip: Drought's End

The men of Kosangbé sat in small groups in the middle of compounds or under the village's palm-leaf *akpa,* peeling long, thick sections of the pink inner bark of a forest tree into thin strips. These strips—called *waleh gobang,* yam ties—were then knotted together, one end to another, into an extended stretch of cord that when coiled into a wide circle could be slung on the shoulder. All this work anticipated the appearance of the first green shoots from the yam mounds. Then a farmer would attach one end of the cord to the tiny shoot, unroll a stretch of the coil to the lowest branch of a nearby tree, and tie it there. Within days the shoot would creep up the cord, its spreading leaves gathering as much sun as possible. I thought this system elegantly efficient: more yam leaves above, fatter yams below.

Kossum, François's younger brother, seemed particularly good at separating the wide strands of bark into thinner and thinner strips. A quiet man, he could sit absorbed for hours. Such relentless, monotonous work, I thought, but I still wanted to give it a try. So I often sat with Yacouba and learned, under his tutelage, how to carefully pull apart the bark, how to follow the grain without ripping, without waste. My fingers tried to accustom themselves to new, delicate movements, until eventually I entered into an almost meditative state that reminded me of my canoeing days nearly a decade earlier, when long hours of steady paddling swept me into a quiet rhythm.

This intense and yet relaxing concentration must have undercut what was also dogged and fatalistic about the work, because no one was sure these cords would be used: despite the various rituals, punishments, and sacrifices the Beng had performed, the drought continued. I didn't want to consider what miseries might eventually be wreaked upon the lives of our neighbors—some of whom still thought our presence in Kosangbé was the cause of the drought. Perhaps these suspicions would finally end when we performed Lamine's prescribed chicken sacrifice on the next *Po fen*—just a few days away—and were thus formally introduced to the Kosangbé Earth.

Alma and I drove to Bongalo and bought a white chicken for the event. But on our return the car shook and creaked, so we turned around and drove cautiously to M'Bahiakro. After locating a mechanic, we discovered that our chassis was once again cracked. For six hours a taciturn old man—whose garage was an empty field—soldered poor Didadi back in shape, while our doomed chicken squawked intermittently on the backseat. Alma sat beside me under a tree and fretfully tallied this small disaster's time lost against the five months we had left in Bengland.

Two days later it rained, the dark, cloudy skies finally releasing their promise. Alma and I swiftly hauled our desk into the house and listened to the clatter on our tin roof, the occasional cheers of the delighted villagers. The forest sex exorcism had been performed about ten days earlier—would the Beng credit that ritual with this downpour?

The rain came down in such thick, luscious sheets that no one dared venture outside. Alma typed up a backlog of field notes, and I cracked open a new book, Roger Angell's *Five Seasons,* a compendium of a half decade's baseball reporting. I knew that pennant races were in full swing back home—the All Star game had come and gone—but I had little access to American sports news. Inexplicably, the Voice of America didn't report baseball standings, so Angell's book was my substitute for the usual summer hours of pleasure. As I read the first few pages, our tin roof thundering from the downpour, I noted with satisfaction that my substitution was, for the moment, an improvement: if I were at a baseball stadium right now, the game would be rained out.

The return of the rains also gave me extended time to work on my new story. I realized now that the first sentence I'd written about that angry family chasing itself out of a house had to be the *last* sentence of my story. Now my task was to create a family that could lose control of itself so completely, and already I suspected that the pace of this budding story would be influenced by the raw energy of the Beng family disputes around me. Over the next few days I invented an American extended family whose members were fictional versions of my own relatives: I raided my memories of a forbidding step-grandfather, who often sat sternly on a chair, his cane resting on his thighs; my favorite grandmother, who pretended to be the Big Bad Wolf and chased the children about her house during family gatherings, her false teeth clacking in her hand; my wild younger brother and his ability to break whatever came his way; and my unhappily married parents, who only minimally coexisted with each other in their own house. These presences had existed for so long within me—why shouldn't they too be affected and transformed by my new life in Africa?

The day finally arrived for our sacrifice to the Kosangbé Earth. Because the sacrifice would take place at a forest shrine, Alma, as a woman, couldn't go with me. I would have to observe carefully, and I liked the prospect of reporting back to the anthropologist. As Alma's informant, I'd get to experience the gentle, curious grilling she put the villagers through.

I walked along a forest path with a small group of men that included San Yao, Kona, Kouakou Kala, and François. We continued for about a mile until, without a word, everyone stopped abruptly—evidently we'd reached a spot that was easily recognizable, though I couldn't see any difference from the rest of the forest. With his machete, François immediately began clearing first one spot, then another, off the side of the path. Once done, he chopped some nearby dead wood and, after starting a fire, left without a word.

San Yao waited until François was out of sight before he knelt and prayed over the chicken. Then he passed it to Kouakou Kala, who prayed as well. Both spoke in low tones that were indecipherable. I wished I'd brought along a tape recorder—though I doubted any of the elders would have allowed it.

The prayers done, Kouakou Kala slit the struggling chicken's neck and sprinkled a circle of blood on the cleared space. When he let go of the dying creature, it hopped about briefly, an inelegant moment in the ceremony, though this seemed to bother no one. Then Kona plucked and gutted the corpse within the circle of blood.

Suddenly a little boy walked down the path toward us—he was returning from the fields. Kona mumbled something to him, and the boy stared straight ahead, passing us silently. When he was gone, Kouakou Kala checked in the chicken's gutted body for the ovaries. They were white, so he declared the sacrifice good. San Yao checked too and murmured agreement.

The body was placed on the fire, and we sat quietly while it cooked. I followed the lead of my companions and said nothing, though I wondered what San Yao and Kona must be thinking about this result of our unusual trial. For my part, I hadn't much faith that past disputes had been settled or past suspicions laid to rest.

Kona laid the roasted chicken across a wide bed of leaves and split the body down the middle. He held out half to me, and I refused what seemed to be an overly generous offering. "It's for everyone," I said. But as the chicken was distributed further, I wasn't offered another piece. I'd only meant to indicate that I should be given a small piece like everyone else, yet who knew what I'd managed to say? Was my refusal to accept Kona's generous offering a faux pas that would affect the ceremony's effectiveness? I couldn't very well grab a piece from someone's hands, so, filled with indecision, I sat and watched the feast. By the time the elders were down to sucking bones, I was furtively examining the undifferentiated forest around me, but there was nothing that I'd be able to remember from this spot. My eyes were not Beng.

François appeared. It was time to leave, so we thanked each other formally and headed back to Kosangbé. Silently I counted my footsteps until reaching ninety-two—the point where an old rotten tree leaned over the forest path. *This* I could remember: from here I'd be able to recount my steps.

Back at the village, Alma was waiting for us in our compound with two large bottles of beer—a gift for the sacrificers, who nodded in approval. We sat in a circle of chairs, and as the glasses were passed around, Alma and I offered our thanks through François. Alma was particularly pleased that we had been formally introduced to one of Kosangbé's sacred Earths, even if we didn't know *which* one. Kona ordered a child to fetch another bottle of beer, then San Yao ordered another, and soon I was tipsy enough to imagine that at least a truce was in effect.

Later I recalled the events of the morning to Alma. Notebook in hand, she peppered my account with questions. "Did the elders pass out the chicken in any particular order?"

I hadn't considered this at all. "Gee, I didn't notice. I don't think it mattered." But I wondered if I'd missed something and tried to re-create the distribution of chicken parts.

"Are you sure you didn't see anything special about the spot?"

"I had a long time to look, and it just seemed like forest to me. But I did count out my steps, so I can take you there."

Alma grinned. "Oh, wonderful thinking. But I'm really not supposed to see it. Maybe you could go back and look around a bit more."

"Sure, but I doubt the place will look any different." Then, as if to apologize for my earlier refusal to witness the forest sex ritual, I added, "What I really wish I'd done was sneak a tape recorder along and tape those prayers."

She paused in her note taking and sighed. Had this idea occurred to her, too? "Well, I hate to say it," she said, "but I'm glad you didn't—that's one of those ethical no-no's."

"You're right," I agreed immediately. Still, I suspected that the unexpected gift of a secret tape would have pleased her.

Alma: Sitting with a Corpse

My mind still orbiting from all the red wine of the morning, I sat in our courtyard trying to memorize some new expressions I'd collected—a secret set of phrases for body parts that adults used when they didn't want children to understand (eyes: "things that see things"; teeth: "things that chew things"; hands: "things that catch things")—when François came over, his usual grin missing.

"Amwé, Kouadio: an old woman has died."

"Oh, *a kunglia*," Philip said—Our condolences. "Who is she?"

"It's old Apisé," François answered. "You know: the one who couldn't even walk to the bush to take a crap anymore."

"Ah, yes," I said, *"a kunglia."*

"The chief has already washed the corpse," François continued. "Soon they'll announce the death on the drums—probably after everyone's eaten dinner."

"Thank you for telling us." After François left, I realized this was virtually the first time that anyone in Kosangbé had told us openly of an event *before* I'd found out about it through my own sleuthing. Perhaps the morning's sacrifice had already begun to do its work? As always, I was on the prowl for that mythic Acceptance.

I decided to walk over to the courtyard where Apisé had lived. Though the funeral hadn't been formally announced yet, I cautiously greeted some women sitting inside Apisé's room.

"Come in, Amwé," they said, and I did. In the middle of the floor was a long, thin bundle wrapped in a black-and-white-striped cotton cloth—a bundle that must have contained what remained of Apisé's frail, tiny body after some ninety years of living. Surrounding the bundle were four women, who all shifted position to make room for me. And so I found myself sitting next to a corpse.

I was in and out of that room for seven hours. During that time I experienced a very different ritual from the first funeral in Kosangbé that I had seen almost eight months ago. This time I too became endangered by the cadaver with its contagious spread of death, I too doused my hands and eyes with an herbal decoction to wash off the smell, touch, and sight of death, I too received the line of men from the village—a line that included our village father as well as Philip—when they came to pay us their condolences. When all but one of the women in the room exited briefly to join in the lively dancing that started in the courtyard, Lanzé Afwé accepted my presence as her only living companion when she spoke softly to the body of the woman who had been her husband's stepmother: "Thank you, Grandmother, thank you for all that you did, thank you for yesterday." And when the other women returned to the room, it was my responsibility to buy them some whiskey. It was then that I sensed another presence in the room: out of a dark corner crept old Makon, to claim her shot glass worth of *kutuku*. A large and rather ugly woman, Makon always had a sad and tender smile for me. Now, on the occasion of her half sister's death, she was grateful for the drink.

Then the young people of the village came to pay their condolences, but they wailed so loudly and histrionically that old Kri Afwé chased them for their mock mourning. I thought how satisfying it was to be on the other side of exile this time, remaining inside with the mourning women to do our serious work of fanning the corpse, waving pungent-smelling *nonu pléplé* and lemon tree leaves over it to ward off the stench of death. But the young revelers weren't deterred by their eviction—immediately the pack began running up and down the road and, to my amazement, screamed outrageously lewd insults to each other.

"You shit pricks!" shouted the girls.

"You red cunts!" the giggling boys yelled back.

In a few minutes the children circled back to us and, standing a scant yard or two outside our doorway, howled even more uproariously while the women inside pretended they could ignore this raucous rebellion.

Finally, at 2:30 A.M., I stumbled out of the room. In the courtyard, two men still drummed to accompany a few women dancing quietly in a circle. Nearby, a few people lay stretched out on bark cloths, dreaming their night air dreams, surrounded by dances of death. In the light of a bright, waxing moon, I trudged across the village to catch a few hours of sleep with Philip in our own bed, before dawn brought preparations for the burial.

Philip: Dancing Dog

"Welcome home," I mumbled as Alma slipped under the mosquito netting and into our bed. "How'd it go?"

"Humpf," she grunted, falling asleep almost immediately. I watched my wife for a few minutes as she slept beside me. I admired her dedication, but I was glad she'd returned.

We woke the next morning to clapping hands and a harsh voice crying, *"Kaw kaw kaw!"* Who was this? I glanced at our clock—we'd overslept. Alma and I crawled out of bed, still tired, and opened the door.

Kri Afwé stood before us, her old face further wrinkled with anger. "Why didn't you come to my compound this morning and give condolences?" she shouted, dispensing with the morning greeting. "Don't you know how to behave? You have to come to my compound!" Before we could answer she stalked off, her small body, as usual, bent forward as though she were struggling against some harsh, private wind.

"Good morning," I said in English, low enough so she wouldn't hear me. "Well," Alma said, sighing, "that was some etiquette lesson, wasn't it?" Still, we took our cue from Kri Afwé and rushed through our morning baths. Then we made a circuit through the village, giving greetings and condolences, working our way as quickly as possible to Kri Afwé's compound.

"Ka kun nini wé"—Our sympathy for being cold from your loss—we said to the old woman. She nodded and returned our greeting, her face both satisfied and bitter.

We continued through the village until storm clouds swiftly approached, then we hurried back to our compound through thick, windswept sheets of rain. Clearly, few visitors from other villages would travel in this weather. The burial was put off until the afternoon.

By late morning, under clearing skies, young women gathered near the village kapok tree and tressed each other's hair, while around them children chased each other, their laughter ringing out. Suddenly the funeral revelry resumed: once again children mocked the corpse while old women sang songs over it; young women marched up and down the road dividing the two halves of the village, tapping canes and happily shouting sexual insults at the men gathered to watch them: "You shrinking pricks! You black dangling testicles!"

Nearby, Kofi Ajua, a young woman not related to Apisé, caricatured the dead woman's doddering shuffle, squinting and talking to herself, bumping into the delighted mourners who crowded around her in a small circle. Beside this slapstick show, Apisé's adopted son, Kwamé, wailed with genuine grief, while a few boys mocked his crying with their own exaggerated version. Alma and I wandered from one cluster of excitement to another, savoring the strange mixture of celebration and mourning. I even joined the young men when they marched along the road and raucously insulted the genitalia of the women of Kosangbé.

Ajua continued staggering about with her cane, imitating Apisé. "I have to take a shit," she croaked in an old woman's voice to howls of laughter. "Where's the path to the forest?" Everyone shouted out conflicting directions, and Ajua wandered this way and that, the crowd of delighted spectators always blocking her way. Less than a hundred feet away, in full view of this comedy, the grave was being dug.

Soon visitors from other villages arrived, and they marched in a solemn line to the seated Kosangbé elders. "God is responsible for the death," announced a speaker for the visiting mourners, "so you shouldn't be too unhappy about it."

"Thank you," the elders spoke in ragged unison.

The long greeting formalities finally completed, arrangements for the animal sacrifices began, with much discussion over who should contribute what—chicken, goat, sheep? Though Alma scribbled away happily, I grew bored, and when San Kofi came by and offered to buy me a drink, I accepted, glad to give him some company. Ever since I'd heard that he had recently lost his eldest daughter, I wondered if his attraction to the intricacies of bird-calls—their weeping—was a form of mourning.

We set off to the other side of the village, where a young man had set up an informal bar in his mud house. Inside were a number of young men who were in the army, back in the village briefly for the funeral. As San Kofi and I entered, I immediately smelled something sweet and tangy, strangely familiar and yet out of place in these surroundings. Then I saw a hand-rolled cigarette being passed, and I knew: marijuana.

"Ah," I said, "what's that?"

"*Ta geng*"—Good tobacco—a young man replied, smiling. "Do you know what it is?"

"Of course!"

They laughed and passed the joint to me. I hesitated at first—I hadn't smoked pot in years—but among the Beng it wasn't polite to refuse an offering. I sat on a stool, closed my eyes, and inhaled, enjoying a moment's nostalgic twinge. Then I handed back the joint and leaned against the cool mud wall. San Kofi brought me a shot glass of *kutuku,* and I bought the next round. When the joint came by again, I sucked in a little more and offered him a hit.

He waved me away with a mock frown. "We have to leave, the animals are going to be sacrificed soon."

When we walked back to the funeral I noticed that the rain-soaked forest surrounding the village blazed with green, its lush smell overwhelming. Then I heard a strangely rhythmic scrunching sound: the suck of my own sandals, thickly crusted with muddy glop. I stopped, imagining I was balancing precariously on stilts. Yes, I thought, the marijuana is certainly taking effect.

I sat on one of the huge, sinuous roots of the kapok tree, feeling remarkably tiny, and the villagers moved in slow motion—due as much to the solemnity of the occasion as to my heightened sense of events—as one by one they walked up to Ché Kofi, made a brief announcement, and then handed him a few coins. I knew all these people around me, yet I didn't know them at all: listening to their speeches, I was struck by the alien contours of the language.

I closed my eyes and for a long time lost myself in a strange map of beautifully unpredictable sounds. Rising out of that musical landscape were words I understood, though I couldn't make out the larger context. Then, behind those words appeared the voices: Kona's mumble; Ché Kofi's sarcastic lilt; the clear, slow tones of Lanzé Afwé; and, in the distance, Moya's stutter as she scolded some laughing children. Suddenly I heard the staccato bite of two men's angry voices, just a few feet away. I listened carefully: Kla Kwana, for sure, and perhaps Egbri Kouassi. I opened my eyes to check. There they were, Kouassi shaking his fist at Kla Kwana's put-upon face.

Alma sat beside me. "Too much to drink?" she asked.

I nodded. "And too much to smoke."

She stared at me for a moment, not understanding. I made a harsh inhaling noise, and then she grinned. "Really? How?"

"Some of the young guys in the army brought some up." I pointed to Kla Kwana and Egbri Kouassi. "What's going on?"

"Kwana's supposed to contribute a sheep, but he says he can't afford to, so he's trying to offer a chicken. Kouassi's pissed at him, says it's against the rules."

"He's being kind of nasty, isn't he?"

"Well, I think I know the reason. Something very interesting is going on about these sacrifices." Alma paused, and I nodded for her to continue. "The funeral donations have become kind of an embarrassment," she said, glancing at her notebook. "Kwamé and Kwana are Apisé's only living relatives. They're the ones responsible for the funeral costs. Under the circumstances, Kwana shouldn't be so stingy."

I watched the two men argue further, their anger so immediate I could almost feel it myself. Finally Kwana walked off, shaking his head, turning once or twice for yet another last word while Kouassi hurled a few more insults at him.

"But there's more," Alma said, "and it's really strange. People are *pretending* to be related to Apisé."

"Pretending?"

"If there aren't enough family donations, then the whole funeral looks bad, so when people go up to Ché Kofi and give him money, they make up a kinship relation. That's what they've all been calling out."

"But they're not fooling anybody. . . ."

"Of course not. It's all just a performance to make the funeral run smoothly!"

I whistled—the villagers around me were assuming roles, creating an entire, extended imitation family for a dead woman who couldn't contradict them. What *wasn't* fiction? I thought. I closed my eyes and let the swirling inside take over again.

"Philip," Alma said, shaking me, "I think the burial's about to begin."

Suddenly the women's wailing once again filled the air: "*Whey! Whey! Whey!*" I looked up to see two of the four grave diggers carrying out Apisé's corpse, which was wrapped loosely in a tan blanket and a white-and-blue-checkered *pagne.* Alma and I followed.

After the two men carefully lowered the body into the nearby grave, San Yaokro, the chief's younger half brother, slit the neck of a sacrificial chicken. When it stopped struggling, he gave it to San Yao, who stood near the covered head of the corpse and prayed over the chicken: "Apisé, Kouassi Kwamé is offering you this chicken. Go to sleep."

His prayer done, he placed the chicken at the foot of the grave, and then Kona poured a calabash of water mixed with white *sepé* powder over the corpse. Apisé was ready to be buried. Yao Ba grabbed a hand hoe and listened to the elders' detailed instructions: only four shovelsful of earth must be pushed into the grave, and only in a particular way.

"Between your legs—and just one shovelful," Kona said. Afraid to make a mistake, Yao Ba tentatively scraped the dirt into the grave.

"Move to your right and shovel again," the elders urged him, and again Yao Ba scraped a clump of dirt through his bent legs.

"Now move to your right! Shovel again!"

His face tense, Yao Ba obeyed and waited for more instructions. This part of the burial was both rehearsal and performance, I realized. Yet who was the audience besides the elders—the spirits, the ancestors, Apisé herself? The tense moment passed with the fourth shovelful, and then the grave diggers set about filling in the grave.

The sheep and goat were quickly sacrificed. Kona and San Yao decided which butchered pieces would go to which mourners, and though there was much potential for disputes, the decisions went quickly: everyone was exhausted from long hours of mourning and revelry.

The next day the funeral wound down further—though more visitors came to Kosangbé, no dances were scheduled. In this quiet aftermath Yacouba came to visit us, and we learned why Apisé's burial had been marked by such excess merriment: when a very old person died, the funeral was considered "sweet" and became a celebration for a long life lived.

But there was a further reason. "Apisé was a witch," Yacouba said quietly.

"A witch?" Alma said.

"Of course. Why else was she childless?"

Yacouba knew of two people who had suffered from Apisé's witchcraft. The first was a friend of his, Nyolé Yao. Yacouba used to work in the fields with him, and one afternoon, as they were returning together from the day's work, they saw a liana, stretched taut about a foot from the ground and tied on both ends to trees on either side of the path. When they returned to the village, Yao's mother, Makon, asked a visiting Jimini diviner to explain what her son had encountered. The diviner said that Apisé—Makon's half sister and therefore Yao's aunt—was performing witchcraft on Yao. She had bound Yao's name to the liana, thus stealing a part of his soul.

That night Yao fled the village. At the time, he had been in the middle of

building yam mounds, which were left to rot in his absence. For years he lived in the nearby Ando region, but he was never the same. During the infrequent occasions he returned to Kosangbé, everyone noticed how he had changed: apathetic, a drunkard with no hopes of ever marrying, spiritually withered away.

Yacouba paused, watching sadly as Alma wrote down his tale. "And who was the second victim?" she asked, looking up from her notepad.

"My first child."

"Oh, Yacouba," I began.

"I was in the army at the time, stationed in M'Bahiakro, and my son was less than a year old. One day Apisé asked Dongi where she slept with our child." Yacouba gestured with his hand. "Dongi showed her the bedroom. That night my son fell sick."

Yacouba spoke so low that we could barely hear him. "Three days later, my mother took the baby to Komena Kouassikro for medicines. He prescribed leaf washes, but they didn't help.

"When I received word that my son was ill, I decided to bring him down to the infirmary. But before I reached the village he was dead. Apisé had eaten his soul."

Stunned by what Yacouba had told us, Alma and I managed to express the proper Beng condolences, but they were empty solace for such a sad story. As Yacouba stared off quietly beside us, lost in his terrible memories, I remembered my friend's dancing the first night of the funeral. I had been struck by the peculiar intensity of his solo as he twirled and spun, his feet pounding the earth, and now I knew why.

Later that morning Alma and I drove to Asagbé, and I kept thinking about that first night's funeral dance and my own solo turn: the villagers had shouted their approval as a few women draped spare *pagnes* over me. Normally proud of my dancing abilities, I now felt somehow shamed, and then I remembered the African fire stoker in Conrad's *Heart of Darkness:* a "savage" dressed as a European, who was "full of improving knowledge" of a world he could never truly enter; Marlow compared him contemptuously to a dog walking on its hind legs. Now *I* felt like a trick dog: I'd merely copied the correct steps of Beng dances, divorced from any wider context, while my friend's furious solo celebrating Apisé's death was his own choreographed revenge for the loss of a child.

The rains continued for days after Apisé's funeral, one monotonous downpour after another. One afternoon a large molasses truck, driving down from a sugar plantation near Groumania, got stuck on the steep and muddy hill just a few hundred yards south of our village. Because it was Kosangbé's rest day—*Po fen*—soon virtually everyone crowded on the hill, watching the listing truck's huge tires spin ineffectually, churning mud into the air.

Another molasses truck approached, its blasting horn warning us off the road. But *its* wheels quickly sank. Both trucks tipped at precipitous angles, and from loose caps at their tops flowed thick, slow streams of molasses. Following the lead of our neighbors, Alma and I hurried back to Kosangbé for cups to collect the sweet windfall. Yao Ba returned with a pail in either hand. Grinning, he told us he intended to use the molasses for hunting: in the forest he'd pour some on a plate and then wait for a sweet-toothed antelope to appear.

By now the spilled molasses formed dark, sticky pools that mingled slowly with the muddy surface of the hill. Swarms of bees swooped and circled over the sweet cargo. Always nervous around bees, I watched the trucks from a safe distance, and those villagers who arrived late with empty cups decided to wait until sundown before trying to collect their share.

Within an hour lines of trucks and cars waited on either side of the jam-up. Crews of drivers and some of the young men of the village teamed up to clear the brush on one side of the road for an alternate path. A caravan of vehicles made their way through, but they quickly turned the path into a boglike mess, so thickened by gobs of molasses that a third truck was mired in the ooze. With the sun about to set, both lines of cars and trucks turned around and drove off.

The next morning a rescue truck from a sugar plantation in the north arrived with thick cables. With much grinding of gears and those taut, coiled cables humming, the first truck finally lurched out, to the cheers of the drivers. But when the second was connected, the rescue truck's wheels spun and spun until it too was mired in the mud.

Again a line of impatient drivers backed up on either side of the muddy disaster. And once again canny villagers laid thick branches and long palm leaves with fanning ribs over the side path's ooze; but now they charged one thousand CFAs for their help. The road became an impromptu carnival, with women walking up and down the lines of waiting cars, selling food to the stranded drivers, and children raced about in the shadows of the great leaning vehicles, their fingers sticky with molasses as they dodged the swarming bees.

Wandering about the festivities, Alma and I recognized one of the stranded truck drivers—back in March he'd given us a ride to M'Bahiakro after one of our car's frequent breakdowns. We reintroduced ourselves and thanked him again for his help. Surprised to see us, Coulibali Ousmane happily accepted when we invited him and his crew over to our compound for dinner.

When Ousmane arrived that evening with his men, he regarded our mud house and quite ordinary-looking compound with politely disguised disappointment—apparently he'd been expecting something grander.

"Do you like it here?" he asked. Perhaps, if village life was a world he had escaped, our presence in Kosangbé seemed truly mysterious.

"Yes," Alma said, describing her work as Moya presented bowls filled with a special meal she'd made for our guests: *foutou* with chicken in a palm-nut sauce.

While we ate I wondered aloud why the M'Bahiakro road crew hadn't yet arrived to rescue the trucks.

"Ah, the roads are bad everywhere," Ousmane said. "They'll come when they can. But that isn't our only problem. We've been told by the old men of this village that the spirits on the hill are angry with us."

"Oh? Why are they angry?" Alma asked. She glanced over at me, and I could see she wished she'd been at that meeting.

He sighed. "We're disturbing them. Our loads are too heavy, and our trucks make too much noise when we drive by on sacred days. We're supposed to sacrifice a chicken."

Intrigued that Ousmane, a Muslim, considered taking the village elders' recommendation, Alma asked, "So you'll do the sacrifice?"

"Of course! Anything to get us out of the mud," he replied. Smiling, he dipped a piece of *foutou* into the sauce.

If Ousmane and his fellow drivers were stuck, so were we: Didadi couldn't make it past the truck-strewed mire, so in order to travel to Asagbé we borrowed bicycles from Yacouba and one of his friends. Alma and I navigated the miles of muddy puddles laboriously, sometimes stopping and walking our bikes along the thick brush at the edge of the road as we chattered away. We were alone: nothing but forest on either side of the empty road, which stretched far ahead and behind us. Though my boots were sticky with mud from skirting my bike around yet another puddle, I said, "I could learn to like this." Letting our trip linger, we pedaled slowly, and we even tried to hold hands while riding side by side.

When Alma and I finally arrived in Amenan's compound, Pascal was waiting for me: today, in partial exchange for his translating Beng stories, I'd promised to help him study for the approaching university exams. I said good-bye to Alma and set off with Pascal to the small thatched house his father had reserved for him during the summer. We hurried across the village—Pascal had little patience for the elaborate greetings, and he hoped to encounter as few people as possible. This rudeness to elders surprised me—often he sped through the greetings while continuing on his way, not even completing the required responses.

But Pascal was now an outsider to his own culture. When he'd completed elementary school in the Asagbé schoolhouse, he'd moved twenty-five miles away to M'Bahiakro, site of the nearest junior high school. Graduating from there, he'd continued on to high school in Bouaké, nearly eighty miles from the Beng region. Now he was in his second year at the university in Abidjan, two hundred and fifty miles away. Asagbé was no longer his true home—he'd lived most of his life away from the village. The Ivoirian system of education ensured alienation, and Pascal was one of its predictable products: French was now his language of choice, and he admitted to me with little shame that there were some nuances of Beng he didn't understand.

That day Pascal wanted me to help him explicate a poem that his professors had announced would be an important part of the fall exams. "This one," he said, handing me the open book. So, during the rainy season in a tropical forest of perpetual greenery, I set about trying to help Pascal decipher Keats's poem "To Autumn." How would I help him understand an evocation of a season he had never experienced, how describe the coming of the cold, the winter months?

I glanced quickly through the poem, then read it more slowly. The archaic language alone—"Who hath not seen thee oft amid thy store?"—was going to be a challenge. "Let's go through the poem line by line," I suggested, and I tried to translate nineteenth-century English into modern American equivalents. Pascal nodded earnestly, but his patient face reminded me that we hadn't really begun to examine the heart of Keats's poem.

The work went incredibly slowly—particularly the middle stanza, with its personifications of autumn—as each line contained poetic allusions to an alien world removed by both time and place. Yet there were similarities: the "thatch eves," the "granary floor," the atmosphere of harvest. Actually, substitute the dry season for winter, and any Beng farmer might appreciate the poem's world better than this city boy sitting beside me. I sighed. Still ahead of us was a discussion of the secret energy of one of Keats's last works: a celebration of life's own autumnal season.

As I tried to help untangle this poem for Pascal, I recalled my reactions to the Beng tales he'd translated for us—some of them containing strange repetitions or abrupt endings, the nuances of the figurative language often elusive. Yet certainly these were also aspects of a literary tradition that were not easily mastered, for the Beng words—like Keats's—were not freestanding but imbedded in culture.

The rain kept falling, and the molasses trucks remained stranded in a thickening, muddy soup. The villagers ventured freely through the daily downpours to neighboring compounds, soaked but friendly, and one wet afternoon

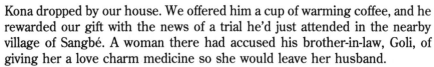

Kona dropped by our house. We offered him a cup of warming coffee, and he rewarded our gift with the news of a trial he'd just attended in the nearby village of Sangbé. A woman there had accused his brother-in-law, Goli, of giving her a love charm medicine so she would leave her husband.

"Her accusation angered her husband so much, he attacked Goli with a log!" Kona said, laughing. "But today at the trial, the bottle which she said held the medicine was found to be empty." He clapped his hands together: *"Paw paw"*—Nothing at all.

"The woman was shamed," Kona finished, flourishing a wicked grin that celebrated his brother-in-law's vindication. Alma grinned back, so happy that he had shared this gossipy tidbit. At least among some villagers we were finally on the delivery route of the local news.

The next morning more than one neighbor told us the truck drivers had performed the necessary sacrifice to the hill spirits, and within a few hours the M'Bahiakro road crew arrived, pounding the road into a firm, flat surface, laying down layers of sand, shoveling new paths, and pulling the trucks with a series of chains. Soon the nearly week-long traffic jam was cleared: an effective mixture of ritual offerings and technology had triumphed.

8

TRANSGRESSIONS

🌀 🌀 🌀

(AUGUST 3–OCTOBER 3, 1980)

Philip: Holes in the Mud Walls

WHILE ALMA AND I SAT TOGETHER AT OUR DESK LATE AT NIGHT IN THE CENTER OF OUR compound, hordes of fat, flying insects—brought out by the rains—dive-bombed our lantern. Boys and girls gathered around us, snatching the occasional luckless creature from the air: they tore off the flickering wings and threw the writhing bodies into a clay pot, then set the pot over a fire. Apparently the roasted insects made a crispy evening snack.

"Amwé, Kouadio," a boy said, his open palm offering us a few of the delicacies. Alma and I were usually adventurous about food—we'd recently tried a tough Leg of Lizard—but tonight we weren't in the mood. We declined, our voices filled with not-so-mock horror, and the children giggled and went back to their happy munching.

The insects continued to swoop about us, oblivious of their possible doom. One flew into my typewriter, where it buzzed and scuttled about. "Damn it!" I shouted, turning the machine upside down to shake out the noisy creature. Plopping down on the desk, the thing scurried across half the length of a typed page before a child's eager, hungry hand grabbed it.

I looked across at Alma. She'd studiously ignored my outburst, instead concentrating on paging through one of her notebooks. I could sympathize. Why offer herself as an audience for another bout of my complaining? We'd been arguing too much lately—a shame, since our wedding anniversary was fast approaching. "Y'know," I said suddenly, "number three is just a few days off."

"Hmm?" she murmured, her head still lowered.

"Let's take a vacation."

"Oh, what a nice idea. But where?"

"Bouaké."

The idea of a short break that wasn't enforced by car troubles actually stunned us. We could rent a hotel room and become a couple again for a few brief days, exploring the city together or, better yet, simply *relaxing.*

The morning before our anniversary, Yacouba walked with us to our car to see us off when a large millipede with ugly claws sped out from behind a front tire and bit Alma on her sandaled foot. She howled in pain and leaned against the door while Yacouba and I smashed the evil-looking thing with rocks. It was a *mledong*—Snake's uncle.

I held Alma's foot and examined the tiny bite. "What a send-off," I said. "What should we do?"

"Don't worry," Yacouba said quietly, "the pain will go away in three hours."

"Three hours?" Alma gasped. "Ooh, it hurts!"

"You think *that* hurts?" Yacouba said, his concerned face breaking into a grin. "I remember when a scorpion bit me—if that happened to you, you'd be on the airplane back to your country tomorrow!"

Alma smiled politely, unconvinced of her good luck.

"We can stop at the M'Bahiakro infirmary," I suggested, "and see if we can pick up some medicine for you."

With my help Alma limped into the car, moaning and grimacing. Yacouba stood at the window and said, "Don't worry, it's not an omen." I thanked him, touched that my friend wanted our excursion to go well. He'd recently confided unhappily that his two wives, Sramatan and Dongi, had barely spoken to each other the past two months.

At the infirmary we managed to pick up a soothing ointment for Alma's bite, and as we continued on to Bouaké her pain subsided. I drove with one hand, massaged her raised foot with the other—not classically romantic, I thought, but the best we could manage under the circumstances.

In the unfamiliar chill of our hotel room's air-conditioning, Alma took a nap to sleep off the last, tiny throbbings of her toe. I settled on the balcony, unfolded a copy of the *International Herald Tribune,* and tried to stir up some angry passion over the latest dead ends in the hostage crisis and Jimmy Carter's deepening political troubles. But the news seemed so far away; I put down the paper and gazed out at the setting sun. Though tomorrow was Côte d'Ivoire's Independence Day, Bouaké's darkening streets were quiet. As always, the holiday wouldn't be observed until four months later, by decree of the government: August was a poor time for a national celebration, since the cash crops wouldn't be harvested for another month, and no one had much money. Only when the farmers were paid for their rice, coffee, and cocoa would the country be in the mood for a rousing party. Still, Alma and I were tickled that the date of our anniversary was the same as the country's official date of independence.

We slept late the next morning, then took a leisurely walk through the city—past long rows of tailor shops, each tailor steadily pumping his foot-powered sewing machine; past school yards of uniformed boys and girls whooping with recess delight. When we came upon a *marché* we bought gifts for some of our village neighbors: a soccer ball for the older children, bullets for hunters who had offered to share the rewards of their catches with us. We spent some time searching for just the right present for San Yao. He'd begun to visit our compound in the mornings—once he'd even brought along his grandson for some malaria pills—and we wanted to return his welcome gestures of peace. We decided on a flashlight and a large supply of batteries.

We also needed to buy a new watch for Alma—her old one had simply stopped, and no shaking or twisting of the tiny dial could make it tick again. But we hesitated before searching further through the *marché*. It was already late in the afternoon—perhaps we should return to our hotel and get ready for dinner. A young man walked by, his shirt a bit ragged, his plastic shoes cracked and dusty, but he wore a watch, and I called to him. *"Excusez-moi, monsieur, quelle heure est-il?"*

The man paused, then pointed at his wrist and muttered quickly, *"Pardon, c'est gâtée"*—Sorry, it's broken.

Then why wear it? I thought as he hurried on. Another man passed by, slightly hunched over, a watch shining against his dark skin. When I stepped forward and asked him the time, he stared a moment, surprised. Then, his eyes downcast, he slowly extended his wrist and I leaned forward to look.

Eleven o'clock. Was his watch broken, too? But I could hear it ticking.

"He can't tell time," Alma whispered, and I nodded. Afraid I'd embarrassed the man, I thanked him, too loudly, and he continued on his way.

A dapper *fonctionnaire*—petty bureaucrat—ambled by; I knew that he could give me the exact time, but now I didn't care. Turning to Alma, I said, "Look, the *marché* is starting to close up, it *must* be late."

As we walked back to the hotel, I thought of how the two men we'd encountered had turned their watches into jewelry: even a broken watch had a pleasing, circular design embossed on its face, and one that worked offered attractive, moving parts that produced a lulling, mechanical music. I could easily appreciate such a transformation: I had always hated how wristwatches bound me too tightly to an awareness of passing time, and I'd long since given up wearing one, agreeing with the writer Julio Cortázar that a watch was a "tiny flowering hell," a "furious bit of something" attached to the wrist.

Certainly Alma and I rarely concerned ourselves with watches and clocks in the village, except for checking the time for a BBC broadcast on the radio. The village was its own timepiece: the morning baths, the pounding of mortar and pestle for breakfast, the staggered lines of farmers marching off to the fields, began a series of daily events that proceeded on its own schedule. Even when Alma made an appointment with Amenan, it was for a no-more-specific time than "early morning" or "late morning": if Amenan wasn't in her compound when Alma arrived, she could easily be found. Still, Alma couldn't help but want a new watch—a quick glance at her wrist throughout the day was a familiar comfort she couldn't give up.

On another of our city walks the following afternoon, Alma and I crossed an open field that served as a bus depot and we heard a faraway music, lilting and oddly indefinable. Soon we made out golden-toned guitars wrapping together in a rhythmic filigree of riffs that became a kind of ecstatic skipping, punctuated by a rising melody from the horn section. The vocal inflections and harmonies of the urgent-voiced singers were vaguely familiar—salsa, perhaps?—but the words were definitely in an African language, not Spanish. On and on, the melody looped and curved. I turned to Alma. "We have to find out what this is."

"I think it's coming from that direction," she said, pointing. We ranged through the narrow streets, an occasional child shouting out, *"Tubabu!"*— White people!

"We're getting closer," I said, "let's hurry before the music stops." Finally, across the street from us stood a single-story shack with a simple, handmade sign above the open double doors: *Musique Afrique.*

We crossed the busy street and entered a tiny room where thousands of dollars' worth of stereo equipment—tape decks, receivers, and turntables— were lined up on shelves. Behind them, on wooden racks that extended over three walls, were rather worn-looking record albums, a world of musicians I'd never before heard of or seen: a trio of guitarists sweating at a live concert; an elegant woman wearing large, circular earrings and a strikingly white turban; a group of smiling musicians wearing identical, Elvis-like costumes. Perhaps a hundred records faced us, yet there seemed to be only a single copy of each one.

A tall, thin man stood behind the wooden counter, smiling at our undis-

guised wonder. He turned down the stereo and, after greeting us, said, "May I help you?"

"Please, what's that music you're playing?"

"That's Luango Franco. So, you like *soukous* music?" He nodded approvingly.

"Yes," I said, "what is it?"

"The music of Zaire. Very popular. Would you like me to make a tape for you? I'll give you a good price."

I paused. This fellow was a bootlegger, his whole shop a shady enterprise. I looked around the room again. No wonder there were only single copies of the records—that's all he needed to make tapes for his customers. What I'd seen for months suddenly became clear: all those young men who sauntered along with their battery-operated tape recorders—in M'Bahiakro and elsewhere—obviously made use of shops like this. With so much poverty, who could afford an elaborate stereo system or, for that matter, records or commercially released tapes? And for villages like Kosangbé, with no electricity, what other choice was there?

"Please, tape the record," I said while silently offering an apology to Luango Franco for his lost royalties.

The man gestured to the wall. "Is there anything else you'd like?"

We stared at the album covers, though we had no idea what treasures they might be hiding. Alma pointed to the woman in the turban. "What about her? Can you play some for us?"

"Fanta Damba, traditional music from Mali. Of course." He set the record on the turntable, and a clear, piercing voice wove among the resonant, tumbling notes of a lutelike instrument.

"Yes, tape that, too," Alma said. We searched the wall of album covers, eager for new finds, sharing in this unplanned anniversary present we'd discovered together.

Almost immediately after returning to Kosangbé, we were met by Yacouba, who told us that a traveling diviner had arrived and was lodging at Kouassikro's compound. Our friend chuckled: "Poor Kouassikro, he's hoping to learn a few secrets." I nodded, knowing that Kouassikro wanted desperately to be considered a diviner: sometimes, at village gatherings, he'd drag out his cowrie shells, only to be shooed away with derisive laughter. I couldn't imagine that this hospitality would help to alter his reputation. Still, Alma and I marched over to greet our intriguing new neighbor.

As we approached I saw a small man hunched over in conference with Kouassikro—already something didn't seem right about him, but it wasn't

until we greeted the two men that I realized the diviner didn't have any toes or fingers. The man's hands ended as rounded nubs of flaking skin; his feet were fleshy slabs. *Leprosy,* I thought, pulling back slightly.

The man ignored my reaction, instead nodding happily as his host praised him. "He really knows a lot," Kouassikro said. "He's very powerful, and I should know, I should know. Come by tonight, he'll tell you the cause of any trouble."

"Thank you, Father," I replied noncommittally. I had no intention of spending any time near that poor man.

But our new neighbor's affliction didn't dampen the villagers' interest in his powers. Over the next few days Alma and I often noted a supplicant heading for the diviner's temporary quarters. At night the light of his lantern shone through the burlap cloth serving as the door to his room, an advertisement for any furtive, nighttime clients.

One evening while relaxing in our compound, staring up at the glorious spread of the Milky Way, Alma and I heard the shouts of women, a baby's wail, then more shouting. We listened carefully—it seemed to be coming from the Jula quarter. Already, curious neighbors scooted past us, and we hurried behind them, eager to catch the latest village dust-up.

Yacouba's compound was crowded with the curious, and we were shocked to see our friend flicking a short whip near his wife, Dongi. She held her hands over her face and edged away, while his other wife, Sramatan, huddled in a corner and clutched her howling baby. She shouted out something, and Yacouba turned to her with his whip cracking in the air, but then Dongi let out a string of insults and he ran back to her.

"What happened?" Alma asked Ajua, Karimu's wife, who clicked her tongue sharply in disapproval. *"Dongi.* She started an argument with Sramatan and started hitting her so hard, Sramatan's baby fell off her back."

Endangering the child of a co-wife was a terrible offense, yet I felt miserable watching Yacouba threatening his wives with a beating. And his fury seemed to accomplish little—Sramatan and Dongi still spit curses at each other. Yacouba ran from one to the other with his whip until he slammed his foot against Sramatan's hearth. He sat down, clutching his toe while the bitter words his wives had nurtured during their months of silence now blossomed.

Tonight was *Po fen* eve, when the village should have been calm. Yacouba and his wives were shaming everyone by this noisy breaching of the rules. Kouassikro—an elder in Dongi's matriclan—made his way through the crowd. "Stop making trouble!" he shouted at her. "Why do you make so much trouble?"

Ché Kofi eased beside him and murmured, "Kouassikro, someone is calling you back at your compound"—a delicate Beng way to say "Mind your own business."

Kouassikro left, but his butting in apparently gave sanction to others. Yacouba's uncle now stood before him angrily. "Why didn't you tell me your wives haven't spoken to each other in months? We could have talked and settled this problem without a public fight!"

Though Yacouba apologized, his uncle stomped off, shaking his head in disgust. A gaggle of relatives offered their heated opinions to each other, drowning out Dongi and Sramatan, and Alma and I made our way to our friend.

He stared up at us, miserable, hands massaging his toe. "It's loose," he said through a grimace. "I'll have to get Anzoumena to fit it back."

"*Ah-heh,*" Alma replied, not quite sympathetic. Then in a low voice she said to me in English, "Serves him right for cracking that whip."

"How's the baby?" I asked.

He smiled painfully. "Fine. Not a serious fall."

Yacouba's uncle returned with more choice phrases. There was little we could do for our friend except spare him our disappointed faces, so Alma and I left quietly.

The next morning Yacouba limped over to our compound, his face tired and sheepish.

"Would you like some aspirin?" I asked, and he nodded. Returning with the pills, I heard Alma ask, "Have things calmed down a bit?"

"Oh, no, it's not over. Because *Po fen* was broken, there's going to be a trial. I know I'll have to pay some large fines."

"What were Dongi and Sramatan arguing about?" she asked.

"Who knows! They won't say—Sramatan says, 'Ask Dongi,' and Dongi says, 'Ask Sramatan.'

"It's my fault," Yacouba continued, and admitted to favoring Sramatan over Dongi during the first year of their marriage. Sramatan was a member of his matriclan, and he played and joked with her "as if she were my sister." Then, when he saw Dongi was jealous, he paid more attention to her, nearly ignoring Sramatan in the process. But still Dongi was jealous, which shouldn't have been surprising. She could often be difficult—this was her third marriage. "What *less* can I do with Sramatan to cool Dongi's jealousy?" he said, shaking his head in frustration.

For months the daughters of both his wives had been ill, one child barely getting better before another fell sick. Yacouba thought this was caused by the "bad atmosphere" in the compound. "If the mud walls have holes, cockroaches get in," Yacouba said with a sigh.

"What does that mean?" Alma asked.

"If a family is constantly fighting, then it's easy for witches to cause further trouble."

I remembered that Yacouba blamed the death of his first child on witchcraft, so I could understand his fears. My friend looked so defeated. Last night's flicking of the whip had been the ineffectual posturing of a powerless man. I wondered if Dongi and Sramatan felt any less powerless.

A few nights later another evening's peace was shattered as Kouassikro and his diviner guest screamed insults at each other in several different languages. Alma and I stood with the rest of our neighbors and watched Kouassikro at his doorway—his figure lit by a nearby lantern—as he howled at the hoarse-voiced leper across the compound. Standing by his own lantern, the leper roared back and waved his clublike hands in rage, and the threatening shadow of his gestures reached out toward Kouassikro's own angry shadow.

I had little idea what they shouted at each other—though the children around us gleefully cheered some of the choicest insults—but I could hear the pain in Kouassikro's voice. Had the diviner refused to reveal secrets, mocking his host's pretensions of spiritual power? Kouassikro could not contain his fury, and for hours he and the leper matched each other word for bitter word, despite the occasional entreaties of sleep-deprived neighbors for them to stop.

When morning broke, the diviner was gone, and Kouassikro remained in his house for the rest of the day, nursing his disappointment.

Alma and I sat on our reclining chairs and searched the cloud-flecked dark sky for the new moon: once the first sliver was visible, the month-long fasting for the Muslim holiday of Ramadan would be over, and the entire village would feast the next day. Though most Beng in Kosangbé were animist, this would be an opportunity to honor their Jula neighbors in the village, who were Muslim.

One of Ché Kofi's sons shouted out, "There! It's there!" and the children of the village trilled their delight. At the edge of a shifting cloud was a thin, shining curve, seeming to gain in brightness as ululations rose up in every compound.

The next morning prayers were offered in the Jula quarter and animals sacrificed. Alma and I avoided the event, assuming we weren't welcome, but Karimu came by afterward dressed in a beautiful white *bubu*. "Why didn't you come along to take photos?" he asked, clearly disturbed that his well-dressed presence hadn't been recorded.

In every compound large pots simmered with delicacies—palm nut, okra, or eggplant sauces, meat of all sorts, and rice, yams, and corn porridge. By late morning plates of food were passed from compound to compound as Muslim and animist households donated food to family and friends. Alma and I received five meals, and we ate all day, determined to finish the gifts: a clean plate would be the best part of our thanks.

The dancing started out with quiet Kossum—who, along with Kwamla Chakro, was one of the village's master drummers—expertly pounding away an interlocking series of rhythms. The Jula women swayed beneath open umbrellas, spinning them slowly in tandem. Under those circles of shade the young Beng women and girls twirled themselves, displaying their flowing scarves, elaborate necklaces and bracelets, colored hair pins and combs—a happy culmination of the day's ecumenical spirit, animists and Muslims celebrating together and sharing in each other's pleasure.

Feasting and festivity were also in the air because in the fields the yam shoots had spread up out of every mound, thick green ladders of vine rising to the trees. Beside every yam mound, thick stalks of corn spread their leaves as the sun's light shifted through the luxurious growth. Soon the animists of Kosangbé would have their own celebration—the festival of the new yam, due in less than a month.

Alma: "The Eggs Are Rotten"

Taking a break from a conversation with Yacouba under our thatched *akpa,* I strode into our kitchen to check on dinner. "Mmmm, that smells delicious," I praised Moya, pleased she'd spiced the tomato sauce with the oregano and basil I'd recently bought in a Bouaké supermarket. The tantalizing scent reminded me of meals I'd eaten in another world, and I walked over to the pot, peered down at the simmering red sauce, and inhaled with gusto. Moya shot me a look of disdain. As far as she was concerned, chili peppers, and chili peppers alone, were the only spice needed for a tasty dish.

"Amwé," Yacouba said when I returned, in that patient but firm tone of voice I'd heard him use often with his two-year-old, "it's very bad manners to smell food."

"Oh, really?" I said. Then, suspecting that my slip might be far worse than a simple faux pas, I asked, "Is it *taboo?*"

"No," Yacouba answered, "but people will gossip about you. If I saw either of my wives smelling the pot while she was cooking for me, I wouldn't touch that dish!"

How uncivilized I must have appeared over these past months: whenever Moya was preparing her most delectable dishes, I'd not only sniffed the steaming pot, but, worse, had made a show of it. What would I think of a guest from another country who flamboyantly licked the stirring spoon from a soup I was cooking?

I was spooning Ovaltine into mugs for breakfast and listening to Philip sloshing water nearby in the bathhouse when Moya's friend N'Au walked up to greet me. I was relieved that she came empty-handed—often she embarrassed me with her gifts of tiny tomatoes or onions, for the teenage girl considered me a potential co-wife. As a monogamous man, Philip was technically still eligible for marriage, but N'Au had chosen to court me rather than Philip—hoping to ensure future good co-wifely relations.

Today N'Au seemed unusually serious. I asked her if something was wrong. "Big sister," she said quietly, "a child has died."

"Ihh!" I sighed. "Who is it?"

"It's Auntie and Uncle's little boy, Félice."

"Whey," I intoned. I'd been dreading this news: with a harsh, hacking cough that racked his frail body, Félice had long exuded a dazed, distracted look that implied his own doom.

As Philip and I readied to offer our condolences to the parents, villagers filed by our compound, recalled from the fields with news of the death. I thought back to a conversation I'd had several weeks ago with Félice's parents—they'd asked me for medicines that might help their young son, almost three years old, finally master the skill of walking. I'd admitted that I knew of no such medicines and commiserated with the worried couple. Later I'd asked Yacouba, "Why do you think Félice still can't walk?"

"It's because of his parents," he'd whispered to me. "They couldn't wait."

"Wait for what?"

Yacouba had gathered his *bubu* around him as he shifted on his seat. "After a baby is born, the parents aren't allowed to sleep with each other until the child learns to walk." He paused. "That's why we have polygamy—didn't you know? At least the man doesn't suffer while the baby's growing up." He chuckled, then turned serious again. "Anyway, you know Kouakou Kala doesn't have a second wife. That's why he and Aya couldn't wait for . . . you know. So Aya became pregnant. But when the new baby was born, Félice still couldn't walk—we say his leg bones were split, because he wasn't meant to have a baby sister yet. If his parents don't get him the right medicines soon, he won't survive."

Now, as I contemplated Yacouba's grim prophecy, our friend stopped by our courtyard on his way back from his farm.

"It will be a special funeral called *fewa,"* he explained, "because Félice was his parents' first child to die. When that happens, we do a lot of ceremonies."

Philip and I walked over to the mourning family's courtyard. Aya's kitchen, normally filled with the tempting smells of bubbling gumbo sauce, was quiet now—no pots nestled on the hearthstones. Instead the cadaver of her son lay stretched out on the dirt floor, set on one white cloth and covered with another. An older woman fanned leaves over the small corpse while a few others sat quietly against the walls, legs outstretched. Among them was Kri Afwé, one of my staunchest critics.

Next door I found the quiet parents exhausted by their sorrow—and, I supposed, their remorse. Aya's hair, normally tressed neatly, was undone and wild. I gently offered my condolences and sat down. But in a few minutes a quiet procession formed outside the doorway—it was time for the burial. Oddly, Kouakou Kala and Aya didn't move. I was tempted to join the procession, but my decision was made for me as a woman entered the room and whispered, "Amwé, you can't go to the grave." So the three of us remained, my friends silent in their suffering, I silent in my awkwardness. Back home I hadn't known parents who had lost a child; not yet a parent myself, I couldn't begin to imagine their grief.

In a short time the procession filed back to the courtyard: the boy was buried. To my surprise, Aya and Kouakou Kala remained stoic, rising wordlessly at the sight of a woman carrying in white bark cloths. The woman quietly offered instructions, and in front of us Aya and Kouakou Kala removed their clothes. Embarrassed, I considered leaving, but I was afraid that might call more attention to myself. So I averted my eyes. The couple stood passively as the woman wrapped them in the bark cloths. Then they all began to leave, and I rose, thinking to follow; but standing just outside the doorway, Kri Afwé wagged her hand at me menacingly and shouted, "No, you mustn't come!"

Over the next days Kouakou Kala and Aya remained in their house, receiving visitors, their heavy eyes, though dry, exuding untold pain. On the fourth day Philip and I set out on our usual morning greetings and reached the funeral compound. Before us sat a new Aya: her head was now almost completely bare, only a perfect pom-pom of hair left in front. Was this to shave away most of the grief, leaving it confined to a small circle of sadness?

A group of women gathered to lead Aya and Kouakou Kala away—to the edge of the forest, someone whispered to me, where they'd do another secret ritual. Today maybe I'd be permitted to attend. But once again Kri Afwé spotted me. "Amwé, you don't belong here!" she said loudly.

This time I asked, "Why not?"

"You just don't!"

"I won't take notes or pictures."

"You just can't be here," Kri Afwé insisted.

Frustrated, I walked back toward our *quartier*. Afwé Ba, who was laying out some okra slices on a drying rack, asked, "What's wrong, Amwé?"

"Oh, it's nothing. I'm just disappointed I didn't get to see one of the rituals, that's all," I said.

Afwé Ba turned to me. "But Amwé, didn't you see I wasn't there, either? And Makola, and your friend Amlan—*they're* not allowed to watch, either."

"Really? Why not?"

Putting down her okra basket, Afwé Ba said quietly, "It's because we've never lost a child. If we saw a *fewa* ritual, we'd soon lose a child ourselves— one that's already born, or even one that's not been born yet. It's good you didn't watch that part of the funeral."

"Big sister, thank you for explaining this to me." I couldn't have misinterpreted my exclusion more. Ironically it signaled my acceptance—I was subject to the same culturally defined dangers as my neighbors. I walked back to my compound to write up the morning's events, but soon Afwé Ba came by and told me, "I just saw them return from the forest; you can go watch now."

I walked back to the mourning compound, where, to my amazement, I found Aya and Kouakou Kala transformed: now they wore several layers of white *pagnes,* bedecked with an abundance of beaded necklaces and bracelets. Any exposed skin—faces, arms, legs, shoulders—was painted with green lines and red dots: their bodies had become canvases on which was drawn the shape of their mourning.

Keeping them company were the women who had dressed the mourning couple in the forest—one of them soon told the couple that the moment had come to tour the village. This time they invited me to join the procession. When we approached my nearby courtyard we all greeted Philip, and one of the women strewed some crumpled leaves from a gourd over the ground. Then Aya walked over to our doorway and stamped her foot on the threshold.

"Ka ma gbria," the women said almost in unison—Thank you for yesterday.

"Maa," said Philip.

We continued to greet each household in the same way, finally ending back where we'd begun. Soon the rest of the village began to file into the house, first greeting Aya and Kouakou Kala and then washing their hands in an herbal decoction. With this ritual the village must have been collectively washing away the death.

Several days later I asked Amenan why the mourning couple had remained in their house during the burial of their child.

"That's because it was a *fewa* funeral," Amenan explained. "Those parents must never attend their child's burial—they'd be too upset. And once the corpse is buried, the parents of any first child to die aren't *allowed* to cry."

"Ah, c'est grave." I wondered if Aya and Kouakou Kala found that this strict rule gave bounds to their grief, and Amenan added, "Since I've never lost a child, I've never been to a *fewa* burial, either, or seen any of those ceremonies the parents do. Amwé, a *fewa* funeral is *grégré"*—difficult.

Ever knowledgeable about her culture's secrets, Amenan proceeded to describe what must have occurred after dark, while the village slept. The very night of the death, and the next night as well, the mourning parents were required to make love to each other in the presence of the old woman who'd prepared all the herbal washes. Had Aya and Kouakou Kala experienced this as an ordeal, or had it unexpectedly eased their pain? Though I'd managed to gain a sense of the *shoulds,* it was often still mysterious how individuals experienced those rules. This, I thought ruefully, was the private part of culture—so compelling . . . and so elusive to anthropologists.

Beneath Kosangbé's enormous kapok tree, Kri Afwé hunched forward on her low wooden stool to face a group of men who'd come from the neighboring village of Manigbé for a trial. Waving her hands at the crowd, Kri Afwé cried, "The eggs are rotten! None of the children that Kobla's had with her husband belongs to him—they all belong to my son because *he's* the man she was supposed to marry!"

The trial hadn't yet begun, but already it was bringing out the worst in the old woman. I knew that the dispute concerned a longstanding grudge that Kri Afwé held toward Kobla, a young woman who had long ago refused to marry her son. These days that long-ago rejected groom, Ali Kouakou, was a sad and damaged man. I wondered if his permanent bachelorhood coupled with his drinking had prevented him from becoming village chief when, some years ago, he'd been next in line. As for Kobla, she'd found another husband on her own, and the couple had fled to Bouaké, far from Bengland; for some fifteen years she'd refused to set foot in her home village. This week she'd returned for the funeral of her mother, who had recently moved to Manigbé to marry a man from that village.

Her mother's death was the subject of much talk. Yacouba told me that many people said she'd died from grief about her daughter's rebellion. Others believed the Earth itself had killed the older woman as a roundabout means to punish Kobla. Whatever the cause, Kobla had returned to Bengland to ask forgiveness, hoping to be readmitted into the circle of lives that, even in Bouaké, must still have inhabited her consciousness. Indeed, she must have remained surrounded by her ancestors, for in the Beng conception of the afterlife, the souls of the deceased went off to live in *wurugbé*—city of ancestors—said to be invisibly located in the heart of large cities, such as Abidjan and Bouaké.

The trial was about to start. I looked around. "Where's Kobla?" I asked Ché Kofi.

"*Eh*, Amwé," he said, laughing, "you ask about everything!"

"But is she here?" I persisted.

"The chief won't even let her in the village until she sends over a sheep," he answered. "If she tried to come before that, she'd be whipped!"

"*Yih!*"

"Do you see those men?" Ché Kofi glanced over to the visiting men from Manigbé. "They're the only ones who'll even speak for her—they're her mother's in-laws." Then Ché Kofi excused himself to start the trial, addressing the assembly: "*Eki a twa an za sé maé*"—God let us understand everything of the affair.

The audience looked around expectantly, and Kri Afwé's brother, Kri Kouadio, began to speak. A slight old man wearing a khaki tunic that barely reached his knees, he leaned forward on his rickety metal folding chair and began formally, "When Kobla's father died, I took over for him, I became her father. Though it wasn't my idea to have her marry Ali Kouakou, I went along with it—but Kobla refused him. There are always some women who do this."

Kri Afwé spat on the ground and continued her brother's lament: "Later, she found another man to marry. I wanted to have a trial in his village so all the children she'd have with her new husband would belong to my son. But no one else from Kosangbé agreed. That's why the eggs are rotten," she concluded.

"Whew! Kobla is *lucky* she's not allowed in Kosangbé today," Philip whispered to me.

"I know what you mean," I answered. Still, I couldn't help feeling a little sympathy for Kri Afwé. If it weren't for Kobla, perhaps the old woman's son would be the chief of Kosangbé today.

Seated on an enormous root of the kapok tree was Kla Kona. He shifted his weight, then added his own lament. "When an uncle of Kobla's fell sick," he recounted, "all his other relatives visited him, but she refused. When he died, I, her *uncle,* sent her a message to come for the funeral. All his other relatives from Bouaké came, but she refused. It was the same with her aunt, the same with her cousin, the same with Apisé just a little while ago—she didn't come to *any* of those funerals."

The villagers nodded. Not participating in relatives' lives was bad enough, but not honoring their passing, it seemed, was even worse.

"Kobla has truly ruined things," said Kouassikro, addressing the elders of Kosangbé. "You yourselves, you haven't created the problem, but the child of your own womb has, and she's inserted you in it." An appreciative murmur rippled through his audience. "Nevertheless," he continued, "Kobla has asked us to forgive her. If we keep examining her and all the terrible things she's done, this affair will *never* be resolved!"

"Okay, let's ask the woman," said Kri Afwé, hands posed defiantly on her knees, "just *what* is she going to apologize with? Isn't that right?"

Ché Kofi answered, "Let's not rush the affair, let's talk calmly!"

"Kobla, she's better than all of us!" Kri Afwé said ironically. She puffed out her chest and shouted: "She should show herself to be a woman. Let's see if she's a woman like me!"

At once everyone began arguing the merits of this challenge, and a dozen voices melted into indecipherable varieties of outrage. Finally Kri Kouadio's voice prevailed: "Let's accept the apology, so we can all speak in harmony."

San Yao addressed him: "It's you who are the oldest among us, and who have the most force. We're all behind you." The chief's humble stance, such a contrast to his usual authoritarian posture, surprised me.

"Thanks to the visitors from Manigbé," another elder said, "she's begun to apologize." The men from Manigbé nodded.

"Yes, and we're grateful to them for that," said Kri Kouadio. "They've thought about it, and they've turned those thoughts into words."

"It's true," said one of the Manigbé men. "We didn't come to your village because the diviner told us to. We ourselves thought about it. . . ." But the man looked rather miserable—I suspected he *had* come at someone else's request.

Now Kri Kouadio asked no one in particular, "If Kobla's brother were here, and not off working somewhere in the country, what gift would he donate for his mother's ghost?"

"A sheep," Yacouba's father answered promptly.

"Good!" said Kri Kouadio. "First, give us a sheep, *then* we can talk! One sheep to sacrifice to her mother's spirit, plus two cases of wine to apologize to her mother and her ancestors."

"Ah, now we're starting lightly, lightly, to finish the affair!" Ché Kofi said with evident pleasure. "Let's thank him! They've cut the tree, and now it's starting to fall. Father, thank you."

"Yes indeed," said San Yao, "now it's time for her to give us two cases of wine. Only yesterday her husband went to Manigbé bearing gifts for the funeral—I heard he brought three cases of drink!"

"Kobla's the child of a dog!" interrupted Ali Kouakou. Dressed smartly in a crisp black pants suit, he had until now managed to avoid what must have been numerous temptations to join in the proceedings. Several people muttered, "Oh, be quiet." Kouakou pouted but remained silent.

The chief continued, "Her husband brought a case of Tip Top soda, a case of beer, and a case of wine, plus a sack of rice, and 12,350 francs!"

"*We* haven't gotten any of those things," declared Kri Kouadio. "Her husband should pay all that to *us* today, or I won't even speak about the situation any more!" At this the trial broke up into several small groups, each caucusing separately around the kapok tree.

Dressed grandly in a green print suit embroidered with golden thread, Kona endeavored to reunite everyone by speaking loudly: "What Kri Kouadio said is good. But I hope he'll forgive me if I ask him to reduce the fine."

Kouassikro joined in. "Once Kobla offers the sacrifice, the problem must be over: remember, if you pick chili peppers and don't wash your hands, you'll probably rub your eyes!"

"Mm-hmm," several people said, apparently contemplating the lesson of this proverb.

"What's happened to the question I asked, though?" Kona said quietly. "Has Kri Kouadio answered?"

"We won't reduce the fine," asserted Kri Afwé. "If it's good for her or if it ruins her, we'll *never* reduce it! If a child does something bad, you must reprimand her. If you don't, you're irresponsible."

Philip shook his head and whispered, "She doesn't give up, does she?"

"All right," Kri Kouadio said in a tone of resolution, "she's got to hand over one sheep, one chicken, six thousand francs, and a case of red wine. That's the last thing I'll say. No matter what, I'll drink a case of red wine today!"

Without a break, several people offered the ritually required thanks to conclude the event . . . uttered so routinely that they completely concealed the passions displayed just moments ago. Soon Ché Kofi appeared with a case of red wine and distributed the twelve bottles. When everyone was pleasantly tipsy, Kri Kouadio presided over the first of the series of sacrifices and prayed over a white chicken. And so the rebellious daughter of the village was collectively forgiven and invited back into the circle of her society.

Later Yacouba and I listened to the tape I'd made of the trial, my friend explaining patiently how everyone was related and why they had taken their particular stances. When we reached the end of the cassette, Yacouba suddenly laughed.

"What's so funny?" I asked.

"They're talking about you!"

"Really?"

Yacouba rewound the tape and listened again. "Kri Afwé's saying, 'She has no shame, putting herself in other people's affairs. She really likes these trials.' "

I laughed. "She's right about that!"

"Now Ali Kouakou's saying, 'That's why she's here.' " Yacouba raised his hand. "And my father's talking—he's saying, 'If it were up to her, there'd be nothing but trials all the time!' Now one of the men from Manigbé is saying, 'We'll all benefit by her work.' "

"Well, that's nice," I said. "Did Kri Afwé respond?"

"I haven't heard her say anything about that—I'm not sure if she heard it," replied Yacouba. "Now Kona is saying, 'She wants to work today.'"

"I wonder what he means by that," I mused. "Do you think he approves?"

"With him, who knows?" Yacouba answered.

The next day I walked over to Ché Kofi's compound to talk about Kobla's trial. But Ché Kofi seemed distracted and after only a few minutes excused himself.

"Is something wrong?"

"It's Mo'kissi. She came to visit her family, but this morning some children said they saw her run off into the forest."

"Oh, no," I said. "Now what'll happen?"

"Her husband has come with some of his buddies to fetch her. They'll wait until evening. By then, she'll be hungry and wet"—he looked up at the sky, thick with dark clouds. "She'll return to the village to dry off, and she'll be hungry!"

Ché Kofi chuckled, but privately I hoped that, as Kobla had done years earlier, Mo'kissi would take another path out of the forest—one leading to some distant town that would welcome her as an unhappy wanderer.

Philip: A Little Rectangle of Power

The trial over the dispute between Yacouba's wives took place in Kona's compound. Dongi and Sramatan sat silently near their husband, who looked as if he'd rather be anywhere else on earth—whatever was decided at this trial would cause trouble for him at home.

San Yao began. "Dongi, what was the argument all about?" Ché Kofi, taking the role of the *Za wo lali*—the Asker of the Case—repeated the question.

"Just ask Sramatan," Dongi replied curtly.

Ignoring her rudeness, Ché Kofi turned to Sramatan and repeated his question.

With a nervous, sidelong glance at her co-wife, she said, "Whenever I greet Dongi, she never answers. She never talks to me. One day I went to my mother-in-law for medicine for our children. But she said, 'Why should I give you medicine when you and Dongi always fight? It is I who have the right to fight with you two, I have the right to rule you, because I gave birth to your husband. But you two don't have the right to fight with each other.'"

Sramatan paused, letting her mother-in-law's words fill the silence. I glanced over at Yacouba: head lowered, he gazed at Dongi surreptitiously. "So I talked to my husband's mother about my troubles," Sramatan continued. "Dongi passed us as we spoke, and she screamed that we were insulting her behind her back. Then she threatened me, shouting, 'You'll hear more about this in the fields.'"

Even though this was by now old gossip, the elders murmured at Dongi's disrespect for the Earth.

"Then she threatened me again," Sramatan added quietly. "She said, 'Today is *Po fen* eve, and I'm going to pollute it by fighting with you tonight!'"

Tolo Kouassi interrupted and said sternly, "Dongi, you must not make any more arguments with Sramatan." Ché Kofi echoed this. Dongi remained silent, so Kona took on the role of *Za ye ma tali*—Closer of the Mouth of the Case—and said, "Dongi, you are in the wrong, and you must ask forgiveness."

Dongi managed to say, in a small voice I could barely hear, *"Ka j'a di"*—Forgive me. Then, scowling, she hurried from the compound, though the trial hadn't formally come to a close.

That night Yacouba came to visit us, quite troubled. "I'm afraid of Dongi," he said. "I'm afraid she'll try to kill me, with either a machete or poison."

Before I could try to soothe his worries, Yacouba continued. "I shouldn't stay with her any longer," he continued, "but then I'd have to give up our child, and I couldn't stand that. Anyway, it's Dongi who must divorce me."

"Why Dongi?" Alma asked, her anthropological antennae out.

"Because it's very difficult for men to divorce women, it's usually the wife who leaves. . . ."

"Yacouba," I broke in, "do you really think Dongi might try to kill you?"

"If she plans to, I'll know: since I came from inside my mother, what's inside someone else can't be hidden from me."

But he didn't sound completely convinced, and when he left us that evening Alma and I watched with sad eyes as he returned to his compound. Yacouba's troubles seemed bound into so many complicated knots, and as outsiders we were powerless to help this man who had become such a good friend.

I was about to finish my morning's medical practice, putting the last strip of tape over a child's bandaged foot, when I heard drunken laughter coming from Bani's compound. The four Mossi laborers who lived in our village swayed against each other, giggling and reeling. Raogo, a tall, lanky man with one blind eye, waved to me. He strode uneasily toward our compound, the other men following, and he slipped and fell at my feet. I crouched down to help him, and he turned over, lifting his laughing face so close to me that I could see the discoloration of his eye.

His fist clutched a thick wad of CFAs—where had he gotten so much money? Grinning, he mumbled something that I had to ask him to repeat. He wanted to buy me a drink.

"No, thank you," I said, hoping that my rude reply would make him leave. But he frowned and insisted, though his buddies had already pulled him up and were tugging him away. He waved them off. *"La,"* he said, pointing to his forehead, *"ka n gba la"*—Give me medicine.

I slipped two aspirins in his hand, hoping this would satisfy him. It did, and I watched the drunken party return to Bani's compound.

"What was that all about?" Alma said. I turned around to see her standing in the doorway.

"I really don't know, but it seems awfully strange. Those guys are usually so quiet."

That afternoon François came to our compound, his lips tight with concern. "Someone killed my chicken," he said. Its neck had been twisted off, the corpse abandoned. Soon we heard that three more chickens in the village had been found dead. But the following day Kosangbé buzzed with talk of another, far greater scandal: Wamya Amo, a neighbor of San Yao's, was missing his life's savings—the equivalent of eight hundred dollars.

It was whispered that the four Mossi laborers had stolen the money and gone on a chicken-killing rampage. This accusation didn't surprise me: I'd seen those wads of bills in Raogo's hand. Others had, too, and this certainly seemed incriminating. Yet if these men *were* guilty, I wondered, why were they still in the village, seemingly oblivious of the suspicions about them?

Mossi people—émigrés from the neighboring country of Burkina Faso—had a terrible reputation among the Beng. "All Mossi were born to be thieves," I remembered Kona saying once during an evening chat in his compound.

"But not our Mossi," another elder had added quickly. Raogo and his friends had lived in Kosangbé without incident for over six years. One even had a child with a Beng woman. But now *"our* Mossi," once a source of village pride, had apparently reverted to stereotype.

Soon the villagers assembled under the kapok tree. Bani stood and declared that the Mossi laborers had come to his compound and asked him to hide a large amount of money for them. "I did this," he said, "but when I heard of the thievery, I knew where their money had come from."

Raogo and his three companions sat among the crowd, their faces oddly blank, as if this meeting were not about them. Their refusal to defend themselves was taken as a confession.

A debate began about whether the gendarmes should be summoned. Many of the older villagers were against the idea—Kosangbé had always solved its own problems. But this was the worst crime in anyone's memory, so it was decided that Kona and Bani would set off for M'Bahiakro.

The Mossi laborers still didn't try to escape, though no one guarded them—surely they could slip away and return to their country without too much trouble? I wondered if they were afraid of the Kosangbé elders' spiritual powers, from which they might never escape.

When the gendarmes arrived the following morning, I understood some of the elders' reluctance about calling them to the village. After parking their paddy wagon by the side of the road, the three gendarmes roughly pushed through the crowd that had gathered, elbowing old men and women, scattering children. They spoke rapid-fire French, ignoring the fact that few people understood them, and they refused to answer any questions posed to them in either Beng, Baulé, or Jula.

The accused men, now chained, were brought out into an open area. I checked the light meter of our camera, ready to take a picture of Ivoirian justice in action: the officer in charge waving his arms angrily in front of uncomprehending faces. But before I had a chance to press a button, the gendarme framed in my lens pointed at me and shouted, *"Pas des photos! C'est interdit! Pas des photos!"*

I lowered the camera, but the officer strode toward me. "What do you think you're doing? It's against the law to take photographs of gendarmes conducting an official investigation!"

"Pardon, I didn't know about this law," I began, stunned by his anger. "But I didn't take a photo, I was adjusting the light meter."

He wasn't listening. "We'll have to confiscate the camera."

"No, you can't do that, we need it for my wife's research."

"No? You're telling me *no?"* He tore the camera from my hand.

"Please, *monsieur,"* Alma broke in, "we live in this village. . . ."

"For your amusement, to make fun of the people and their poverty."

"That's not true! I have research papers signed by the—"

"You," he said, gesturing to me, "come along. We're taking you down to prison, too—there's a three-month sentence for what you've done."

Stunned, I stared at the Mossi men crouched inside the paddy wagon. They shifted down the bench to make room for me. "Wait, *monsieur,* we have many friends who can attest to our good intentions," I said, and I took out from my wallet the business card of Marcel Gross, an assistant to Phillippe Yaçé, the head of Côte d'Ivoire's General Assembly. Alma and I had been introduced to him by a mutual friend during our first week in the country, and we'd enjoyed a relaxed lunch at his home. Now shamelessly pulling rank, I handed the card to the officer. It was a little rectangle of power I'd never intended to use, but I didn't want to visit an Ivoirian prison.

He glanced at the card, then screamed even louder than before. "I don't care *who* your friends are! I don't care if you know the president himself! You broke the law!" But he was already backing down: "At the very least, we'll expose the film." He started fiddling with the camera.

"Please, monsieur, there are photos in there that are important to my wife's research. I didn't take a picture of the gendarmes. We can prove it if you'll let us develop the film."

"Yes," Alma added quickly, "we have prepaid mailers. We can have the developing lab mail the film to you directly, and you can see for yourself."

"Bring one to me. And quickly," he barked, and Alma hurried off to our house. The officer scowled at me, then turned away dismissively. Though he must have been relieved at this face-saving arrangement—*I* certainly was—he couldn't relinquish his angry pose of authority. The villagers regarded me with a mixture of surprise and sympathy—I too was being treated badly by the gendarmes. The officer had actually done me a favor, I realized. He'd whittled me down in size a bit in the eyes of our neighbors.

Alma returned with the mailer and a sheaf of her stamped research papers. The officer poked through them, feigning disinterest, while she addressed the mailer to the M'Bahiakro *gendarmerie.* We popped the roll of film inside, and the officer released our camera.

"We will notify you when the film arrives," he said, dismissing us coldly.

He returned to the paddy wagon. Kona and Bani sat beside him on the front seat. I watched the chained Mossi men, bent low in the small compartment.

The gendarmes roared off, and wiry little Kwamla Chakro hurried over to me. "Kouadio," he said heatedly in his hoarse voice, "if they had tried to take you away, I would have run home for my shotgun!"

"Thank you, Father," I said, quite touched, "but you see, I'm still here."

I didn't have time to mull over my narrow escape—Alma and I were due in Asagbé to translate more Beng stories with Pascal. But soon after arriving we were summoned to Bwadi Kouakou's compound with a request for help: his cousin had fallen off a bike on the way to the fields, smashing his mouth into the handlebars. Accompanied by our Asagbé village father, we helped lead the injured man—who held a bloody towel against his mouth—from his compound to our car.

We were speeding along on this latest emergency trip when a truck rushed past us as we turned a curve, its tires churning pebbles at our car. The windshield shattered, cracks swiftly zigzagging before us.

"Not *again!"* Alma cried out.

By now Didadi had been informally renamed the Damn Car. Just weeks before, an electrical fire in the engine had forced us temporarily to abandon the car in a Baulé village. Worse than the time spent on these repairs was the drain of money—we might go broke long before Alma's fieldwork was scheduled to end.

After dropping off our passenger at the M'Bahiakro infirmary, we stopped by Honoré's tailor shop—he'd appreciate hearing our village gossip, particularly the morning's incident with Côte d'Ivoire's finest. But Honoré not only knew, he gave us an update: at the *gendarmerie,* the Mossi laborers had accused Bani—*their* accuser—of operating an illegal still and selling them whiskey.

"Now Bani is in prison, too!" Honoré said with an I've-seen-it-all expression. "The village elders are all here in town. They're meeting at Kofi Kala's compound to decide what to do."

Honoré accompanied us to a large, cemented house with painted wooden shutters over the windows, an electric light brightening the wide porch. In the courtyard, a number of Kosangbé's elders gathered together under a small tree, in the middle of an intense discussion that barely stopped for our greetings.

"It was a mistake to bring the gendarmes to our village," San Yao said, disturbed by the news that they intended to return to Kosangbé the next day to search Bani's house for evidence of the alleged whiskey still. Alma and I sat down—it felt good to be part of the inner circle, clucking at what havoc strangers could wreak.

San Yao paused for a moment and looked past us all. I turned around and, through the distant open door of the porch, saw a half circle of children, rapt before a television. The black-and-white images of sailors chasing some sort of seaweedy monster through a submarine's interior looked familiar, and I kept glancing back at the bizarre chase until I made the connection: *Voyage to the Bottom of the Sea,* one of my boyhood television passions. Though I'd grown blasé about balancing cultural disjunctions, I simply had to shake my head, amazed.

The monster's screams, punctuated by gunshots, caused the rest of the elders to turn, and for a moment we all watched the creature's flailing arms as it raced through the submarine's dim interior. Finally the discussion resumed, Kona presenting an intricate strategy of how best to defend Bani. Yet throughout all the plotting, an occasional elder once again found his attention temporarily drawn to another drama—those fantastical images flashing from a television screen.

The next morning we drove to Bouaké, where Dramane quickly replaced our windshield. We immediately set off for Kosangbé, anxious not to waste any more time away from the village, but just before we reached Bengland this new windshield suddenly shattered by the swift trajectory of yet another churned-up rock.

I pulled the Damn Car over to the side of the dirt road. "What are we going to *do?*" Alma moaned, tears of frustration staining her cheeks.

"Sell it?" I offered, at once alarmed and excited by this sudden inspiration. "You're right—let's sell it."

"Wait," I said, reconsidering, "how will we get around?"

"The *taxi-brousse.* Or bicycles—we can buy bicycles."

"And the money we make will help stretch your grant," I added, beginning to convince myself. "Maybe there's someone in M'Bahiakro who'd want this thing."

"It's a great idea," Alma said, wiping her face with an edge of *pagne.* "But I don't want to waste any more time. Let's get back to the village. The next time we go to Bouaké, we'll just leave the thing with Dramane. We'll ask him to sell it for us and offer him a commission."

"Sounds okay to me. But whatever we do, this Damn Car is history."

With Didadi's name changed officially and its fate decided, we drove the remaining stretch of road back to Kosangbé. Still, we had misgivings. What if there were further emergencies? With our car we had helped save three lives. I hoped fervently that we wouldn't regret our decision.

Back home, we hoped to see Bani next door in his compound, but Bayo, his second wife, stood alone, her round, normally friendly face puffy from crying as she pounded yams with her wooden pestle.

Yacouba was already marching toward our courtyard to welcome us. As we sat down together he looked over at Bayo and shook his head. Apparently, when the gendarmes had returned to the village to search Bani's house, Yaa, his first wife, had refused to let them pass the door. Taking this incriminating behavior as an admission of guilt, they'd left.

"She had nothing to hide, so why did she do such a thing?" Yacouba marveled. "Some people say she wants Bani to stay in prison so she can marry a lover, but I don't believe it."

"Hasn't Yaa explained why she kept the gendarmes out?" Alma asked.

"Not to me. You can ask her, but she's not here, she's gone to the *marché* for a chicken."

"A chicken?"

Yacouba nodded. "A diviner has told her that Bani will be released only if she gives a white chicken to the first stranger who walks past Kosangbé. She can't say a word when she does this, or it won't work." He sighed. "What's happened to Bani is terrible—he'll be in prison for five years if he's judged guilty. And Bayo," he added, nodding in her direction, "is pregnant."

Alma: Washing Away Witchcraft

Perhaps Yaa's odd chicken sacrifice worked, for soon afterward Bani returned to the village, happy but haggard—he'd been beaten regularly, along with the four thieves. Perhaps this was to induce confessions . . . or simply to inscribe the authority of the State on the bodies of suspected lawbreakers. During Bani's absence we realized how much we'd come to care for him, and we joined the others of our *quartier* in cheering his return.

One Mossi migrant to the village hadn't participated in the theft, so he hadn't been arrested. But seeing his compatriots chained and herded into the paddy wagon must have undone him. One day I found him standing in his host's courtyard, a faraway look in his eyes. Idly he picked up a bunch of green plantains lying on the ground nearby and, with a machete, proceeded to hack off chunks of the thick fruit, peel and all, then scatter them randomly. The poor man, alone in an alien village, had gone mad. Perhaps he was wasting those unripe plantains as his friends had thrown away their lives.

A few days later Philip and I stood in the back of a hot M'Bahiakro courtroom—the day had arrived for the thieves' trial. The four men, now manacled, stood awkwardly on the sidelines, impassively awaiting their turn. Finally their case was announced and they moved forward, dragging their chained feet. The judge asked the suspects perfunctorily if they had committed the theft, and they all obligingly pleaded guilty. Then, after hearing Bani's testimony for the prosecution, the judge spouted a slick but rapid French heavily seasoned with judicial terms I strained to catch. Someone whispered a translation of the sentence to the men in a language they understood: ten years in prison, immediately commuted to five, plus fines of up to $1,500 each—sums they could never hope to amass. The men remained stony-faced. I knew they were all guilty; still, I couldn't help but pity them, wondering how many would survive five years in an Ivoirian jail.

That evening, on his way back from the fields, Yacouba stopped by our courtyard. "Tomorrow's the big day!" he said gaily.

"What big day?" Philip asked.

"Didn't I tell you? We're all going to Asagbé—it's to thank them for giving us Karimu's new fiancée, Fatima."

"We'll be there," Philip promised.

As Yacouba walked off, I thought of how, months earlier, Karimu had steadfastly rejected Akissi, Kona's choice of a bride for him. Kona had angrily declared that he wanted nothing more to do with Karimu's efforts to find a second wife, and a short time later Karimu had selected Fatima—it was this new engagement that we'd celebrate tomorrow.

In the evening I walked over to Karimu's courtyard, where I found him sitting on a low stool, mending a torn *bubu*.

"You know, Amwé," he remarked, "I'm happy that I'll be marrying Fatima. I know she likes me, and she's a member of my matriclan—that should help the marriage. But I'm also worried."

"About what?"

"Where will she live? You see my house, it's not even big enough for Ajua and me." He gestured to what was indeed one of the smallest houses in the village—I guessed it contained just two tiny rooms.

"I'd like to build a second house for Fatima," he continued, "but I don't have the money right now. I'll have to wait until I can sell my coffee in a few months. I hope there'll be enough cash for a tin roof. Otherwise the two women will just have to live together in there—that'll be trouble, for sure." He sighed, then looked at me earnestly. "What do people do about this in *your* country?"

"Karimu," I said softly, "men don't have two or three wives in my country—just one."

"*Tey eh?*" he exclaimed—Is that true? "But why not?"

"Well, for one thing," I said, curious to hear his response, "if a man married two women, he'd be arrested and put in jail."

"*Yih!*" Karimu shook his head and smacked his lips in staccato fashion—a Beng form of disapproval—then declared slowly and clearly, "Your country is very bad."

Hoping to provoke him, I offered my own opinion. "But polygamy isn't fair to women. Why should a man be allowed more than one wife if a woman can't have more than one husband?"

"*Eh,* Amwé," he said, laughing, "that's just the way God made us. Anyway, some women like it."

"Does Ajua?" I asked.

"She's going along with it. I *hope* she'll like her co-wife," he said. "But for now, only God knows."

The next morning I woke early, to the sunrise bleating of goats outside our window: I was curious to see the medicine that Kwamla Chakro had promised he'd give us today—a medicine that was so powerful, he said, it would always keep us healthy. After a hurried breakfast, we walked over to his courtyard, Philip carefully holding a small ceramic pot that Kwamla had asked us to bring. The pot fit nicely in his cupped hands, its reddish clay shining through some spots that had blackened in the firing—we took this charring as a sign of character.

We found Kwamla Chakro in his courtyard, adjusting one of his drums. After our good mornings, Philip said, *"Aba,* here is the pot you told us to bring you. Is it all right?"

Kwamla Chakro turned the bowl around in his hands, running his fingers over its incised lines. *"Ah-heh,"* he said, stomping his foot and grinning a toothless smile. "It's good, very good, truly!"

A slight man, Kwamla Chakro spoke in bursts of energy that were often barely understandable even when he was sober. Now, early in the morning, we could already detect the sweet smell of palm wine on his breath.

"I'll fill this up with the medicines for you today. Come back tonight and it will be ready!" He shook our hands vigorously.

"Thank you very much, Father," we said, and we returned to our courtyard just as Yacouba arrived, puffing out his cheeks to blow on a soccer whistle.

"Hurry up, hurry up, hurry up!" Yacouba exhorted. "It's time to get ready for Asagbé! Come on, go get your fanciest clothes. Get dressed, get dressed, get dressed!"

Surprised to see our friend suddenly playing this ritual role of hurrier— he'd told me last night that Karimu had asked him to do so, but I hadn't known exactly what he meant—we scuttled inside. Philip picked out a colorful handmade shirt, I chose an indigo batik outfit that I saved for special occasions.

Once dressed, we ran into Yacouba again, now on his second tour of the village. He took a break from his shrill whistle to complain that the elders in Karimu's patriclan refused to go to Asagbé to offer thanking speeches because Kona was boycotting the entire event. "He's still mad about Akissi. You know Kona's a lot older than Karimu; well, ever since their father died, Kona's been like a father to him—and how can you have an engagement thanking party without a father? So last night, the family sent over Andama as a mediator—he begged Kona to participate today. No one knows what Andama said," Yacouba continued, "but Kona tried to beat him up!"

"Andama probably already had a few shots of *kutuku,"* I said.

"Ça, c'est sûr. Anyway," Yacouba concluded, "if *someone* doesn't get to Asagbé soon, it'll really be insulting." He returned to his whistle.

Philip and I came upon our friend, Egbri Kouassi, a soft-spoken man who enjoyed chatting about village affairs. After exchanging greetings, I said, "So, we hear none of the elders has gone to Asagbé."

"Oh, they'll go," he replied, "it's still early." I looked at my watch: almost noon. I guessed the walk would take well over an hour each way. And the darkening clouds seemed less and less likely to cooperate.

"But who will go, now that Kona has refused?" I asked.

"Oh, Ché Kofi, for one," he said.

I thanked him for his tip, and Philip and I walked over to Ché Kofi's courtyard.

"Me? Mm-mm. I'm on my way to the *marché* at Bongalo!" he said evasively.

The more Philip and I talked with people, the more this ritual seemed to be in shambles. Soon we found Yacouba again, who reported that the female elders had left for Asagbé. "They'll just do the job themselves," he said.

"They can do that?"

"Oui, oui," he answered. "They're elders, too, aren't they?"

"Of course! Which ones went?" I asked.

"It's Makola, Kouassi Ajua, and Busu Amla," Yacouba answered. This was an odd list indeed. First of all, these women were hardly "elders": at about forty, Makola was the senior member. The second member of the expedition, Kouassi Ajua, was Karimu's first wife. I wondered if she was really pleased at this outing or merely fulfilling her duty. And Busu Amla was Kona's junior wife—considering her husband's adamant refusal to join in the ritual himself, I was surprised that he hadn't prevented her from participating.

At two o'clock Yacouba announced they couldn't wait any longer, it was time to go. For the first time, Philip would bike with the men of the village, and I'd walk with the second wave of young women. Since my group would take longer, we'd have a head start; the men could catch up in a short while.

I laced up my hiking boots and waved good-bye to Philip, looking forward to the five-mile walk. This would be a good opportunity to spend time with some women I hadn't gotten to know well: I'd practice my Beng, and we could chat about the ritual, maybe sing walking songs.

We started down the long road. "Look at that waddle!" said one woman, shifting her weight from foot to foot in imitation of another's gait. Everyone around her laughed, including the butt of the joke herself.

"And look at *that* walk!" another woman said, dragging along with exaggeratedly leaden steps as if she were wearing muddy sandals . . . or canvas hiking boots. The woman looked at me: now it was my turn to laugh at myself, see how I appeared in Beng eyes. How different were the gaits of my companions, with their light stepping of flip-flops snapping in the air or their rounded barefoot strides, feet embracing the dirt road's dips and bumps.

Our light banter continued as the women wandered in and out of their small groupings. Moya walked with Mo'san for a while, then Mo'san fell behind to nurse her baby and take a pee in the woods. This accomplished, she made no effort to catch up with Moya but just fell in step with another

friend. I'd assumed that my major challenge would be to insert myself into a single, tightly knit ensemble of lifelong friends. How romantically I'd envisioned their relationships—there *was* camaraderie, but it was casual and contingent, continually dismantled and reinvented.

In a little while the men caught up with us. Philip waved as he pedaled by, flanked by Yacouba and François. It hardly seemed fair that the men should have such an easier trip. I'd never asked anyone why Beng women and girls didn't ride bikes; now the inequity glared at me.

But no sooner had they cleared a curve to pedal out of sight than the men returned in our direction. We whooped with delight as boyfriends, husbands, and brothers stopped to pick us up so we could ride sidesaddle into Asagbé, still about two miles off. One by one we gave up our group for the luxury of a ride, each attaching herself to a partner. I seated myself behind Philip, my arms encircling his waist.

Finally we reached Asagbé. Quickly we formed a motley line and began snaking through the village to sing lovely Jula wedding songs: "The bride is beautiful, the groom is beautiful!" We greeted every household: "Good afternoon, we've come to say *Good afternoon,* and to thank you for before." In a village of Asagbé's size, this long round of greeting and thanking was an ambitious task in the best of circumstances. But storm clouds were gathering, and our pace increased correspondingly, with women in the rear leapfrogging to pass those in front or taking shortcuts to shave off yards. By the time we reached the farthest outpost of the village, we were literally running.

We ended up underneath the public canopy. Catching our breath, we leaned against the log pillars of the thatched overhang and watched two men face each other: the speaker for the bride and the speaker for the groom. Hands at his sides, Karimu's speaker began: "We are honored that you have agreed to this union, and we beg your forgiveness for not having sent male elders to thank you this morning." His counterpart accepted the elegant apology, and each proceeded to set forth the virtues of the day's match. I took notes studiously on the protracted figures of speech and eloquent metaphors.

But soon the clouds turned from gray to black. The men abruptly cut their speeches short, and we all hurried away from the plaza. Having begun inauspiciously, the ritual now concluded with little grace—by Beng standards, it wasn't "sweet." With little time before the inevitable storm, the other women and I clambered onto the backs of the men's bikes.

But we lost the race with the clouds—with two miles still to go, the rain assaulted us relentlessly under a sky nearly as dark as night. Flash lightning lit up the forest, and trees swayed ominously in the howling wind. I wiped streams of rain from my face with one hand as I clung to Philip's waist with the other, and he huffed and cursed, nervously looking left and right for signs of any trees about to topple onto the road. Finally we reached the large rise right before Kosangbé, and Philip and the other men hunched forward, putting all their weight into pedaling us up that slippery, spirit-laden hill. By the time we arrived in Kosangbé, we were all thoroughly drenched, bedraggled, and exhausted. Meanwhile a very dry Kona must have felt some satisfaction—his delaying tactics had thoroughly spoiled Karimu's celebration.

Back in our house, we peeled off our sopping clothes, slipped into dry outfits, and warmed our hands around the kerosene lamp. I halfheartedly heated a packet of miso soup that my mother had sent—sometimes those anxious gifts came in handy—and Philip and I sipped distractedly at the warm broth and picked at sardines straight from the can—already we were anticipating bed.

As we wearily cleared the table, there was a knock at the door: it was Kwamla Chakro, grinning and looking as lively as ever. Without much enthusiasm, we invited him in. Kwamla sat down and began formally, "This morning I told you I'd give you some medicine. Now I've come to tell you that it's ready—I'll bring it right away." Of course! I cringed to think how in our fatigue we'd forgotten all about that morning's promise.

In a few minutes Kwamla Chakro was back with the pot . . . and with Jimblé, Yacouba's uncle. We were in for a long evening, for Jimblé had come as a Speaker—that formal role reserved for solemn occasions, when the main participants speak to a third person as if they hadn't heard what had just been said. Though Jimblé didn't know a word of French, his speech was much clearer than Kwamla's. We offered them seats and turned up our kerosene lamp. Then I snuck a peek into the ceramic pot: it seemed to be filled with long pieces of tree bark coiled around and around.

Kwamla began his speech, which Jimblé then restated: "There are a few things you must know about this medicine."

"Father, thank you," Philip said. "Please tell us about it."

Again Kwamla Chakro addressed Jimblé, who repeated: "He says that next Friday you must awake before dawn, open the door to your house, and sit naked on the threshold of the door. While there, you must bathe very quickly with this medicine."

An unwelcome *"Yih"* escaped from my lips.

"It's very important that you do what I say," Kwamla said sternly, this time addressing me directly.

"Yes, Father," I said obediently, all the while casting a look of dismay to Philip.

Kwamla Chakro turned back to his friend, who repeated: "The elder says that when you wash with this medicine, you should pour just a very little bit of the water from the pot into this half gourd that he's giving you. Take the gourd and quickly splash yourselves all over, then get dressed.

"After the first time you use it, you can wash with the medicine in your regular bathhouse on any day you want to, but it should always be early in the morning, never in the evening. It's especially good if you'll be traveling that day—to another village or to town. It'll protect you from any evil—even bullets."

Turning to me, Kwamla said, "The only time you can't use the medicine is when you're menstruating—then it's taboo. Outside of that, you can use it any day." I nodded, blushing. Turning to Philip, Kwamla added, "There are no days that are taboo for you."

Now he instructed us both: "Every time you wash with the medicine, you should immediately replace the water you've used—don't forget, because if the pot dries out, the medicine will be totally ruined. Also, never heat the pot, and only pour fresh water into it. If you fill it with boiled water, it will heat your body when you wash with it, and you'll fall sick. Rainwater is fine. In fact, go get some right now."

I opened the door and, holding a bowl, extended my arm into the down-pour—within a minute the bowl was filled. I poured the water into the pot.

"Good. Now go put the pot in a safe place in your house and don't touch it until next Friday. After you wash with the medicine for the first time, you can touch the pot whenever you need to."

We agreed, and Philip asked me, "Where do you think we should keep it?"

"How about in the far corner of our room, near the bed?" I said.

"Okay."

"The first time you wash with the medicine," Jimblé quoted Kwamla, "you'll notice that the bark in the pot has a pretty strong smell. But you mustn't say anything about that, or even sniff it: if you do, the medicine will be ruined."

I reflected in shame how often I'd smelled Moya's cooking pots. At least by now I'd learned my lesson.

"If you follow these instructions and wash with the medicine regularly," Jimblé said, repeating Kwamla's words, "you'll never fall sick or have to see a doctor. Also, your work here and back in your own country will go well—if anyone tries to ruin it for any reason, he or she won't succeed."

Then Kwamla addressed us directly. "I'm happy to give you this medicine pot. It was my father who told me about it. He taught me that when I collect the medicine I must embrace the tree trunk before stripping its bark."

Then Kwamla turned back to Jimblé, who reported: "The elder says that for this medicine, the price is five hundred francs plus one red rooster."

Philip nodded and reached into his pocket.

Now Kwamla addressed us directly: "Make sure you give me the chicken before next Friday. Have you understood all the instructions?"

We said we had and thanked him profusely. The two men parted, and Philip and I, utterly worn out, prepared for bed.

"Well, what do you think?" Philip said, lowering the wick in the lamp.

"I'm just so touched—Kwamla's been incredibly sweet to us. Somehow I feel like we have a protector."

I untucked the mosquito netting and sat on the edge of our narrow bed, staring at the pot perched a few feet away on the floor. Already I detected the strong odor that Kwamla had warned us of, but dutifully I refrained from comment. We lay down, and I reflected on my decision to use the medicine: if I washed like a Beng person, I might come one step closer to knowing what it felt like to inhabit a Beng body. Silently I thanked Kwamla Chakro once again for the gift.

The next morning we brought a beautiful red-and-brown-feathered rooster to Kwamla's courtyard. He was listening to a loud tape of what sounded like village drumming, but the batteries in his old tape deck were so weak, the music lurched and wobbled.

I turned to Kwamla. "Father, we've brought you the rooster and a bottle of beer." I paused to regard the noisy machine and put my hands over my ears. Kwamla rose to my challenge and mischievously turned up the volume—perhaps he was hinting. "Also," I added, "we'll give you some new batteries."

Kwamla responded, "Thank you, we'll have the beer as soon as we kill the chicken." Then he led us into a small room in his house that served as a chicken coop and deposited a tiny egg in the middle of the room. He slipped a knife out of an animal-skin sheath hanging from his belt loop and deftly slit the bird's throat. Holding it upside down over the egg, he let the blood drip down from its neck until the shell shone red. Then he let the rooster slump to the ground. But suddenly it squirmed, and he hurriedly flung it out the doorway. In a final burst of life, the bird majestically flapped those glimmery red-and-brown wings before finally collapsing.

Kwamla said, "That's a *very* good sign that he flapped about with his wings spread out." Then he singed the feathers off the bird, carved it up, and inspected the testicles. "They're white," he said, pleased. We all shook hands and opened the beer.

"This is a very, very powerful medicine," Kwamla said between sips. "My father was never sick and lived to be a very, very, very old *kalabé* because of it. When he finally died, it wasn't anyone who killed him—it was just God." Then, handing half the carcass to Philip, Kwamla said, "You know, I haven't given this medicine to many people at all—just a few friends. And you're the first woman, Amwé."

"Aba, ka nuwaliaa," I said—Father, thank you.

"You haven't forgotten the instructions I gave you about the pot, have you?"

"Nn-nnn."

"Good. Make sure you don't touch it before next Friday. If you do, I'll know about it," he said mysteriously.

Two days later I went to see Amenan in Asagbé. I found her sitting on her usual bark-cloth mat, tressing little Amwé's hair in the *gbofloto* style: small, round tufts in rows all over her head, named for the fried balls of dough that young girls sold in the market. Now six months old, Amwé was sitting up nicely on her own. Today she looked too cute to escape my camera: I took it out and began to focus. Amenan held her up and pointed to me.

"Look at your mama," she told the baby. "Go ahead, there's your mama."

Amwé gazed at me obligingly, and I clicked, touched. Then I sat down on the mat to do "This Little Piggy" with Amwé's toes, and she giggled with pleasure. All Amwé's toes accounted for, Amenan and I settled down for a serious day's work. This time it was I who started off our session with news.

"Amenan," I said, "one of our friends in Kosangbé has given us a medicine pot."

"What sort of pot is it?" she asked, and I told her.

"Ah," Amenan said, lowering her voice as she always did when she was about to tell me something of grave significance, "that's *kraw ti* medicine— it's very special. There are two kinds of *kraw ti*. One kind is evil: it's to let you kill someone by witchcraft. If anyone uses this kind of medicine against you, nothing can save you. The witch casts the medicine by throwing a small piece of iron against a tree, saying, 'When so-and-so walks under this tree, may the leaves fall on him.' At that very moment, even if you were perfectly healthy, you'll suddenly get sick and start dying."

"*Yih!*"

"The other kind of *kraw ti* is to protect you *against* sickness and witchcraft. You always have to kill a chicken for this kind of medicine pot. Did your friend kill a chicken for you?"

"Yes, he asked us for a red rooster," I said.

"*C'est bon,* you have the right kind of pot," she said.

Philip: Caught by Spirits

I sat under the palm branch veranda of the men's lounging area, enjoying a short break from writing. I looked at the men around me: some were sleeping on straw mats, exhausted from the hard work of the fields, while others gossiped quietly to themselves. Alma had gone to Asagbé for the day, and as I enjoyed the shade I wondered what new cultural revelations she'd come back with. Last week Amenan had told her that anyone dancing at a funeral was especially susceptible to witchcraft, and she'd given the example of a young girl, Duti Ajua, who'd been killed this way. During the funeral dance a gunshot was heard to go off—a common funeral practice—but no one could see where it had come from. The next morning Duti Ajua had a terrible headache, and the following day her mouth began bleeding, her teeth fell out, and she swelled up alarmingly. The third day she fainted and died. The guilty party, Amenan told Alma, was Duti Ajua's own grandmother, a woman who'd been at the dance. As part of her dancer's costume, the old woman had worn a colorful turban and held a baton—but the turban was really a Gabon viper, all curled up, and the baton was actually a gun. With these invisible weapons she'd bewitched her granddaughter.

I recalled all the funerals I'd danced in, never suspecting that my fellow dancers worried about witchcraft. I *did* know that funerals were an important source of Amenan's witchcraft tales: no witch could die without first confessing his or her crimes. Otherwise the witch's dead victims would block the path to *wurugbé*—the city of ancestors—and the witch would have to return to the land of the living. Recently in Asagbé an old woman had come to life twice during the first day of her funeral, sitting up and startling the women who were fanning what they'd thought was a corpse. Only after the old woman admitted her witchly misdeeds did she finally lie still and enter the Beng afterlife.

Though to me this all seemed exotic, to the Beng it was as ordinary as air. Would there ever come a time when I would live and breathe their culture without an outsider's awe? I stretched and had just thought of returning to my compound to write when Kona sat down beside me, offering a handful of warm, freshly roasted peanuts.

"Aba, ka misiala," I said, a special thanks reserved for the gift of food.

The nuts were marvelously tasty, almost sweet, reminding me of beer nuts back home. So when I finished I thanked Kona again and returned to my compound, where I began shelling a large bowlful of peanuts. Before long a few children wandered over to help, and soon they were roasting the peanuts at the smoldering hearth in François's compound.

When the peanuts were browned just right I split the batch with my helpers and asked one of the boys to fetch me a bottle of beer. Then I ambled over to Kona's compound, beer and bowl of peanuts in hand, and delivered the formal speech I'd been reciting to myself: "Father, your affairs are good, I like you. Accept my offer of beer and peanuts."

It wasn't my most eloquent speech, nor was it entirely true. Though I liked the man, I didn't quite trust him. But Kona appreciated the sentiments, and we filled our glasses, drank, and grabbed handfuls of nuts. Then Bani joined us. His face was still raw and puffy from the beatings he'd received in prison, but he was *home,* thanks to bribes paid to the gendarmes and Yaa's gift of a chicken to a passing stranger.

Kona whispered something to one of the hovering children, who ran off and quickly reappeared with a bottle of wine. It was the notorious Valpierre—Le Roi du Vin du Table, the label shamelessly claimed—a wine so vile that Peace Corps volunteers theorized it must have come from a powdered mixture. But it was an expensive gift by village standards, so I hid my dismay and thanked him.

Since we were still working on the beer, Kona—remarkably nonchalant—poured the wine into our half-filled glasses, creating a perverse sangria that horrified me. How could I drink such an unappetizing brew? But Kona and Bani downed their glasses, so before they could notice my reluctance I took a cautious sip.

The peculiar concoction wasn't bad at all—the wine disguised the fact that the beer was warm, and the beer masked the wine's turpentinish bouquet. I raised my glass in appreciation of Kona's innovation and ordered another child to chase down one more bottle of beer so we could keep this mixture going. Then, peanuts done and bottles empty, I gave and received thanks and walked very slowly back to my compound, hoping for my stomach's forgiveness.

Alma finally returned, with a potpourri of information that she recounted over a dinner of rice with fish in a tomato sauce. Amenan was worried about her uncle: in the old days kings never worked in the fields, otherwise, they'd go blind. But these days Bondé Chomo occasionally went to the fields because he didn't have enough sons to help him.

"And then there's this baby disease Amenan told me about," Alma said. "It's called *gbri.*"

"Dirt?"

"That's right, a baby gets it if she's touched by a woman who's considered sexually polluted."

"Really? What do you make of *that?*"

"Well, I have some ideas. The same women who cause the disease are also the only ones who can cure it. There's something interesting going on here—it seems to contradict the standard theories about women and pollution. But I'll have to ask Amenan a lot more questions."

I nodded my head sympathetically and refilled our glasses—insurance against Moya's spicy sauce—and then Alma continued, now telling me that the Asagbé chief had recently announced no one could work in the fields on Monday, for fear of offending the spirits and ruining the coffee crop. "The only exceptions are men who need to check their animal traps, but they have to wear white *pagnes,* to appease the spirits."

Alma paused. "How could I have forgotten? Amenan says that Kwamla's medicine pot is the real thing, very powerful."

"Well, that's good to know."

"I have *so* much stuff," Alma said, spooning more rice onto her plate. "Let's see, what else? Oh, yeah, the best times for sex at night are either before

eleven or after three. Amenan said it's bad to have sex in the dead of the night because the spirits are walking around the village. If they pass by a house where people are making love, they'll eavesdrop, and if a child is conceived then, it won't be a good child."

"Jeez, you mean the spirits are *voyeurs?*"

"I suppose," Alma said, scrunching up her face. Apparently she hadn't considered this possibility.

"Okay, okay," I said, laughing, "first Fridays, now this. Any more interviews and we might as well take a vow of celibacy."

Gba Apo, still resentful that the male elders had appropriated the porch of her house for Mo'kissi's trial, increasingly felt that the privileges of the house were slowly being claimed by her extended family. One afternoon Au, the wife of Gba Apo's grandson, wanted to fetch something from the house. Since the door was locked, she borrowed a key from her husband.

When told of this, Gba Apo released her pent-up fury. "It's *my* house," she said, "Au should have asked *me* for the key." When Ché Kofi returned from the fields, he sided with Au.

"I'm tired of you storing rice in *my house,*" Gba Apo shouted at him. "They only attract mice. Too many people are taking over!" Ever the hothead, Ché Kofi aimed one of those choice Beng sexual insults at his mother—an appalling breach of respect. Enraged, Gba Apo ordered everything to be removed from the house.

By the time her house was about to be emptied a few days later, Gba Apo—still stung by her son's words—had decided to vacate it as well. Honoré came up from M'Bahiakro and sat on the porch, sick with regret that his village monument to his success in town was being abandoned. Ché Kofi, trying to hide the shame of his behavior, gruffly supervised his older sons in the removal of the bags of rice. His wife, Asaw, grumbling all the while, carried out the lanterns, piles of clothing, and small pieces of furniture.

I watched, stunned by this Beng echo of my current story in progress— another family deserting a house. Slowly I approached Ché Kofi, and with the peculiar feeling that I was entering into a foreign translation of my fiction, I joined the procession and helped tote bags of rice out of the house. That afternoon François's uncle Andama rebuked me for interfering in other people's business. He was right, and I apologized. Yet I'd needed to sidle alongside that family's estrangement, for I suspected something of their angry energy might help me arrive at the final paragraph of my story that I'd been working toward for so long.

Everyone in Kosangbé was relieved that Anayaa, the celebration for the new yam harvest, had finally arrived, for in the past few months they'd made do mainly with rice and corn porridge. Karimu was especially pleased, confessing, "If I go just three days without eating yams, I don't feel right."

On the eve of Anayaa, animal sacrifices would be offered in the forest, and the following day people could finally cook succulent meat dishes with the new, fresh yams of the season. But before these impending rituals, a meeting of animist priests and supplicants from various villages would take place. Alma was forbidden from this event; as we were often told in the days preceding Anayaa, she—or any other woman—would die if she tried to attend. Galled at her exclusion, Alma left broad hints that perhaps I should go in her stead.

"Don't worry, of course I'll go," I finally told her, though I was sure I wouldn't be able to follow the intricacies of the speeches.

The meeting began after dark, on the chief's side of the village. At the last minute I decided to sneak a tape recorder to the meeting—if I returned with a tape, how could Alma refuse my gift? So I wore a light jacket with deep pockets, hoping no one would notice the bulge in one of them, and joined the elders just as they were about to begin. By now I had doubts about the whole enterprise, but Komena Yao, an older man I barely knew, gave me a friendly smile, so I sat next to him.

The leader of the meeting, a thin-faced elder from another village, didn't appreciate my sudden presence. "Kouadio, *ka ta!*"—Go away—he said brusquely.

I pretended I didn't hear him, and he repeated his command. I turned to him and, as if I didn't understand, said, "Good evening, Father."

Exasperated, he went through the evening greetings with me. Then, again, he said, *"Ka ta!"*

I smiled and nodded my head. The elder sighed.

"He can barely speak Beng," someone said behind me, "why not let him stay?"

"Aiee! If he's going to stay, I want a thousand CFAs to buy beer later."

I was so pleased he'd relented that I reached for my wallet and pulled out a bill. Luckily no one paid any attention to my sudden fluency.

When the meeting began I could understand a few phrases here and there, though I didn't try very hard to follow: the tape recorder was secretly running in my jacket pocket. Yet as one long speech followed another, I began to worry that my tape might soon run out and stop automatically with a loud click that would surely give me away. With no watch, I didn't know how much time I had left, and I certainly couldn't examine the tape recorder to check.

"I'm going to take a piss," I said in a low voice, standing up—a public announcement that is perfectly polite among the Beng. I walked off toward the forest, and behind a bathhouse I took out the recorder and tried to examine it.

It was too dark to see, though just a few feet away from me the ground was dimly lit by the lanterns at the meeting. Yet if I stepped away from the bathhouse, the elders would see me, tape recorder in hand. I closed my eyes, hoping to adjust my sight to the dark. I opened them, but no luck, so I closed them again, trying to imagine why I'd ever thought this secret taping would be a good idea. Then I worried that someone might notice I was taking a long time, so I simply turned the tape over in the recorder—coughing to disguise any telltale mechanical sound—and hoped for the best.

I returned to the meeting, my arm stiff over my bulging pocket, and sat down again. Before a minute passed I felt a hand lightly touch my jacket. It was Komena Yao. A surge of fright spread over my body.

"Kouadio, why?" he whispered in my ear.

Sliding my hand down to the jacket pocket, I pressed the off button. I could just make out the muffled click. Then I leaned over to Komena Yao and whispered, "Big brother, I'm sorry. It's over."

He nodded, said nothing. No one else seemed to notice our exchange, yet as the discussion continued I resisted the urge to rush off, afraid Komena Yao might announce my misdeed.

When the meeting ended, everyone stood and thanked each other. Expecting an accusing arm on my shoulder at any second, I hid my nervousness with a fixed smile. Then, as preparations began for the evening's sacrifices, I hurried back to our compound.

"What's the matter?" Alma asked when she saw my pallid face. I pulled out the recorder.

"You *didn't*."

I nodded and told her what had happened.

"It's my fault," Alma said. "I should have said something before you left." She sighed. "Now what do we do?"

"Wait, I suppose."

Two hours passed, but no group of angry elders arrived to demand the return of the tape. Komena Yao had kept the secret. Or perhaps the elders, being told, felt certain no one would dare help us translate a recording of such a secret meeting. And they were right—who would? The cassette I held in my hands was worthless.

Alma and I prepared to go to bed. I set the alarm for four A.M.—just before dawn, as Kwamla Chakro had instructed; for in the morning we were supposed to wash with his medicine pot. Initially I'd been charmed by this arrangement—there was little that Alma wouldn't try in order to enter the Beng world. But now, after having violated the privacy of a ritual, I wanted a cleansing bath to wash off my shame.

We woke to the insistent, high-pitched beeps of the clock. Opening the door to the quiet night, Alma placed the pot on our doorstep. "Hurry up," I whispered, nervous that some early riser might wander by. But the village was asleep, and any wandering spirits had cleared out an hour ago. Alma crouched down and dipped the small gourd into the pot, quickly splashing the medicinal water over herself. Then it was my turn, and I rushed through my ablutions in the chilly, early morning air.

The herbal water felt faintly sticky. Finished, I stepped back and shut our door. I'd hoped to wash away my transgression, but instead I was left with a thin film covering my body. Yet what had I expected? The clingy feeling on the skin surely reassured Kwamla Chakro and whoever else subscribed to this medicine, for this bathing wasn't designed to clean, it was supposed to protect, perhaps creating an invisible wall between the body and the world. As for my feelings of guilt, I'd need more than a bath to assuage them.

Early the next morning, drums sounded in the village: important news needed to be announced. Alma and I walked across the village to the kapok tree, where a crowd was already gathered. I sat down and regarded the suppressed curiosity on the faces of my neighbors. I half feared that Komena Yao might stand up and denounce me, just as Bani had denounced the Mossi laborers a month earlier. But the Beng world certainly didn't revolve around my behavior, for when everyone was settled, San Yao reported that a death had occurred last night in the village of Ndogbé, and the funeral would begin today. Small groups then gathered, discussing the news, calculating their ritual obligations as near or distant kin.

Alma and I returned to our compound, and before long Kona came by to greet us. "Kouadio, I'm going to Ndogbé. Come along with me—Akwé Sié was a very old man, so the funeral will be sweet."

Surprised but also pleased that he wanted me to accompany him, I accepted. The celebrations for Apisé's funeral had also been "sweet," and Kona had obviously noticed how much I'd enjoyed the revelry. I hurried to Yacouba's compound to borrow a bicycle, and he helped me locate the same rusted, wobbly affair, with only half the front brakes working, that I'd borrowed for Karimu's wedding thanking party. I didn't care—I was used to the thing.

I joined Kona at the road dividing Kosangbé, and together we set off for

Ndogbé, four miles away. A short distance from the village, we stepped off our bicycles and began to climb the steep hill. I was happy to be alone with Kona, hoping he might tell me something interesting during our long trip. So as I pushed my bicycle along, I casually mentioned the spirits who lived on the hill.

"No spirits live here," he said quietly.

Astonished to hear this, I continued in my best Beng, "Yes, they do, remember the molasses trucks and the sacrifice?"

"There are no spirits here," Kona insisted.

I knew that Kona was normally cautious about speaking on religious subjects, but since we were alone I continued to press him, annoyed at his denials.

"You say there are spirits here," he said in a low voice. "Have you ever seen one?"

Eager to show off my knowledge, I replied, "No, they're invisible. I'd die if I saw one!"

Kona said nothing.

He must have been relieved when we reached the top of the hill and climbed back on our bikes. Soon we were speeding down the other side of the hill. But a foolish stubbornness had taken hold of me, which I couldn't resist.

"Kona," I said, "there *are* spirits here, can't you hear them? They're calling us!" And then I jokingly shouted out his name.

The look of alarm on his face surprised me, so at once I added, "No, don't worry, they're calling me, too." As I shouted out my own name—"Kouadio!"—I realized I was speeding down the hill too fast. I pulled on the brakes. They snapped, the front wheel turning in sharply. I tumbled through the air, then twisted my body and rolled when I hit the hard ground.

Lying on the dirt road, quite shaken and afraid to move, I stared up at the sky—so nicely blue—and the dark green crest of trees. Kona ran to me. Picking myself up gingerly, I discovered only a few cuts and bruises on my arms and legs, and I dimly understood that I'd received far less than I deserved. But it was clear I couldn't continue on to the funeral. Kona accompanied me back to the village in silence.

"What *happened* to you?" Alma asked when she saw me limping toward our compound. Still a bit dazed, I told her the story as she dressed my slight wounds. When Yacouba came to join the crowd that had gathered, I repeated the story, and a smile crept across his face. "Didn't Kona tell you?" he asked.

"Tell me what?"

"Today is a very sacred day. It's dangerous to travel because the spirits come out of the forest. They were on the road listening to you!"

So that was why Kona had invited me to accompany him, I realized—he'd

wanted company on the dangerous, spirit-infested road to Ndogbé. Well, I'd certainly spoiled his plans.

Laughing, Yacouba told my story to the small crowd, and word quickly passed around: *"Bonzo Kouadio kuna"*—The hill spirits caught Kouadio. Kwamla Chakro arrived to examine my minor wounds and grinned—his medicine pot had obviously protected me from far greater harm.

As I limped about the village that day, I began to understand my accident's complex pedigree: I had flown from one world into another, from a world of rickety bicycles and unreliable brakes to a world of angry spirits who meted out swift punishment. Still, while I was unwilling to explain away spirits as mere abstract "beliefs," I was also unwilling to acknowledge that spirits actually existed.

The young men in the village had a different reaction to my accident. Impressed with my minor injuries after such a serious fall, they were once again certain that I knew karate.

"Kouadio," Yapi Yao said one morning, disappointment filling his face, "why won't you teach us?"

"I really don't know karate, I just had a lucky fall. *C'est vrai.* " Actually, what I did know was far simpler—after all those gymnastics classes in high school, I'd somehow learned how to tumble. But this explanation might only engender a different set of requests that I couldn't fulfill.

"C'est vrai," I repeated. But I could tell Yapi Yao wasn't convinced. He left for his compound, surely pondering the mystery of my inexplicable refusal.

9

METAMORPHOSES

❧ ❧ ❧

(OCTOBER 4, 1980–SPRING 1982)

Alma: "Everything Inside Was Crushed"

WE DROVE ALONG ON THE NEWLY PAVED ROAD TO BOUAKE, SQUINTING AGAINST THE WIND that now replaced our windshield: this was our last trip with the former Didadi, for our mechanic, Dramane, had agreed to sell it for a commission. Perhaps a taxi fleet owner would have better luck with our worn-out jalopy . . . surely it would be more content on the paved roads of a city.

I wished Philip could drive faster. We'd just met with the M'Bahiakro gendarmes to painstakingly examine our supposedly suspicious slides for any illegal example of police activity—now I wanted to put as many miles between us and that experience as possible. The officer in charge had been gracious enough—when no offending picture was found, he returned the slides—but throughout the meeting I kept thinking of poor Bani's battered face when he'd finally been released from custody.

Finally arrived in Bouaké, we stayed at a modest hotel, and to further economize we eschewed air-conditioning, opting for a room with an electric fan and a can of Raid. The manager was curious: Why would we deny ourselves the pleasures of air-conditioning? I explained that Philip and I weren't tourists—I was an anthropologist, and we were living *en brousse* in a tiny Beng village called Kosangbé.

"You live *where?*" He stared, perhaps groping for a new category in which to locate us. Again I explained to him our circumstances.

"*Mon vieux,*" he exclaimed, "those people are *forts!*"—strong.

"*Ah, bon?*"

"*Oui, oui*—they can overturn a car just by witchcraft. Once, a Jula man drove past a Beng village and didn't stop for someone who tried to wave him down. About two miles later, the car rolled over. That Beng man he'd passed by had bewitched it."

"Yes, they're *fort,*" I agreed, wondering if our Beng friends and neighbors saw our current Bouaké jaunt to unload our doomed car as a flight from witchcraft.

In the hotel room that night, Philip—eager for comments—read me his latest draft of "The Deserted House." I knew how much he missed the community of writers he'd left behind in America—though he did exchange work with friends through the international mails. But this year I'd been his primary audience. I always loved listening to the successive versions of his stories: watching the characters develop, I could imagine they were people I knew. Now Philip turned off the noisy fan, and in the hot room, with no whooping children to interrupt us, he settled down to read his story. Listening to that madcap family's increasingly desperate domestic adventures, I was reminded of the purposely silly ditty Philip sang whenever our lives in the village were particularly hectic: "There's never a dull moment in Kosangbé." As he continued to read aloud, I was struck by how much his fictional American family was an improbable mixture of my in-laws and our village neighbors. Philip had somehow transformed people I knew into characters who, however different, were still recognizable. I couldn't imagine how he was able to do this.

Yet were the differences between Philip's work and mine really so stark? For much as I tried to remain true to what I saw, I knew that it was *I* who decided what to take notes on and what to leave unsaid, I who sketched out my own analyses of all I heard and witnessed—like Philip's stories, the characters populating my notebooks were, at least to some extent, my inventions, too.

Back in the village, the long-awaited national elections were coming up: President Houphouët-Boigny was running unopposed for reelection. At first the event seemed an intrusion on village consciousness by a remote world— its main effect was to require villagers to spend money replacing lost ID cards, which they'd need in order to vote. But the Beng were able to claim the election as their own by casting the protagonist in a role they knew well: the president, some people confided to me, was a powerful witch.

By now I knew that Beng kings, queens, and village chiefs were all said to practice sorcery. Indeed, within a year of taking up the position, each new officeholder was obliged to bewitch three close relatives. In this way the new ruler warned the other sorcerers of the kingdom: Beware, don't threaten me or my subjects, for my own greater powers will defeat you—I will sacrifice even my family, those who are part of my very identity, for the sake of my office. Houphouët, people told me, must be the greatest witch of all, for unlike virtually every other head of state in Africa, he'd remained in office since the country had gained independence—in his case, for twenty years.

For the Beng region, the election was held in Sangbé, a village four miles down the road from us. All morning people traveled on bike or foot, and when they arrived they stood on a long line leading to a table—on the other side sat a few government functionaries from M'Bahiakro. Aware that few people on line knew how to read or write, I introduced myself to one of the officials and asked him how the villagers would be able to participate.

"We give each voter an envelope and a little card with an elephant and the president's name printed on it," he explained, holding out samples to show me. "When their turn comes, they just hand in the envelope."

"I see," I replied. "And what if they want to vote against Houphouët?"

"In that case, they just turn in an empty envelope to the man in the booth."

I thanked him and walked away from the table to embark on an informal survey of voter preference. The people I questioned stared at me blankly: *Could* they vote against Houphouët? Yes, I understood they could turn in an empty envelope. They stared again. Clearly they hadn't been told of this possibility. In any case, why would they want to? Their lives, while desperately poor, were better off materially than they had been in many years: the government paid the farmers relatively well for their cash crops, had built wells or water pumps for most villages, maintained upkeep of the dirt roads, and recently paved the road from Bouaké to M'Bahiakro; there was even talk about installing electricity in some villages. The present regime was doing its job decently enough. Besides, who would dare vote against someone so powerful?

The next day Amenan and I settled in our usual spot under the coffee trees. My friend's store of gossip was unusually scanty, so I questioned her on something I'd long been curious about: the classic Beng house style. Amenan explained that about fifteen years ago, the newly independent government had ordered the villagers to destroy their enormous round houses, because the thatch on the inverted crown-shaped roofs occasionally caught fire. They were instructed by government officials to replace the old-style houses with smaller square buildings sheltered by tin roofs. I tried to envision how dif-

ferent Asagbé must have looked to a teenage Amenan: a large village filled with enormous round structures, a maze of narrow dirt paths leading from circle to circle.

A pained look passed over Amenan's face. "Amwé, a lot of elders really suffered. When the bulldozers came, the elders refused to take their *fétiches* outside, and all their old power objects, their treasures—*everything* inside was crushed. It was too much. Some old people died just a few days after they saw their houses collapse. Less than a year after our family moved into the new house, my own aunt, Akissi Kala, was dead."

I knew that Beng religious icons were associated with an absolute taboo: they must not be exposed to any light, either sunlight or moonlight. If the object's owner violated the taboo, he or she would immediately go blind. Those old people must have been caught in a classic double bind: remove the icons and lose their sight, or keep them inside to meet the bulldozer's broad shovel. They obeyed the taboo but suffered a fate worse than blindness: their vision of their own future was denied them.

I gazed at the nearby courtyards, appalled at the destruction that was hidden behind these ordinary mud brick houses. And for what purpose had they been built—so that a newly emerging Third World nation could proclaim to the West that it was now civilized, because the square of the nuclear family had replaced the circle of the extended family? Here was another way that European colonialism had extracted precious resources from the Third World—not crops or minerals, but the aesthetic sense of a people that transformed an architectural space into a home.

I thought back to yesterday's elections. The children and grandchildren of those elders who'd died of sorrow had just voted for the same president whose officials had ordered the destruction of the round houses. I wondered if any felt secret resentment as they cast their ballots.

Philip: Metamorphosis

I walked along the forest path with Yacouba, Dongi, and Sramatan, the two wives carrying their daughters on their backs. Watching the toddlers' sleeping heads swaying slightly to the lulling pace, I hoped their mothers would be able to keep their rivalry in check today. Soon we arrived at their stand of coffee trees, where thick clusters of green, ripe beans hung from the branches, ready for harvest.

Under the shadow of a huge termite mound we set to work. I watched Yacouba grab a branch, one hand holding fast while his other hand stripped off the beans in a long, stretching motion—and with them fell great bunches of coffee leaves. I reached for a branch and gave a try. The nubby beans snapped off easily, the leaves protecting my hands from scratches, and everything tumbled down to the burlap sacks on the ground. Dongi bent over, her child balanced snugly on her back, and painstakingly gathered these unwanted leaves, tossing them away. Sramatan joined her, and to my surprise the two wives worked well side by side, joking a bit—they even laughed together at my flapping arms when I brushed against a nest of red ants. Had their troubles finally eased?

After a long stretch of work, Dongi and Sramatan set off in search of firewood while Yacouba and I staggered back to the village with huge sacks slung over our shoulders. I sang out "I've Been Working on the Railroad," and my friend made an attempt at the lyrics, gleefully tripping me up with his inventive pronunciation. Back in his compound, we emptied the beans onto a large patch of ground lined with logs to make a shallow bin. Over the next few weeks the beans would dry here in the sun.

I bade Yacouba good-bye and walked back home, already anticipating a warm pail bath. I passed Kouassikro, who thwacked the earth in his compound with a wooden mallet, trying to make the ground as hard as possible for his own coffee bin. He was late: most villagers had finished theirs—some held coffee beans that were already darkened by the sun. More than a few chickens poked about those curing beans, searching for any insects that might be lurking among them. Walking daintily among the piles, the chickens pecked and occasionally shat oozy trails on someone's future beverage. It was no coincidence that I had recently switched to tea for breakfast.

Nearby, Kossum and his family sat together in their compound, slamming thick bunches of rice stalks against burlap mats to dislodge the grains. Fine particles of white dust floated in the air, and the entire family coughed back and forth, a harsh antiphony from irritated throats. From other compounds came the sound of wooden mortars ringing against huge pestles: women preparing fresh new yams for the evening meal. Kosangbé was filled with the work and rewards of harvest, and I wondered what Alma and I had harvested in this past year; what had we gathered into us?

I already had more than an inkling, having recently read a prose translation of *Metamorphoses,* Ovid's epic compendium of mythological transformations that made an oddly comfortable fit with Beng daily life. When Arachne turned into a spider, her hair, nostrils, and ears fell off and new limbs multiplied out of her shrinking body; as Daphne ran from Apollo, her hair grew into leaves while her arms became branches, her legs slowed and settled into the earth as roots; and Cadmus's body stretched "into the long belly of a snake, his skin hardened and turned black in color, and he felt scales forming on it, while blue-green spots appeared, to brighten its somber hue. Then he fell forward on his chest, and his legs, united into one, were gradually thinned away into a smooth, pointed tail." These transformations from the ordinary to the fantastic echoed the interpenetrations of different realities that abounded here in every village, where some people were really snakes who could be turned back into their original, snakish form by a diviner; a woman's turban at a funeral dance could actually be a Gabon viper; forest spirits bewitched young brides into rejecting their grooms; and viewing a corpse could make a child grow ill.

I remembered Yacouba detailing for us the dangers of traveling while spirits roamed free. Nighttime was especially dangerous, he'd said, which was why no one ever left the village after sundown. Yet I knew that occasionally a car drove past Kosangbé at night, the clank of its engine announcing its unusual presence from afar, the headlights illuminating clusters of sheep sleeping by the side of the road.

"Then why do cars sometimes drive by the village after dark?" I'd asked Yacouba, thinking I could catch him in a contradiction.

My friend had remained unfazed. "Any person driving at night is a witch," he'd said casually, "and the car is the witch's victim."

"The witch's victim?"

"Yes, the witch turns his victim into a car and then drives him along the road." He'd thought a moment, then added, "An airplane flying at night is a witch's victim, too."

Touché, Ovid. Yet metamorphoses weren't restricted to Ovid's world or that of the Beng—would those stories be so powerful if they didn't also echo the secret knowledge of our own inner mutations? I had changed from my experiences here—though a detailed mapping of that change was still beyond me. For months I'd struggled to maintain a kind of amphibious consciousness, trying to fuse the insistent call of my stories with the call of the odd and exciting events around me. While attending with Alma a three-day funeral, I found myself perversely longing to return my attention to the fate of a character in a story. Yet when seated back at my desk, in the midst of the pleasures of uncurling a stubborn sentence, I felt the need to tour the village, to see if the unhappy snake child was up to some mischief, or to help a neighbor wash newly harvested kola nuts.

My recent bicycle accident was the most graphic example of this amphibious consciousness, for that small disaster held within it two mutually exclusive yet complementary explanations: while trying to coax Kona into speaking, I'd forgotten how fast I was speeding, and when I'd finally pulled on the uncertain brakes it was too late; yet I'd also insulted the hill spirits on their own territory, violating the most sacred day of the year. The two contrasting worldviews embraced by those explanations reminded me of the week when butterflies invaded Kosangbé: thick, fluttering curtains that parted, just out of reach, wherever I walked. Now my amphibious conscious-

ness had become my own elusive, transforming curtain, endlessly parting inside me.

The drenching Alma and I had received at the end of Karimu's wedding party was a revelation of how removed we'd been from the daily tribulations of our neighbors. No longer did we breeze from village to village in our car, and this change became a blessing. Now, when we wanted to visit Amenan's uncle, King Bondé Chomo, we walked there from Asagbé; during our leisurely five-mile hike, Amenan revealed her voluminous knowledge of the plants and flowers we passed along the road—which ones were herbal medicines and what they cured—an opportunity we would have missed had we simply zoomed by.

We also entered into local commuter culture: on our trips to the M'Bahi-akro *marché* we now took the *taxi-brousse,* a small bus with seats for twenty-two people and space for newborn babies in bassinets, huge sacks of rice or yams, squawking chickens bound by the feet, an occasional goat, and plastic cans filled with palm wine or kerosene for lanterns. The lot of our fellow passengers was The Long Wait, because a driver wouldn't leave until that final, twenty-second passenger appeared, which sometimes took a few hours. If the passengers didn't like the delay, they complained—in Jula, French, Baulé, Ando, and Beng—and this opened up a world of protest about the way the apprentice loaded the baggage, the bus driver's skills, the condition of the road, the dust seeping in through the windows. Now two new voices grumbled in English, but we did so with secret satisfaction at our newest immersion in the local frustrations.

At 2:30 A.M. our alarm clock beeped, and Alma and I crawled sleepily from under the mosquito netting. We settled at our table in the kitchen and turned on the short-wave radio to listen to the presidential debate on a live Voice of America broadcast. The spirits were still wandering about the village—would they invisibly join us by the radio, and if they did, what would they make of this American ritual?

In recent months I'd followed with dismay the broadcasts chronicling Reagan's peculiar rise to political power and Jimmy Carter's increasing ineffectuality. Now, by the dim glow of our oil lamp, we listened—with some trepidation—to the two sparring candidates. Suddenly the audience laughed as Carter, responding to a question about the dangers of nuclear war, cited his young daughter, Amy. Though this easy disrespect worried me, I still

thought Carter won the debate—his command of the facts clearly foiled Reagan's easy platitudes. So Alma and I listened, incredulous, as the postdebate pundits seemed to give the nod to Reagan.

"How can they *say* that?" I groused, and Alma and I repeated for each other choice moments in the debate, as if our impeccable logic could somehow affect those distant commentators.

"What did we miss?" Alma asked, hands up in exasperation. "Wait," she added, "it was a television debate, right? Reagan's an *actor.*"

"Maybe," I muttered, "but I have a different theory. The spirits are responsible."

"The spirits?"

"Yeah," I replied only half-jokingly. "Supposedly they were right here next to us, listening, too. If they can spoil the babies conceived from late night screwing, then why couldn't they ruin the outcome of a debate?"

"Ha. If I were you, I wouldn't plan an alternate career as a political commentator," Alma said with a yawn, already heading wearily back to bed.

Electioneering had arrived in Bengland as well—the first contested popular elections in this single-party government's history for the deputies in the National Assembly. Until now the deputies had been elected unopposed, just like President Houphouët-Boigny's cakewalks every five years. The incumbent in the Beng area, Loukou Yasso, was widely disliked, for during his years in the government he had done little to help develop the area he supposedly represented. His main presence was two horses he owned, which were allowed to roam freely down the streets of M'Bahiakro. Years ago one of them had trampled a child, and now everyone gave the dangerous creatures wide berth as they lazily clopped along.

The challenger was a young unknown trying his hand at politics for the first time and, like Loukou Yasso, a Baulé. The incumbent quickly devised his strategy: because the Baulé vote was likely split, the Beng—an ethnic minority he'd previously given no attention—might very well be the swing vote in the election. Loukou Yasso's supporters hustled off to all the Beng villages, offering cases of beer and wine or, in those villages with large Muslim populations, Tip Top soda. They also passed out facsimiles of U.S. dollar bills, printed in purple, with Loukou Yasso's portrait on the reverse side. Most of these worthless bills were quickly discarded by the unimpressed villagers or passed on to children.

When this largesse didn't quell his constituents' skepticism, Loukou Yasso's political operatives returned with real money—up to fifty thousand CFAs per village. Finally the Beng were receiving some of their deputy's plunder. Yet when some villages compared their differing takes and complained about how little they'd received, Loukou Yasso sent a stand-in, who offered formal apologies for his boss's past, neglectful behavior. This was another shrewd campaign tactic, for the Beng were great believers in the power of apology; our friends and neighbors were finally inclined to believe that Loukou Yasso should be returned to the National Assembly, if only for one more term.

Though the vote for the National Assembly was still a week away, the day of the presidential election in our own country had arrived. Once again Alma and I woke in the middle of the night—it was now nine P.M. in America—to listen to the election returns. The race had been reported as close, and I expected a long night of anxious listening, as with the squeaker of '76. But when I finally tuned in to the Voice of America, I was shocked to hear commentators already describing Carter's concession speech. *Reagan* had won? The actor? My clearest image of him was his weekly television hucksterism for soapsuds when I was a child: a tiny, twenty-mule-team Borax wagon raced before him as he smilingly plugged the detergent. Why not elect Ed McMahon?

"You won't believe this—it's over already!" I called out to Alma, who was still in bed, struggling to wake up.

"What? Who won?"

"Reagan," I barely managed.

"Oh god."

We sat together at the table and listened to the dismal election results—Reagan's landslide, the Republicans winning a Senate majority and making large gains in the House of Representatives. What had happened to cause such sweeping change? "Home," I realized, had no guarantee of permanence: our country had strangely transmuted during our absence.

Soon after, the deputy elections were held in the Côte d'Ivoire. The vote took place in the village of Sangbé, a festive occasion that everyone dressed for—the women displayed their best *pagnes* and the young girls their most inventive hairstyles; the men wore formal dress suits usually reserved for funerals or important trials. Many of our friends still couldn't believe the power that had been placed in their hands—their vote could actually decide the fate of powerful men, one of whom had courted them with gifts and apologies, and this new power was just the beginning. A wobbling Kwamla Chakro, already drunk by late morning, shouted too loudly as he stood on line to vote, "If Loukou Yasso doesn't do a proper job this time, we'll chase him out in the next election!"

With a long sigh, a sad-faced Honoré settled his large bulk on one of our chairs. Earlier, I'd seen him walk toward Gba Apo's compound, so I thought I knew the source of his unhappiness.

"How goes the dispute between your mother and your older brother?" I asked.

"The situation is hard, very hard," he replied, and then he enumerated his recent attempts to end the stalemate between them. Honoré had consulted a diviner in Sangbé, determined to do anything to restore peace so his beautiful house could once again be occupied. "The diviner recommended a sheep sacrifice. Even though I'm a Muslim, I've agreed to this."

Then he traveled to Manigbé and asked his aunt if *she* would apologize for Ché Kofi. His aunt agreed, and the following day she visited Gba Apo in Kosangbé and begged her sister to move back into the house. But Apo refused. "The house is no longer mine," she declared. "I don't want it anymore."

A few days later Honoré traveled to Manigbé to thank his aunt for her failed attempt at mediation. "I am a *Muslim,* but I gave her a gift of red wine and offered to sacrifice to the souls of their ancestors! Then I came here and gave *more* red wine to my mother!"

"Did this help?" I asked, already suspecting the answer.

"No," he replied, his lips twitching slightly, "she said, 'I don't care one way or another about your sacrifice. There's nothing more to be done.' "

Honoré sighed again, clearly miserable. I split a kola nut and offered him half. We sat and chewed for a while, spitting out the bitter juice, and I pondered the contrast between the two brothers. Ché Kofi was his usual cheerful and sharp-tongued self, seemingly undisturbed by the continuing estrangement from his mother. Yet stubborn as he was, he'd eventually have to ask her forgiveness—his culture would demand it. Perhaps, by delaying this apology, Ché Kofi was purposely making his brother suffer—this younger brother who had built a monument to his success right beside Kofi's compound.

Like Honoré's trials, my new story, "The Deserted House," also lacked resolution, even though it was now completed. My characters had circled each other warily for a long time—the two young brothers' midnight games of hide-and-seek in the dark, the parents idly clutching each other's hands yet finding no firm grip as they sat together, the father's incessant rearranging of the furniture, were their own form of procrastination. Finally their odd patterns tumbled into complicated, forward motion, and they took the final steps toward that paragraph I'd first written of a furious family chasing itself out of a house. Yet their angry, ragged line was the ending's still life, for they hadn't caught each other. Now they could do so only in a reader's imagination; I'd decided to grant them all the unwritten possibilities that their troubles might bring them, remembering the words of the short-story writer Grace Paley: "Everyone, real or imagined, deserves the open destiny of life."

Dust particles settled everywhere in the oppressively hot, still air of the dry season, particularly on many of our neighbors, who sat in their doorways, their legs alarmingly bloated, gazing at the compounds they were too weak to cross. An epidemic of Guinea worm had struck Kosangbé, caused by drinking water that was infested with worm eggs. The larvae, Alma and I read with horror in one of our medical texts, could penetrate the stomach and intestinal walls and eventually lodge in the legs of the victim, where the mature worms could grow to lengths of three feet or more. Then a blister formed, finally breaking when the parasite exited painfully.

"I've had Guinea worm many times," Yacouba told us, rolling up his pants leg. "You see?" He pointed to dark circles that speckled his leg; radiating from each round scar were shiny stretch lines resembling photos of the impact craters on the moon. All year I'd seen these scars on so many of the legs of our neighbors—only now did I understand their origin.

"This one is from two years ago," Yacouba said, his finger following the irregular pattern of scars, "and these two are from the year before that." He clicked his tongue. "A terrible time."

Alma and I told Yacouba, and anyone else who would listen, that boiling their water would protect them from this disease. Whether or not they followed our advice, the epidemic continued. One afternoon I came upon a crowd of children surrounding Kwana, Yacouba's younger brother. As I drew closer I saw that the thin white head of a worm poked out of a raw, round scar on his leg and the taut, surrounding skin resembled a glazed, ceramic surface. Kwana's silent face was a terrible, shifting mask of pain: beside him, one of Ché Kofi's sons dipped a cloth into a pail of hot water and pressed the steaming cloth near the scar, trying to draw out the worm.

It urged up into the air a few more centimeters, then a few more, until a finger's length of worm writhed above the wound; then Kwana's younger sister deftly twisted it around a small twig. Kwana sucked in frantic sips of air as his sister gently pulled and eased the worm out farther. She paused, careful not to tug too quickly, for otherwise the worm would split and the rest of its long, thin body would remain in Kwana's leg to spread further infection.

I couldn't watch any longer. Without a word I eased away from the small gathering. That night, as I lay in bed with Alma, I said, "There must be some medicine for this disease." We made a special trip to Bouaké, but the only medicine we could find was primarily preventive, so it wouldn't help any villagers already afflicted, and it was so prohibitively expensive that we couldn't afford more than a few doses—Dramane hadn't sold our car yet, which was beginning to worry us.

Back in Kosangbé, queasy with the feeling that we were playing God, we gave out the boxes of pills with clandestine caution to Yacouba and a few other selected friends. But of course no secret was safe in such a small village—soon more of our neighbors arrived in our compound, requesting this medicine they'd heard would cure their ravaged limbs.

"It doesn't work unless you don't have the disease yet," I said, wincing that this unconvincing conundrum was all I could offer. "And besides," I added sadly to their disappointed faces, "we have no more, the medicine is too expensive."

But the people of Kosangbé weren't relying on us to combat the Guinea worm plague—they consulted a Jimini diviner from the north. They wanted to know the underlying cause of the outbreak, and for them that meant the spiritual world. One evening, as the full moon cast its glow over the village, some neighbors told us, "The spirits are coming tonight."

Alma and I hurried over to the Jula quarter. On our way we were stopped by several concerned neighbors. "Amwé, Kouadio, this diviner is powerful—you mustn't take photos or tape-record him. If you do, you'll die."

We glanced briefly at each other in disappointment, but we'd learned our lesson about secret taping. "Oh, well," Alma said, "we'll just have to watch especially carefully." We thanked our friends for their warning and returned the equipment to our house.

By the time we arrived at the gathering, the entire village had formed a circle around the towering figure of the Jimini diviner. Over six feet tall, he wore a pointed raffia hat that made him seem even taller. His face painted white, he sported a raffia shirt and skirt, and bells jangled at his knees and ankles. More bells were woven into his shirt, while thick strands of sheep hair dangled lazily from his wrists.

Slowly he moved an arm, a leg, and announced that he was ready to dance "sweetly," to attract the forest spirits. The diviner seemed to have independence of movement for all parts of his body—he twisted and shook so that only his knee bells jangled, then only the ankle bells, then the ankle bells rang together with those attached to his shirt. Finally he stood quite still: the invisible presences had arrived in the village. He asked permission to utter a divination, which the elders granted, and in a dramatic voice he intoned the revelation he was receiving.

"What's he saying?" Alma whispered to Asaw.

"All the Guinea worm in the village was caused by a bad fetish planted in the ground." She smiled ruefully, understanding that she had just become Alma's informant of the evening.

The diviner's body shook once again in shimmering motion, alternating with strange, mechanical movements that were almost robotlike or astonishingly high leaps into the air. Then, unexpectedly, he blew on a small antelope

horn in front of the battery of drummers—a beautiful yet eerie sound, its swift trill inspiring the drummers, who pounded out rhythms more fluid than any I'd heard before. Women in the crowd now sang, and their keening voices, along with the seething drums, became another circle for the diviner to dance within.

Suddenly he stopped. The singing and drumming immediately ceased as well, and in the stunning silence the diviner listened to the night air, his body absolutely still. Then he spoke, and Asaw translated for us: "The spirits recommend many remedies for this terrible fetish. First, one ram must be sacrificed to the Earth. . . ."

The diviner danced again in furious abandon, the drums and singing accompanying him for long, entrancing minutes. Then he stopped, listened, and announced that a chicken had to be sacrificed to the soul of whoever had planted the fetish. Once more he danced, making several writhing circuits; when he stopped he said that two red kola nuts and one frog must also be offered in order to catch either the planter of the fetish or one of the culprit's children.

The diviner leapt in the air, shaking all his bells. Suddenly Kouassikro—who so much wanted to be a diviner—broke through the crowd, so drunk he wobbled, and stood inside the circle. "He doesn't know anything, he's no good," Kouassikro groused. A few people tried to pull him back, but he evaded their hands with an awkward shrug and moved farther into the open space. He continued complaining, but the rhythms of the drums and bells couldn't be ignored—Kouassikro began to dance, too, shuffling toward the diviner, who still hadn't noticed the disturbance. We all stared, silently stricken by Kouassikro's intrusion. He drew closer, then slipped in front of the diviner and resumed his complaints.

Without showing surprise, the diviner reached out for Kouassikro's hand and continued dancing. Kouassikro beamed a grin of vindication—here, before the entire village, his own spiritual power was being acknowledged! But the diviner was merely leading his drunken partner back to the edge of the crowd, where he released him and then returned to the center of our large circle, shivering even more ecstatically.

The diviner stopped before the elders and spoke, "The spirits tell me there have been many difficult childbirths in this village." Soon they would suggest remedies, for he turned and swooped and shivered, playing the haunting scales of his antelope horn, summoning further revelations from the spirits. Meanwhile Kouassikro danced alone in a corner, his own small side show ignored except for the occasional insult thrown his way. Finally he skulked off in the direction of his compound—once again he'd failed in his quest to become a diviner.

After another extended, whirling display—silence again. The drummers' eyes were fixed on the motionless figure of the diviner while he pronounced the remedies: whenever possible, all women should be taken down to M'Bahiakro to deliver their children there. Also, a villagewide sacrifice should be held for the spirits, with every woman offering a meal of rice and peanut sauce. Then, without warning, the diviner slipped past the drummers into the shadows—the divination was over, and we all stood, exhausted, as if his extraordinary energy had sapped *us*. Slowly the villagers dispersed, our magic circle now unraveling into individual families returning to their compounds.

"Hurry," Alma said, pulling me along, "I want to write this all down right away."

"You bet," I agreed, unwilling to forget a moment of that performance. We made our way through the crowd, the gleaming moon illuminating all our spent faces in a strangely calming light.

I found it hard to believe that Alma and I would have to leave in a little more than a month. We were growing increasingly adept in the language, the villagers felt more at ease with Alma's nosy presence, and even San Yao and Kona's rivalry had abated. The past two months had moved swiftly, and as I sat in my compound, book forgotten on my lap, watching a troop of children build their own miniature mud house, I truly felt settled in the life of the village.

Yacouba also seemed content—though Dongi still had her sharp moments, she had finally made peace with Sramatan. For weeks after Dongi's *Po fen* provocations, Yacouba had refused even to speak to her, and I suspected that she'd been thoroughly alarmed by the threat of his deepening coldness.

Now, whenever Yacouba and I spent time together he taught me new phrases that he thought might make me laugh. "You're as stupid as a bat," was one choice insult he offered—the Beng caution against hubris. "Bats sleep upside down with their asses in the air," he explained, "because they're trying to shit on God. But all they can do is shit on themselves."

Yacouba paused. "They're stupid, but delicious." The look of disgust on my face surprised him, and he couldn't help adding, "I'll have one of my wives roast you a few sometime—four or five make a nice meal."

A week later he dropped by just before dinnertime and announced that a plate of roasted bats was on its way from his compound. Alma and I were revolted by the prospect—though we knew it was extremely impolite to refuse an offering of food, how would we manage even to look at the things?

"You think you won't like them, but wait, you'll see," Yacouba said, rubbing his belly. But the misery on our faces as we barely forced out thanks for this upcoming gift undid our friend, and he giggled wildly with the pleasure of having fooled us.

Once, when Yacouba and I bicycled together to the Bongalo *marché,* he went too far. As we walked our bikes up the spirits' hill outside Kosangbé, Yacouba suddenly chanted in a singsong voice, "He's here, he's here, he's come back to visit you." I waved to him, silently urging caution.

Yacouba only laughed. "What's your name?" he asked me.

I said nothing. Whether spirits existed or not, I was in no mood to test their hypothetical patience.

"I've forgotten your name," he insisted. "Please tell me, and anyone else who might be listening!"

"My name is Yacouba," I finally replied, pushing my bike ahead of him, and this stopped his teasing. We remained silent until reaching level ground, when we could no longer contain our laughter.

Soon after, I took further revenge. Often Yacouba visited with us until late at night, chatting and joking, as did many of our other friends. Once Au Ba and Dawni dropped by—young women who often traipsed about together through the village in the evening with their sleeping babies on their backs. It had rained that evening—a rare, dry-season downpour—and Yacouba, Alma, and I were seated around the table in our kitchen.

"You'd better tighten your *pagne,* or your baby will fall to the ground. Don't you know how to be a proper mother?" Yacouba teased Dawni.

"You're always insulting me," she complained, pouting in mock anger.

"He always insults *everyone,*" I joined in with pretended exasperation. "He doesn't speak words, he speaks farts."

Yacouba began to protest, but I held my nose. "See? He's doing it again!"

He chuckled, and Au Ba waved her hand in the air at these new gusts. Yacouba laughed harder, and we all mock choked from the imagined fumes, our faces scrunched up every time Yacouba, his eyes now teary, tried to speak.

Yet my laughter was fueled by suppressed regret. Already I missed my friend, for soon we would be leaving Bengland for a world he couldn't imagine. I remembered when Alma had spent an afternoon collecting women's favorite recipes, all the while carefully uncovering, through offhand questions, the patterns of food exchanges between compounds. Yacouba sat beside us, commenting on the various delicacies the women offered; one dish in particular met his approval. "Make sure you write it all down carefully," he'd insisted. "Once you're back in your village, all the women will hurry to your compound to see what you're cooking!" Alma and I had smiled ruefully at each other—our friend imagined that our home was much like his own.

But how far off was he? Though in many ways I was anxious to return to America and resume my life, my life now included the Beng. Perhaps I'd

carry an African village within me, the people in its various compounds continuing their lives through my nostalgic imaginings.

Alma: Feeding the Spirits

Today, the women of Kosangbé, following the Jimini diviner's instructions, were preparing the special meals of rice and peanut sauce for the forest spirits; if they were pleased by the offerings, the spirits would ensure easy future childbirths of the village's women. As Moya was stirring the thickening sauce, my neighbor Afwé Ba came over to our kitchen. "Is it done?" she asked.

"Just finished," Moya said.

"I think we're supposed to put all the sauce in one dish and all the rice in another," Afwé Ba commented.

"Ah, thank you, big sister," I said, touched that my friend had come to share these instructions with me—she must have thought that my own contribution to this ritual somehow counted, too. Afwé Ba left, and Moya and I began ladling out the sauce.

But in a few minutes Afwé Ba returned. "I just heard we're supposed to split each of the dishes into two meals, so there will be four bowls altogether," she said, and left in a hurry. I was surprised by Afwé Ba's nervousness—she was usually so calm. Moya and I began reapportioning the rice and sauce.

In a few minutes my neighbor was back again—she wanted this offering to be just right. "Four plates are too many," she said, a bit shamefaced, "let's stick to the two dishes after all." Now *I* was nervous, and Moya and I followed Afwé Ba's instructions carefully.

When Afwé Ba returned yet again, she announced, "It's time to go," and we joined all the *quartier*'s women in procession to the chief's courtyard. There, we deposited our dishes under the huge kapok tree, adding to a growing collection of steaming bowls, all filled with rice and peanut sauce. Soon the entire village was gathered around the tree.

Imperious in his finest outfit, a bright red-and-green print, San Yao sat on an intricately carved chair set under the tree. He waved a hand, and instantly all the women and children rushed toward the dozens of brightly colored dishes and grabbed any food they could, gobbling down mouthfuls. Undoubtedly the children snatched for the sheer pleasure of it, but why were the women so voracious? I wondered if they competed for the forest spirits' favor: did they reason that the more food they ate, the more the spirits would protect *them?* And perhaps the spirits were eating, too, invisibly and quickly, and the women rushed to share in those spirits' unseen meals. Meanwhile the men hung back, eating more slowly with spoons they'd brought along. As for me, by the time I finished scribbling notes, the bowls were completely empty.

All the bowls, that is, but two—my friend Busu Amla frowned as she collected her two plates, the only ones still full. "People wouldn't eat my sauce because I put chili peppers in it," she lamented. "No one told me that these spirits don't like spicy food."

I commiserated with my friend. She'd already lost several children, and her one young daughter was frequently sick. If the spirits hadn't accepted her food, Busu Amla must be worried that the spirits might not protect her during her next childbirth.

Later I typed up my notes on the day's events, and when I reached the bottom of the page, I pushed a switch on the typewriter to change the ribbon to red and typed *QUESTIONS/IDEAS*. Then I tried out a thought: In involving everyone in the village, this ritual transformed childbirth into a collective event—its risks were now shared, to be combated by the village. Through the sacrifice, the body of almost every Beng woman was socially claimed, communally protected.

Did this sharing of experience extend to other aspects of Beng culture? My intuition was supported one evening when Yacouba came by to chat later than usual. Philip sat outside on a palm-rib chair, finishing up a chapter of *Lord Jim;* I stood nearby, brushing my teeth. Yacouba stared. "Amwé, you mustn't do that," he chided.

"Why not?" I asked.

Yacouba explained, "It's very dangerous to your first spouse if you brush your teeth after the late morning. Kouadio *is* your first husband, isn't he?"

"Oui, oui."

"Well, it could kill him."

"Yih!" Immediately I rinsed, then called over to Philip, repeating what Yacouba had just told me.

"Put that thing away!" he called back teasingly in English.

Yacouba didn't need to understand Philip's words to grasp their meaning. *"You* mustn't brush your teeth late at night, either," he rebuked Philip. "You don't want to kill Amwé, do you?"

"Of course not!" Philip said.

Another evening soon after, our neighbor Ajua walked past us on her way to the bush, muttering to no one in particular, "There's nowhere to pee."

Sitting in our courtyard, Yacouba shook his head. "She'll go mad someday if she keeps doing that."

"Keeps doing what?" I asked.

"Talking to herself," Yacouba answered.

"But why?"

"Talking is for people," Yacouba explained, then glanced at Philip. "That's why I always tell you not to talk to the chickens when you chase them. What would you do if a hen answered you one day?"

"Cluck back?" Philip suggested.

"Eh, Kouadio," Yacouba answered, "this is serious! If the hen talked to you, you'd go mad, just like Ajua might. Speech isn't for animals, and it isn't for yourself—it's for other people."

It was a good lesson, a lesson that summed up much of what I'd learned that year: to be Beng was to be part of a society that claimed each member as a participant with a continuing commitment to the whole. Now, in my last months of fieldwork, I was finally beginning to achieve a sense of what it must be like to inhabit a body made Beng every day, all day, in the momentous and trivial acts alike that we all, as embodied people, performed. I was even beginning to dream in Beng.

And I'd come to know far more of Beng religion than my Kosangbé hosts realized—more than I would ever allow myself to write about, considering the secrecy surrounding that knowledge. Those who had shared their knowledge with me made it clear exactly what I might and might not publish; it was unthinkable to betray their trust. Still, I worried that I hadn't amassed enough information for a dissertation. For several nights I paged through my copy of *Notes and Queries on Anthropology,* an old guide detailing every possible topic that should be investigated. I was alarmed to realize major gaps: I hadn't measured fields, hadn't charted friendship networks, hadn't asked enough about precolonial trade patterns. And undoubtedly these forays into Beng society would lead to more questions. How would I know when I had enough information to understand Beng culture? Indeed, would I ever have enough?

And if I did, would I piece together everything into a dissertation? Constantly interviewing people, or taking notes on what I observed others doing and saying, I rarely had the time to sit down and think about the underlying, grander themes. I couldn't even imagine a table of contents for my dissertation, let alone a general argument that might illuminate or refute current theoretical models. Worse, once I did start writing, I knew I'd think of questions I couldn't answer—but the Beng would be thousands of unbridgeable miles away.

I resolved to patch the obvious gaps in the time remaining. I read and reread my field notes, alert to whatever didn't make sense. I came across some pages I'd written on a funeral we'd attended soon after arriving in Bengland—the funeral of Wamya Kona's brother, who'd lived in a neighboring village. One evening I walked over to Kona's compound.

"You know, Father," I began after settling down on a wooden stool, "I've been looking over my notes on your brother's funeral—"

"You're lying," Kona interrupted.

"Excuse me?"

"You're lying," he repeated. "Why would you look over those pages now? That funeral was months ago."

"I know," I explained, "but I've been reading my notes from other funerals, too, and there's something different that happened at this one that I don't quite understand—"

"You've been here a long time," Kona interrupted again. "I *know* you understand everything that happens at funerals. Come, have some *si blé.*" And so we spent the rest of the evening in a daze of palm wine, my question about that long-ago funeral quickly forgotten. But I did learn that Kona had come to see me as part of his community—no longer would he permit me the luxury of displaying my ignorance.

Although I was touched by Kona's confidence, I couldn't possibly believe I merited it, and I continued to collect data madly—as if "information" came packaged only in bundles of four-hour interviews, as if simply living in a small village, watching women serve food to invisible spirits to reduce their risks in childbirth, learning when to brush my teeth and when to talk, weren't "information," too.

I now biked to Asagbé as often as possible. Aside from all the serious matters I wanted to discuss, I also wanted finally to hear a joke that Amenan had once promised me. But at the time she couldn't tell it because her mother was nearby, polishing the floor of her kitchen with a fresh batch of shiny mud, and, as Amenan explained, giggling, "It's not the kind of joke a mother should hear!" It seemed that whenever I visited Amenan, her mother was around—shucking dried corn, pounding dried okra slices into a powder, chopping wood. Finally, one day, Amenan said that her mother had just left to gather some crops in the fields and should be gone for a while—it was a good time for that story.

I glanced at Amenan's younger brother, who was patching a hole on his bicycle tire nearby. "What about Boka?" I whispered.

"*Ça va,* he can listen," Amenan answered.

"But won't you be embarrassed?"

"Oh, no, not with him," Amenan answered, laughing. "It's only your mother you'd be embarrassed with."

"*Ah, bon,*" I said.

"So, Amwé," Amenan began, "they say that in the old days, Penis, Testicles, and Vagina were friends; they spoke with one mouth."

Sure enough, Boka immediately dropped his knife and rubber patch and came over to join us on the bark-cloth mat.

"One day," Amenan continued, "they were going to the village, and they carried on their heads some banana-corn pudding that they'd cooked. They took to the road and started going rather far."

Amenan started giggling. "Now, Vagina had a big mouth. She said, 'Hunger is killing me.' So she divided up her pudding and ate some. They went a little farther on ahead, and she said, 'Hunger is killing me.' She cut off another chunk of the pudding and ate it. Soon, she ate the rest. They kept going, kept going, and again she said hunger was killing her. She begged Testicles to give her some of his pudding, but he refused. Then she begged Penis, 'I'm sorry, please give me a little bit of your pudding to eat.' Penis divided up the pudding and gave her some.

"They kept going, and in a little while the sky started getting dark, it started getting windy. Penis and Testicles said, 'Oh, we're afraid of the wind.' Vagina said, 'Penis, don't worry about it, I'll hide you.' It started raining, and she caught hold of Penis and hid him in her big hole. Then Testicles said he wanted to enter, too, but Vagina said, 'No, you're selfish, you're not coming in.' And even now, when a man sleeps with a woman, Testicles stays hanging outside.'" Already grinning, Amenan joined our laughter, and the three of us hooted until tears streamed from our eyes.

Finally, still chuckling, Boka said, "Well, I'd better get back to that tire." Wiping his wet cheeks, he walked across the courtyard, and I whispered to Amenan, "You know, if I had a brother, I think I'd be too embarrassed to tell a story like that around him."

"*Ihh?*" Amenan said, wondering at my culture's oddities. A sense of shame might be universal, I reflected, but who caused it certainly was variable.

Soon, Amenan's mother came walking slowly along the path from the forest, a heavy basin of yams atop her head. Amenan rose quickly to help her mother down with her load. When she returned to our bark-cloth mat, Amenan said, "You know, even though I wouldn't tell that story around my mother, *she* says I'm not her *leng ling ti paw*"—her real daughter.

"*Ihh,* why is that?" I asked.

"It started with the day I was born," Amenan said cryptically.

"Go on," I urged.

"You know that I'm the oldest child," Amenan began.

"*Oui?*"

"Well, my mother had a very difficult labor with me. I wasn't coming out and I wasn't coming out, so my grandfather went to consult a diviner. The diviner said that someone was bewitching my mother. He didn't say who, but my grandfather knew: it was my mother's aunt. The aunt had a boyfriend she wanted to marry, but she couldn't because of my mother."

"How's that?"

"The boyfriend was related to my father, so he was an in-law of my mother's aunt, and we're not allowed to marry that kind of in-law—it would be incest. Well, my aunt blamed my mother for her unhappiness. So that's why she decided to bewitch my mother.

"*En tout cas,* once my grandfather heard the diviner's news, he offered an egg to the Earth right there and then, and he prayed that whoever was bewitching my mother should die that very day. Soon, my mother's aunt went into the forest with a friend for firewood. But as she was chopping a tree, it fell on her head and she bit her tongue hard—right away, Amwé, her tongue fell out of her mouth!

"Her friend ran to the village for help. But when they got back to the forest, they found my mother's aunt lying on the ground, dead. A few minutes later, back in the village, I was born."

"*Mon dieu!*"

Amenan paused to let me take in this news, then she continued, "When I wasn't quite two years old, my mother gave me to her sister, who didn't have any children of her own. I stayed with my aunt through my childhood, and then I married. I only started living with my mother a few years ago, after I divorced my first husband. But my two married sisters aren't living with her—Mo'kwe and Aya are both in the city, with their husbands. I'm the one who takes care of my mother—when she's sick, I find her medicines, I help her in the fields, I cook. But still, she says I'm not really her daughter."

Amenan stopped, a pained look on her face. Here was an Amenan I'd never seen before—usually so cool, she was nevertheless still hurt by her mother's continuing rejection. I thought of my own mother, who'd always been *too* involved in my life. Now I was in Africa, thousands of miles from my mother, while Amenan was back home, trying to make up for years of distance from hers. But only later, back in Kosangbé, did I realize sadly that I'd been so busy writing down Amenan's story, I hadn't confided my own.

I soon had another opportunity. Caught up in his own work, Philip lagged behind me in Beng. I could imagine how frustrating it must be for a writer not to be able to speak for himself, but sometimes as I interpreted for Philip, I resented his insistence that I translate every word or phrase. One day our frustrations burst out while biking to Asagbé to see Amenan, our mutual accusations flying in the space between us as we pedaled.

"When you censor me, I feel like I've been rendered mute!" Philip began.

"I'm an anthropologist, not a translator!" I countered.

Our bitter words continued until we reached Asagbé. Arrived at the village, Philip rode off to the boutique for a Coke, and I continued on to Amenan's courtyard. I must have offered my greetings indifferently, for Amenan asked me, *"Paw mi maé?"*—What's on you? This time, I confided in her.

"Don't worry, Kouadio won't be mad long," she said confidently. "I can tell he loves you, he'll be back soon to *gbeka*"—ask forgiveness. Then Amenan proceeded to recount how her current husband, Kofi, disappeared periodically without explanation, though he always returned. For a few moments I forgot I was in a foreign land, speaking a foreign tongue: Amenan and I were just two women sharing an intimate moment.

The officially deferred celebration of Côte d'Ivoire's Independence Day had finally arrived. Women in all the villages had saved up money for matching *pagne* outfits so they could dance together, and I loved watching them move in slowly shimmering lines, then bright, rotating circles. But the dancers celebrated their citizenship in a country whose constitution they could never read; whose official language, French, they didn't speak; whose laws many of them broke daily, simply by being a co-wife; and whose official court system they avoided at all costs.

Still, the Beng legal system could be just as forbidding. Two months earlier Mo'kissi had fled from her husband—and Bengland. Aiming to show her determination to divorce Domolo, she had traveled hundreds of miles to San Pedro, a coastal city near Liberia. There, she'd picked up some French and had found a job as nanny for a wealthy Ivoirian family. Still, her heart was in her homeland—soon after the Independence Day dances, a troubled Mo'kissi returned to Kosangbé to try the village elders' court one last time.

But, to her dismay, the verdict of this trial was final, and drastic: if she was to live in Bengland, it must be as Domolo's wife. Without any evident hesitation, Mo'kissi quietly made a bitter choice for exile, announcing: "I'll just remain on my own, I won't have any family."

The evening before she planned to leave, Mo'kissi came to my compound, and we exchanged the usual greetings as if her life weren't in upheaval—whatever her anguish, her serene face betrayed nothing. "What are you going to do?" I asked.

"There's a rich woman I know who's offered me a job as a cook," Mo'kissi replied diffidently. "Maybe I'll take it."

"Ah." Realizing I might never see Mo'kissi again, I went into the house to fetch a small parting present. I came out with a chopping knife I'd bought recently and said, "Please take this small gift."

Mo'kissi fingered the sharp blade carefully. "Ah, it's a good one," she said quietly, "it should cut well. Thank you."

I said, *"Eki mi gba yong pu"*—May god give you luck. We hugged awkwardly, and Mo'kissi walked off into the night, perhaps her last in Bengland.

The next morning, when I reached her courtyard, Mo'kissi was already gone. I walked back to cook breakfast. Stirring the bubbling oatmeal, I hoped Mo'kissi wouldn't have to stay away for fifteen years, as Kobla had done.

If the village system of justice had failed Mo'kissi, I doubted if it would fail San Au, for not only was she a *kala leng*—an older woman—she was also the sister of our village chief. When someone stole a large bundle of palm nuts that she'd set down on a forest path, hotheaded San Au first accused a young woman, then cursed her with the vengeance of Kosangbé's Earth. Though the terrified thief immediately confessed, a trial was still held in the village.

Under the kapok tree, the thief's mother insulted San Au's barren womb, and the older woman sputtered in disbelief at this public disrespect. Wamya Kona announced that because the thief's relatives were now hurling *sisen voni*—rotten insults—at the victim of the crime, they must offer a chicken and a goat to the Earth, plus a whole case of wine as an apology to the village. Thus Beng justice was served—the thief punished, the curse lifted.

This trial reminded Philip of his own obligation to that exacting Earth. Back in February, the diviner Akissi had instructed Philip to offer the Earth a goat as thanks once his writer's block was cured. But these past months had been so packed with emergencies, illnesses, and just the dailiness of life that we'd forgotten this obligation; now, time was running short.

Within days we bought a small goat from a neighbor and led it, bleating unhappily, to the kapok tree, where old Wuru San sat waiting. Watching the dying animal's blood drain out over the large stone under the tree, I thought with gratitude how, despite the initial resistance of the villagers, despite our illnesses, our linguistic frustrations, even the trial with our own chief, Philip and I had both become bound to these people, this Earth we'd come to know over the past year. As San Kofi carved up the goat's carcass, I thought with regret how inopportune a time it was to plan our departure. Philip had found a way to balance his immersion in the Beng world with his own work, and I'd amassed a few thousand pages of field notes. My two thousand vocabulary cards had finally sunk in—I could say almost anything I needed to say in Beng, and I usually understood all that people said to me. I was even starting to include some proverbs in my own speech; when I did, inevitably my partners in conversation would exclaim *"Yih!* You sure can speak Beng— you've become one of us!" In my weaker moments I enjoyed pretending that this was true. But the options for staying any longer had run out, I reflected sadly as we took our share of the goat meat. My grant money was all but used up, and the money from Dramane's recent sale of our car had gone immediately to pay for our return plane tickets.

On our final trip to Bouaké, we bought as many parting presents as we

could afford—in particular, I wanted to find something especially nice for King Bondé Chomo. On my next visit to the king, I presented him with a string hammock.

"Father, I'll soon be leaving," I said, "and I want to give you this."

The king fingered the rope, then stretched out a section of the hammock between his arms. "Eh, Amwé," he said, *"e geng"*—it's good. Though his appreciation pleased me, I knew how uneven our exchange was: how could any commodity possibly be the equal of even a tiny portion of a person's lifetime store of knowledge?

One late afternoon Kossum brought his drum into our courtyard, tying it to a post of our thatched overhang. Immediately he began tapping with his notched drumstick, and within minutes our neighbors, dressed in their finest outfits, filled the courtyard: they'd come to dance us good-bye. The women clapped hands in counterrhythm to the drums while Yacouba expertly twirled around the courtyard, his raffia skirt splayed out, the bells at his knees jangling as he danced. San Kofi joined Yacouba, and the two men crouched and leaped in the center of the encircling chorus; even San Yao looked on approvingly. My notebook untouched on the desk, I sniffled to hold back my tears, while Philip swayed to the drumming, wishing that he could dance, too. That night, long after the last of the dancers had gone home, it was with waves of regret—though mixed with some longing as well—that I turned my eyes to a wintry world across a wide ocean.

The next day Philip and I dusted off our suitcases. I'd never been a very efficient packer, always agonizing: Should I take this shirt or that one, maybe pack for hot *and* cold days? This time the necessary choices were momentous, since we had decided to give away virtually all our possessions—a house's worth of parting gifts to our neighbors.

We began to sort everything into piles on the floor and table: Philip's clothes, my clothes, kitchen items, stationery supplies ... I didn't know where to begin. Slowly we earmarked items: a pot for Nguessan, wooden spoons for Asaw, water bottles for Aya, a calculator for François to keep the government's coffee buyers honest.

A few curious children came to watch, and I addressed one of the girls, *"Mo,* go take this dish to Little Aunt—you know, Jata's mother—and tell her it's from me." The girl nodded and skipped off, obviously pleased to have been picked as an errand runner.

Philip nodded to one of the older boys. *"Maa,* go take this machete to Little Uncle, Kofi's father."

"Yo," the boy said, and hurried away. Meanwhile the first courier returned,

reporting, "Little Aunt says *'Ka nuwaliaa'* "—Thank you. Then she stood close to the doorway, hoping for another errand.

I looked at my pile of clothes—on top was my best outfit, whose indigo-and-white floral print Busu Amla had often admired. "Go bring this over to Father Kona's compound," I said. "It's for his second wife." My young helper bundled the outfit into her arms and bounded off.

As our gifts circulated around the village, more and more children crowded into the courtyard to play this exotic game of Empty the House. Soon adults began lingering in our compound, and we handed out some of our presents directly. As they inspected and compared what they'd received, more villagers arrived. We were diverting drastically from what we'd intended—a simple way to thank our hosts and hostesses for their year of hospitality. Desperate to quickly end what was now an embarrassing public handout, we made decisions hastily. Philip gave a shirt and two chairs to Yacouba; catching sight of Moya in the crowd, I was reminded that I had yet to give anything to her mother, Sunu. Spotting a plastic jug, I asked Moya to bring it to her mother. Then I turned back to my pile of clothes, searching the growing crowd for a good match for each *pagne*.

Soon Moya returned with the plastic jug. "My mother says she w-won't take it," she stuttered.

"What? Why not?"

I felt the many pairs of eyes in the crowded courtyard on me. But Moya didn't have to explain: I understood my faux pas. Not only was the jug a rather shabby gift, but an hour earlier I'd sent that beautiful outfit to Sunu's junior co-wife. How could I have done this? I had often chatted with Busu Amla and commiserated over her sickly daughter, while Sunu's forbidding demeanor had usually kept me from exchanging much more than greetings. Clearly my own personal affections had won out over what, for a Beng, was more structurally appropriate.

"Tell her that she shouldn't be insulted," I said to Moya. "Tell her we're going to give your family our large bookcase—this will be for her, too." Stony-faced, Moya walked off to relay this message, but Sunu had already stormed into our compound.

"How could you give me such a thing!" she shouted shrilly.

"N'a, ka j'a di," I said—Mother, forgive me. "I know my part wasn't sweet, but this wasn't the only thing we planned to give you—"

Sunu interrupted. "Shame on you—how dare you insult me like this! All year long *my* daughter has cooked for you, and . . ." Sunu shouted a string of enduring resentments, and as they gushed forth, our audience clucked and commented, some siding with Sunu, others with me.

Mediators were fetched and apologies offered, but with this mistake—made publicly, and in our final hours in the village—I felt as if I'd erased all

that I'd learned these fourteen months. I wanted to pack myself into one of our suitcases and be carried out of the village incognito.

Two days later we were high above Abidjan's glittering evening skyline, in a plane that was a marvel either of aerodynamics engineering . . . or of witch-craft, its pilot the sorcerer who was flying us all somewhere for his dinner. Feeling the rush of the engines accelerating as we climbed higher and higher, I closed my eyes and let my mind fill up with images of the life we'd left behind. Our sad parting from Yacouba at the M'Bahiakro bus depot had been so unsatisfactory—but how could it be otherwise? And Amenan—my final memory was of her sad eyes regarding me as I left her courtyard for the last time. Images of Moya, Kona, and Busu Amla tumbled over one another as I drifted off in exhausted sleep.

At dawn the captain turned up the lights and a stewardess announced, "We are now flying over Manhattan, and we'll be coming down the aisles to hand out customs cards."

I accepted the small card, dreading the thought of government agents peering into our suitcases, fingering our carved statues and spoons, brass bracelets, and wooden beads as if they were mere objects. It was just as well we hadn't brought Kwamla Chakro's medicine pot. Wincing, I remembered the hurt look on Kwamla Chakro's face when we'd returned the pot to him. "If we take it on the plane, we'll have to empty the water and the medicine will be ruined," I'd explained—but he wasn't convinced. Even if we *had* figured out a way to keep the pot filled with water en route, I now thought, surely the customs agent would confiscate it, alleging some dangerous plant disease harbored in that pungent herbal decoction.

As the plane taxied down the runway, I turned to the card the stewardess had handed me, and so my fifteen months in Africa were reduced to checking a box certifying that I had nothing to declare. What a lie: I had more to declare than could ever fit on any form.

Philip: The Alien Snow

I gazed out at the frost-lined window as we drove from the airport, trying to answer my parents' questions as they chatted away on the front seat, happy to see me. We were passing the sprawling edges of Manhattan, but instead of drawing me back home, this sight returned me to the Beng. I recalled driving Talé, San Kofi's young wife, to M'Bahiakro—she'd cut herself while working in the fields, and San Kofi had wanted her to have a tetanus shot.

Talé had never traveled in a car before, so I drove as slowly as possible to help her adjust. As we passed the first Baulé village, Talé gaped, surprised at how similar it looked to her own, and I realized she was leaving the Beng area for the first time. When we reached M'Bahiakro, everything in that wider world seemed to intimidate Talé—paved roads, a large bridge spanning the M'Bahia River, the sprawling *marché,* electric lights, and the *sous-préfecture* office—a modest enough structure, but the largest building she'd ever seen. The poor woman glanced about nervously all afternoon, as if disaster might arrive at any moment.

Now, gazing at New York's urban landscape, I better sympathized with Talé's fears. Three weeks before we'd left Bengland, Alma and I had awakened one morning to the BBC's news that John Lennon had just been murdered. The shared drama of this shocking death seemed to draw us closer to America, yet for the next week or so the radio regaled us with stories about street violence in America; suddenly "home" was filled with dangers comparable to those we'd anticipated before leaving for Africa.

But now I knew how to follow a winding trail through the rain forest, stepping deftly over any thin column of army ants that crossed my way; I'd endured my share of tropical diseases; and I'd long ago internalized the simple rule for how to avoid snakebite: never put your hand or foot where you can't see it. Those real and possible dangers now seemed far less threatening than the thought of navigating the busy streets of a city.

Alma and I spent our first week home shuffling from one set of suburban parents to the other, staying indoors, staring out a window at a world we weren't yet ready to enter. Sometimes I watched the alien snow drift down through the night air and felt an urge to walk out into the cold and leave footprints across the white expanse.

One night I slipped on a coat and stepped outside before I could change my mind. The cold assaulted my face and lungs, and the curious scrunch of my steps echoed in the dark as I tramped across snowy yards. Slogging through drifts, bending low under the thick branches of evergreen trees, I reawakened to the once familiar cold weather. Finally, after crossing a field, I looked back to see where I'd been, and the moonlight revealed my wanderings: a long, curving trail of tiny shadows formed by my footprints. But nothing in those prints could reveal who I had become in the past year. I shivered in my bulky coat, my arms hugging the thick layers, and imagined I was in a cocoon threaded with the interwoven strands of two cultures.

The privacy and personal isolation of our own culture had once been a second skin we'd worn without giving it much attention; now, returned from Africa and trying it on again, we were aware of the poor fit. When we passed

strangers on the street, of course no elaborate greetings were exchanged—
there were no greetings at all, just the occasional, suspicious sidelong glance.
What's wrong with these people? I thought, though I was silent, too.

Alma and I now found ourselves longing—perversely—for the lack of privacy that had initially oppressed us among the Beng. Every day, when we
climbed the steps to our new suburban apartment, we knew we'd be alone
until the next morning: no one would casually drop by with a story to tell
or gossip to share, no one would offer us a small gift of food or come by
to thank us for a recent favor, no gangs of children would invade our living
room with their games, showing off for our foreign eyes. At best, a phone
might ring.

We had lost the drama of an African social world we couldn't re-create: if
we wanted to speak with friends, we'd have to call them up and enjoy their
disembodied voices, and if our friends wanted to visit, they'd call us and make
an appointment a few days or even a week or two in advance. Though Alma
and I had much to talk about, our words didn't seem to fill the small apartment. Often we kept on the radio and television, competing voices and faces
that sometimes soothed us into imagining we were surrounded by noisy,
talkative neighbors: the financial expert on the radio who intoned his interpretation of the whims of "The Market," an unpredictable entity that fussily
worried over inflation figures and Soviet troop movements in Afghanistan; or
the television weather reporter who made predictions, with an impressive
array of electronic wizardry, that would quite likely prove wrong—I suspected that Lamine's divinations had a greater rate of success. Even the
canned laughter of sitcoms, that background noise of amusement, was oddly
comforting, though it competed with our own unspoken background noise:
memories of another world shared by no one else around us.

We were in danger of becoming exiles from our own experience. Alma, just
beginning to analyze the thousands of pages she'd collected, stared at her
piles of field notes; as the months passed and I began free-lance teaching
again and writing scenes for new stories, I knew I was merely marking time,
waiting for the arrival of something I couldn't predict.

It came in the mail: a new issue of the *Paris Review,* featuring an interview
with Gabriel García Márquez. I had fond memories of rereading *One Hundred Years of Solitude* while in Africa—the fantastic events of the novel had
seemed perfectly normal, considering my surroundings. I remembered in
particular one morning after a heavy rain, when a Ghanaian puppeteer strode
down the road to our village, his cap tilted archly on his forehead. A large
crowd had encircled him, the children giggling and weaving among the
adults' legs for a better view. He reached into a cloth bag and drew out a
small statue of a woman, her figure painted a bright red, and a male puppet,
his hair striped black and yellow, a red tie painted on his blue-and-white body.

Their faces were starkly sculpted, their painted features chipped and worn. Pulling and twisting the strings, our guest performer led the puppet on a dance around the statue and sang a brief, sweet song; his voice then alternated between the man and the woman as he made them speak in musical, almost lulling tones. Alma and I couldn't understand the language, but the villagers laughed with a knowing pleasure that made me suspect these wooden creatures were enjoying a smutty exchange. The man's arms stroked the woman's face, she said something high-pitched, then soothing, and the audience howled gleefully. Soon the female statue was down on the ground, the puppet's body upon her, thrusting to her caressing cries. Coins fell all about them—our neighbors' applause—and the clinking mingled with rippling laughter. *I'm in Macondo,* I'd thought at the time, and the gypsies have come to our small, faraway corner to delight us with their tricks.

Now, I eagerly read through the García Márquez interview, stopping at the page where he justified the magic realism of his novels by claiming "there's not a single line in all my work that does not have a basis in reality. The problem is that Caribbean reality resembles the wildest imagination." I read it again, replacing "Caribbean" with "African," and felt I'd discovered a great truth: life had indeed lost its mad pace since we'd returned to America. Whenever I trotted out my African stories for friends, I repeated García Márquez's words. Yet even as I quoted them approvingly, something inside me dissented—a small voice that slowly grew louder.

Once, while waiting on line at a drugstore's prescription counter—more medicine for our lingering African maladies—I examined the racks of paperback books: row after row of horror novels faced me. The gruesome, eerie covers, held snugly in little wire compartments, announced a world of hidden dangers, of supernatural beings ready to haunt the weak or unaware. Ah, I thought, I know something about this. I'd always dismissed such novels as poorly written trivialities; but why were they so popular? There had to be more to them than the desire for a temporary thrill.

That book rack beckoned me to reexamine my assumptions. However trashy, those novels sanctioned an invisible world of significance. Though we all hold inside us hidden fears, intuitions, and superstitions, we live in a culture that doesn't sanction such private quests for meaning and order—the word *superstition* itself is used to deride or shame. Yet "unreasonable" fears are unreasonable only to those who don't share them. And who *doesn't* nurture a private ritual of some sort? Slipping a lucky penny in a pocket, scanning the horoscope, saving a fortune cookie's propitious words, searching a road sign or storefront for a lottery number, wearing a charmed blouse or shirt on an important day, all these are small protections against a larger, interior unruliness that can never truly be tucked in, pinched, or constrained.

All reality resembles the wildest imagination. Or, rather, our incessant inventiveness—our wild imaginations—*makes* reality, whether in the Caribbean, Africa, North America, or anywhere else. It's just more obvious in the tropics. Most Beng live all their lives together in the same small village—how hard for secrets to be kept, how easy for grudges to develop and fester, for passions to reveal themselves. But what if an American kindergarten class grew up, intermarried, and grew old together? What if *any* American family were forced to live together for generations in close quarters? I could certainly imagine the readily available turmoil *my* extended family might create, could remember the turmoil my parents, brother, and I had managed all on our own.

With the onset of warm weather, Alma and I began taking walks at night through our neighborhood. Over the course of an excursion we'd pass church after church—in another time these would have served mainly as architectural markers, but now they reminded me that many of the people I passed in the supermarket or the post office carried within them the otherworldly presences of angels and devils. And each long row of houses on every block might once have appeared more nondescript than the last, but I had been given new eyes by the Beng. Now I found it hard *not* to imagine each of those homes as a little village with its own secrets and convoluted history: their windows were glowing rectangles of light, radiating the excess energy of the complicated lives within.

PART TWO

RETURNING

10

A PARALLEL WORLD

🌀   🌀   🌀

(JUNE 11–AUGUST 13, 1985)

Alma: Retrieved in the Moonlight

TINGLING WITH ANTICIPATION, I SAT NEXT TO PHILIP IN THE CROWDED BUS THAT RATTLED along the dirt road from M'Bahiakro to Bengland, that washboard route whose every bump and twist we still knew by heart, even after a near five-year absence from Côte d'Ivoire. Almost as a nervous gesture, I took out a thick pack of index cards from my briefcase and, slipping off the rubber band, flipped through them, browsing through the hundreds of questions about Beng culture I'd accumulated over the past five years in writing up my notes. But I was too excited to concentrate—my expectations for the summer's stay in Asagbé, not to mention my fellow passengers in the bus, all beckoned for my attention. Across the aisle a young woman nursed her infant and a trader clutched a bundle of used clothes he clearly planned to sell; behind them a Muslim elder fidgeted with his prayer beads, perhaps over some private dilemma. Their poverty was unmistakable—while Philip and I had vowed never to own a car in rural Africa again, our busmates didn't have the luxury to choose between a private car or a bush taxi for their travels.

As we passed a tiny Baulé village, Philip nudged me with his elbow. "Look, this is where Didadi's wires burned out."

"Mmm," I muttered, preferring my own, more idyllic memories of life among the Beng: languorous afternoons chatting with Amenan, bowls of tasty palm nut sauce, evening pail baths under the stars. I thought with pleasure how this time we would join Amenan's compound as live-in guests for the summer. I'd already imposed myself once before on Kosangbé—this time I was going to stay where I was wanted.

Philip's elbow tickled me again. "Getting closer. This is where we had that blowout, remember?"

"Oh, you and that car," I said, laughing. Still, Philip's banter was infectious, and my own recollections of emergency trips taken in that rattletrap tumbled out of my memory—Nguessan screaming in labor as we rushed to the M'Bahiakro dispensary or Wamya Kona calmly holding a bleeding bandage to his eye for his own hospital trip. I hoped this summer's stay would be free of such traumas. Still, in receiving letters from Amenan and François, I knew that life had become much tougher for our hosts. In the years since we'd lived in Côte d'Ivoire, the country's economy had begun to collapse. While the west African drought of the past three years had been most disastrous farther north in the Sahel, it had also affected the crops in Côte d'Ivoire, and with a cruel twist of fate, world market prices for coffee and cocoa had lowered drastically at the same time. Still, the Ivoirian government had done little to alleviate the suffering of the farmers, while allowing itself to rack up a hefty debt.

While the Beng suffered, Philip and I had thrived, I reflected guiltily. I'd completed my dissertation, and Philip's collection of stories had been published; miraculously we were both teaching at the same university, and we'd even bought a house. But now I yearned to shed my new identity of professor for my former role—student of Beng culture.

"Hey, look," Philip said, interrupting my reverie, "isn't this where that tree fell across the road, right in front of us? Yeah, it was right . . . here!"

In spite of myself, I looked out the window. "My god, we're almost at Bongalo." I fell silent and tried to think in Beng. Back in the States, I did this often: walking down a street, I often imagined being a tour guide to village friends, explaining in their language the baby carriages, schoolchildren without uniforms, regular strips of grass bordering cement sidewalks, fire alarm boxes, and countless other images that would seem odd to a Beng visitor. But I knew these invented dialogues were hardly real conversations. As our bus neared Bengland, I whispered the afternoon greetings to myself, much as I used to memorize the lines of a part I was learning for a high school play. But this time I wasn't sure of the script: would we be greeted as visitors to a new village, as fellow villagers having returned home after a long voyage, or as something in between?

The *taxi-brousse* stopped on the dirt road bisecting Asagbé, and I stared out the window: there was the small boutique where we'd bought cans of sardines and warm bottles of Coke; nearby was a lovely flowering tree, its fan-shaped orange petals radiating above the village; off in the distance was the elementary school, flanked by mud brick houses. Ah, Asagbé: this time it would be our home.

A boy recognized us and tore down a path toward Amenan's compound. Philip and I busied ourselves with our baggage, undoubtedly to conceal our nervousness and excitement as a small group gathered. Soon I spied Amenan approaching calmly in the distance, surrounded by children. I wanted to run toward her, then reconsidered—perhaps my impulse was too American. When we finally met, Amenan said, "Eh, Amwé, *bienvenue!*" and we hugged, but not too tightly—for on Amenan's back was her two-month-old daughter, Lucy, nestled in a *pagne* and leaning her head over in peaceful sleep. I stared in wonder at this new creation, then looked down: another addition to Amenan's family tugged at her mother's skirt and stared at me, wide-eyed. She would be Rose, another daughter born since my departure—surely she was three by now. And holding Amenan's hand was a beautiful little girl with a serious gaze: could it possibly be Amwé, whom I'd left as a happy, crawling nine-month-old almost five years ago?

"Mi da nua," Amenan said quietly to Amwé—Your mama's come. Silently the girl let go of Amenan's hand, padded over deliberately, and reached toward me. I grasped her hand, and my small namesake and I walked together along the narrow path as Amenan explained: "Ever since you've been gone, she's been sad. Now that you're back, she's content. She knows you're her mother. But we don't call her Amwé anymore—Kofi's Ghanaian name for her, Esi, has stuck."

We continued on the path, surrounded by children hustling along with our lighter bags or proudly dragging the heavier ones, and I contemplated Amenan's words. Was I really responsible for a four-year-long *tristesse?* When Amenan had playfully told baby Amwé, "Look, here's your mother," she might have meant her words more seriously than I'd imagined, and she'd continued this sweet fiction even in my absence. If my friend was really bestowing a kind of motherhood on me, her childless friend, it was the most valuable gift she could offer.

Our small group arrived at Amenan's compound, where our hostess pointed to a small mud brick house, its facade cemented over, and she instructed the children to put our bags inside—this would be our lodging for the summer. The children brought stools into the courtyard, and Amenan embarked on a lengthy formal welcome, her husband and mother beside her—after all, in the Beng world hugs couldn't replace proper etiquette.

"Kouadio, ka kwaba; Amwé, ka kwaba"—Welcome, welcome—Amenan be-

gan, and then in formal tones asked us how our time away had been and if we brought news from the world.

"When we left you last time," I said, "we returned to America. But *ka ka an dé, deh*"—We missed all of you terribly—"and so we've returned."

"Yo." She nodded and welcomed us, *"Ka nu blaa"*—Get yourselves settled. Ah, those words, just the ones I'd hoped to hear: Amenan had offered us the greetings to welcome a native son and daughter back home after a trip.

The formalities over, Amenan nodded in the direction of our new home. "I hope you'll be comfortable."

I was sure we would. The tiny house faced onto the courtyard, so we'd be part of the household, yet we'd still have some privacy. The arrangement seemed ideal.

The sun was lowering rapidly on the horizon, and Amenan brought out dishes for dinner. Taking the single stew pot off the cooking fire, Amenan turned away from me and half whispered, "I'm sorry, but we weren't expecting you until tomorrow. There's only rice—"

"Oh, Amenan," I murmured, "I know how hard it's been. My grant has given me money for the household—tomorrow we'll buy a chicken."

"Merci," she said quietly.

I sensed my friend's embarrassment—but we both knew this was not a normal year. Even with a bumper crop, many African farmers lived on the margin; where was the space in their economy for three years of poor harvests? Since the beginning of the drought, young people from every village had left for the cities in search of work so they could relay their earnings back to their families. Philip and I had also sent cash periodically to Amenan and other village friends—all the while feeling helpless in the face of that distant, widespread suffering.

After dinner Philip and I realized we had nothing to sleep on in our new, empty house—we'd have to buy a mattress in M'Bahiakro. But what to do for tonight? "Is there anyone in the village," I asked Amenan, "who might loan us a mattress for a few days?"

"Well," she answered slowly as if measuring out her words, "I know Bwadi Kouakou has an extra one. Maybe he'd let you use it."

"Why don't we go over and see him right now? We have news for him—we just saw Pascal in Abidjan."

Amenan hesitated, and I thought about our sad encounter with Bwadi Kouakou's oldest son last week. Pascal had told us wearily that after his mother, Jokwa, had died, his father's junior co-wife, Kla, suddenly evicted her senior co-wife's young children from the compound—they were now being raised by a married sister.

Amenan remained silent, and Philip asked, "Do you think it's too late to go see him?"

"No, that's not the problem." She paused. "Actually, he's angry with me."

I was struck silent for a moment—Amenan had always been quite close with Bwadi Kouakou, a member of her matriclan. "But what's happened?" I finally asked.

"Do you remember that just before you left, Bwadi Kouakou began flirting with my daughter Evelyne and giving her little gifts?" she began.

"Yes, of course. He even told me he wanted to marry her." But I hadn't put much stock in his declaration—I couldn't imagine him appealing to the teenager I knew, an attractive girl who could be charming one minute, feisty the next.

"Well, after Pascal's mother died, Bwadi Kouakou announced it was time to make plans."

"So he was serious all along."

"*Ah, oui.* But Evelyne protested that he was too old."

"*Mm-hmmm.* What did *you* say?" I asked. When Amenan and I had discussed Nakoyan's and Mo'kissi's unyielding families last time, I'd never considered that as the mother of quite a few daughters, my friend might one day face similar decisions.

"I was opposed to the match," Amenan answered, "because Evelyne and Bwadi Kouakou aren't related the right way—it would be a bad marriage. But my mother was in favor of it. She and I fought a lot about it."

"*Ah-heh,*" I said. Amenan's answer unnerved me: would she have opposed the match if the couple *were* related in the right way? I decided not to ask.

"Anyway, Evelyne married someone else. But soon after, she came down with terrible stomach pains—she almost died. Thank goodness she got the right medicine from a pharmacy. Then her husband turned out to be impotent! She left him and went to M'Bahiakro so she could live with another man, an old boyfriend who works as a tailor in the *marché*. But as soon as she began to live with him, she became sick again—it got so serious she couldn't move at all."

"Oh, *mon vieux,* she's really suffered."

"Finally she recovered." Amenan moved closer and said, sotto voce, "Now, people are saying there was witchcraft involved. Evelyne's first husband said *I* bewitched him to become impotent!"

"You?" Philip said indignantly.

"A little while later, he took back the accusation."

"*Ah, merci!*"

"But now people are saying that it's Bwadi Kouakou who bewitched Evelyne to fall sick both times." My mind whirled with this new, equally distressing accusation. Our village father considered a witch?

Amenan continued, "That's why our families aren't talking much to one another these days. And that's why I don't know if Bwadi Kouakou will loan you his mattress—since it would be moved to my house. Especially because I've asked Evelyne to come back to the village for the summer so she can cook for the family."

"Mmm, thank you," I said, though silently I questioned the wisdom of my friend's plan. Having a daughter cook for the family would indeed free her for our work together—but of all her older daughters, why Evelyne? Surely this could only make things worse.

"I can't believe it—we've stepped into *another* crossfire," Philip whispered in English. "Kosangbé all over again, eh?"

Shaken, Philip and I set out on the path to Bwadi Kouakou's compound. I should have been happy at the thought of seeing our village father again after almost five years—instead I had to admit I dreaded the encounter.

We found Bwadi Kouakou and Kla in their compound, each chatting quietly with a friend. We all shook hands and exchanged greetings, then we gave them news of Pascal—at this Kla looked away disinterestedly.

The courtyard was eerily quiet: none of Bwadi Kouakou's young children by Jokwa was in sight. Our last time in the village, I'd somehow missed the two women's jealousy. Or had I? Now, standing in the quiet compound, I recalled that famous meal of rotten meat that we'd eaten here. I knew the dinner had been prepared by Kla. Suddenly I understood that this had been the work not of a bad cook, but of a resentful co-wife: why should Kla have entertained guests who'd been visiting on account of her rival's college boy? I glanced over at Kla, who was now chatting with a daughter. That woman was responsible for my first sickness, which had set off months of stomach cramps. I didn't want to stay in this compound any longer than I had to.

Very nervously I told Bwadi Kouakou that we would be lodging with Amenan during the summer.

"*Bon,*" he said coolly, displaying no reaction.

"There's no mattress in the room," I almost whispered. "We're planning to buy one when we go down to M'Bahiakro, but we were wondering if we could borrow a mattress from you for tonight." Looking away, I muttered, "I've heard that you might have an extra."

"*Oui, oui.* It belongs to Pascal, but as long as he's in Abidjan, you can use it."

"*Merci beaucoup,*" Philip said, and we shook hands on it. I thought sadly how Pascal had told me with sorrow, "I don't think I'll go to the village for a very long time. With my mother gone and Kla taking over the compound, I don't feel welcome anymore."

The next morning Philip and I embarked on what we knew would be a day-long tour of the huge village: at every courtyard we stopped to say a formal hello. It was exhilarating to be enmeshed in those long rounds of greetings that renewed our relationships with old friends, especially André and his family. But by late afternoon, after repeating the same greetings hundreds of times, the tedium of the ritual started to wear on us. Still, when we lay down to sleep that night, our exhausting welcome also felt delicious.

Though Asagbé already felt like home, we did have one regret in not returning to Kosangbé: we both missed Yacouba terribly. After sending word of our arrival, we waited impatiently for the next Asagbé market day, when our friend could bike over to visit us.

When Yacouba arrived, accompanied by François, Philip rushed to them, and for a moment we were all hugs and handshakes. Yacouba still sported the same youthful grin, though François had aged—I could see some of his skinny uncle Andama coming out in him.

Amenan came over to welcome our guests, then stood back and looked on smiling as we four sat at a table under the *akpa* and exchanged the formal greetings. "And how are your wives?" Philip asked.

"Oh, Dongi will always be Dongi," Yacouba said with a shrug, "but they're getting along."

"Ah, Dieu merci," Philip said, and I sighed in relief at the news. Then I turned to François.

"How are Makola and the children?" I asked.

"Everyone's fine. Do you remember my oldest son, Bertin? He's in high school in Béoumi now—the first one from our village! He's very good in English. But tell us your news, too."

"Our families are all healthy," I said, "and our work has gone well." I paused, wondering how my next words would be received. "Let me show you what I've written from all the notes I took last time."

I brought out my dissertation, bound between stiff black covers, and nervously placed it on the table: this would be my first reaction from a villager of Kosangbé. But ironically, of course, the words meant nothing to them—Yacouba had never learned to read, and François was literate only in French. They flipped rapidly through the pages; but when they reached the photographs, they stopped to discuss animatedly the image of Moya cooking over a hearth, Yacouba intently carving a wooden rasp. Then I showed François the acknowledgments, and he grinned at the sight of his own name and Yacouba's, then read through the long list of people I thanked.

"Bon, Amwé, I have to go now," François said, quickly closing the stiff black cover. Abruptly he was off to the *marché.*

Baffled, I asked Yacouba, "Why did François leave so suddenly?"

"He was embarrassed," Yacouba answered, shifting on his chair.

"Ihh—why?"

Yacouba was silent for a moment, then he said cryptically, *"Ngwo zra kpandré o, na ngwo ta sra maw blé lu"*—They threw it out into the darkness, and they retrieved it in the moonlight.

"What does *that* mean?"

"The last time," explained Yacouba, "people didn't really know why you were here. Now, François sees that all you did was write a book, and you thanked us by name. He's embarrassed that people in our village were so suspicious of you and Kouadio."

"Ah, I see," I said. Though I wasn't sure I wanted to hear the answer, I asked, "But why *were* they so suspicious?"

"Well," said Yacouba, looking away, "some people said you were asking us all those questions to start up forced labor again."

"What!"

"The last time anyone wrote down all our names and ages," Yacouba said quietly, "that's what it was for. People thought you were working for the government, and they'd make us abandon our farms to build roads and grow cotton without being paid, just as the French did. Of course *I* didn't believe that, but some people couldn't be convinced—"

"Oh, Yacouba!" I stared dumbly at my notebook, my scrawled handwriting a blur. Then I recalled how old Wuru San, the chief's father, had once confided his fear that forced labor would someday return—he must have been testing me to see how I'd react. All those stamped government papers, which had taken me weeks of bureaucratic wrangling to obtain, had reawakened memories of colonial rule—when villagers were required to pay a tax so onerous, the Beng term for it was *nen zra:* "to throw away one's soul."

Philip: A Strange Dream Dreamt Again

Alma and I quietly contemplated Yacouba's stunningly simple explanation for so many of our difficulties in Kosangbé. Yet I doubted we could have allayed the villagers' fears so easily, even if we'd known earlier—only now, with our return, did we seem to have achieved credibility. I regarded Yacouba carefully, so happy to see him again—he seemed unchanged, though I knew from the letters François had written for him that his life had been hard these past years of drought and crop failure. I asked him for news of Kosangbé, thinking how odd it was to be, in effect, Yacouba's host in another village.

"Nguessan has died," he began.

"What?" Alma interrupted, now torn from her reflections—she'd always

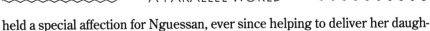

held a special affection for Nguessan, ever since helping to deliver her daughter Amla in M'Bahiakro.

"Yes," Yacouba murmured uncomfortably, "she had another difficult delivery, much worse than when you were here. She died during childbirth."

"A kunglia"—Our condolences—we said, this ritual phrase inadequate to our sadness. After a few shocked moments Alma asked, "What about her daughter, Amla?"

Yacouba winced, waved away a fly. "Dead. She was always sickly."

"A kunglia," we repeated, miserable. They were *both* dead. Suddenly a suspicion rose in my mind, and I blurted out, "And Apu, how is little Apu?"

"He was bitten twice by snakes since you left," Yacouba replied, sighing. "The second time, he died."

"A kunglia," we both managed to say, and then fell momentarily silent, the joy of our reunion dulled by this terrible news. How proud we'd been of saving those three lives, and yet in the intervening years they had died of the same circumstances: snakebite and childbirth—even little Amla's frailty could be attributed to her traumatic birth. Our rescue attempts had merely delayed the particular fates that awaited them all.

"Kouadio, Amwé," Yacouba murmured at the sound of a distant, shrill soccer whistle, "let's go watch the high school boys get beaten." He rested his hand on my shoulder.

"Yes, let's," I agreed, and Alma nodded. The Asagbé high school students, back home for vacation, had challenged their farmer brothers and cousins to a soccer competition, to be held each market day. We set off with Yacouba for the village soccer field: watching a little friendly roughhouse, punctuated by cries of *"But! But!"*—Goal! Goal!—might, if only for the moment, ease us from our sadness.

Alma and I swiftly established the rhythms of our new life, and like a strange dream dreamt again, the world of the Beng enveloped us once more. Every morning we awoke to the resonant call and response of mortar and pestle, and we opened the wooden shutters of our bedroom for the sunlight. But this time the view through our window wasn't the jousting goats of Kosangbé, balanced precariously on a termitary; instead the grassy, unkempt courtyard of Amenan's mad neighbor Amwé faced the back of our house.

"What's she doing?" one of us would whisper while the other peeked through the slats. Often the thin, dazed woman slapped the ground aimlessly with a stick; one morning she bathed scandalously in the open, and I turned away quickly.

Alma and I always dressed quickly and took our place in Amenan's extended family of six adults and sixteen children: a comforting dailiness of tressing hair or washing clothes, gossiping, returning from a forest well with a huge brimming pot, nursing babies. Amenan's husband, Kofi, stripped long cords of bark into yam ties, and neighbors walked through the compound on the way to and from the fields, greeting us as they passed. Children played with a pet monkey, sculpted little dolls from mud, singed the fur off a squirrel they'd just killed, and engaged in teasing games: Amenan's two-month-old daughter, Lucy, was dubbed La Radio—the Radio—because her cries reminded the older children of a radio's static, and Esi's nickname was Tobi—automobile—since her frequent whining resembled a car's anxious, stalled motor. While Evelyne prepared the meals, chickens, goats, and sheep wandered by as close as they dared, in search of lucky scraps. Once while sitting near the courtyard's open hearth, I gathered different treasure: overhearing Amenan and her daughter discuss the evening meal, I learned that charcoal, in Beng, was *sie a ti*—Black piece of fire—and the word for "barely simmering" was the wonderfully musical *féféfé*. Our hosts' large family gabbed in counterpoint, arguing, joking, and singing, and sometimes the mad Amwé wandered by, mumbling and mangling the various intricate greetings. Alma's interviews and my typing merely added to the hubbub.

Now I was working on a new short story about a woman who, falling in love with a geologist, is also seduced by his professional ability to see the invisible past and future landscapes in any terrain. Yet she grows increasingly unsettled as she realizes that if even mountain chains can appear and disappear over aeons of time, then *everything* around her is fluid, transmutable. This was a story I couldn't have written if I hadn't lived in Africa, for now I had a better sense of how so much of our lives is invisible: it's people's beliefs that make the world resonate and vibrate. As I eased my way into this new story, I chuckled silently when I thought of the question I'd been asked repeatedly over the past five years: "Have you ever written about Africa?" I'd always replied, "Well, not directly, but Africa is in every word I write." My reply usually drew a silent reaction. I seemed to be offering a riddle few people cared to solve. I understood their reaction—I'd be solving this riddle all my life.

In Kosangbé I'd often fretted over interruptions while I worked, but here in the commotion of Amenan's compound there was simply no private space to interrupt. Though I typed out what I could, sometimes I gave up and escaped into the forest with Amenan's husband. Kofi was an excellent teacher who was happy to have a helper, and we tapped palm wine, set animal traps, or attached long cords from yam mounds to nearby trees.

Kofi had his own reasons for taking a break from the compound. During the worst two years of the drought, he'd deserted his family and returned to Ghana. Though he was now back in Asagbé, the continuing resentment over his behavior was palpable—one night a minor dispute with his mother-in-law quickly accelerated, and her biting contempt so shamed him that he spent the following day in bed, suffering from migraine.

Kofi was doing his best to make amends—he'd become the compound's gofer, accepting any errand his in-laws needed done. When Amenan fell ill with a fever, Lamine told her that her medicine pot had to rest on the base of a termite mound in order to be effective, so Kofi set off into the forest, and I accompanied him. The thick mud stuck to the bottom of our sandals as we trooped along, courtesy of the almost daily, heavy rains—this year the harvest would be good. After less than a mile, Kofi stopped and pointed out a small termite mound, less than three feet tall, that resembled a huge brown mushroom.

"That's it—the right one." He grinned, displaying the space where his front teeth should have been. With a machete he neatly severed the mound from the earth, then hefted it onto his shoulder. We returned to the compound, where he chopped off the fanning, umbrellalike top and presented the base to Amenan for her medicine. Then he ambled over to the center of the courtyard, announcing, "Time to feed the chickens," and dashed the top of the mound onto the ground. The brittle, dried mud shattered into pieces, and out poured a teeming white puddle of termites. Squawking from all corners of the compound, chickens raced over and pecked away, gobbling up the wildly scurrying insects.

I picked up a few of the craggy pieces and examined the intricate tunnels and interconnected rooms, growing steadily glum at how this beautifully complex world had met its end: Kofi and I had stolen a little city and then served up its helpless inhabitants to ravenous chickens as a snack.

The sight haunted me for hours, and then, ruefully, I realized why—the little drama reminded me of the plight of the villagers, beset by increasing government corruption. Even the most insignificant official now displayed an arrogance usually associated with the gendarmes, able to abuse their power because their victims were poor and often spoke little French. Agricultural extension workers, whose duties ostensibly were to help farmers grow cotton, were interested primarily in stealing the profits of harvest; elementary school teachers often took advantage of their students, using them as unpaid labor for their farmwork; petty bureaucrats now demanded large bribes for processing the paperwork for children's required identity cards. "People are afraid to go M'Bahiakro," Amenan once told me, "because we're afraid we'll be cheated."

Though I suspected that my efforts might never provide anything more than a temporary balm for lives that would always be hard, once again I began to treat the various illnesses of the villagers. One afternoon Sopi, a stocky woman sporting a sharp gaze beneath her heavily lidded eyes, requested that I treat a cut on her calf. I agreed, with some trepidation—the forest leaf she'd placed over the wound was quite large—and when I carefully peeled away the poultice I saw an eerily even-edged, rectangular wound, so deep it seemed as if five or six layers of skin had simply been lifted out of her leg. The exposed flesh was red and raw.

"Alma," I blurted out, "come look at this."

"My god," she said, peering at the wound, "I've never seen anything like it."

As Alma and I tried to decide whether or not to recommend that the woman travel to the M'Bahiakro infirmary, Amenan interrupted us. "She's had it for years," she said diffidently in French, "for as long as I can remember. It's from witchcraft, and medicine won't help."

Amenan's words annoyed me. Too many people's lives had been destroyed even by the simple suspicion of witchcraft, and there was no reason not to treat this woman—she had, of course, asked for help. I slathered the wound with antibiotic cream, then applied a bandage.

"Here," I offered, holding in my hand a vitamin E pill to aid the healing, "take this and come back tomorrow."

Sopi thanked me and left. Amenan said nothing: if I'd ignored her advice, she was content to let me discover for myself the wisdom of my decision. Perhaps I *was* foolish to believe that my small stock of medical supplies might have an effect on this woman's life, but I couldn't allow myself not to try. So when Nakoyan, still living in Asagbé with her husband, Gaosu, came to us for help, I was determined to do what I could for her.

She still had a hint of her old, mischievous smile, though deep worry lines now scarred her forehead—I knew from Amenan's store of village knowledge that Nakoyan's first child had died in infancy. This young woman had been visited too often by trouble, and now her second child, a one-year-old son, was ill and bloated—he hadn't been able to piss in three days. I was certain that this was a problem far beyond my small powers—the child might be suffering from uremic poisoning. "I'm sorry, little sister, but your son's illness is *grégré*"—serious. "You have to take him to the M'Bahiakro infirmary."

Though understandably disappointed that I offered no easy remedy, Nakoyan and Gaosu took my advice. When they returned that afternoon, Alma and I walked to their compound to welcome them back. But the little boy looked no better, and I couldn't understand why they hadn't stayed in M'Bahiakro. The next morning we were summoned to Nakoyan's compound, and when we arrived I was shocked at the sight of her child: his arms and legs seemed inflated, and his light brown skin had a greenish tinge.

"Nakoyan," I said, "I can't help you. You have to go back to the infirmary. Your child is very ill and needs new medicine."

"But, Kouadio," she said, her face so miserable, "the bus to M'Bahiakro is too expensive."

"Nakoyan," I managed, almost too stunned to reply, "your child is deathly ill." I looked at the others gathered in the courtyard, sitting on stools or some of the larger rocks—those basaltic outcroppings that eerily speckled the village. Zang, her father, and her older sister, Ajua, were present, a sure sign of an emergency, yet no one seemed willing to urge Nakoyan and her husband to further action. Alma and I left, disturbed by what seemed an inevitable outcome. Yet why did this have to be so?

As we settled back in Amenan's compound, I realized guiltily that I should have immediately given Nakoyan the money for the bus fare—because of the recent poor harvests, most villagers had very little available cash. How could I have been so insensitive? I was about to return when Zang appeared and thanked us for our visit.

I offered him a seat. He was as thin as ever, his sunken cheeks still a startling sight—a bony little man filled mostly, as I remembered, with bile.

"Oh, it's terrible that my grandson is ill," he began, his words both emphatic and slurred—he'd been drinking. "Children," he said, with a clap of his hands, "can die so quickly."

I was sure he was here to ask for the bus fare. Ashamed, I interrupted what I assumed would be a long speech and pulled a one-thousand CFA note from my wallet. Zang's eyes widened at the sight of the bill. "Father, please accept this money. It's for your daughter and her husband, so they can return to the infirmary. But they have to leave right away."

Zang pulled the bill from my hand and thanked me.

"If they need more, let me know," I called to his retreating figure.

A few hours later Amenan announced that the child had just died, adding with disgust, "Nakoyan never even saw the money you gave to Zang. He drank it up, the rotten man."

"He used the money to buy *beer?*" Alma shouted. "How could he do that?"

Silently reproaching myself for contributing to this latest addition to Nakoyan's tragic life, I said nothing. Though I couldn't have predicted Zang's monstrous behavior, I should never have given money to such an untrustworthy man. As if reading my thoughts, Amenan shook her head and said, "Even if Nakoyan had received your gift, she wouldn't have gone to M'Bahiakro. Her first child died the same way: she and Gaosu didn't want to spend the money to go to the infirmary."

"But *why?*" Alma asked.

"They knew the child would die," Amenan replied matter-of-factly. "Some say Nakoyan's younger sister, Amlakro, the snake child, eats the souls of her babies. Others say the forest spirit who fell in love with her is still jealous and kills all the children she has with Gaosu."

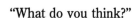

"What do you think?"

Amenan shrugged. "Her children die."

Angered by Nakoyan's unfair lot, I tried to escape from the Beng world by plunging into my preparations for a course on the nineteenth-century short story that I'd teach in the fall: Gogol, Hawthorne, and Melville, among others. Each long sentence of Henry James became an involving world of its own, a counterbalance to the leisurely chaos of Amenan's compound. Yet once, while in the midst of a passage's ornate logic in "The Jolly Corner," I heard children calling out, "Snake! Snake!"

Following their voices, I rushed from Amenan's courtyard, my eyes darting about in search of something heavy enough to break the back of a snake. I grabbed a log from a pile of firewood, but the snake was only a young girl, her hair filthy, who wore the slightest of G-strings—one of Asagbé's snake people. Surrounded by a crowd of kids, she crouched down, picked little dark balls of sheep dung, and, to derisive laughter, slipped one after another into her mouth. The children started up a repetitive, mocking song, and the snake girl, prodded by sticks, danced an awkward, improvised dance like a poorly manipulated marionette. I turned away from the cruelty of her audience because I understood it: this girl wasn't considered human; instead she was a despicable imposter, an incompetently disguised alien who, like Nakoyan's younger sister, was surely capable of eating the souls of babies.

Soon after, I once again encountered my old friend, malaria, and I rested in bed for a day, reading through *The Dick Gibson Show,* Stanley Elkin's cruelly hilarious novel about the adventures of a traveling radio personality. But apparently Amenan's compound was unnerved by the feverish man who lay in bed and laughed so loudly that he could be heard through the walls of the mud house. Alma came inside and sat beside me.

"Hey, keep it down in here," she murmured, stroking my forehead as she took my temperature. "You're giving everybody the creeps."

Nodding apologetically, I promised to be quiet. But minutes after she left I returned to the wicked acrobatics of Elkin's prose, and my laughter—manic and joyless, alarming even me—bubbled up and burst through the filigree of mosquito netting. I needed to release my pent-up sadness, trying to erase what could not be erased.

Alma: The Work Village

Philip and I marched along under the hot sun, dejected after our visit to Kosangbé. I knew the source of Philip's sadness—he'd hoped for more time alone with Yacouba; but because we were returning from a five-year absence,

our obligations were to the entire village, extending elaborate greetings to every compound. My own feelings were not so easily understood. I'd been happy to offer gifts to Wamya Kona and San Yao; delighted to see Moya, now a young mother, proudly turn around to show me the infant on her back; Philip and I had even played a running game with the children who tagged alongside us everywhere—we pretended we couldn't recognize them now that they were older and grown up. And many of our friends—Kwamla Chakro, Busu Amla, Ché Kofi—seemed genuinely sad that Philip and I had decided to live in Asagbé this summer.

Yet the people of Kosangbé had somehow lost their hold over me, if only because I knew I would no longer share in their daily lives. This seemed so unfair, but I had made the choice not to return. I sighed, looking at the long road ahead of us, and trudged on. My entire day in Kosangbé, though amply leavened with greetings, had actually been an extended good-bye.

When Philip and I finally arrived at Amenan's compound, we found Esi weeping inconsolably in the courtyard, tears dripping down her dirt-stained shirt.

"What's the matter?" I asked Amenan, who was helping Evelyne pound *foutou.*

"Esi wants 'women's bread,'" she said, frowning, "and I said I don't have any money to buy it." I couldn't blame Esi—those small loaves, made fresh every day by the village's Ghanaian prostitutes, were always tasty.

"I'll treat her," I offered. "Come on, Esi, let's go!" The little girl walked over, wiping the tears from her pouty face, and we crossed the village hand in hand.

I enjoyed indulging Esi, but this past month I'd been troubled by her whining—Beng children rarely complained so often. When we returned to the house, Esi happily munching her treat, I mentioned her behavior to Amenan.

"I know she's difficult, but there's nothing I can do," my friend lamented. "Lamine explained it all. Before my last three girls were born, his cowrie shells showed that Esi will always be willful and Rose will always be a glutton. Little Lucy will always be a help to me, and she'll be my last child."

"Do you think he's right?" I asked noncommittally.

"Mm-hmmm," Amenan said earnestly. "You see for yourself how stubborn Esi is. And Rose has a good appetite, even when she's sick. I never have to threaten that the witches will come after her if she doesn't eat—"

"What witches?" I interrupted.

Amenan laughed. "We tell picky eaters that the old ugly women of the village who have hairs on their chins are witches! A lot of the children are terrified of them—but Rose isn't, because I don't need to scare her to eat. As for Lucy, she's already such an easy baby, I can tell she'll always be sweet."

Though I nodded, I was disturbed by the self-fulfilling nature of Lamine's prophecy. Surely if a mother assumed her child was unalterably stubborn because of some inborn character trait, she'd be more lax about discipline than otherwise—why fight fate? Although I wasn't a mother and knew nothing of how to raise a well-behaved child, I wondered if Amenan had accepted Lamine's prophecy too easily—perhaps she'd used it as an excuse to let Esi run wild. Yet were my own culture's categories of "fussy babies" and "quiet babies" any less formative? And my own unspoken criticism troubled me for another reason, for I so much wanted to fit in seamlessly with Amenan's compound—especially after the day's visit to Kosangbé.

Still, I found myself disapproving of how another villager was treated: whenever Amwé, the madwoman who lived next door, came by the compound, my hosts often treated her with amusement or even barely concealed derision. I felt sorry for this unfortunate woman, so one day, when an itinerant salesman came through the village selling fresh fish, I bought several and, on a whim, chose one for Amwé as well.

As I presented my gift, Amwé muttered something that vaguely resembled *"Ka nuwalia"*—Thank you. A few moments later she entered our courtyard a bit unsteadily and gently grasped my hand. But all that emerged from her smiling mouth were incomprehensible gurgles. I responded as if she'd offered the appropriate thanks.

The next day Amwé returned, her untucked blouse hanging loosely over her *pagne,* and she offered me a few ears of corn. Touched by this present, I thanked her profusely. This time Amwé didn't even attempt language, just smiled and nodded before she walked away. Yet by this simple exchange, my namesake and I had taken a first step, however unlikely, toward something resembling friendship.

As I grew more adept at interpreting Amwé's peculiar speech, I noticed that in a single mangled sentence, my neighbor seemed to alternate between her own voice and that of another person. Sometimes I thought that second voice was meant to anticipate my own words; other times it clearly belonged to Amwé's own private vision. The poor woman's identity seemed shattered . . . unapproachable.

Amwé wasn't the only visitor to Amenan's compound, for my friend was as much a social magnet as ever. Even when there were no visitors, a gaggle of children played, giggled, and bickered constantly in the courtyard around us—Amenan and I couldn't possibly work in the midst of all this noisy energy. Finally Amenan had an inspiration: why not use an empty room in her uncle's compound next door?

The building belonged to Kokla Kouassi, an animist priest whom Amenan addressed as "Aba Kouassi"—Father Kouassi. Soon we settled into the unfinished mud brick room, spreading out a bark cloth mat on the dirt floor for Amenan and Lucy. In one corner Amenan stretched out and I crouched on a low stool; in another corner a hen guarded her eggs jealously, taking breaks to scratch in the dirt and run outside for stray corn kernels. Sometimes Philip came in and joined us—when he wasn't helping Kofi tap palm wine in the fields or watching a market-day soccer match during one of Yacouba's weekly visits. The room's open doorway connected us to the village: no one could accuse us of locking ourselves inside to harbor witchly plans when normal human beings should be in sight of others. From time to time a sobbing Rose or Esi might enter and, between tears, inform us of their latest dispute. But mostly we were left to work—indeed, the room became known as our "work village." When we emerged at the end of the day, people greeted us as if we'd just returned from laboring in the fields.

Since we were working in Aba Kouassi's compound, he was our host of sorts, and I thought it appropriate to present him with a gift.

"The *pagne* is beautiful," he thanked me. "Too bad it won't last as long as the old-style *pagnes:* they stood up to hundreds of my wife's hand washings before they tore."

"I'm sorry—I should have looked for one of those in the market," I apologized.

"No, no," he said, laughing, "everything has its time, Amwé. The time for those old *pagnes* is past."

I longed to know more of this animist priest's response to the modern world—and to his own. And I wondered how much of the pattern on that colorful *pagne* Aba Kouassi could see, for his eyesight was failing. He'd tried one local cure after another—herbal washes from a local healer, sheep sacrifices to his father's ghost, eye cream from a traveling merchant. Nothing had worked—indeed, the cream had made his eyesight even worse. Lately Aba Kouassi had all but abandoned his work in the fields, ceding his coffee plantation to Amenan and his son, Petit. Most days, when he wasn't sacrificing chickens to the bush spirits, he sat on a bench in the center of the village, chatting with the old men.

Once Amenan and I established ourselves in the henhouse, Aba Kouassi came in for a short while each day, chatting casually. Soon he joined in my conversations with Amenan as we puzzled out the complexities of the Beng arranged marriage system. At first Amenan translated her uncle's Beng into French, but fortunately my Beng had returned—working with my vocabulary cards and field notes during the intervening years had helped keep the language alive.

For a week we three pored over a manuscript on arranged marriage that

I'd drafted before leaving the States. Paragraph by paragraph, I translated the article into Beng for Amenan and her uncle, double-checking each rule of the complicated marriage system by scrutinizing Amenan's and Aba Kouassi's own genealogies: Would So-and-so be permitted to marry So-and-so? Occasionally I predicted wrong, but once, when Amenan and I disagreed about a particular form of cousin marriage, Aba Kouassi settled the disagreement. "Amwé's right," he announced.

"*Ihh*—you're a better Beng than I am!" Amenan said, and I laughed, trying to hide my pride.

Finally, after considering the possible spouses for every aunt and uncle, every first, second, and third cousin of Aba Kouassi and Amenan, none of us could stand our game of genealogical checkers any more. I was confident I knew the rules—it was time to move on to another topic. Many subtleties of the Beng religion still eluded me, but this was always a delicate topic. I decided to approach it by inquiring about Aba Kouassi's own biography. Delicately I asked him, "*Aba,* how is it that you became a priest to the Earth?"

"My father was a priest," he answered immediately, "and after he died, I took over his position."

"*Ah-heh,*" I said, hoping to encourage him further.

"But these days," he continued, a sad look in his clouded eyes, "a lot of people have become Muslim. When I'm gone, who will take over *my* position? You know, it's not just anyone who can be an Earth priest."

"*Ah-heh. E lé loa?*"—How's that?

"First, the priest must be a man. He must be right-handed, and he must respect the Earth spirits—no Christian or Muslim could do it. Also, he must not be circumcised. That's a problem: lately, even the young men who aren't Muslim have gotten themselves circumcised."

"*Ihh*—why is that?"

Aba Kouassi chuckled, and Amenan jumped in. "The girls won't sleep with them if they don't!"

Aba Kouassi nodded, then turned serious again. "Amwé, that's why I've decided to talk to you. If you can write down what I tell you, someday our grandchildren and great-grandchildren will read your papers and understand *an za*"—our affairs. "Maybe they'll even return to sacrificing to our forest spirits."

"*Aba,* thank you," I said, wondering if he sensed my excitement. "I'll try to listen carefully so I can write my book well."

And so I became an apprentice to an Earth priest. Aba Kouassi, who was going blind, had access to the invisible spirits of the forest as few others did, and in his increasingly solitary state he'd decided to share his vision with an unlikely acolyte.

During our first stay in Bengland, I'd been told that the forest spirits never entered Beng villages except to do harm; now Aba Kouassi told me that every *Bafen* or *Pofen* eve—the two days of Beng worship—the spirits entered the village and hovered right above his compound. There, they eavesdropped: villagers brought chickens and sheep to the priest for him to sacrifice the next morning—and so the spirits obtained a preview of the offerings. When the last of the visitors had gone, the spirits flew back to the forest.

"Their path takes them directly over the room you and Kouadio sleep in this summer," he added casually. "Once every six nights, the bush spirits pass over you."

Sitting on his low wooden stool, Philip was scribbling away on a story, oblivious of Aba Kouassi's words, but I knew he'd want to hear about this. I was about to interrupt with a brief, whispered translation when a boy biking through the courtyard stopped to peek into our room. "Hey, Monsieur Damang," he called out, then swiftly pedaled off. Aba Kouassi frowned.

"Who's Monsieur Damang?" I asked Amenan.

Trying to hide her smile, she whispered in French, "I'll tell you when my uncle's not around." Before long, Aba Kouassi excused himself to go pee, and Amenan said quickly, "Once, Aba bought a bike with four bags of his coffee beans. Everyone thought he'd paid too much, and some people started to tease him, calling him *Kleh sieng*"—Four bags.

"*Ah, bon.*" I chuckled.

"Well, that *really* made him mad, and he told people to stop calling him that. So they started calling him *Damang* instead—but it means the same thing, in Jula!"

As we waited for her uncle to rejoin us, I was amused to realize that this Earth priest could be the butt of a village joke, even as he was respected for his religious knowledge. Soon Amenan interrupted my thoughts: "I'm going to have to do a sacrifice soon, I've been a little dizzy lately. Lamine told me I should sacrifice a *mleh senzen.*"

"*Mleh senzen,*" I repeated, writing it down. "What's that?"

Just then Aba Kouassi came in. "It's a chicken that has only a few feathers," he explained. "They're very good to sacrifice because there's a kind of forest spirit that especially likes them—in fact, if you sacrifice a *mleh senzen,* it counts the same as a sheep sacrifice."

"*Ah-heh.*"

Then Amenan continued, "The diviner also told me to wear a white *pagne* every Wednesday. The spirits behind me want this."

"Behind you?"

"Everyone has spirits behind them. Whenever you see a baby wearing a cowrie bracelet, it's because the spirits behind them told the diviners they want cowrie shells." Amenan paused. "But adults have spirits, too. You should always find out what they want."

Philip: The Spirits Within

Alma and I sat with Aba Kouassi in his courtyard, shucking dried corn for his wife—later she'd cook it into sweetened corn pudding. As we flicked the dried kernels off the cobs, Aba Kouassi's daughter-in-law, Au, approached, about to greet us. But she stumbled badly and fell, one of her sandals skitting away from her along the hard dirt surface of the courtyard.

Aba Kouassi looked up at the commotion, but his eyesight was so poor that he couldn't recognize his son's wife. "Who is that?" he asked.

"It's me, Aba," Au said, picking herself up.

He shook his head slowly, murmuring, "This is a bad omen."

Disturbed by her father-in-law's words, Au gathered up her sandal and cut her visit short. Within an hour word came that Siagbé Yao, her uncle, had just died.

Many people were relieved by the man's passing, Amenan told us quietly, because he'd been a notorious goat thief—the mourning at his funeral would be more obligatory than deeply felt. Early that evening Kofi and I sat with the men of Asagbé, underneath the large public space shaded by a grand roof of palm fronds, and listened to the formal announcement of the death. A thin, unshaven man near me suddenly stood up and shouted, pointing in the air as if at invisible assailants. "Siagbé Yao was killed by witchcraft! *Witchcraft!* And I know who did this!" He began to name names, and a few embarrassed relatives tried to lead him away, just as a line of wailing women approached. The men joined in quickly, drowning out the angry accusations.

If Siagbé Yao had been killed by witchcraft, as some believed, then he exacted a small revenge from beyond the grave the following day. Tiny, stinging *kpotokpé* insects swarmed about the dead man's compound, and the assembled mourners, arms flapping, grumbled bitterly that Yao's ghost had incited the creatures. Alma always had a strong reaction to a *kpotokpé*'s bite, so we cut short our condolence greetings. Returning to Amenan's compound, we saw a trio of happy boys holding strings that lifted in the air and twisted as if alive, swooping over their heads—mutating, magic wands that buzzed.

Drawing closer, we saw that the strings were attached to flying insects, larger and rounder than a cicada, though just as noisy, and I remembered seeing them once before: last week, while I'd walked along a path to a funeral in a distant corner of Asagbé, a low-flying swarm had passed lazily by. Today I could imagine how the boys had easily caught them; now the things were tied and flying like kites—great fun on an otherwise solemn occasion.

When we returned to Amenan's compound I mentioned those insects turned into toys. "Ah," she said wistfully, perhaps remembering her own childhood games, "those are *tining kaka*"—visitors' insects—"they only appear when guests arrive from other villages. Today Siagbé Yao's relatives are here for the funeral."

Increasingly unnerved by the uncanny events around me—Aba Kouassi's successful prediction, the timely appearances of the *tining kaka*—I concluded grudgingly that there was much in this tight-knit belief system that I couldn't explain. Whether the connections the Beng saw were empirically based or not didn't seem to matter—what mattered was that everyone accepted their culture's explanations. For a month now I'd been treating Sopi's deep leg wound, and the red, raw skin hadn't healed in the slightest. It hadn't worsened, either, as if the wound inhabited its own circle of time, different from ours. Sopi accepted this stoically, undoubtedly concluding that my bandages and antibiotic creams were no match for the witchcraft she'd suffered from for so many years. Whatever the reason for this lack of progress, I began to regard my almost daily efforts as futile.

Now that Aba Kouassi was sharing his knowledge of Beng religion with Alma, I often joined them, in an empty room that also served as shelter for a hen and her clutch of eggs. Sitting in a corner, I would scratch away at a manuscript, putting it aside frequently to listen, delighted, as Aba Kouassi revealed to Alma, in greater detail than she'd ever received before, the world of spirits. Those otherworldly presences governed so much of Beng behavior, and the relationship began at birth: spirits communicated with every baby until the child began to speak; only with the acquisition of language did a child finally, truly become Beng, become human.

Of course the two worlds never stopped intermingling. There was a little boy in Asagbé, Bonzo Kofi, who went to the fields with his grandmother one day and mysteriously disappeared—one moment he was beside her and the next, gone. Villagers searched the nearby forest into the night, without success, but the following morning Kofi reappeared, in the same spot where he'd vanished. In place of his red underpants was a belt made of hand-spun cotton, from which dangled tiny deer horns, cowries, and ancient beads. Little Kofi was too young to speak, so diviners were consulted, and they discovered that a barren spirit woman, attracted by the boy's red pants—spirits loved the color red—had stolen him away, hoping to adopt him. But her spirit husband grew angry and ordered his wife to return the child, arguing that if the Beng thought children would be abducted in the nearby fields, they might abandon those farms; if this happened, the spirits would no longer be able to steal food, and they'd go hungry. Reluctantly the spirit woman set the boy free, the elaborate waist beads serving as an apology.

Aba Kouassi was filled with such tales, often tossing them out as if they were casual asides. Once, while Alma paused in the middle of a question, trying to backtrack and correct her Beng, Aba Kouassi pointed out the door and asked, "Can you see a large iroko tree from here?"

We followed the line of his finger. "Yes," Alma replied—the tree easily towered above the surrounding forest.

"Spirits live there," he said, describing how they could be heard singing at night, a whistling wind. But unluckily for the spirits, their homes were coveted by loggers, for faraway strangers had a taste for the irokos' rich hardwood grain. Recently teams of loggers had arrived in the Beng area, indiscriminately cutting down trees, and the angered spirits swiftly exacted vengeance. "The spirits caused trees to fall on the last two teams of loggers. Many of them were killed."

"Now that the news is out," Alma said, "maybe the loggers will stay away."

"No"—Aba Kouassi laughed bitterly—"they'll keep coming, spirits or not—there's good money to be made chopping down our trees."

He paused, then continued his spiritual mapping of the forest, telling us that near the iroko tree was a spirit village, the home of a polygamous male spirit who flew at night once a week from one invisible village to another, visiting each of his two wives. His path took him right through our courtyard—the sound of the wind on those nights was the sound of his flight. The wind itself was the very movement and sound of all spirits, and in the forest encircling the village, each swaying tree and shaking branch was their transfigured presence. I recalled Amenan rushing about in the compound, frantically collecting pots, sandals, whatever lay about, whenever a heavy wind presaged an approaching storm.

Once, Alma's session with Aba Kouassi was interrupted by shouts from the compound of our mad neighbor, Amwé. Alma and I ran to the commotion and joined the steadily gathering crowd. Amwé and her son—not much older than ten—howled at each other as they circled the hearth. Amenan stood beside us and said with disdain, "She refuses to give her son any of the yams she's cooked." The screams of mother and child increased until their waving hands became fists and they exchanged blows—a sight so shocking that some villagers gasped.

Kofi and a few other men broke up the battle, and Alma and I returned to the chicken coop, depressed by what we'd seen. "What happened?" Aba Kouassi asked, and Alma explained in her increasingly fluent Beng. His face tightened in pain.

"*Aba,*" Alma ventured, "do you know why Amwé went mad?"

"It all began many years ago," he said in a low voice, "when Amwé was a young girl. She had a bitter argument with her father."

"Like the argument she just had with her son?" I asked.

Aba Kouassi nodded. "Her father was so angry that he cursed her."

"Yih!" Alma said, knowing that a father's curse could never be rescinded. "And that's why she went mad?"

"Not at first. The curse began after Amwé grew up and married, a long time after her father died. One day Amwé was burning the underbrush in the forest for the new yam mounds. Her fire spread too quickly, and before she could stop it she'd burned down a spirit village."

"Whey," I gasped, imagining those invisible creatures fleeing from the flames and Amwé's terrified face.

"Her husband demanded that they consult diviners to find out how Amwé should apologize to the spirits. But they all told her there was nothing she could do—now the spirits cursed her."

"And then she went mad?" Alma asked.

"Yes," Aba Kouassi replied, his clouded eyes staring past us.

Over the next few days, remembering Amwé's violent argument with her young son, I wondered how many generations her tragedy might repeat itself, for spirits were so imbedded in the inner lives of the Beng that there seemed little possibility of shedding their influence. André, our first host in Asagbé, was a devout Christian—recently he'd been chosen by the M'Bahiakro *pères* to take part in a forthcoming, church-sponsored trip to Rome. But unknown to the *pères,* André had been struck by a mysterious illness last year that responded to no medicine or prayers. Regarded as virtually dead by most villagers, André finally gave in to his wives' entreaties and allowed a diviner to offer sacrifices to the spirits who inhabited his matriclan's forest shrine. He quickly recovered.

Alma and I grew increasingly attuned to the order of invisible beings as Aba Kouassi continued recounting the cosmology that was carried inside every person we passed on a village path or bargained with in the market: another universe—a parallel world—in familiar bodies and the multiplication, in a crowd, of strange, shared secrets. Now, whenever I awoke in the middle of the night and listened to the convoluted rustle of wind—as complex as speech—I imagined that someone in another compound might also be lying awake, trying to interpret the hushed movement of spirits. I'd long believed that spirits were creatures of the imagination; now I felt that spirits indeed existed—*because* they were creatures of the imagination. The spirits lived *within* the Beng and therefore outside them as well, for those interior presences also filled up their outer world.

During another session, Aba Kouassi told Alma of the different methods that diviners employed to attract spirits—laying out red cloth, white powder, small statues. Drawn to these enticements, spirits then spoke to diviners, revealing the causes of an illness or who was bewitching whom. I'd heard many such descriptions before, so I continued to write in my notebook, only

half listening. But when Aba Kouassi said that diviners were the point where the spirit and human worlds communicated, something clicked.

As Alma wrote this down, I remarked, "It sounds a bit like what a writer does. We hear voices, too."

"Right," she agreed, turning to Aba Kouassi. "That's like what Kouadio does."

"Kouadio?" he replied, his eyes squinting and skeptical in the dark room.

"Yes," said Alma, suddenly excited, "voices try to tell him their stories. And that's what he writes down."

"And my paper, and pen," I said to her, and she understood.

"His paper and pen and typewriter," she repeated to Aba Kouassi in Beng, "these are what he uses to draw the voices to him."

Aba Kouassi regarded me carefully as I sat with my notebook in hand. I could see he understood. He had often seen me sitting silently in a corner, then suddenly scribbling furiously: a plausible enough sign of possession.

I turned to Alma, ready to speak, but she knew as well as I did what to say. "Yes!" she exclaimed. "That's why he shouldn't be interrupted when he's working, because then the voices leave, and their stories can't be written."

The next morning, as I sat at our desk in the middle of the compound, no one interrupted me while I wrote, for in the eyes of the Beng my typing was now a physical act that revealed a hidden world. I realized that in the past I had made the mistake of defending my writing solely as labor, as if my typewriter were some sort of tiny, mechanical farm, each line of words another row of crops. But the Beng also understood the invisible world, and now, sitting at my typewriter, I was both outside their world and within it: I wrote for hours without distractions, visited by spirits the Beng could now imagine. After all these years I had finally found a complementary fit with my own culture, for what writer would disagree that we *are* possessed—by our imaginations, our interior voices, those gifts that surge up from within? Our characters call us, as we call them, and from that invisible, intuitive relationship our stories grow. And once created, those creatures of the imagination make their place out in the world—on a page, in a reader's mind.

Alma: The Circle

Aba Kouassi wasn't the only Beng person worried about village culture. With the large number of young people migrating to the cities in the face of rural hunger, many villagers worried that few émigrés would return. But those who did had imported city ways. Some of the changes seemed to me trivial

or even welcome: teenagers enlivened the evenings dancing "disco" to a generator-powered record player; village women now rode bikes.

But other transformations were troubling. Some high school students spoke less Beng than I did. And the returned urbanites were impatient with the drawn-out rounds of greetings and sometimes balked at helping their parents in the fields. I wasn't convinced that any of these, separately or together, meant the dissolution of Beng culture, for I had come to appreciate the regenerating and transforming abilities of culture. Still, I understood why the older villagers were nervous.

Ironically, the years of drought and hardship contributed to my welcome: the most conservative villagers now wanted me to document traditions they feared would soon vanish. Aba Kouassi's son, Petit, proud that he knew how to make a traditional bark-cloth mat, invited Philip and me to follow him into the forest and record his work. It took all day, even with Philip's help: chopping down the *zo* tree, carefully tapping the trunk to loosen the outer layer, then peeling off the bark carefully without tearing it, separating and then soaking the inner layer, wringing out the softened bark and pounding it with a special wooden mallet to stretch it, finally laying the mat out in the sun to dry.

Until recently, Beng men had cut down *zo* trees regularly to make into clothes, mats, hunting bags. Bark cloth had several virtues, Petit explained: after several washings it softened nicely to hug the body; and it was far sturdier than the flimsy factory-made *pagnes*. Even now, Amenan mentioned to me, some old men in the villages still wore bark-cloth underwear. But otherwise, manufactured cotton *pagnes* had all but replaced bark cloth. After seeing Petit work, I understood why: the labor involved was just too demanding.

Amenan was amused that I'd methodically photographed Petit's every step. "Since you're interested in these old-fashioned things," she said, "the children should make you some *kpraw kpraw* lamps."

"*Kpraw kpraw* lamps?"

"That's what we used before kerosene lamps. They're made from the *kpraw kpraw* fruit—it has an oily seed that burns well. We used to skewer a few seeds onto a reed and light it, then carry it as a torch." Then she called over a few of her young daughters and nieces who were playing nearby. They buzzed with excitement as they ran off to the forest, soon returning with handfuls of round yellow fruits that they'd picked from a vine. After laying them on the ground, the children cut each one open to the two black pods inside. Then they set the pods out in the sun to dry.

The next morning the children gently tapped stones against the dried hulls to loosen the seeds within. Then they pierced the dried white seeds, one by one, with a thin reed. That evening the children begged matches from their parents and proudly lit their seed torches, illuminating a corner of the compound with a soft yellow glow.

For a few days the children of our *quartier* competed to see who could make the most *kpraw kpraw* torches. But their enthusiasm soon waned—it was a lot of work for a short-lived reward. And their parents could buy kerosene in the *boutique*—though only after working long hours cultivating their coffee trees so the crop could be sold for cash. What had once been necessities were now relegated to anthropological curiosities: bark-cloth *pagnes* that withstood the rigorous hand washings of Beng women, seed torches that lit up a moonless night sky.

The old style of round house was barely even such a curiosity—the bulldozers had long ago done such a thorough job, there was only a single fragment left in all Asagbé. One day I asked Amenan to come along with me to take a close look at the sad shell. We arrived at the house's remnants, its mud walls and thatched roof caved in forlornly: what remained seemed no more than a small fraction of the house's former self. The owner, Kwamé Ba, was relaxing on a palm-ribbed lounge chair. I asked him if I could have a look at the remaining rooms, maybe photograph them.

"Oh, Amwé," Kwamé Ba said, laughing, "why do you want to take photos of this old thing? Look how it's falling apart—my family is only living here because I don't have the money to build a new home. But you can take pictures if you want—who knows how much longer it will last?"

Amenan and I started our tour at the entrance's corrugated-tin door. "Look," Amenan said, pointing at a weatherbeaten wooden plank lying on the ground nearby, "that's the kind of door all the old houses used to have! I used to feel so safe inside the house because of our door—it was a lot bigger and heavier. It was closed all day, and I always knew it kept the bush spirits and thieves and forest animals out."

We pushed open the creaky tin door and entered. Walking around the edge of what would have once been an interior courtyard, peering into rooms with partially collapsed walls, Amenan murmured, "Every day around dusk, my uncle opened our door to let in the chickens and sheep, and also the *wuru*"—ancestors. "At dinner, we always put a bowl of food out for the *wuru*, and at bedtime they slept alongside us. In the morning, everybody left: the family went to the fields, the animals roamed around the village, and the *wuru* went back to *wurugbé*"—the city of ancestors.

We'd reached the last of the intact rooms—beyond was the open space where other rooms had once been. There was no more to see, no longer any shelter for the invisible ancestors of the extended family. Amenan and I walked back in silence to her courtyard while I tried to imagine—and Amenan, I suspected, tried to remember—a past that had vanished.

With Amenan's help I sketched out how the round house must have once appeared. Staring at the drawing, I was reminded of similar sketches I'd made of Beng farms; for, like the old houses, Beng fields were also round, and they were divided into slices radiating out from the center like the spokes of a wheel—one or two sections served as each farmer's plot. This summer I'd planned to measure a few fields to get a sense of their dimensions, for up until now I hadn't measured much of anything—the questions I cared about weren't often those that could be answered with numbers. Still, I was afflicted with some collapsing remnants myself: vestiges of a once popular notion, hanging on by a thin but tenacious thread, that an anthropologist should do a little of everything during fieldwork.

I told Amenan I'd like to measure some fields.

"Bon, let's go to my family's farm," she suggested. "I have to check on my rice anyway."

So we set off on the narrow path along with Philip and Kofi, and we walked for miles beneath the shade of the overhanging rain forest. When we arrived I reached into the dusty backpack for tape measure, notebook, and pen. Then I stared inside, chagrined.

"Oh, no, I don't believe it. . . ."

"What?" Philip asked.

"I forgot everything!" I started to laugh. "I guess *this* mistake isn't hard to figure out. . . . But what am I going to do? It's too late now to go back to the village."

"Wait a minute," Philip said, lifting his foot, "how about if we measure with this?"

"It's a good idea—but how will I remember all the numbers?"

Challenged by my ridiculous predicament, Kofi pointed out an old camp-fire and said in his lilting Ghanaian English, "Here: some lumps of charcoal—good as a pencil!"

"You think?"

"Oh, yes, no problem at all. And here's your paper," he added, breaking off a strip of bark from a log.

"Fabulous, thank you!" I said, grateful for Kofi's ingenuity.

So Philip set about walking slowly, heel to toe, heel to toe, around the circle as he called out his footsteps and I scrawled the numbers with fat charcoal chunks on pieces of bark. And so it went, a communal effort to cope with my initial forgetfulness.

"But Amenan," I asked as I recorded the measurements, "why are the fields round? You know, in our country, fields are mostly square."

"Ihh—ours are *always* round. That way, misfortune can be shared."

"How's that?"

"Well, if an animal comes to eat some of your crops, it'll just walk all around the circle and eat a little from each farmer's section—that way, no one's crop is ruined, but neither is anyone's spared."

By the end of the afternoon, my hands black, I'd amassed quite a collection of tree bark, and I delicately stuffed them into my pack. Back in the village, I found my tape measure—on the table where I'd left it, of course—and measured Philip's shoe from tip to toe at 11½ inches. I set about deciphering my charcoal scrawls, typing them into statistics, but somehow the process seemed to violate the very experience of having collected those numbers. While the figures would be useful, I knew that they were not at the heart of my work. Of the many sorts of anthropologies, this wasn't the one that I was drawn to practice. No, my interests lay in the culture behind those numbers: the work songs that farmers sang to encourage them in their hard labor; the charmed circle that once enfolded a family's ancestors and that still apportioned crop failure equally; the spirits that farmers avoided once a week by staying in the village, far from those fields I'd just measured.

If those spirits were the creation of Beng minds, that didn't prevent individual Beng from sharing those spirits with visitors. Our last days in Asagbé, Amenan told me she intended to sacrifice an egg to the Earth to ensure us a safe trip back home. I refrained from asking questions, didn't even enter the event into my notebook—it was liberating, for a change, to accept Amenan's gracious offer as a Beng person might.

"Eki mi gba lenni kpang kpang kpang," said Amenan's mother, Akissi Kro— May god give you many, many, many children. I thanked her—this time I was grateful for the wish.

Still, much as I'd been accepted this summer by the villagers of Asagbé, I could never imagine myself as one of them—nor, I was sure, could they imagine me so. There was always some invisible border that prevented me from gaining full citizenship in the Beng circle: my American otherness and my commitment to anthropological distance both asserted themselves, nudging me to question and probe further and above all to avoid the temptation to accept anything as final. Of all that the Beng people had taught me, this stood out: "The spirits will protect you," Aba Kouassi told me, "if you believe in them." He, too, understood the relativity of faith, of knowledge.

Philip: A Public Reading

While resting in Abidjan a few days before our plane flight, Alma and I stayed at the diplomatic residence of Cary and Marianne Caldwell. Actively curious about the cultures in which they found themselves—Marianne had actually come to visit us in Asagbé one day—the Caldwells were in the grand tradition of Al and Eszti Votaw, our American embassy friends from our first time in Africa. But the luxury of our accommodations unsettled us—the Caldwell home was a virtual mansion, three stories of interior space for so few people—a family of four, a maid, a cook. Alma and I thought of our own far smaller home awaiting us in Illinois—in our memory it also seemed more than two people deserved.

Alma and I spent most of the day walking about Abidjan; though we were far from Bengland, I remembered that we were also walking through *wurugbé,* one of the Beng's invisible cities of ancestors: elders, reunited husbands and wives, young mothers, children and infants, even witches who had finally confessed their crimes were gathered together in Abidjan for an afterlife that was a bustling—and transparent—parallel community. Surely every Beng visiting or living in Abidjan felt their presence; even I now knew some of the inhabitants. I could imagine a ghostly Nguessan regarding us from a street corner, cradling a frail Amla in her arms. And perhaps Apu was now playing with his invisible companions in a side street somewhere, mimicking the games of tussling schoolchildren. I knew that many older Beng worried that the young people living in towns and cities were losing interest in traditional ways. Were the *wuru*—who now had no access to the enfolding family comfort of the old Beng round house—also assimilating in this city, or were they still reminders for any Beng of a distant, vibrant village?

Our first evening as guests, Marianne organized a dinner, inviting the director of the Abidjan branch of an international bank and a representative of the World Bank. Though these men must have been fairly typical guests for a diplomatic dinner party, Alma and I certainly weren't, and I suspected that perhaps Marianne had an ulterior motive in introducing us.

They indeed found us quite exotic. Jean-Claude, the bank director, was an elegant Lebanese man who, when he wasn't making exaggerated complaints about how nothing ever worked in Africa, expressed frequent amazement that Alma and I could have lived so "primitively"; William, the World Bank representative—a thin-faced American—listened quietly, occasionally bemoaning how far removed all of us were from "culture."

Alma and I countered their comments as politely as we could, deciding not to argue—we were, after all, guests of the Caldwells. Still, I quickly grew tired of these self-assured, powerful men who seemed to know so little about this part of the world. I chafed throughout the dinner—the maid's efficient attentiveness underlined my uneasy sense of privilege, and each new course of the delicious meal made me recall ruefully the Spartan meals that were the Beng villagers' daily fare.

Over coffee, Jean-Claude sighed and announced, "You can educate the African, but you cannot change him. I've learned this after years of trying." He turned to the World Bank representative. "You remember Suleiman, don't you?"

"Ah, yes," William replied, "Suleiman."

Jean-Claude faced us, a smile of satisfaction on his lips, his hand brushing over his dark, short-cropped hair: he was about to tell a story that clearly gave him pleasure. "Suleiman had the best education, the best training. We sent him abroad—Paris, London—at company expense. We considered him one of us—civilized. Who would have known? We discovered that someone was embezzling funds, a rather sophisticated siphoning that took us some time to discover, and even then Interpol had to be called in. Oh, when I think of the cost! Suleiman was, of course, the responsible party. His dishonesty was certainly a terrible thing, but it was the nature of the dishonesty that was most upsetting. And it proves my point."

He leaned back, savoring the impending triumph of his argument. "Suleiman was being blackmailed—by a quite clever type who claimed he'd had a *féticheur* cast a dangerous spell over Suleiman's mother. She'd be killed if Suleiman didn't produce large sums of money.

"This man was *educated,* our best hope. But he turned out to be just another African. How can we ever achieve proper security if we can't trust a single African employee? How can they possibly be given positions of responsibility? They can never be changed."

"Why would you want to change them?" Marianne asked.

"Excuse me?" He was certain he'd misheard her.

"Why try to change them? If you really want to protect your employees from that sort of scheme, then hire your own in-house *féticheur.* You're in Africa—it's an African security system that you need."

Jean-Claude said nothing for a moment. Perhaps he was waiting for all of us to laugh, for Marianne must certainly be joking. Alma and I sat silently, enjoying his discomfort.

"Security system?" he finally ventured, eyeing a quiet William for support.

"Why not?" Marianne continued. "If criminals are using *féticheurs* to rob you, then employ one for protection. . . ."

He waved his hand dismissively. "That's impossible."

"Why? You yourself said that Africans can't be changed. So why not respect their beliefs?"

"And it will save you money," I broke in, eager to support Marianne. "No more embezzlement, and a *féticheur* must be less expensive than an Interpol investigation."

He regarded us coolly: we were lost souls, another line of defense breached in this dismal continent. I stared back: he was a man destined to be forever foiled by his bigotry, a man transplanted in another world but unable to bend to it. Clearly, no one's mind would be changed, and Cary quickly broke the quiet stalemate. "How was your trip to Liberia?" he asked William, and the peace of the dinner party wasn't further threatened.

I sat back, both disturbed by the story of Suleiman's downfall and relieved that the world of the village was indeed alive and thriving in the city. But by the end of the evening I grew more and more depressed by my encounter with these two men who wielded so much power in a world about which they knew so little. How could their decisions ever be more than the blind pecking of chickens? Would they ever visit a small village and take in the poverty of the people who lined up in curiosity to see them, then share a small pot of rice with a large family and go to bed hungry? I thought of our friends in Kosangbé and Asagbé: when would their plight, and the plight of so many villagers like them, ever be taken seriously?

Late the following afternoon I felt a familiar wave of chills rippling through my chest—malaria's going-away present for my last full day in Côte d'Ivoire. I searched through our already packed bags and found the bottle of quinine pills; swallowing the prescribed handful, I took to bed in the guestroom, apologizing in advance to the Caldwells for the dinner I'd have to miss.

My fever broke the next morning, just two hours before Alma and I finally boarded our plane—the pills had done their work, suppressing the effect of the malarial parasites in my blood. But I also knew that those parasites would remain inside me for months while I underwent a regimen of more pills for a cure.

As I gazed out the ascending plane's window at the city of Abidjan, I realized that once again I was leaving Africa and taking some of it along with me. When we rose above the cloud cover, I pulled down the tray from the seat before me and tried to write a little in my notebook, hoping to invoke my own private spirits. Then I set down my pen, suspicious that this explanation of inspiration seemed a little too neat: if I'd learned anything about Africa, it was that a new revelation or irony always awaited discovery. I closed my eyes and hoped for sleep—soon we'd be in Paris for a brief stopover. While there, I was scheduled to give a public reading of my fiction at the Village Voice, an English-language bookstore—this would be the belated last leg of a book tour I'd completed just before Alma and I had left for Africa.

The following evening, still weary and recovering from malaria, I sat before an audience composed mainly of American and British tourists with a literary bent, our small gathering framed by shelves of books. I began with "Waiting for the Right Moment," that gift bestowed on me after consulting a diviner. Then I began another story, which recounted a dead husband's ghostly presence in the home he couldn't bring himself to abandon; though written in America, the story was certainly influenced by Beng tales of spirits and their concept of the afterlife.

As I continued to read, my tired voice steadily grew softer, and when I finally finished, nodding gratefully to the brief applause, I wondered how "public" this reading actually was, for I was host to far more than malaria. Who would know, to look at me, that two full African villages teemed within? Yet more than ever before, that world's unfolding secrets had joined my inner voices, a secret harmony that was now a dual passport: forever I'd be an ethnographer of my own imagination. Suddenly no longer tired, I paged through the book on my lap, looking for another story to tell.

GLOSSARY

❧   ❧   ❧

aba	father
ah-heh	polite response when someone speaks
A kunglia	Our condolences
Ah leh paw doi	No reason
akpa	a free-standing veranda
alufyé	type of forest spirit
A oukwa	Thank you for your lie (Baulé)
attieké	cooked manioc dish
Ba fen	religious rest day, occurring every six days (for Beng savanna region)
bidon	plastic jug (French)
blofwé	white person (Baulé)
bofloto	snack of fried flour
bonzo	type of forest spirit
boutique	village general store (French)
boyena	request for a traveler's news
bubu	Muslim-style men's robe
bundingyéké	wooden rhythm instrument
CFA	Ivoirian currency (50 CFA = 1 French franc)
chéché	bitter
Dih a pey mi ni?	Who told you that?
duti	chief (Jula)
e bling	many
E geng	It's good
eki	sky/god

eki a twa ka le kpekpeaa	May god grant you good health
eki mi gba dring	May god give you tomorrow
eki mi gba lenni	May god give you children
eki mi gba yung pu	May god give you good luck
e nini	it's delicious
E nyana	It's finished
féticheur	powerful practitioner of animist rituals (French)
fewa	funeral for death of a first child
fonctionnaire	Ivoirian petty bureaucrat (French)
foutou	cooked yam dish
gagon	type of forest spirit
galee	corpse; also, a disease caused by contact with a corpse
gbaya	arboreal rodent
gbeka	to ask forgiveness
grégré	difficult, strong, serious
Ihh?	Really?
jimisan	bitter berries, used for a sauce
Ka j'a di	Forgive me (literally, "please pass over it")
kaka	insect
Ka ka an dé	We'll miss you
kalabé	an elder
Ka ma!	Courage!
Ka ma gbria	Thank you for yesterday
Ka n gba zreh	Give me the road
Ka niché	Thank you (Jula)
Ka nu batwa	Come back quickly
Ka nuwaliaa	Thank you
Ka ta poblé	Go eat
Ka ta wala	Go home
kpalé	hand hoe
kpesékpesé	type of chili pepper
kraw ti	herbal medicine
kutuku	potent, still whiskey
lolondalé	children's dance
marché	market (French)

mleh	snake
mon vieux	a popular Ivoirian French phrase (literally, "my elder")
N kana	I'm full
Ngwo blo	I'm here
ngwo mi popolo	please (literally, "I beg of you")
Ngwo n si paw?	What's my name?
nn-nnn	no
pagne	length of cloth, adaptable to many clothing styles (French)
paw paw	nothing
Po fen	religious rest day, occurring every six days (for Beng forest region)
quartier	particular section of village or town (French)
Sahel	semidesert band of West Africa, just south of Sahara
si blé	palm wine
soukous	popular music of Zaire
sous-préfet	local government official, comparable to mayor (French)
taxi-brousse	rural bus
Ta zro!	Go wash!
tubabu	white person (Jula)
vlong vlong	slippery
voleur	thief (French)
whey!	mourning cry
wuru	ancestor; ghost
wurugbé	city of ancestors; the Beng afterlife
Ye ta!	Be quiet!; Shut up!
yih!	exclamation of appreciation or surprise

ACKNOWLEDGMENTS

WE ARE GRATEFUL FOR SUPPORT IN THE RESEARCH AND WRITING OF THIS BOOK FROM THE following agencies:

AG: National Endowment for the Humanities, Social Science Research Council, American Association of University Women, Woodrow Wilson Foundation (Program in Women's Studies), United States Information Agency, and several units at the University of Illinois: Department of Anthropology, Program for the Study of Cultural Values and Ethics, Center for African Studies, and the Research Board.

PG: National Endowment for the Humanities, Yaddo Artists' Colony, Arts America, United States Information Agency, United States Information Service, and the following units of the University of Illinois: Department of English, Program for the Study of Cultural Values and Ethics, International Programs and Studies (William and Flora Hewlett Summer International Research Grant), and the Research Board.

Short extracts of this book have appeared, in slightly different form, in the following publications, to which we are grateful for reprint permission:

AG: "Interviewing a Diviner," in *Discovering Anthropology* by Daniel Gross (Mayfield Press, 1992).

PG: "A Writer in a World of Spirits," in *Poets & Writers Magazine;* reprinted in *Writer's Digest* and *Annual Editions: Anthropology 90/91,* Elvio Angeloni, ed. (The Dushkin Publishing Group, 1990).

"The Alien Snow," in *Cream City Review.*

We are grateful to Chuck Stout for preparation of the maps. We would also like to extend our thanks to the following individuals who, each in his or her own way, helped or otherwise inspired us in the writing of this book: Ralph Alexander, Edward M. Bruner, Sharon Decker, Kate Doughty, Walter Feinberg, Wilson Henley, Janet Dixon Keller, Julie Kosarin, Kevin MacDonaugh, Erica Marcus, Enrique Mayer, Stuart Muir, Robert Dale Parker, Etya Pinker, Helaine Silverman, Geri Thoma, Leon Waldoff, and the students in Alma's course, Fieldwork in Cultural Anthropology: Theory and Method.

We presented portions of the book to the Red Lion Seminar, organized by the Program of African Studies at Northwestern University and the Department of Anthropology at the University of Chicago, and to the Program for the Study of Cultural Values and Ethics at the University of Illinois at Urbana-Champaign; we are grateful for all comments.

We also wish to express our loving gratitude to our son, Nathaniel, born in 1987, whose continuing ethnographic explorations of the strange world he was born into have inspired us in recounting our lives among the Beng.

Finally, our deepest gratitude to the Beng people—to those who appear in our book as well as those who do not: *Eki a twa ka le kpekpeaa.*

INDEX

❀ ❀ ❀

319

Komena Kouassikro, 63–64, 122–23, 155,
162, 163, 204, 213–15, 216, 222–23,
253, 261
Kona (Wamya Kona), 51, 62, 71–73, 94–
96, 100, 101, 103, 114–17, 118, 122,
123, 128, 131–32, 139, 141, 183, 184,
186, 188–90, 193, 196–97, 201, 203,
208, 224–26, 228–30, 233–35, 237,
241–42, 246–48, 254, 262, 266–67,
271, 274, 282, 295
Kosangbé: decision to settle in, 47, 48–
49, 50–51, 128; gendarmes in, 228,
230; political rivalry in, 71, 116, 131–
32, 189, 262; return to (1985), 281,
294–95; vendetta against Asagbé,
185–86
Kossum, 51, 61, 173, 194, 217, 253, 272
Kouadio (son of Akwé Amenan), 93,
130, 168, 175–76
Kouakou Ba, 73–74, 80–82
Kouakou Kala, 176, 196, 218–21
Kri Afwé, 199–200, 219–20, 221–25
Kwamla Chakro, 178, 217, 229, 233–34,
237–39, 242, 245, 248, 257, 274,
295

Lamine (a diviner), 153, 157–58, 174–76,
181–83, 184, 185, 187, 190, 195, 276,
291, 295, 296, 299
Language: difficulty vs. translation, 16,
30, 33, 35, 63, 71, 73, 81, 155, 156,
163, 180, 188, 191–92, 206, 207, 229,
237–38, 269, 282, 298; and madness,
265–66; multilingualism, 80, 255;
progress in learning (by AG and
PG), 262. *See also* Beng language;
Etiquette
Lanzé Afwé, 153, 160, 198, 201
Lévi-Strauss, Claude, 68
Livestock, 118, 127, 133, 140–41, 169
Lord Jim (Conrad), 265

Maat, 30–32, 33, 37, 38, 41, 45, 46, 56,
57, 93
Makola, 68, 220, 235, 287
Maps: of Beng region, 8, 24, 25; of ethnic groups, 9; by Kona Kofi Jean, 35
Marie, 30, 32, 37, 39, 45, 50
Marriage: among relatives, 47, 147, 152,
156, 177, 233, 285, 298; Beng arrangements for, 36, 54, 91, 129, 139,
147, 155, 176, 285, 297–98; and divorce, 226, 269; and engagement,
54, 55, 122–23, 176; and incest taboos, 268–69; to non-Beng, 94; and
polygamy, 218, 233
M'Bahiakro: description of, 21, 275; infirmary in, 22, 40–41, 56, 76, 130, 143,
159, 161–62, 210, 230, 262, 275, 292–
93; mayor of, 36–37; storing snake
serum in, 19, 143–46, 148; transpor-
tation to, 16, 255, 293
Mead, Margaret, 124

Media, 13, 22, 34, 52, 56, 89, 111, 132,
166, 195, 230, 255, 257
Medicine: aspirin, 215, 227; during childbirth, 120; circumcision as, 168; and
divination, 175; and doctoring by
PG, 63–64, 68, 78, 80, 99, 114–15,
125–26, 165, 192–93, 226, 291–94;
failure of vs. faith in, 183, 259, 303;
for Guinea worm, 259–60; herbal,
104–5, 121, 175, 183, 204, 255, 297;
love charm, 208; as magical protection against harm, 234, 237–38, 240,
245–46, 274; massage therapy, 160;
and medical emergencies, 80, 114–
17, 229, 282; payment for, 83–84;
quinine pills, 56, 64, 75, 311; traditional (nonherbal), 121, 160, 291.
See also Diseases and illness; Sacrifices
Melville, Herman, 294
Menstruation, 158, 183, 238
Metamorphoses (Ovid), 253–54
Miguel Street (Naipaul), 99
Mo'kissi, 176–78, 225, 270, 285
Mossi ethnic group, 226–28, 229, 230,
232
Moya, 65, 78, 103, 127, 201, 206, 217,
235, 242, 264, 273, 274, 287, 295
Music, 71, 72, 73–75, 80–82, 107, 137–
38, 176, 198, 199, 261, 272; inspiration for, 82; payment for, 75, 81–82;
soukous, 212–13; tapes, 212–13

Naipaul, V. S., 99
Names: and name calling, 117; and
namesakes, 109; for PG and AG, 30;
rules for, 45, 92; and secrecy, 68;
stealing of, 203–4
Native Son (Wright), 180
New Yorker, The, 116
Nguessan, 130, 272, 282, 288–89, 309
Njál's Saga, 75, 76
Notes and Queries on Anthropology, 266
Nuer ethnic group, 67–68

Okot p'Bitek, 167
One Hundred Years of Solitude (García
Márquez), 276
Ovid, 253–54

Paley, Grace, 258
Palm-Wine Drinkard, The (Tutuola), 29,
96
Paris Review, The, 276
Pascal (Kouakou Kouadio Pascal), 14–
17, 25–26, 27, 29, 179–80, 190–94,
206–7, 229, 284, 286
Peanuts (comic strip), 9–10
Performance, 70, 276–77; and scripted
behavior, 71; storytelling, 42–44,
162–63, 311–12
Personal hygiene: after childbirth, 121;
bathing, 32, 37, 56, 78, 79, 103, 127,